3RD EDITION

ESSENTIALS FOR LIVING

The Complete Package for Junior Certificate Home Economics

Eilis Flood

Gill & Macmillan
Hume Avenue
Park West
Dublin 12
www.gillmacmillan.ie

978 07171 6451 6

Design and print origination by Design Image

The paper used in this book is made from the wood pulp of managed forests. For every tree felled, at least one tree is planted, thereby renewing natural resources.

Any links to external websites should not be construed as an endorsement by Gill & Macmillan of the content or view of the linked material. Furthermore it cannot be guaranteed that all external links will be live.

For permission to reproduce photographs, the author and publisher gratefully acknowledge the following:

© Advertising Archives: 218BL, 218BR, 219TL, 219TR, 219CL; © Alamy: 3C, 3R, 5, 8T, 13T, 35, 54, 62TR, 65CR, 72B, 74T, 75, 92BR, 94R, 100, 101B, 103TR, 108CR, 108TR, 108BR, 118, 120TR, 136L, 136C, 138T, 138B, 144TC, 144BL, 146, 149, 154T, 154BR, 154BL, 156TL, 189, 190, 196, 198, 210TL, 210TR, 210BL, 210BC, 211, 218T, 219, 235TR, 235CL, 235BL, 236B, 241, 252BL, 260, 261, 265B, 270R, 275, 276T, 279TCL, 279BL, 283T, 284T, 284B, 287B, 297, 298BL, 298BR, 299T, 300C, 301TR, 301B, 304T, 304B, 308, 310T, 310CL, 313, 316TL, 318T, 318BL, 319CR, 319BL, 319BR, 325BR, 328T, 330C, 330R, 337T, 337BC, 337BR, 338, 339T, 339CTL, 347, 352, 359B, 364TC, 364CL, 364C, 365BL, 373T, 375L, 375R, 386C, 386B, 387, 388C, 394CR, 394B, 400, 412B, 414, 415C, 416B, 417T, 420BR, 421, 423T, 425, 434BL, 437L, 235BC, 235BR, 236TL, 236TCL, 236TCR; © Corbis: 9; © Getty Images: 11T, 13B, 29, 38, 92BL, 326, 340L, 340C, 340R, 342T, 342B, 364BL, 365BR, 374, 386T, 418B, 443; © Imagefile: 305; © Jen Patton: 40B, 212, 212, 406, 407; © McDonald's: 219CR; © Mother and Baby Picture Library: 419B, 420BL; © Photocall Ireland: 210TC, 225, 349TL; © Rex Features: 285; © Science Photo Library: 3L, 22, 265C, 276B, 388T, 410, 411T, 411C; © Shutterstock: 4, 6–7, 10, 11B, 12, 13C, 14, 25–28, 30–31, 41, 48–50, 58, 62TL, 62BL, 63–64, 65TLL, 65TL, 65CL, 65CR, 65CRR, 65B, 67, 72T, 73, 74B, 76, 92T, 92C, 93, 94L, 98, 101TL, 101TR, 103LT, 103LC, 103LB, 103BC, 103BR, 103TC, 104B, 111–112, 115, 117, 119, 120TC, 120TL, 120CL, 120BL, 120BC, 120BR, 120CR, 121, 123–124, 130–135, 138C, 144TL, 144TR, 144BC, 155, 156TR, 156C, 156B, 163–169, 171–176, 178–179, 181–186, 188, 193–194, 197T, 200–203, 207, 210BR, 226T, 235TL, 239, 243T, 244, 248, 250, 252TL, 252TC, 252TR, 141BR, 265T, 269, 270L, 279TL, 279TCR, 279TR, 279BC, 279BR, 280, 282, 283B, 298T, 299B, 300TL, 300TR, 300B, 301TL, 309, 210B, 311, 314–315, 316TC, 316TR, 316B, 317, 318CL, 319T, 320, 325T, 325CT, 325CB, 328CL, 330L, 335, 337BL, 339CT, 339CB, 339CBL, 339B, 348, 349TR, 350BL, 357–358, 359T, 360–361, 364TL, 364CR, 366–367, 372BL, 373B, 376–378, 379B, 389, 396, 399, 406, 412T, 412C, 415T, 415B, 416T, 417B, 418T, 419T, 422T, 422B, 423C, 446; © Shutterstock/abimages: 8B, 108CL; © Shutterstock/Anton Oparin: 365T, 371TR; © Shutterstock/ChameleonsEye: 364TR; © Shutterstock/dean bertoncelj: 207; © Shutterstock/Featureflash: 371; © Shutterstock/LunaseeStudios: 159; © Shutterstock/M. Unal Ozmen: 236TR; © Shutterstock/Paul McKinnon: 379T; © TopFoto: 287T; Courtesy of An Post: 242; Courtesy of Australian Wool Innovation: 226BL, 370, 370; Courtesy of Avent: 420CR; Courtesy of Avonmore: 136R; Courtesy of Bank of Ireland: 213, 243B; Courtesy of Bord Bia/Irish Food: 104C; Courtesy of British Standards Institution: 233BR; Courtesy of Carraig Donn: 434BR; Courtesy of Coeliac Society of Ireland: 40C; Courtesy of Competition and Consumer Protection Commission: 229CT; Courtesy of Consumers' Association of Ireland: 229CB; Courtesy of Ecobaby: 423C; Courtesy of euecolabel.eu: 350TR; Courtesy of Eugene + Anke McKernan: 434BC; Courtesy of Excellence Ireland Quality Association: 233TL; Courtesy of François Micheloud: 74C; Courtesy of Glanbia: 107, 109; Courtesy of Guaranteed Irish: 226BCL, 233TC; Courtesy of LennonLines/Catherine McAviney Photography: 388B; Courtesy of Moya Mc Guigan: 197B; Courtesy of National Standards Authority of Ireland: 233TR; Odlums: 116; Office of the Ombudsman: 229T; The Restaurants Association of Ireland: 229B; Simplicity: 439.

The author and publisher have made every effort to trace all copyright holders, but if any has been inadvertently overlooked we would be pleased to make the necessary arrangement at the first opportunity.

Contents

Introduction

What is involved in Junior Certificate Home Economics?

Structure of Course:

Junior Certificate Home Economics can be taken at two levels – Ordinary Level and Higher Level. There are some sections of the course that are not included at Ordinary Level. Higher Level only material is highlighted clearly in this textbook. The course you are studying is divided into **two sections** – although this is set to change in 2018 when the new Junior Certificate Home Economics course is introduced for first years.

Section 1 – Compulsory for all students

Unit 1:	Food
Unit 2:	Consumer Studies
Unit 3:	Social and Health Studies
Unit 4:	Resource Management and Home Studies
Unit 5:	Textile Studies

Section 2 – Students pick one area of study

Option 1:	Childcare
Option 2:	Design and Craftwork
Option 3:	Textile Skills

How Junior Certificate Home Economics is Examined

Junior Certificate Home Economics is examined in **three ways**. The total marks awarded at both Higher and Ordinary Level is **600** marks, but they are awarded in different ways.

Exam component	Higher level	Ordinary level
Written exam	50% (300 marks)	40% (240 marks)
Practical cookery exam	35% (210 marks)	45% (270 marks)
Project	15% (90 marks)	15% (90 marks)

Written Examination

At both Ordinary and Higher levels the written examination is divided into two sections.

Section	Type of Questions	Higher Level	Ordinary Level
A	Short questions asking for precise pieces of information – across all core sections of the course	Answer 20 of 24 (Most students attempt all questions – lowest marks will be eliminated)	Answer 16 of 20 (Most students attempt all questions – lowest marks will be eliminated)
B	Long questions – usually one topic divided into sections (a), (b), (c), (d) and sometimes (e)	Answer 4 of 6 Long questions take more time so it is usually advised to decide which ones you think you can answer best and only answer these. Answers are written in a separate answer book.	Answer 4 of 6 Unlike at Higher Level, long questions at Ordinary Level are not as time-consuming. Students often complete all six as lowest marks will be eliminated. Answers are written into the same answer book as section A.

The Higher Level written exam lasts 2½ hours. The Ordinary level exam lasts 2 hours.

Practical Cookery Examination

This is a chance for students at both Higher and Ordinary Level to pick up marks. You will know at least two weeks before the examination what you have been asked to cook (usually in April). If you want to achieve good marks it is therefore advisable to practice the dish/dishes you have to cook in the exam as much as possible beforehand. Chapter 9 of this book provides detailed guidance on achieving high marks in this exam. Do not neglect the written material that must be completed as part of this examination as marks will be lost.

The practical cookery examination lasts **2 hours**. This involves ½ hour preparation time and 1½ hour actual examination time. An external examiner will come to your school to examine your cooking skills.

Project

Students have three options to choose from for this project: Childcare, Design/Craftwork and Textile Skills options. Chapters 37, 38 and 39 of this textbook provide detailed guidance on achieving high marks for this section. Again, as with the practical cookery examination, hard work pays off and students can gain excellent marks by putting effort into their projects. An external examiner will come to your school to examine your project.

eTest.ie – what is it?

A revolutionary new website-based testing platform that facilitates a social learning environment for Irish schools. Both students and teachers can use it, either independently or together, to make the whole area of testing easier, more engaging and more productive for all.

Students – do you want to know how well you are doing? Then take an eTest!

At eTest.ie, you can access tests put together by the author of this textbook. You get instant results, so they're a brilliant way to quickly check just how your study or revision is going.

Since each eTest is based on your textbook, if you don't know an answer, you'll find it in your book.

Register now and you can save all of your eTest results to use as a handy revision aid or to simply compare with your friends' results!

Teachers – eTest.ie will engage your students and help them with their revision, while making the jobs of reviewing their progress and homework easier and more convenient for all of you.

Register now to avail of these exciting features:

- Create tests easily using our pre-set questions OR you can create your own questions

- Develop your own online learning centre for each class that you teach

- Keep track of your students' performances

eTest.ie has a wide choice of question types for you to choose from, most of which can be graded automatically, like multiple-choice, jumbled-sentence, matching, ordering and gap-fill exercises. This free resource allows you to create class groups, delivering all the functionality of a VLE (Virtual Learning Environment) with the ease of communication that is brought by social networking.

Unit 1
Food

Slide presentation • Student activity pack with revision crossword • Class test • Student learning contract

Key words

It is a good idea to keep an indexed notebook of key words with their definitions included for revision purposes.

- ✓ Malnutrition
- ✓ Nutrient
- ✓ Macronutrient
- ✓ Micronutrient
- ✓ Nutrient composition
- ✓ Nutrient source
- ✓ Nutrient function
- ✓ Recommended daily allowance
- ✓ Empty-calorie foods
- ✓ Deficiency diseases
- ✓ Oxidation
- ✓ Energy balance
- ✓ Basal metabolic rate

Learning outcomes

After completing this chapter and the homework, assignments and activities that accompany it, you should:

- Understand why we need food. Be able to list the factors that influence our food choices.
- Have a good understanding of each of the six nutrients, including their composition, classification, sources, functions in the body and their RDA/GDA.
- Understand and be able to describe the effects of over-consumption of certain nutrients on the body (fat, sugar and vitamin/mineral supplements).
- Know the nutrition-related causes of the following deficiency diseases and be able to describe their symptoms: constipation and bowel disease, scurvy, rickets, neural tube defects, tooth decay, osteomalacia and osteoporosis, anaemia and goitre.
- Understand the term *energy balance* and be able to describe how it can be maintained by the individual.

Why we need food

Food serves three functions in the body:
1. Heat and energy
2. Growth and repair
3. Helps fight disease

Factors that affect our food choices

- **Cost:** Some foods are too expensive to buy regularly, such as fillet steak.
- **Foods that are readily available**, such as potatoes in Ireland. (Foods very commonly eaten in a country are often called **staple foods**.)
- **Foods in season**, like strawberries in summertime.
- **Lifestyle:** For example, convenience foods are now more common because of our busy lifestyle.
- **Culture and tradition**, such as pasta dishes in Italy.
- **Religious rules:** For example, strict Hindus do not eat meat.
- **Nutritional value:** Some people choose foods because they know they are good for them, such as low-fat food.
- **Personal likes and dislikes**.

Malnutrition – what is it?

Too little of certain foods, e.g. lack of fresh fruit and vegetables – scurvy

Too much of certain foods, e.g. too much sugar and fat – obesity

Too little food – starvation

Nutrients

All food contains one or more of the six nutrients. The names of the nutrients are:

1. Protein
2. Fat
3. Carbohydrate
4. Minerals
5. Vitamins
6. Water

Each and every one of the six nutrients must be taken in to keep our bodies healthy. Protein, fat and carbohydrate are eaten in large amounts. They must be broken down by the body during digestion and are called **macronutrients**. Minerals and vitamins are needed in smaller amounts and need no digestion. They are called **micronutrients**.

Protein
Composition of protein

Protein is made up of chains of **amino acids**. Each amino acid is made up of the elements carbon, hydrogen, oxygen and nitrogen (CHON). Of these, nitrogen is the most important because it is needed for growth.

 Chapter 2, page 20 – during digestion, enzymes break the links between amino acid molecules

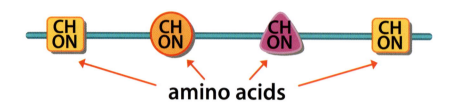

amino acids

Classification of protein

First-class protein (usually from animals)

Sources of animal protein: meat, fish, eggs, cheese, milk, meat alternatives

Second-class protein (usually from plants)

Sources of vegetable protein: peas, beans, lentils, pasta, nuts, brown bread, rice, breakfast cereals

Essential amino acids

You learned earlier that protein is made up of chains of amino acids. While all amino acids are good for the body, some are more important than others. The most important are called **essential amino acids**.

High and low biological value protein

Some protein foods contain most or all of the essential amino acids. These are called **first-class** or **high biological value (HBV)** protein foods. These foods usually come from animal sources, such as meat. (The main exceptions are TVP and mycoprotein foods, such as Quorn, which are vegetable proteins with a high biological value.)

Other protein foods do not contain all the essential amino acids. These are called **second-class** or **low biological value (LBV)** protein foods. These are usually from vegetable or plant sources, such as beans.

Functions: What does protein do in the body?

- Promotes growth of the body.
- Repairs worn-out and damaged cells, such as when you cut yourself.
- Makes enzymes, hormones and antibodies.
- Provides heat and energy.

Meat alternatives

There are many different high-protein meat alternatives on the market today. Textured vegetable protein (TVP) is made from soya beans. TVP is an excellent food because it is high in protein and calcium, yet low in fat. It is available in steak, chunk or minced form. Mycoprotein foods (the most common of which is the brand Quorn), which are made from edible fungi, are also available. Quorn is produced both as a cooking ingredient and as a range of ready meals.

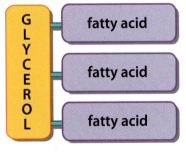

Quorn mycoprotein product

Recommended daily allowance (RDA) or guided daily amount (GDA)

RDA and GDA tells us how much of each of the nutrients we need every day. The table below shows the RDA/GDA for some of the nutrients needed by the body.

Nutrient	RDA
Protein	1g per kg of body weight
Fat	No more than 30% of energy intake
Carbohydrate	Depends on how active the person is
Fibre	30g
Vitamin C	30mg
Vitamin D	2.5–10mg
Vitamin A	750–1,200mg
Iron	10–15mg
Calcium	500–1,200mg
Sodium (salt)	2g

Fats
Composition of fats

Fats are made up of fatty acids and glycerol. Each glycerol molecule has three fatty acid molecules attached to it. Fats contain the elements carbon, hydrogen and oxygen (CHO).

GLYCEROL — fatty acid

GLYCEROL — fatty acid

GLYCEROL — fatty acid

Composition of fat

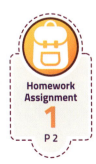

Homework Assignment
1
P 2

Chapter 2, page 20 – during digestion, enzymes break the links between the fatty acid and glycerol molecules

Classification of fats

Saturated fats – sometimes called animal fats   **Unsaturated fats** – sometimes called vegetable fats

Sources of saturated fats: meat (rashers, sausages), fatty red meats (many minced meats contain large amounts of fat), cream, butter, eggs

Sources of vegetable fats: polyunsaturated margarines (Flora), beans, nuts, oily fish (salmon), fish liver oils such as cod liver oil, cereals

Functions: What does fat do in the body?

- Fat gives us lots of heat and energy.
- A layer of fat under the skin called adipose tissue insulates the body (helps keep the body warm).
- Delicate organs such as the heart and kidneys have a layer of fat around them. This layer can protect them from injury.
- Vitamins A, D, E and K dissolve in fat. When we eat fat, we are also eating these vitamins.

How to cut down on fat

- Grill, bake, boil or microwave food instead of frying.
- Use polyunsaturated fats (such as Flora) instead of butter.
- Cut fat off meat.
- Cut down on foods like crisps, burgers and chips.
- Use low-fat foods.

Homework Assignment
2
P 5

Carbohydrates
Composition of carbohydrates

Like fats, carbohydrates are made up of the elements carbon, hydrogen and oxygen (CHO). Fats produce more energy than carbohydrates because they have more carbon. Carbohydrates are made up of chains of simple sugars.

 Chapter 2, page 20 – during digestion, enzymes break the links between glucose molecules

Composition of carbohydrate

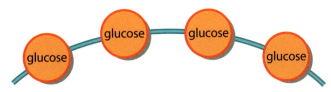

Classification of carbohydrates

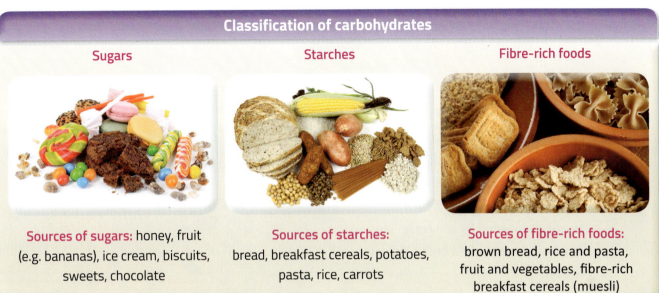

Sugars	Starches	Fibre-rich foods
Sources of sugars: honey, fruit (e.g. bananas), ice cream, biscuits, sweets, chocolate	**Sources of starches:** bread, breakfast cereals, potatoes, pasta, rice, carrots	**Sources of fibre-rich foods:** brown bread, rice and pasta, fruit and vegetables, fibre-rich breakfast cereals (muesli)

Functions: What does carbohydrate do in the body?

- Fibre provides heat and energy.
- Fibre-rich carbohydrates fill you up.
- Fibre helps stop constipation and other bowel problems.

Fibre

Fibre is very important in the diet because it helps waste pass easily through the intestines. If we do not eat enough fibre, we risk constipation and diseases such as bowel cancer.

It is recommended that we eat 25–30g of fibre per day, yet on average Irish people eat only 15–20g.

Refined or processed carbohydrates

Refined or processed foods rarely contain much fibre. To increase fibre intake:

- Eat brown bread and rice instead of white
- Eat more fresh fruit and vegetables
- Eat high-fibre breakfast cereals, such as bran flakes

Chapter 4, page 37 – detail on high-fibre diets

Empty-calorie foods

Most of the foods pictured contain lots of sugar but very little goodness. These foods are all high-calorie foods but do not supply any of the other nutrients needed by the body. This is why they are called **empty-calorie foods**.

Empty-calorie foods

Hidden sugar

The foods pictured above are obviously sugary foods. Sometimes, however, foods have hidden sugar: watch out for the words sucrose, glucose, maltose, fructose and dextrose – these are all types of sugar.

Did you know that ketchup is one-quarter sugar?

Homework Assignment

3

P 7

Vitamins

Vitamins are needed in small amounts by the body. There are two groups of vitamins:

- **Water-soluble:** These dissolve in water (vitamins C and B group).
- **Fat-soluble:** These dissolve in fat (vitamins A, D, E and K).

Fat-soluble vitamins can be stored in the body, but water-soluble vitamins cannot be stored and need to be eaten every day.

Water-soluble vitamins

Vitamin	Functions	Sources	RDA/GDA	Deficiency diseases
C	• General health • Healthy skin and gums • Helps wounds to heal • Helps absorb iron	• Fruits: blackcurrants, grapefruits, lemons, orange juice, oranges, peppers, strawberries • Vegetables: cabbage, coleslaw, new potatoes, peppers, tomatoes	30mg for adults; more for adolescents	• Scurvy • Wounds slow to heal
B group (6 vitamins)	• Growth • Healthy nervous system • Controls the release of energy from food	Nuts, peas, beans, lentils, yeast bread, brown bread, meat, fish, milk, eggs, cheese	Varies with each vitamin	• Beriberi (nerve disease): May appear with alcoholism • Pellagra: Sores on the skin and tongue
Note: Extra folic acid needs to be taken during pregnancy	The B vitamin folic acid helps prevent neural tube defects (spina bifida). It is usually taken in tablet form for three months before and three months after conception.	Some breakfast cereals are fortified	0.4mg daily (one folic acid tablet)	Increased risk of neural tube defects (spinal) in babies

 Chapter 3, pages 29–30 – diet during pregnancy and breastfeeding

Scurvy

Scurvy is a disease caused by a lack of vitamin C. While rare, scurvy still occurs in infants and people living on poor diets that do not contain fresh fruit and vegetables. Babies, especially bottle-fed babies, should be given diluted fruit juice in a cup or from a spoon.

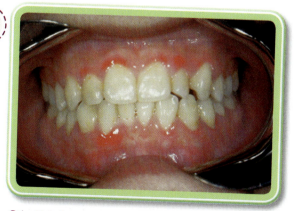

Scientists have recently begun to recommend 10 a day instead of 5 a day (particularly vegetables) for optimal health. Fruit and vegetables prevent scurvy.

The symptoms of scurvy are:

- Poor healing of wounds
- Frequent bruising
- Sore, bleeding mouth and gums
- Anaemia

Fresh fruit and vegetables contain vitamin C, which prevents scurvy

Preventing vitamin C loss

Vitamin C is easily destroyed. To help prevent this loss:

- Don't buy wilted vegetables.
- Cook vegetables soon after buying them.
- If boiling vegetables, cook in a small amount of water, bring to the boil and then simmer.
- Don't overcook vegetables.
- Don't use bread soda when cooking cabbage, as it destroys vitamin C.
- Eat vegetables soon after cooking – vitamin C is lost if they are kept warm for a long time.

Fat-soluble vitamins

Vitamin	Sources	Functions	Deficiency symptoms
A	• Pure vitamin A: eggs, fish liver oils, kidney, liver, margarine, milk, oily fish • Carotene: brightly coloured vegetables (carrots)	• Growth • Healthy eyes • Healthy skin • Healthy linings of the nose and throat, etc.	• Slowed growth • Night blindness • Linings of the nose and throat become dry and irritated
D	Cheese, eggs, fish liver oils, liver, margarine, oily fish, sunshine	Works with calcium for healthy bones and teeth	• Rickets (children) • Osteoporosis (adults) • Osteomalacia (adults)
K	Made in the bowel, green vegetables, cereals	Helps blood to clot	Problems with blood clotting

Rickets

The disease rickets is caused by a lack of vitamin D. It was first diagnosed in the 1650s and was common in children living in the industrial smog-filled cities at the beginning of the 20th century. Because vitamin D is needed to absorb, or use, calcium, and calcium is needed to harden the bones, a child with rickets will have soft, badly formed bones (bow legs) and teeth that are prone to decay.

Due to better nutrition after World War II, rickets was thought to be practically eradicated in Ireland. However, a 2014 report from the Irish Food Safety Authority found a recent reappearance of rickets amongst infants in Ireland and widespread low levels of vitamin D in the Irish population as a whole. There are three reasons for this:

- As always, infants are most at risk, as they are the most unlikely to be exposed to the sun (because they are covered in clothes or kept inside). In addition, the weaning diet is often low in foods containing vitamin D (fish, egg yolks, fortified cereals).

- Most of our vitamin D comes not from food, but from the action of sunlight on the skin. Because of Ireland's climate (particularly in winter), we do not get enough sunlight to manufacture enough vitamin D. This is made even worse by the fact that many people now lead predominantly indoor lifestyles.

- Ireland has now become a multicultural society, and darker-skinned people living in Ireland are particularly at risk, as they need more sunlight to produce vitamin D (10 to 50 times more). Also, some religious practices (such as strict Muslim women) forbid exposed skin.

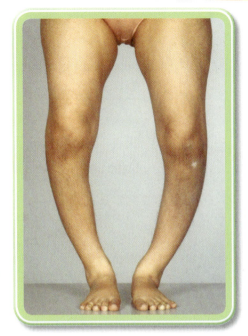

Rickets was common in Victorian times, but recent studies have seen it reappearing in Ireland

While most people living in Ireland do not have full-blown rickets, milder forms of the disease are evident, such as unhealthy bones and teeth. Most Irish dieticians now say that if they were to recommend one dietary supplement for Irish people, it would be vitamin D.

Osteomalacia

Osteomalacia is the adult form of rickets. In developing countries, this disease is found in women who have low intakes of vitamin D and calcium. Many of these women have had several closely spaced pregnancies followed by long periods of breastfeeding.

Hypervitaminosis

Because fat-soluble vitamins dissolve in fat, they can be stored in the fatty tissue of the body. Therefore, it is possible to have too much in the diet and a condition called **hypervitaminosis** results. There have been cases of hypervitaminosis A and D in people who eat foods high in vitamin A and D and also take food supplements in tablet form. The effects are dry skin, reduced bone density, hair loss, headaches, skin problems, birth defects and liver problems.

Homework Assignment

4

P 10

Minerals

Minerals, like vitamins, are needed in small amounts by the body for growth and general good health. Important minerals include:

- Calcium
- Iron
- Iodine
- Fluorine
- Sodium
- Phosphorus

Calcium

Sources: What foods contain calcium?

Cheese, milk, tinned fish, water, yoghurt, beans, bread and cereals contain calcium.

Functions of calcium

Calcium is needed to build strong bones and teeth.

Deficiency symptoms and diseases

If you don't get enough calcium, you risk getting rickets, osteomalacia (adult rickets), osteoporosis (brittle bones) and tooth decay.

Which would you prefer?

Iron

Sources: What foods contain iron?

Red meat, offal (liver and kidney) and green vegetables contain iron.

Functions and deficiency of iron

Sources of iron

There is a substance called **haemoglobin** in our blood. Haemoglobin carries oxygen to all our body's cells. Iron is needed to make haemoglobin. If there is not enough iron in our diet, anaemia is the result. The symptoms of anaemia are tiredness, paleness, weakness and dizziness. A survey conducted by UCD and UCC in 2008 found that approximately 75% of Irish teenage girls are not getting enough iron.

Vitamin	Sources	Functions	Deficiency symptoms
Iodine	Cereals, milk, sea fish, sea salt, seaweed, vegetables	Needed for a healthy thyroid gland (in the neck)	Goitre (see the photo below)
Fluorine	Sea fish, tap water, toothpaste	Helps prevent tooth decay	Tooth decay
Sodium (salt)	Salt added to food, bacon, snack and convenience foods	Needed for water balance in the body	Cramps, bloating
Phosphorus	Some is found in most foods, especially high-protein foods	Works with calcium for strong bones and teeth	None known

Salt

Too much **salt** (sodium) is linked with high blood pressure and strokes.

Vitamin and mineral link
Vitamin C is needed to absorb iron.
Vitamin D is needed to absorb calcium.

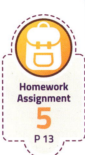

Homework Assignment **5** P 13

Goitre

Water
Sources of water
Food

All food contains water, except solid fats, such as lard, and dried foods, such as cornflakes.

Drinks

Coffee, fruit juice, milk, soft drinks and tea all contain water.

Properties of water			
Pure water is tasteless and has no smell.	Water boils at 100°C.	Water changes to steam at 100°C.	Water freezes at 0°C.

Functions: What is water needed for in the body?

- Body fluids, such as blood, are mainly water.
- Water is often a source of calcium and fluoride.
- Water removes waste from the body (in urine).
- Water helps keep the body at the right temperature. For instance, we sweat water when we are too hot.

Dehydration

Dehydration is when the body loses more than 2% of its normal volume of water. It is particularly dangerous in babies (the main sign of dehydration in babies is a depressed soft spot on the top of their head). Dehydration can occur after a long period of vomiting or diarrhoea or if people consume too much alcohol.

The main symptoms of dehydration are bad breath, dark-coloured urine, headaches, cramps, lowered blood pressure, dizziness, dry, itchy skin, constipation, rapid heart rate and tingling in the fingers and toes.

To prevent dehydration, you should drink eight glasses of water every day.

Energy
How energy is produced in the body

Food is burned in the body's cells and energy is produced. Oxygen is needed. This process is called **oxidation**.

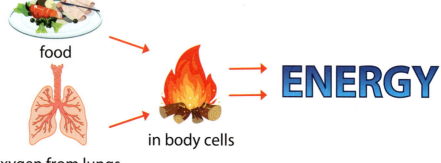

food

oxygen from lungs

in body cells

ENERGY

Energy balance

Energy balance, as the name suggests, is all about energy input (food) equalling energy output (BMR + activity).

BMR is explained on page 16.

Healthy Eating **Calories In** **=** Being Active **Calories Out**

Kilocalories and kilojoules

Just as the amount of milk in a carton is measured in litres, the amount of energy provided by food is measured in **kilocalories (kcal)** or **kilojoules (kJ)**. 1 kcal = 4.2 kJ.

Food labels

All foods that contain protein, fat or carbohydrate produce energy and are said to contain calories. Food products must display nutritional information on the package. One piece of information displayed is the food's energy value. Food labels give energy values per 100g of the food. Food labels often give values for a serving of the food as well.

How much energy do I need?

The amount of energy (number of kilocalories or kilojoules) needed by an individual depends on their size, whether they are male or female, their age and how active they are. Pregnant or breastfeeding women and people living in cold climates need extra energy. However, there are **average** recommended/guided daily allowances (RDA/GDA) for energy.

Approximate daily energy requirements (in kilocalories)

| Toddler 2 years 1,300 | Child 7-10 years 2,000 | Adolescent female 11-18 years 2,100 | Adolescent male 11-14 years 2,600 15-18 years 2,900 | Adult male sedentary 2,600 active 3,000 | Adult female sedentary 2,100 active 2,300 | Adult female pregnancy 2,400 lactation 2,700 |

Energy output

The body needs a basic amount of energy to stay alive – this is called a person's **basal metabolic rate (BMR)**. Extra energy is needed for activities. Look at the graph to see the amount of energy (kilocalories) needed for various activities.

Homework Assignment **6** P 15

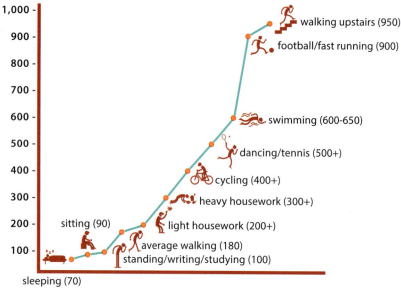

Energy consumption per hour for various activities

1. We need food for heat and energy, growth and repair and to fight disease.
2. **Factors that affect food choices:** Cost, availability, food in season, lifestyle, culture and tradition, religious rules, nutritional value, likes and dislikes.
3. **Nutrients:** Protein, fat, carbohydrate (macronutrients), minerals, vitamins (micronutrients) and water.

4. **Protein**
   - **Composition:** Chains of amino acids (CHON).
   - **Classification:** First-class or animal protein (meat, fish and eggs) and second-class or vegetable protein (pulse vegetables).
   - Essential amino acids are important for body function and are mainly found in animal protein foods. Foods that contain most or all of the amino acids are called high biological protein foods (meat). Foods that contain few essential amino acids are called low biological protein foods (mainly vegetable protein foods).
   - **Functions:** Growth, repair, manufacture of hormones, enzymes, etc. Provides heat and energy.
   - **Meat alternatives:** TVP and mycoprotein foods (Quorn) provide high-protein, low-fat alternatives to meat.

5. **Fats**
   - **Composition:** Each fat molecule contains one glycerol molecule and three fatty acids (CHO).
   - **Classification:** Saturated (mostly animal sources, such as butter and meat) and unsaturated (polyunsaturated margarines).
   - **Functions:** Heat and energy, insulates body, protects internal organs and a source of fat-soluble vitamins (A, D, E and K).
   - **To cut down on fat:** Grill, bake, boil or microwave. Use polyunsaturates, trim meat, cut down on fatty foods (chips) and use low-fat foods.

6. **Carbohydrate**
   - **Composition:** Chains of simple sugars, such as glucose (CHO).
   - **Classification:** Sugars, starches, fibre-rich foods.
   - **Functions:** Heat and energy. Fibre-rich foods fill you up and prevent bowel problems.
   - **Fibre** is vital for a healthy bowel. 25–30g a day is recommended. To increase fibre, eat brown bread and brown rice, fruit and vegetables and high-fibre breakfast cereals.
   - **Empty-calorie foods** contain lots of calories, yet few nutrients (cakes). Many foods contain hidden sugar.

7. **Vitamins**
   - **Classification:** Water-soluble (C and B group), fat-soluble (A, D, E and K).
   - **Vitamin C:** Sources are citrus fruits, berries and some vegetables. Functions: General health, healthy skin and gums, heals wounds, iron absorption. RDA: 30mg+. Deficiency diseases include scurvy and wounds are slow to heal.
   - **B group:** Sources are high-protein foods and fortified breakfast cereals. Functions: Growth, healthy nervous system, energy release from food, folic acid helps prevent spina bifida. Deficiency diseases include beriberi and pellagra and an increased risk of spina bifida.
   - **Vitamin A:** Sources: Pure (eggs, fish, offal), carotene (highly coloured vegetables). Functions: Growth, healthy eyes, skin and linings of nose and throat. Deficiency diseases include slowed growth, night blindness and dry, irritated linings.
   - **Vitamin D:** Sources include sunshine and foods that contain fats. Functions: Works with calcium for healthy bones and teeth. Deficiency diseases are rickets, osteoporosis and osteomalacia.
   - **Vitamin K:** Made in bowel, needed for blood clotting.
   - **Hypervitaminosis:** Excessive consumption of fat-soluble vitamins. Symptoms: Dry, itchy skin and hair, headaches, liver problems and birth defects.

8. **Minerals:** Important minerals are calcium, iron, iodine, fluorine, sodium and phosphorus.
   - **Calcium:** Sources are dairy products, tinned fish, fortified bread and cereals. Functions: Healthy bones and teeth (works with vitamin D). Deficiency diseases are rickets, osteoporosis, osteomalacia and tooth decay.
   - **Iron:** Sources are red meat, offal and green vegetables. Functions: Necessary for the manufacture of haemoglobin, which carries oxygen in the blood. Deficiency diseases: Anaemia.
   - **Iodine:** Needed for a healthy thyroid gland – prevents goitre.
   - **Fluorine:** Prevents tooth decay.
   - **Sodium (salt):** Needed for water balance in the body. Too much salt results in high blood pressure.
   - **Phosphorus:** Strong bones and teeth.

9. **Vitamin–mineral links:** Vitamin C and iron, vitamin D and calcium.

10. **Water:** Sources include drinks (eight glasses of fluid per day), fruit and vegetables. Functions: Part of all body fluids, source of calcium and fluorine, removes waste (urine) and temperature regulation. Dehydration is dangerous, particularly for babies.

11. **Energy:** Food is burned in the body's cells. Oxygen is needed – this is called oxidation.
    Energy balance: Energy input (food) must equal energy output. Energy is measured in kilocalories (kcal) or kilojoules (kJ). Food labels indicate energy values. Energy requirements vary depending on age, gender and activity levels. **Basal metabolic rate (BMR)** is the amount of energy required at rest.

1. List the three functions of food in the body.
2. List five factors that can affect our choice of food.
3. What is malnutrition?
4. What are the six nutrients found in food?
5. What is the difference between macro and micronutrients?
6. Describe the composition, classification, and functions of protein in the body.
7. What do the letters RDA and GDA stand for?
8. Name two meat alternatives and explain their advantages in the diet.
9. Describe the composition, classification, and functions of fat in the body.
10. Suggest four ways fat could be reduced in the diet.
11. Describe the composition, classification, and functions of carbohydrate in the body.
12. On average, how much fibre should be eaten daily? Why is fibre important in the diet? Suggest ways in which fibre may be increased in the diet.
13. Name the water-soluble and fat-soluble vitamins.
14. Describe the sources, functions and deficiency symptoms of each of the following vitamins: A, B group, C, and D.
15. Name six minerals needed by the body.
16. Describe the sources, functions and deficiency symptoms of each of the following minerals: calcium, iron, iodine, fluorine, sodium and phosphorus.
17. How much sodium should be consumed daily?
18. What are the risks associated with consuming too much sodium?
19. List six sources of water in the diet.
20. What are the four main functions of water in the body? What is dehydration and what are its symptoms? How much water should be consumed daily? Describe four properties of water.
21. What is oxidation?
22. What is meant by energy balance?
23. What do the letters BMR stand for and what does the term mean?
24. How is energy measured?
25. List five factors that affect energy requirements.

Test Yourself
eTest.ie

*Higher Level only chapter

Teacher's CD

Slide presentation ▪ Student activity pack with revision crossword ▪ Class test ▪ Student learning contract

Key words

- ✓ Physical digestion
- ✓ Chemical digestion – enzymes
- ✓ Alimentary canal
- ✓ Amylase
- ✓ Maltose
- ✓ Oesophagus
- ✓ Gastric juice
- ✓ Chyme
- ✓ Hydrochloric acid
- ✓ Pepsin
- ✓ Peptides
- ✓ Peristalsis
- ✓ Pancreatic juice
- ✓ Bile
- ✓ Intestinal juice
- ✓ Villi
- ✓ Lymph system
- ✓ Colon
- ✓ Faeces

Learning outcomes

After completing this chapter and the homework, assignments and activities that accompany it, you should:

- Understand the terms *physical digestion* and *chemical digestion*.
- Understand what a digestive enzyme is.
- Know what protein, fats and carbohydrates are broken down into during digestion.
- Be able to list and locate the areas of the alimentary canal on a diagram.
- Be able to describe the passage of food through the alimentary canal from mouth to rectum.
- Know what the following substances are and what part they play in the digestive process: salivary amylase, hydrochloric acid, pepsin, pancreatic juice, bile and intestinal juice.
- Be able to describe how digested nutrients are absorbed and transported to body cells from the small intestine.

As we saw in Chapter 1, food contains the following six nutrients:

- Protein
- Fat
- Carbohydrates
- Minerals
- Vitamins
- Water

Protein, fat and carbohydrate must be **digested**, or broken down, before they can be used by the body. Minerals, vitamins and water, on the other hand, do not need to be digested and can be used by the body as they are.

Food is **physically** broken down by being chewed in the mouth and churned around in the stomach. Protein, fat and carbohydrate are **chemically** broken down by **enzymes**.

Digestive enzymes are chemical substances that break down food. Enzymes themselves do not change in the process. Each enzyme can only work on one nutrient. For example, an enzyme that can break down fats has no effect on protein.

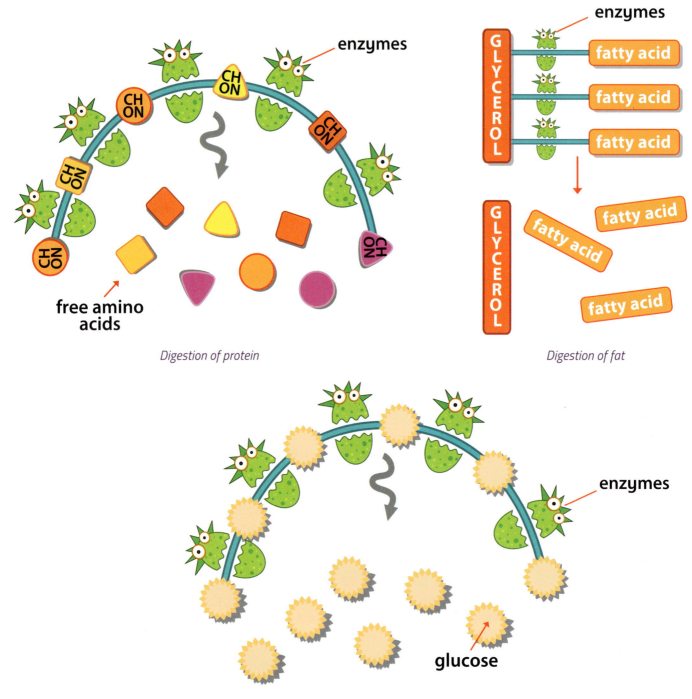

Digestion of protein

Digestion of fat

Digestion of carbohydrate

The alimentary canal

Digestion takes place in the alimentary canal. The alimentary canal consists of the:

- Mouth
- Oesophagus
- Stomach
- Small intestine (pancreas and liver)
- Large intestine
- Rectum

1. The teeth physically break food down in the mouth. The tongue mixes it with saliva from the **salivary glands**. Saliva contains the enzyme **amylase**. Amylase breaks down long chains of cooked starch, such as bread, into short chains called **maltose**.

2. Food is then swallowed and passes into a long tube called the **oesophagus**. The walls of the oesophagus move in and out, squeezing the food along – this is called **peristalsis**.

3. Food then passes into the **stomach**. The stomach can be described as a muscular bag that lies in the left-hand side of the abdomen under the **diaphragm**. Food is churned about in the stomach until it turns into a liquid called **chyme**. The walls of the stomach produce **gastric juice**. This juice is made of a strong acid, **hydrochloric acid**, and two enzymes. One of these enzymes is called **pepsin** and it starts to digest protein by breaking the long amino acid chains into shorter ones, called peptides.

4. Next, food passes into the narrow, but very long, **small intestine**. Again, peristalsis keeps the food moving along. Three digestive juices work here to complete the digestion of our food: pancreatic juice (made by the pancreas), bile (made by the liver; works on fats) and intestinal juice (made by the intestine itself). All three juices work together to change:
   - Protein and peptides to free amino acids
   - Carbohydrates to monomers (simple sugars)
   - Fats to fatty acids and glycerol

   Digested nutrients are then absorbed into the blood. They travel to our cells, where they carry out their various functions, such as producing heat and energy.

5. Waste that is not absorbed now passes into the **large intestine** (**colon** or **bowel**). As it passes into the large intestine, the waste is still very liquid. Some of this water passes back through the walls of the intestine into the bloodstream. This causes the waste to become more solid. It is now called **faeces**. Faeces passes out of the body through the rectum and anus.

The small intestine

The walls of the small intestine are like a very fine carpet. They are covered in a huge number of hair-like projections called villi. Each villus has a tiny blood vessel and a lymph vessel. Digested nutrients pass into these vessels.

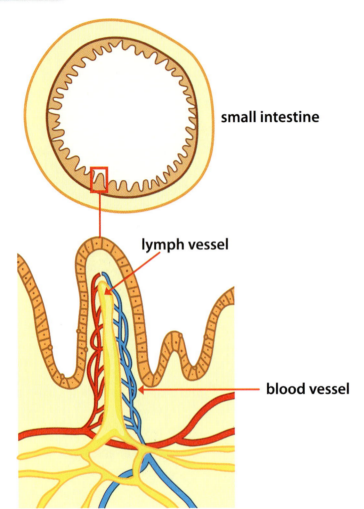

small intestine

lymph vessel

blood vessel

The small intestine

Close-up of the small intestine showing the villi

The absorption and transport of protein and carbohydrate is simple:

small intestine → blood vessel of villi → bloodstream → body cells

Fats are more complicated:

small intestine → lymph vessel of villi → lymph system → bloodstream → body cells

Rapid Revision

1. **Macronutrients** (protein, fats and carbohydrates) are broken down by both physical and chemical digestion.

2. **Digestive enzymes** chemically break down foods without being altered themselves. Each enzyme works on only one nutrient.

3. The **alimentary canal** consists of the mouth (salivary gland – turns cooked starch into amylase), oesophagus, stomach (turns food into chyme and mixes it with gastric juice; pepsin turns proteins into peptides) and small intestine.

4. There are **three juices in the small intestine**: pancreatic juice, bile (works on fats) and intestinal juice. These fully digest all macronutrients: protein to amino acids, fats to fatty acids, and glycerol and carbohydrates to simple sugars (monomers, such as glucose).

5. **Nutrients** are absorbed into the bloodstream from the small intestine. Proteins and carbohydrates are absorbed directly, whereas fats are absorbed via the lymph system.

Revision Questions

1. Name the parts of the alimentary canal.
2. How is food physically and chemically broken down?
3. What are digestive enzymes? What is their function?
4. What is the movement of the wall of the alimentary canal called?
5. Describe the process of digestion in the stomach.
6. What is chyme?
7. Describe the digestion of protein, fats and carbohydrates.
8. Explain how digested protein, fat and carbohydrates are absorbed into the bloodstream.

Test Yourself
eTest.ie

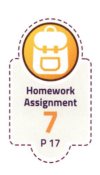

Homework Assignment
7
P 17

Teacher's CD — Slide presentation ▪ Student activity pack with revision crossword ▪ Class test ▪ Student learning contract

Key words

- Balanced diet
- Food pyramid
- A serving
- Food groups
- Folic acid
- Sedentary worker
- Manual worker
- Invalid/convalescent

Learning outcomes

After completing this chapter and the homework, assignments and activities that accompany it, you should:

- Be able to describe the food pyramid and know how many servings are required from each shelf.
- Understand what each of the food groups on the pyramid are needed for in the body.
- Be able to explain general healthy eating guidelines that should be followed by everyone.
- Be able to describe more specific dietary requirements for each of the following groups: babies, children, teenagers, adults, pregnant and breastfeeding women, elderly people and invalids/ convalescents.
- Be able to create a daily menu for each of these groups taking account of their specific needs.

To have a balanced diet, we need to eat the correct amount of each of the six nutrients. The food pyramid pictured on the next page is designed to make planning a healthy, balanced diet easy. It divides food into four groups and then advises us how much of each group we need every day. The number of servings to be eaten from each group will depend on the individual. For example, a pregnant woman will need extra servings from the meat and milk groups.

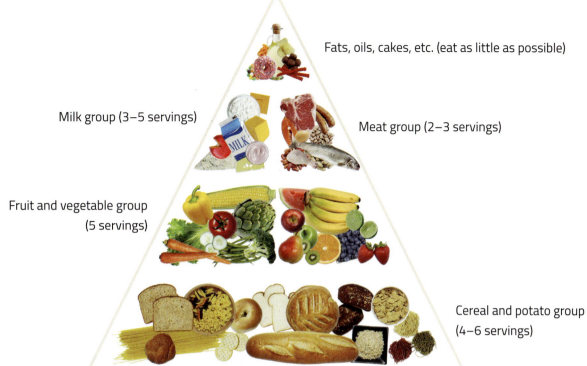

Fats, oils, cakes, etc. (eat as little as possible)

Milk group (3–5 servings)

Meat group (2–3 servings)

Fruit and vegetable group
(5 servings)

Cereal and potato group
(4–6 servings)

General healthy eating guidelines

- Reduce intake of salt, sugar and saturated fat.
- Increase intake of fibre, fruit and vegetables, water, iron, calcium and vitamin D.

The food groups

	Meat group	Milk group	Fruit and vegetables	Cereal and potato group
Why we need this group	The foods in this group are good sources of protein, which is needed for growth and repair of the body's cells.	The foods in this group are good sources of calcium and protein. Calcium is needed for strong bones and teeth. Choose low-fat options (except for children under five).	The foods in this group are good sources of some vitamins and minerals. Many contain fibre to prevent constipation and other bowel disorders.	The foods in this group are needed for energy. Choose wholemeal options, as they contain more fibre to prevent constipation and other bowel disorders.

	Meat group	Milk group	Fruit and vegetables	Cereal and potato group
A serving is:	• 50g meat or chicken • 50g Cheddar-type cheese • 75g fish • 75g TVP • 75g Quorn • 75g nuts • 2 eggs • 8 dessertspoons beans or peas	• 1 glass milk • 1 carton yoghurt • 25g cheese	• 1 small glass fruit juice • 4 dessertspoons cooked vegetables • 1 bowl homemade soup • 1 piece fresh fruit • 4 dessertspoons cooked or tinned fruit	• 1 small bowl cereal • 1 slice bread • 4 dessertspoons rice or pasta • 1 potato
Servings per day from this group	Child 2 Teenager 2 Adult 2 Pregnant woman 3 Breastfeeding mother 3	Child 3 Teenager 5 Adult 3 Pregnant woman 5 Breastfeeding mother 5	Child 5 Teenager 5 Adult 5 Pregnant woman 5 Breastfeeding mother 5	Child 4 Teenager 6 Adult 6 Pregnant woman 6 Breastfeeding mother 6

A balanced diet for each age group

Babies

🍴 Breastfeed if possible for the first six months. If bottle feeding, then use a suitable formula milk, as cow's milk should not be given to babies.

🍴 Do not allow babies and toddlers to sleep with a bottle in their mouth. This causes 'bottle rot' and they could choke.

🍴 Wean onto puréed solids at four to six months. Introduce one food at a time. Avoid using convenience baby foods (jars), as babies become used to their taste and may refuse fresh, home-cooked food (see also weaning on page 423).

🍴 Babies need vitamin C. Serve juice in a cup or from a spoon – never from a bottle, as it rots teeth. Stewed, puréed fruit is also a good source of vitamin C.

🍴 From six months, a baby's natural store of iron runs out. They therefore need iron-rich foods such as dark green vegetables and liver from six months.

🍴 Do not add salt or sugar to a baby's food.

🍴 By one year, babies will generally be eating the same foods as the rest of the family. Remove the baby's portion before adding seasonings, especially salt.

Children

🍴 Have regular meal times.

🍴 Children need more protein, calcium, vitamin D and iron for their size than adults.

🍴 Serve small, attractive portions. Each meal should contain a nutrient-dense food. Nutrient-dense foods are foods that contain a number of different nutrients but with little bulk. They are sometimes called superfoods. Examples of nutrient-dense foods are cheese, eggs, chicken and fish.

🍴 Do not fuss about food refusal. It only makes it worse.

🍴 Serve healthy snacks such as fruit or unsalted popcorn.

🍴 Continue to use whole milk, as it contains vitamin A for growth and vitamin D for healthy bones.

🍴 Try to serve healthy packed lunches and avoid junk food such as sweets or crisps. Children should be given these foods only very occasionally, especially due to the fact that approximately 22% of Irish children are overweight or obese.

🍴 Set a good example yourself, as children imitate adults in their eating patterns.

Adolescents/teenagers

🍴 The growth spurt during the teenage years means teenagers need plenty of protein, calcium and iron.

🍴 Some very active teenagers will need lots of high-energy foods, but choose foods that provide other nutrients as well (brown bread, rice and pasta). Inactive teenagers, however, need to monitor their carbohydrate and fat intake to avoid weight gain. Ideally they would introduce an activity such as walking into their daily routine, even if they are not particularly interested in sport.

🍴 Girls need to eat iron-rich foods such as red meat and green vegetables to avoid anaemia because of periods (menstruation).

🍴 For healthy skin, avoid fried foods, chocolate, etc. Eat fruit and vegetables and drink plenty of water (eight glasses per day).

🍴 Choose healthy snacks such as yoghurt and fruit.

Sedentary worker

Manual worker

Adults

🍴 Weight gain becomes more common as people enter adulthood. People with sedentary jobs should cut down on what they eat to avoid weight gain.

🍴 Many people stop taking regular exercise once they leave school. Adults should try to take some form of exercise at least three times per week.

🍴 Eat plenty of fibre-rich foods such as brown bread, fruit and vegetables, as they prevent bowel disease and are low in calories.

🍴 Do not eat too much salt. It can cause high blood pressure and strokes.

🍴 Avoid foods that have too much saturated fat, such as butter and sausages. Saturated fats contain cholesterol, which is linked to heart disease.

🍴 Women in particular should eat calcium-rich foods such as milk, yoghurt and cheese to avoid brittle bones in later life. Also, because of monthly blood loss, all women risk anaemia and so need to eat iron-rich foods such as meat, cereals and green vegetables. (**Note:** Vitamin C is also needed to absorb iron.)

🍴 Avoid drinking too much alcohol (women maximum 14 units per week, men 21 units).

🔗 Chapter 24, page 286 – healthy alcohol consumption

Pregnant and breastfeeding women

🍴 Pregnant women are not eating for two. The expected weight gain during pregnancy is 12kg (2 stone). Anything more than this (except with multiple births) is just extra body fat.

A recent study conducted by the Coombe hospital and UCD found that almost half of all pregnant women in Ireland (43%) are overweight; 13% of these women are obese and 2% are morbidly obese. Gaining too much weight during pregnancy can be harmful to women and their baby and will be very difficult to get rid of after the birth.

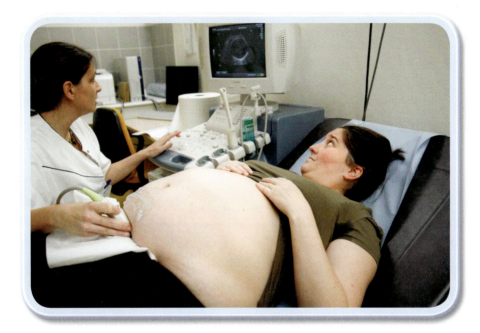

Obese pregnant woman

🍴 Avoid smoking, alcohol, strong tea, coffee and spicy foods. Avoid lightly cooked eggs, unpasteurised cheeses and cook-chill foods because of the risk of food poisoning.

🍴 Eat iron-rich foods such as green vegetables to avoid anaemia. Vitamin C is needed to absorb iron, so fresh fruit and juices should be eaten.

🍴 Take vitamin D to help absorb calcium. Vitamin D is found in cod liver oil and oily fish such as mackerel, and is made in the body in the presence of sunshine.

🍴 Eat calcium for healthy bones and teeth. It is found in milk, tinned fish and cheese (pasteurised only).

🍴 Because of the extra weight bearing down on the bowel, some women experience constipation during pregnancy. To avoid this, eat plenty of fruit and vegetables and fibre-rich cereals such as brown bread, pasta and rice.

🍴 Breastfeeding women should eat a healthy diet so that they can produce good-quality breast milk. Extra fluids should be taken. Alcohol, smoking and drinking too much caffeine should be avoided, as they all pass into the breast milk.

Folic acid

Approximately 84 babies are born every year in Ireland with serious neural tube defects such as spina bifida. Folic acid helps prevent spina bifida and other conditions and should be taken in tablet form for three months before becoming pregnant and for the first 12 weeks of pregnancy. Some foods, such as breakfast cereals, are fortified with folic acid (this means that folic acid is added artificially by manufacturers).

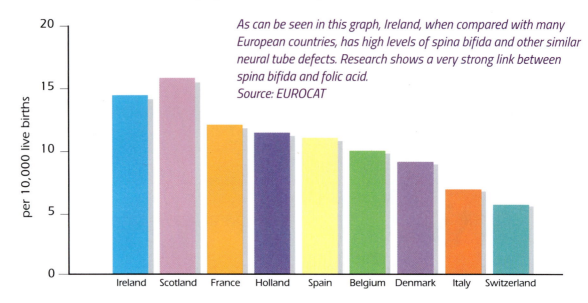

As can be seen in this graph, Ireland, when compared with many European countries, has high levels of spina bifida and other similar neural tube defects. Research shows a very strong link between spina bifida and folic acid.
Source: EUROCAT

Elderly people

🍴 Some elderly people, especially those living alone, have nutritionally poor diets. They may have arthritis, which makes shopping and cooking difficult. They may have difficulty chewing food or lack the motivation to cook balanced meals. Elderly people should try to eat three nourishing meals a day.

🍴 Choose low-fat cheese, milk and yoghurt, as these foods are high in calcium and low in fat. Calcium prevents osteoporosis (brittle bones).

🍴 To prevent heart disease, limit high-cholesterol foods such as butter and sausages. Choose polyunsaturated spreads instead, such as Flora.

🍴 Eat plenty of fruit and vegetables. Many elderly people lack vitamin C.

🍴 Reduce salt, fat and sugar intake.

🍴 Choose high-fibre foods such as brown bread and fruit, as elderly people can be prone to constipation.

🍴 Limit intake of processed foods such as tinned foods, white bread and butter.

🍴 Get outside as much as possible as sunlight is needed for the manufacture of vitamin D – needed for strong bones and teeth.

Invalids and convalescents (those recovering from illness)

- Follow the doctor's or hospital dietician's advice.
- Eat protein-rich foods such as chicken, fish and pulse vegetables to repair damaged cells.
- Eat or drink vitamin C-rich foods such as fruit and fruit juices to help fight infection, repair wounds and absorb iron.
- Eat iron-rich foods such as offal, green vegetables and brown bread to prevent anaemia if blood has been lost.
- Foods should be easily digested, such as white fish, chicken, custard, milk, light soups such as broth and fruit juice.
- Drink plenty of fluids, especially with fever.
- Boil, bake, grill or steam food. Do not fry, reheat or add spices.
- Prepare small, attractive portions.
- Remember, food hygiene is very important.

Rapid Revision

1. A **balanced diet** means eating the correct proportions of the six nutrients. The food pyramid helps make this easier for us.
2. The **food pyramid** has five shelves containing different food groups: cereal and potato (4–6 servings), fruit and vegetables (5 or more), milk and milk products (3–5), meat, chicken, fish and eggs (2–3) and empty-calorie foods that should only be eaten sparingly.
3. **Each shelf of the food pyramid has a different primary function in the body.** Cereals and potatoes provide heat and energy; fruit and vegetables are a source of vitamins, minerals and fibre; milk and milk products are a source of calcium for bones and teeth; meat has protein for growth and repair; and empty-calorie foods should only be eaten sparingly because they have no function that other groups cannot fulfil.
4. There are **general healthy eating guidelines** that everyone should follow: reduce salt, sugar and saturated fat and increase fibre, fruit and vegetables, water, iron, calcium and vitamin D.
5. **Babies:** Breastfeed and use home-cooked foods for weaning. Babies need vitamin C, so serve diluted juice from a cup or puréed fruits. Iron-rich foods are needed after six months. Do not add salt or sugar.

6. **Children:** Serve home-cooked meals and small, attractive portions, nutrient-dense foods (eggs, fish, chicken), healthy snacks, whole milk for calcium and healthy packed lunches. Set a good example.

7. **Teenagers:** Teenagers need plenty of protein, calcium and iron due to growth spurts. Energy intake should match activity rates. Girls in particular need iron-rich foods to avoid anaemia. Choose healthy snacks and drink lots of water.

8. **Adults:** Avoid weight gain by taking regular exercise and reducing empty-calorie food intake. Eat plenty of fibre-rich foods. Reduce salt and saturated fats (to avoid high cholesterol). Women in particular should consume enough calcium to avoid brittle bones later in life. Avoid too much alcohol.

9. **Pregnant and breastfeeding women:** Avoid excessive weight gain because it causes problems for mother and baby. Do not smoke and do not drink alcohol or too much tea or coffee. Do not eat spicy foods, unpasteurised cheeses or cook-chill foods. Consume plenty of calcium and vitamin D (bones and teeth), iron, vitamin C (to prevent anaemia) and fibre to prevent constipation (common in pregnancy). Drink extra fluids when breastfeeding and avoid alcohol, too much caffeine and nicotine because they pass into breast milk. Folic acid/spina bifida link.

10. **Elderly:** Many factors prevent elderly people from following a balanced diet. Choose low-fat products. To avoid high cholesterol, eat plenty of fruit and vegetables for vitamin C and fibre. Reduce salt, fat and sugar intakes. Limit processed foods. Get out in the sunshine.

11. **Invalids/convalescents:** Follow the doctor's orders. Eat easily digested, protein-rich foods for repair (chicken or fish). Consume vitamin C to fight infection and help wounds to heal. Consume iron-rich foods to replace blood loss. Drink plenty of fluids. Boil, bake or steam foods. Serve small, attractive portions. Food hygiene is vital.

Revision Questions

1. What is the purpose of the food pyramid? Name the four food groups represented on the food pyramid.
2. What types of food are at the very top of the food pyramid?
3. List six general healthy eating guidelines.
4. Explain why each of the food groups is important in the diet: meat group, milk group, fruit and vegetable group, cereal and potato group. How many servings from each food group should be consumed by the following groups of people: (a) children (b) teenagers (c) adults (d) pregnant women (e) breastfeeding mothers?
5. Why is the meat group important in the diet? Describe a serving from this group.
6. How many servings from the meat group should be eaten daily by (a) children (b) teenagers (c) adults (d) pregnant women (e) breastfeeding mothers?
7. Describe five specific healthy eating guidelines for each of the following groups of people: (a) babies (b) children (c) teenagers (d) adults (both sedentary and manual workers) (e) pregnant and breastfeeding women (f) elderly people (g) invalids and convalescents.

Test Yourself
eTest.ie

Homework
Assignment
8
P 19

Teacher's CD

Slide presentation ▪ Student activity pack with revision crossword ▪ Class test ▪ Student learning contract

Key words

- ✓ Lactovegetarian
- ✓ Vegan
- ✓ Coronary heart disease
- ✓ Stroke
- ✓ Sodium
- ✓ Empty-calorie foods
- ✓ Dietary fibre/cellulose
- ✓ Obesity
- ✓ Coeliac disease
- ✓ Gluten
- ✓ Diabetes (type 1 and 2)
- ✓ Insulin

Learning outcomes

After completing this chapter and the homework, assignments and activities that accompany it, you should:

- Know what the different types of vegetarians are and be able to plan a menu for a day for a vegetarian (both lacto and vegan), taking account of suitable dietary guidelines.
- Understand the diet-related causes of the following health issues: coronary heart disease and strokes, obesity, coeliac disease and diabetes.
- Be able to suggest at least four dietary guidelines that should be followed by people at risk of or with the other related issues above.
- Be able to plan a suitable daily menu for each of the above.
- Understand the benefits of having a diet low in saturated fat, sugar and salt and be able to suggest at least four ways of reducing each of these in the diet.
- Understand the need to increase fibre in the diet and be able to plan a menu for a person who wants to improve this aspect of their lifestyle.

People follow special diets for many different reasons. The following diets will be studied in this chapter:

- Vegetarianism
- Diet-related conditions such as coronary heart disease and obesity and their diet-related treatments, i.e. low-fat, low-salt, low-sugar and high-fibre diets
- Coeliac disease
- Diabetes

Vegetarianism

Vegetarians, for various reasons, do not eat meat or fish. There are two main types of vegetarian:

- Lactovegetarians do not eat meat or fish but do eat animal products such as milk, cheese and eggs.
- Vegans, or strict vegetarians, eat only plant foods such as fruit, vegetables, nuts, cereals and soya milk. Vegans usually take vitamin B supplements because this vitamin is not found in plant foods at all.

There are also subdivisions. Pesco-vegetarians will eat fish, pollo-vegetarians will eat chicken and lacto-ovo vegetarians will drink milk and eat eggs.

Case study

Hi, my name is Rian and I'm a lactovegetarian. I became a vegetarian about three years ago. Some people don't eat meat for religious reasons, but my decision was based more on health grounds. I believe it's wrong to kill animals, and it also scares me when I read about all the hormones that are pumped into animals these days.

Being vegetarian has its advantages. My diet is a really healthy one: it's low in fat and high in fibre, which will help prevent bowel disorders and heart disease later in life. It also keeps me at my correct weight. I do have to be careful that I get enough iron and protein, though, so I eat plenty of dark green vegetables and brown bread for iron and foods like cheese, beans, TVP and Quorn for protein.

Generally I find being a vegetarian fine. There are lots of different foods to choose from. I don't feel restricted just because I don't eat meat.

Suitable vegetarian dishes

- Vegetable soups such as carrot, mushroom or mixed vegetable
- Vegetarian pizza, quiche, risotto, lasagne or curry
- Salads
- Stir-fries

Problem diets

Most diet-related problems are linked to the following:

- Eating too much saturated fat (heart disease, obesity and type 2 diabetes)
- Eating too much salt (high blood pressure and strokes)
- Eating too much sugar (obesity and type 2 diabetes)
- Eating too little fibre (bowel diseases such as colon cancer)
- Drinking too much alcohol (heart disease, liver disease, obesity and type 2 diabetes)

Coronary heart disease and strokes

A **heart attack** happens when an artery becomes totally blocked by the fatty substance known as cholesterol. A **stroke** occurs if the blocked artery is in the brain.

Ireland has the highest death rate from heart disease in people aged under 65 in the EU (see the bar chart below).

Most heart attacks happen within a few hours of the symptoms first occurring and before the person can reach a hospital. Prevention is therefore vitally important.

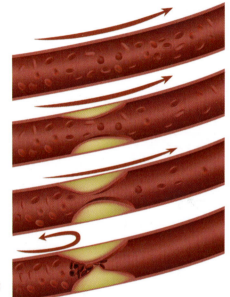

STAGES OF ATHEROSCLEROSIS

A healthy artery

Healthy artery

Build-up begins

Plaque forms

An artery clogged with cholesterol

Plaque ruptures; blood clot forms

Death rates per 100,000 people from coronary heart disease in the EU (age 0–65) Source: World Health Organisation)

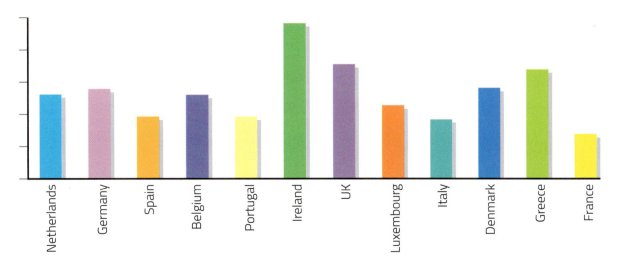

Netherlands · Germany · Spain · Belgium · Portugal · Ireland · UK · Luxembourg · Italy · Denmark · Greece · France

Heart disease is linked to:

- A high-fat diet
- Being overweight
- Smoking
- Drinking too much
- A stressful lifestyle

Tips for a healthy heart: A low-fat diet

Eat fewer foods from the top of the food pyramid

Bake, grill, boil, steam or microwave food – avoid frying food

Use low-fat products

Use polyunsaturated margarine (e.g. Flora)

Eat plenty of fruit and vegetables

Drink eight glasses of water every day

Choose chicken and fish instead of fatty red meats

Low-salt diet

According to the Irish Heart Foundation, if everyone in Ireland reduced their salt intake by half a teaspoon (3 grams) per day, it would prevent 900 deaths per year from stroke and heart attack.

Salt is the common name for a substance called sodium. Sodium is sometimes represented by the letters Na. Adults need a maximum of 4–6g of sodium per day according to the Irish Heart Foundation. Children should have less. Many of us, however, take up to 20g. Too much salt in the diet can cause high blood pressure (hypertension), which can lead to heart attacks and strokes.

To reduce salt in the diet:

- Reduce the amount of salt added during cooking or at the table. Use low-sodium alternatives such as LoSalt.
- Flavour dishes with herbs, spices and pepper instead of salt.
- Choose fresh meat and vegetables – these have a naturally low salt content.
- Avoid foods high in salt, such as ham, bacon, rashers, sausages, frozen burgers, packet soups and sauces, instant noodles, stock cubes, crisps, popcorn and salted nuts.
- If in doubt, look out for the words *salt*, *sodium* or *Na* on food labels.

Low-sugar diet

Sugar is not needed in the diet. Sugar and sugary foods and drinks are often called **empty-calorie foods**. This means that they provide a lot of calories but very little goodness.

Unfortunately, many of us are encouraged to develop a sweet tooth as children, when we are rewarded with sugary foods for being 'good'. Too much sugar in the diet causes weight problems and tooth decay.

To reduce sugar in the diet:

- Avoid fizzy drinks (especially non-diet), sweets, bars, sugary breakfast cereals, cakes, etc.
- Use artificial sweeteners such as Canderel for cooking.
- Snack on healthy foods such as fresh fruit and unsalted nuts.
- Be careful of 'hidden sugars'. Read labels – glucose, fructose and sucrose are all sugar.

High-fibre diet

Dietary fibre (cellulose) is found in plant foods such as cereals, fruit and vegetables. However, once foods, particularly cereals, are processed, they lose much of their fibre content. Therefore, wholesome, unprocessed foods should be eaten.

A high-fibre diet has many benefits: it helps prevent constipation, piles and other serious diseases of the bowel, such as colon cancer. Fibre absorbs large amounts of water when eaten, creating a feeling of fullness. In addition, it contains no calories, so fibre-rich foods are excellent to include in the diet for anyone trying to lose weight. Fibre-rich foods include wholegrain breads and breakfast cereals (All-Bran), brown rice and pasta, fruit and vegetables, nuts and seeds.

Rates of colon cancer worldwide

Region/countries	Rate per 100,000 population
Australia and New Zealand	45.0
Western Europe (Austria, Britain, France, Germany, Ireland)	36.4
Southern Europe (Greece, Italy, Malta, Portugal, Spain)	29.7
Eastern Europe (Bulgaria, Latvia, Poland, Romania, Ukraine)	25.1
Eastern Asia (Iran, Saudi Arabia, Syria)	25.1
South Central Asia (India, Nepal, Pakistan)	4.1
South Africa	10.1
Northern Africa (Cameroon, Chad, Ethiopia, Nigeria, Sudan)	4.5

What sort of food is traditionally eaten in countries with low/high incidence rates of colon cancer?

Obesity

Obesity means being 20% or more above the normal weight for your height and build.

Adults

A recent study sponsored by the Department of Health and Children found that two out of five Irish adults (39%–45% of men; 33% of women) are overweight. One in four (24%–25% of men; 26% of women) are obese. The trend towards obesity in Ireland is increasing. Between 1990 and 2000, the prevalence of obesity increased by 67% overall, up 1.25 fold in women (from 13%) and up 2.5 fold in men (from 8%).

Why do you think Ireland has seen this huge increase, particularly in men?

Children and teenagers

In total, 22% of 5- to 12-year-olds are overweight or obese. One in five teenagers is overweight or obese (11% overweight and 8% obese). Did you know that in 1990, only 1% of teenage boys and 3% of teenage girls were obese?

Why do you think Ireland has gone from having very few overweight children and teenagers in the 1990s to the situation as it is today?

The thyroid gland in the neck controls the rate at which we burn food. People who are naturally thin burn food quickly, but some people burn food more slowly and are therefore prone to put on weight.

Obesity can be caused by an unhealthy thyroid gland. More often, though, the cause is overeating and lack of exercise.

People who are obese suffer an increased risk of:

- Chest infections
- Low self-esteem
- Diabetes
- Problems when under anaesthetic
- Fertility problems

- Strokes
- Heart attacks
- Varicose veins
- High blood pressure

Body mass index (BMI)

Body mass index (BMI) is a measure of body fat based on height and weight that applies to both adult men and women.

$$BMI = \frac{\text{weight in kg}}{\text{height in m}^2} \quad or \quad \frac{\text{weight in pounds}}{\text{height in inches}^2} \times 703$$

BMI categories:
- Underweight = < 18.5
- Normal weight = 18.5–24.9
- Overweight = 25–29.9
- Obesity = BMI of 30 or greater

Guidelines for sensible weight loss:

- Avoid crash or fad diets, as they do not work in the long term.
- Exercise more – at least three times per week.
- Plan your meals each day in advance. If you do not do this, you may get hungry and eat unwisely, such as buying a takeaway.
- Always have healthy options easily available (fruit) if you want to have a snack between meals. Do not buy junk food, and if it is in the house, keep it out of sight.
- Use a smaller plate and try to eat more slowly. If you eat quickly, you will eat more because your body has not had enough time to realise it is full.
- Eat less butter, fatty meats such as sausages and burgers, sugary foods such as biscuits and chocolate and calorie-laden convenience foods such as pizza and garlic bread.
- If you do buy biscuits, go for low-fat varieties and perhaps individually wrapped portions so that you are not tempted to eat more than one or two at a time.

🍴 Eat more fruit and vegetables, white fish and chicken.

🍴 Eat bread, potatoes and nuts only in moderation.

🍴 Drink more water – at least eight glasses per day.

H Coeliac disease

During normal digestion, long protein chains are broken down into lots of tiny amino acid units. These single units pass easily through the walls of the small intestine and into the bloodstream.

Gluten is a type of protein found in wheat and some other cereals. A person suffering from coeliac disease cannot break gluten down. The big undigested gluten molecules damage the walls of the intestine as they pass through.

The symptoms of the condition are pains in the abdomen, diarrhoea, failure to thrive and anaemia.

There is only one way to treat coeliac disease: avoid all foods containing gluten.

Foods to avoid:

🍴 All wheat products: biscuits, bread, cakes, pasta, many breakfast cereals

🍴 Rye and barley

🍴 Processed meat products such as sausages and fish or anything in batter or breadcrumbs

🍴 Packet soups and sauces, many snack foods

Gluten-free symbol

Gluten-free foods and foods very low in gluten:

🍴 Fruit, vegetables and dairy products, such as milk and cheese

🍴 Rice, soya products such as TVP

🍴 Plain meat and fish

🍴 Maize products such as cornflakes

🍴 Specially made gluten-free products such as bread and cakes

Gluten-free products

Diabetes

Diabetes is a disorder that occurs when the pancreas (a leaf-shaped organ under the stomach) does not produce any/enough insulin to meet the body's needs or stops being able to use insulin, causing abnormally high levels of sugar in the blood.

Normally when you eat carbohydrates, such as bread, pasta, fruits or vegetables, these foods are broken down into glucose (sugar). This fuel then travels in the bloodstream until it is 'unloaded' into your cells by insulin, which functions like a little team of removal men. With diabetes, however, the body either stops producing any/enough insulin or becomes unable to use it properly. This makes it difficult for the sugar in the blood to get into the cells, so it builds up in the bloodstream. Body cells do not get enough fuel to function properly and literally begin starving to death. If left untreated, diabetes can lead to heart disease, kidney disease, chronic infections or other life-threatening conditions. While there is no cure for diabetes, it can be controlled.

There are two types of diabetes: type 1 and type 2.

Type 1 diabetes, also called insulin-dependent diabetes, occurs in about 0.5% of the general population. With type 1, the body produces little or no insulin and so insulin injections need to be taken daily. Type 1 may appear at any age but usually begins in childhood or early adulthood, most often among young people with a sibling or parent who also has the disease.

Type 2 diabetes, also called non-insulin-dependent diabetes, occurs in 2–3% of the general population. You are most likely to develop the disease if you are obese, are over the age of 45 or have a family history of diabetes. While type 2 diabetes used to be practically unheard of in people under 30 (it was actually called adult onset diabetes), it is now appearing in adolescence and even childhood because of increased obesity levels. Studies show that a hormone produced by fat cells called resistin

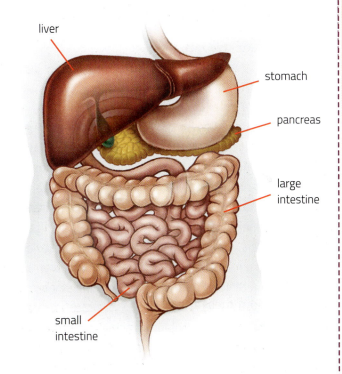

The pancreas is the leaf-shaped organ directly under the stomach in the diagram above

causes body cells to resist insulin. Thus, the more fat cells there are, the more resistin there is and the greater the likelihood of developing diabetes. Most people with type 2 diabetes do not have to inject insulin, but some do.

Controlling diabetes centres around three things: injections or tablets, diet and exercise.

Dietary guidelines for diabetics:

- Reach and maintain your ideal weight and get plenty of exercise.

- Eat regularly – don't skip meals.

- Keep to a low-sugar diet – some artificial sweeteners (Canderel) may be used.

- Eat high-fibre carbohydrates such as brown bread and pasta.

- Diabetic foods, such as diabetic chocolate, are available, but it is a good idea to get out of the habit of eating sweet-tasting foods.

1. **Vegetarians:** Lacto-vegetarians do not eat meat or fish but will eat dairy. Vegans eat no animal products at all. A vegetarian diet is a healthy one – low-fat and high-fibre. Vegetarians must be careful to get enough iron and protein – they should eat plenty of dark green vegetables and protein-rich foods (nuts, beans, Quorn). Suitable dishes: vegetarian quiche, curry and lasagne.

2. **Coronary heart disease (CHD)** occurs when arteries become blocked with cholesterol. A **stroke** occurs if the blockage is in the brain. Ireland has a very high rate of CHD. To help prevent CHD, avoid saturated fats, fried and junk foods, being overweight, smoking, too much alcohol and stress. Choose low-fat products, chicken and fish, eat plenty of fruit and vegetables and drink lots of water.

3. A **high-salt diet** causes high blood pressure, which can lead to strokes and heart attacks. Reduce salt by not adding it at the table, choosing low-sodium products and by flavouring dishes with herbs and spices. Fresh fruit, vegetables and unprocessed meats are all low in salt. Avoid foods that are high in salt (rashers, packet soups) and salty snacks (crisps). Look for salt, sodium or Na (all salt) on food labels.

4. A **high-sugar diet** causes obesity and tooth decay. Avoid sugary drinks and foods, use artificial sweeteners, snack on healthy foods (fruit) and be careful of hidden sugars. Look out for glucose, fructose and sucrose on ingredient lists – they are all sugar.

5. **Fibre** is needed in the diet for a healthy bowel. Choose unprocessed cereals and eat plenty of fruit and vegetables. Fibre-rich foods are usually low in calories, so they can help maintain a healthy weight.

6. **Obesity** is a major problem among all age groups in Irish society. Obesity increases the risk of CHD, diabetes, chest infections, fertility problems and low self-esteem. A body mass index between 18 and 25 is healthy. To maintain a healthy weight, avoid crash or fad diets, exercise regularly, plan meals in advance to avoid poor food choices, have healthy snacks available, avoid fatty or sugary foods, eat more chicken, fish, fruit and vegetables, and drink plenty of water.

7. **Coeliac disease** is an inability to digest gluten. Gluten is a protein found in cereals such as wheat, rye and barley. Many processed foods contain gluten, such as sausages, fish in breadcrumbs, packet soups and sauces. Gluten-free products are available – look for the symbol.

8. **Diabetes** occurs when the pancreas does not produce any or enough insulin to meet the body's needs. Insulin regulates the amount of sugar in the blood. There are two types of diabetes: type 1 and type 2. Type 2 is associated with obesity. Diabetics must try to maintain a healthy weight, eat regular meals and maintain a low-sugar diet.

1. Name the two main types of vegetarianism. List three advantages of being a vegetarian.
2. Describe three nutritional precautions that should be remembered by vegetarians wishing to have a balanced diet. Name six dishes suitable for a lactovegetarian.
3. List five factors associated with coronary heart disease and suggest five ways it can be prevented.
4. What is the scientific name for salt? What is the RDA for salt as recommended by the Irish Heart Foundation? Suggest five ways of reducing salt in the diet.
5. Describe two problems associated with a high-sugar diet. Suggest four ways of reducing sugar in the diet.
6. Describe two advantages of a high-fibre diet.
7. Define obesity. What percentage of Irish children are currently considered to be obese? What are the main causes of obesity? List six problems associated with obesity.
8. What do the letters BMI stand for and what do they mean? List eight guidelines for sensible weight loss.
9. What is coeliac disease? Name six foods that should be avoided by coeliacs.
10. What is diabetes? Describe the two different types of diabetes. What are the main differences between them? List three ways diabetes can be controlled.

Homework Assignment

9

P 25

Meal Planning

Slide presentation ▪ Student activity pack with revision crossword ▪ Class test ▪ Student learning contract

Key words

- Dietary restrictions
- Appetiser
- Accompaniments
- Table d'hôte
- À la carte
- Buffet
- Time/work plan
- Condiments
- Garnish

Learning outcomes

After completing this chapter and the homework assignments and activities that accompany it, you should:

- Know what factors affect meal planning.
- Know the difference between a table d'hôte, an á la carte and a buffet menu. Be able to design one of each, taking account of the rules for writing menus.
- Be able to correctly set a formal table setting.
- Know what garnishes and/or accompaniments are suitable for the following: soup, fish, lamb, turkey, beef, pork and duck.
- Be able to suggest a variety of ways to decorate sweet dishes and carry this out in practical classes.

Factors that affect meal planning

- Dietary restrictions, such as coeliac, diabetes, low-fat.
- Nutrition – meals should contain many different nutrients.
- Amount of time available to shop and cook.
- Money/equipment available.
- Climate and the availability of foods in season can also be a factor in meal planning. In cold weather, serve hot dishes such as stew. In hot weather, serve cold dishes such as salads.
- Ability of the cook.
- Occasion or type of meal (lunch or dinner, formal or informal).

Meals: Courses

Main meals are usually divided into courses. In medieval times, when banquets lasted for days, meals had as many as 12 courses. In modern times, two to five courses are more common.

1. Starter or appetiser

This course should be something tasty and not too filling, such as soup, melon, fruit juice or pâté. This course gets the digestive juices flowing.

2. Main course

A meat, fish or vegetarian dish is central to this course. **Accompaniments** are also served, such as:

- Potatoes, pasta or rice
- Vegetables or salad
- A sauce or gravy

3. Dessert or cheeseboard

- Hot or cold desserts such as trifle, cheesecake or warm apple pie with ice cream
- A cheeseboard is a selection of three or four different cheeses served with crackers
- Tea or coffee

Menus

There are basically two types of menu:

- Table d'hôte
- À la carte

Table d'hôte is a set-price menu. It is usually cheaper than the à la carte menu, although you pay the full menu price even if you do not have all the courses. Two to five courses are usually on offer, with a limited number of dishes to choose from for each course (see the sample on the next page).

On an **à la carte** menu, each item is priced separately. The menu may be several pages long, with a separate page with lots to choose from for each course (see the sample on the next page).

Table d'hôte menu

Starters

Pan-fried garlic mushrooms

Bruschetta
Toasted ciabatta bread topped with tomato, basil and olive oil

Deep-fried Brie with red onion relish

Main course

Pork medallions
Medallions of pork fillet pan-fried with julienne of onion, peppers and mushrooms in a pepper sauce

Poached salmon
Fillet of salmon poached in a light cream sauce

Vegetable risotto

Chicken piri piri
Chargrilled corn-fed chicken fillet in a lemon and chilli sauce

Desserts

Meringue nest with fresh fruit

Profiteroles with hot chocolate sauce

Hot apple pie with fresh cream or ice cream

Tea or coffee

Price: €38

One page from a Table d'hôte menu

À la carte

Starters

Pan-fried garlic mushrooms €4.50

Homemade roasted winter vegetable soup €3.75

Bruschetta €3.75

Toasted ciabatta bread topped with tomato, basil and olive oil

Tiger prawns in filo pastry €7.25

Tossed in garlic butter and served with a sweet and sour dip

Deep-fried Brie with red onion relish €5.25

Greek salad €3.75

Fresh vine tomatoes with peppers, onions, cucumber, feta cheese and oregano dressing

One page from an À la carte menu

Guidelines for writing a menu

- Write down the centre of the page.
- List courses in the order they are eaten.
- Write the main dish of the course first and then the accompaniments.
- Leave a line or place a motif between courses.
- Describe dishes in some detail – give the cut of meat or fish and the cooking method, such as 'roast loin of pork'.

Buffets

When catering for large numbers, such as a twenty-first birthday party, a buffet is often best. Food should be laid out in a logical way, with drinks served at a separate table or at the end.

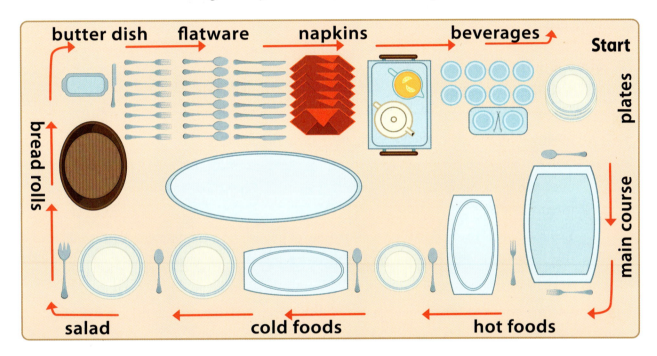

Hot main course	Salads	Desserts	Other
Beef, vegetable or chicken curry, pizza, quiche, cocktail sausages, chilli con carne, chicken à la king	Cold meat salads (ham or turkey), Waldorf salad, pasta salad, potato salad, rice salad, coleslaw	Cheesecake, fresh fruit flans, mousse, fruit salad and cream, apple and rhubarb crumble or tart	Boiled rice, rolls, bread, salad dressings

Setting the table

- Everything should be spotless: cutlery, glasses, tablemats, tablecloths, etc.
- They should match if possible.
- Fill clean salt and pepper containers (condiments).
- Keep flower arrangements low.
- Place a jug of iced water on the table just before the meal begins.

Formal table setting

🔧 Cutlery used first is on the outside.

🔧 When serving, serve food to the left of the person eating and clear empty plates from the right.

Planning a meal

Once you have decided what you are going to cook, you now have to shop for the ingredients, store them correctly before use and then prepare the meal using an effective time or work plan.

Shopping for food

🔧 It is best to shop for food only once a week, as this reduces buying things that you do not really need (impulse buying).

🔧 When you have planned out your meals for the week or for the special occasion, make out a **shopping list** of all the ingredients you need. Check that you do not have any of them already.

🔧 Buy food in clean shops with a wide variety of goods and a high turnover (this means that fresh foods are being put on the shelves regularly).

🔧 Stick to your shopping list – something is not a bargain if you do not need it.

🔧 Avoid pre-packed fruit, vegetables and meat, as you cannot examine them for quality.

🔧 Check use-by dates and that food in supermarket freezer cabinets is stored below −18°C and below the load line (this is usually a red line; food should not be piled up above this mark, as it will not be cold enough).

🔧 Pack foods away at home as soon as possible after purchase.

Time/work plans

Both time and work plans list all the tasks involved in preparing, cooking and serving a meal in the order it makes sense to carry them out. Time plans, unlike work plans (see Chapter 9, page 85), include specific times. Basically, with both plans you work out how long it will take to make the various dishes on your menu and begin with the dish that takes the longest to make. For example, if your menu includes prawn cocktail, Irish stew and apple crumble with ice cream, you would start with the stew because it takes the longest to cook, then the crumble and last the prawn cocktail.

 Chapter 7 – guidelines on preparing, cooking and serving food

Presenting food

Before we taste food, we see it. How food is presented is very important. All tableware must be **spotlessly clean**. Wipe spills from dishes or plates before bringing them to the table. Garnish or decorate food attractively, but do not overdo it.

- **Garnish:** Savoury foods
- **Decorate:** Sweet foods

Garnishes can either be items placed on or beside food, such as lemon twists, or sauces, such as fillet steak with pepper sauce.

A garnished savoury dish

Dish	Suggested garnish
Soup	Parsley, swirl of cream, croutons
Fish	Lemon wedges or twists, tartare sauce, tomato roses
Lamb	Mint sprigs, mint sauce
Turkey	Cranberry sauce
Beef	Horseradish sauce
Pork	Apple sauce
Duck	Orange sauce, orange twists

Lemon and lime loops

Spring onion tassel

Lemon/lime twist

Herbs

Tomato roses

Tomato collar

Sweet dishes are decorated in lots of ways:

- ✎ Piped cream
- ✎ Pastry decorations, such as leaves
- ✎ Fruit, such as strawberry fans or slices, cherries, or fruit coulis
- ✎ Sugar-based decorations, such as angelica, grated chocolate or hundreds and thousands
- ✎ Icing, such as feathered glacé icing, royal icing on Christmas cake, dusting with icing sugar on sponge cake

Piped cream

Glacé icing (feathering)

Strawberry fans

Dessert with a fruit coulis

1. **Factors that affect meal planning:** Dietary restrictions, good nutrition, time, money and equipment available, climate, ability of cook and the occasion.
2. **Meals are usually three courses:** Starter, main and dessert or cheeseboard.
   Two main types of menu: Table d'hôte (set price) and à la carte (items priced separately) as well as buffets.
3. **Menu writing rules:** Centre down the middle of the page, list courses in order, write main dish and then accompaniments, space out well (use a motif) and give detail on some dishes.
4. **Setting a table:** Everything should be spotless. Fill condiments. Flower arrangements should be low. Put a jug of iced water on the table. Place the cutlery used first on the outside. Serve to the left and clear from the right.
5. **Meal planning:** Make a shopping list. Buy from shops with a high turnover (freshness). Avoid pre-packed foods. Check use-by dates and that frozen foods are below the load line. Store foods correctly as soon as you get home.
6. **Time and work plans:** Work plans just give the order or work; time plans also include times. Start the dish that takes longest first, then next longest, etc.
7. **Presentation of food is essential:** Garnish savoury and decorate sweet.

1. List six factors that affect meal planning.
2. Name the three most common courses in a meal and give two examples of dishes suited to each course.
3. What are the two main types of menu and what is the difference between them? List the five main rules for writing menus.
4. When is a buffet most likely to be the chosen option? How should a buffet be laid out?
5. Describe six guidelines for a formal table setting.
6. List four rules that should be followed when shopping for food.
7. What are time/work plans and what is their purpose?
8. Are savoury dishes garnished or decorated?
9. How would you garnish or what would you use to accompany each of the following?
   (a) Soup (b) Fish (c) Lamb (d) Turkey (e) Beef (f) Pork (g) Duck
10. Name three ways of decorating a sweet dish such as a cake or trifle.

Homework Assignment **10** P 31

Unit 1 Food

CHAPTER 6
Good Food Hygiene and Storage

Teacher's CD

Slide presentation ▪ Student activity pack with revision crossword ▪ Class test ▪ Student learning contract

Key words

- ✔ Food spoilage
- ✔ Enzymes
- ✔ Moulds
- ✔ Yeast
- ✔ Bacteria
- ✔ Food-poisoning bacteria
- ✔ Conditions for growth of micro-organisms
- ✔ Cross-contamination
- ✔ HACCP
- ✔ Perishable foods
- ✔ Semi-perishable foods
- ✔ Non-perishable foods
- ✔ Frozen foods
- ✔ Star markings (fridge and freezer)

Learning outcomes

After completing this chapter and the homework, assignments and activities that accompany it, you should:

- Know what food spoilage is and what causes it (enzymes, moulds, yeasts and bacteria).
- Know the names of common food-poisoning bacteria and how they generally enter the human food chain.
- Know the five conditions that bacteria need to grow successfully.
- Understand the four ways that food usually becomes infected.
- Know how to keep food safe: rules for food handlers, safe practices with food preparation, cooking and storage, and how to keep food preparation areas hygienic.
- Understand the concept of HACCP and be able to give an example of HACCP and how it works.
- Understand the following food types and what they mean for food storage: perishable, semi-perishable, non-perishable, frozen.
- Know what the star markings on a refrigerator or freezer mean in terms of length of storage.
- Be able to name a variety of packaging materials for food cooking and storage and know what each is suitable for.

Food spoilage

Food spoilage is when food goes rotten or bad. It is caused by enzymes and micro-organisms (moulds, yeast and bacteria).

- **Enzymes:** Enzymes are naturally present in fruit and vegetables. They cause them to ripen and eventually rot.
- **Moulds:** Moulds cause a fluffy beard to grow on bread, fruit and vegetables. Many moulds are useful. For example, they are used to make the antibiotic penicillin and blue-veined cheeses such as Cashel Blue.
- **Yeast:** While yeast will attack some foods, such as jam, yeast has a positive use in bread making, brewing and wine making.
- **Bacteria:** Bacteria are everywhere. If they multiply too much, they cause food to go off. They can also cause food poisoning.

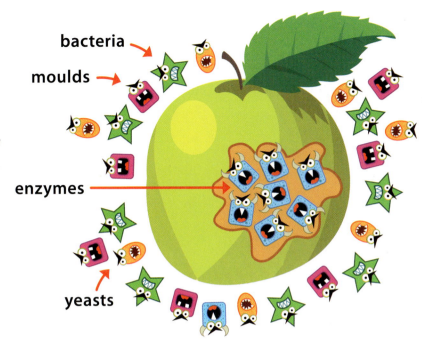

Food poisoning

Food poisoning occurs when bacteria multiply to unacceptable levels on food and then the food is eaten. Our bodies respond to this invasion with symptoms such as cramps, nausea, vomiting and diarrhoea.

Some food-poisoning bacteria

Campylobacter

- *Campylobacter* can be found in raw poultry and meat, unpasteurised milk and untreated water. Pets with diarrhoea can also be a source of infection.
- *Campylobacter* is the most commonly identified cause of food poisoning.

Salmonella

- *Salmonella* occurs naturally in the intestines of animals and humans. It is found in human and animal faeces.
- It causes no problem until faeces (even tiny amounts) get onto food and food is not cooked, or not cooked enough, to kill the *Salmonella*.

Staphylococci

- Often found in the nose, throat and skin of humans, especially on boils and sores.
- When people sneeze or cough over food or handle it with uncovered sores, they risk causing this form of food poisoning.

Listeria

🔧 *Listeria* likes to grow on foods such as soft cheese, pâté and coleslaw.

🔧 It also likes cold temperatures and can multiply even in the fridge.

🔧 Babies, pregnant women and the elderly are most affected. They should avoid the foods mentioned above.

E. coli

🔧 *E. coli* is the name given to a large family of bacteria commonly found in the intestines of humans and animals. Most *E. coli* are harmless, but one in particular, *E. coli 0157*, can cause serious illness in humans, ranging from diarrhoea to kidney failure and death.

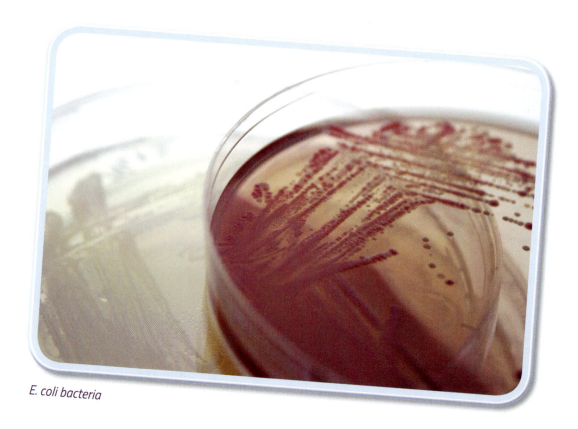

E. coli bacteria

Ireland has one of the highest rates of disease-causing *E. coli* cases in Europe, according to a new report by the European Food Safety Authority. The number of *E. coli* cases reported in Ireland is more than four times the EU average. In 2007, 167 such cases were reported, of which 115 were confirmed. Ireland's average of 2.7 cases per 100,000 inhabitants is exceeded only by Sweden and Denmark. Irish cases have doubled in three years.

Micro-organisms (germs) need five conditions to grow successfully

Conditions for growth of micro-organisms

1. Food
They like high-protein foods.

2. Warmth
30°C–45°C is ideal for most micro-organisms.

5. Moisture
Micro-organisms cannot grow well on dried foods such as cornflakes.

4. Air
Most need oxygen to survive.

O_2 O_2 O_2 O_2

3. Time
Micro-organisms multiply every 20 minutes.

The four main ways food is infected by bacteria

1. **Unhygienic people:** Not washing hands, especially after using the toilet; not covering cuts; coughing or sneezing over food.

2. **Pets, vermin and insects.**

3. **Dirt and grease:** Dirt on surfaces, equipment and cloths provides food for bacteria to multiply.

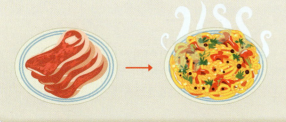

4. **Cross-contamination:** Preparing or storing raw food, such as chicken, with food that will be eaten without being cooked or cooked again. Bacteria cross from the raw to the cooked food and this now-contaminated food is eaten, resulting in food poisoning.

Food hygiene guidelines

Food hygiene guidelines relate to the food handler **(1)**, the food itself **(2)** and to the kitchen **(3)** in which the food is prepared.

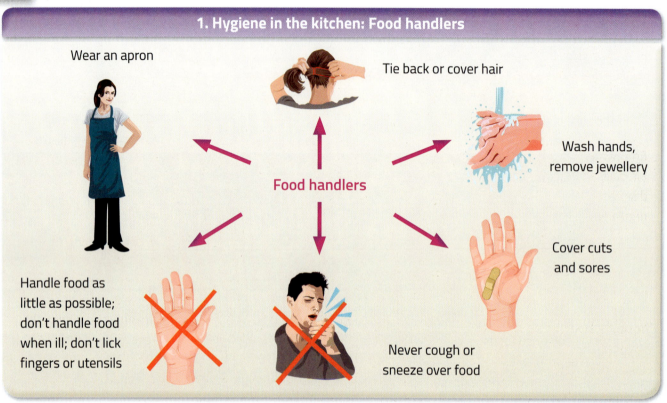

1. Hygiene in the kitchen: Food handlers

Wear an apron

Tie back or cover hair

Wash hands, remove jewellery

Food handlers

Cover cuts and sores

Handle food as little as possible; don't handle food when ill; don't lick fingers or utensils

Never cough or sneeze over food

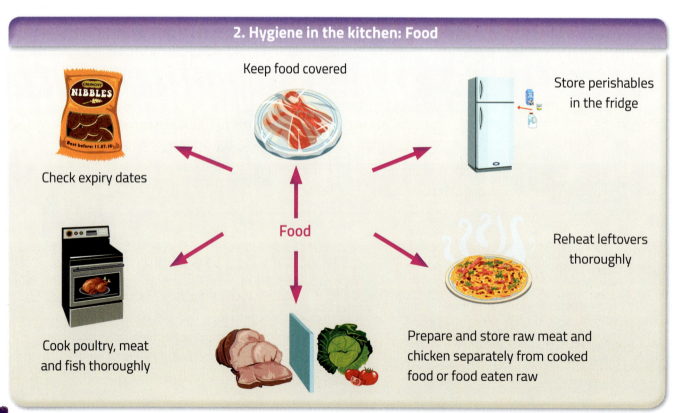

2. Hygiene in the kitchen: Food

Keep food covered

Store perishables in the fridge

Check expiry dates

Food

Reheat leftovers thoroughly

Cook poultry, meat and fish thoroughly

Prepare and store raw meat and chicken separately from cooked food or food eaten raw

3. Hygiene in the kitchen

No smoking in the kitchen.

No pets in the kitchen.

Disinfect the floor, sink and fridge regularly.

Kitchen

Empty the bin daily and disinfect regularly.

Keep all surfaces, equipment and utensils spotlessly clean and dry.

Cloths and mops should be very clean.

Chopping board colour coding

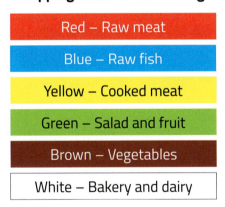

Red – Raw meat

Blue – Raw fish

Yellow – Cooked meat

Green – Salad and fruit

Brown – Vegetables

White – Bakery and dairy

Food safety in industry

Anybody involved in the food industry must be extremely conscious of food hygiene and safety. **HACCP** is an international food safety system that is required by law in Ireland for any business selling or providing food to others. HACCP stands for **h**azard **a**nalysis **c**ritical **c**ontrol **p**oints. The HACCP system works by identifying potential risk areas in advance and then putting systems in place to minimise their risk. One example is the use of colour-coded chopping boards to reduce the risk of cross-contamination between raw and cooked foods.

Storing food

The **shelf life** of food (how long it remains fit to eat) depends on storing it correctly. How a food is stored depends on what type of food it is.

- **Perishable:** Food that goes off in three or four days, such as meat, milk, poultry, fish, cream and bread. Store in the fridge or freezer.
- **Semi-perishable:** Food that lasts a week or so, such as fruit, vegetables, cheese, eggs and cakes. Store fruit and vegetables in the fridge or on a vegetable rack in a cool, dark, ventilated place. Store cheese and eggs in the fridge. Store cakes, etc. in an airtight tin.

Always follow the instructions on the food label.

🍴 **Non-perishable:** Food that lasts unopened for a month at least, including dried foods such as breakfast cereals, flour, rice, dried fruit, tea and tinned foods. Store in its own package in a clean, dry, wall-mounted press. Once opened, store dried food in an airtight container. Treat tinned food as perishable once opened.

🍴 **Frozen at –18°C or below:** Many perishable and some semi-perishable foods are frozen to prolong their shelf life.

Star markings

Star markings are found on frozen food and on freezers. They tell us how long a food can be stored for.

* One week
** One month
*** Three months
**** One year

Packaging for cooking and food storage

🍴 **Kitchen paper:** Use to mop up spills and drain grease off fried foods.

🍴 **Aluminium foil** (also commonly but incorrectly called tin foil): Use to cover food in the fridge and for packed lunches. Wrap vegetables, such as carrots, in the fridge to prevent wilting.

🍴 **Polythene (plastic) bags:** Use for packed lunches. Stronger bags are used for storing frozen food.

🍴 **Clingfilm:** Use for packed lunches and for covering food for fridge storage.

🍴 **Plastic boxes and containers:** Use for food storage. Old ice cream tubs are useful for frozen food storage.

🍴 **Greaseproof paper:** Use for lining cake tins and wrapping cheese.

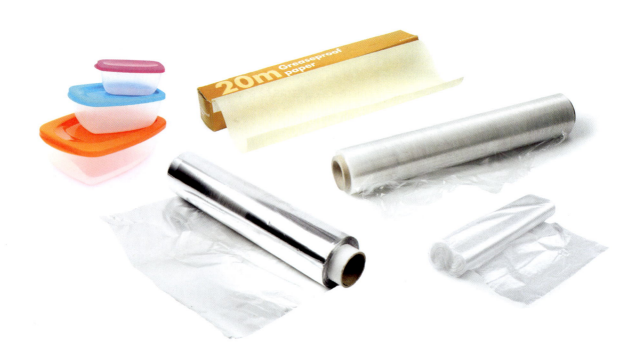

Rapid Revision

1. **Food spoilage:** Food spoilage (when food goes rotten or bad) is caused by enzymes or micro-organisms such as moulds, yeast or bacteria.
2. **Food poisoning:** Food poisoning occurs when bacteria multiply to unacceptable levels on food. Food-poisoning bacteria that cause infection in humans include *Campylobacter*, *Salmonella*, *Staphylococci*, *Listeria* and *E. coli*.
3. **Conditions for growth of micro-organisms:** Food, warmth, moisture, time and oxygen.
4. **How food is infected:** Unhygienic people, pets, vermin and insects, dirt and grease on surfaces and equipment, and cross-contamination.
5. **Food hygiene:** Food handlers should wear an apron, tie or cover hair, wash hands and remove jewellery, cover cuts, never cough or sneeze over food and handle food as little as possible.
6. **Food hygiene**
   - **Food:** Keep food covered. Store perishables in the fridge or freezer. Reheat leftovers thoroughly. Prepare and store cooked and raw foods separately. Cook high-risk foods (meat, chicken and fish) thoroughly. Check expiry dates.
   - **The kitchen:** Disinfect the floor, sink and work surfaces regularly. Cloths and mops should be clean. Empty the bin daily and disinfect regularly. Do not smoke in the kitchen.
7. **HACCP** is the food hygiene and safety method used by industry. It identifies potential danger points and puts systems in place to prevent risk, such as using colour-coded chopping boards.
8. Foods can be **perishable** (milk), **semi-perishable** (cheese), **non-perishable** (flour) or **frozen**. This affects where food is stored.
9. **Star markings** on fridges and freezers tell us how long food can be stored.
10. **Packaging for cooking and storage:** Kitchen paper, foil, polythene bags, clingflim, plastic boxes and containers, greaseproof paper.

Revision Questions

1. What is meant by food spoilage? How do each of the following spoil food:
   (a) enzymes (b) moulds (c) yeasts (d) bacteria?
2. What causes food poisoning? What are the usual symptoms? Name four different food-poisoning bacteria.
3. List the five conditions needed for micro-organisms to grow.
4. What are the four main ways food is infected by bacteria?
5. List 10 rules that should be followed when preparing, cooking and serving food in order to minimise the risk of food poisoning.
6. What do the letters HACCP stand for? What is meant by cross-contamination? How can it be prevented?
7. What is meant by the term *shelf life*? What is meant by each of the following in relation to food:
   (a) perishable (b) semi-perishable (c) non-perishable?
8. What temperature should food be frozen at? What do star markings 1 to 4 mean on a fridge or freezer?
9. List five different types of packaging for food storage.

Test Yourself
eTest.ie

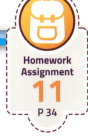
Homework Assignment
11
P 34

Teacher's CD

Slide presentation ▪ Student activity pack with revision crossword ▪ Class test ▪ Student learning contract

Key words

- ✔ Grams (g)
- ✔ Millilitres (ml)
- ✔ Recipe modification
- ✔ Preheating
- ✔ Conventional oven
- ✔ Fan oven

See also the glossary of terms on pages 67–68.

Learning outcomes

After completing this chapter and the homework, assignments and activities that accompany it, you should:

- Understand the rules for kitchen safety and implement them in your practical classes.
- Know how to set up and prepare to cook. Put this into practice in cookery class.
- Know how to measure both solid and liquid ingredients.
- Be able to suggest ways that recipes can be modified to make them healthier (reduce fat, sugar and salt, increase fibre).
- Be able to identify a range of common cooking utensils and know what they are for.
- Know the routine for washing up and clearing away after cooking. Put this into practice in cookery class.
- Be able to set an oven to the temperature stated in the recipe.
- Know the meaning of a range of cooking terms commonly found in recipes.

Kitchen safety

Most household accidents occur in the kitchen. When in the kitchen, take care and be safe.

Kitchen safety guidelines

1. Never leave a frying pan unattended. If overheated, oil will spontaneously burst into flames. Use a deep fat fryer instead of a chip pan.

2. Never touch anything electrical with wet hands.

3. Use oven gloves.

4. Keep saucepan handles turned in to the back of the cooker.

8. Never run in the kitchen.

7. Wipe up spills immediately.

Kitchen safety

6. Never walk around holding a knife or a hot saucepan.

5. Curl fingers in when chopping.

Follow this work routine before you start to cook:

1. Study the recipe before class. That way, you will know what ingredients you need and the basic steps involved in making the dish.
2. Tie back or cover your hair.
3. Wash your hands and remove jewellery.
4. Gather all equipment. Is it clean? Set the table (see diagram).
5. Weigh ingredients accurately.
6. Preheat the oven.
7. Wash and clear away waste, such as egg shells, as you go.

Recipes

A recipe includes:

- ✎ The name of the dish
- ✎ A list of ingredients
- ✎ The method (instructions on how to make the dish)
- ✎ Oven temperature and cooking time
- ✎ Serving suggestions
- ✎ Sometimes a picture of the finished dish

Before starting to cook, read the recipe well.

Weighing (solids) and measuring (liquids)

Weighing solids

1,000g = 1kg

Solids are weighed in grams (g). Since a gram is a very small amount, you will rarely see less than 25g written in a recipe. If less than 25g is needed, the recipe will usually say a teaspoon (5g), dessertspoon (10g) or a tablespoon (15g). Recipes mean a level spoon unless otherwise stated.

Weighing

Spring scales

Make sure the dial is at 0 after you place the empty bowl on the scales.

Balance scales

Select the weight you need, such as 100g. Add the ingredient to the other side until the scale is level or balanced.

Digital scales

Place the the ingredient to be weighed on the scale. Add or take some away until the scale reads the correct amount.

Measuring butter/margarine

Blocks of butter or margarine are usually marked out so that you do not have to use a weighing scales.

Measuring liquids

Liquids are measured in millilitres (ml). There are 1,000ml in one litre (l). A measuring jug is used to measure liquid; again, less than 25ml is rare in recipes. Teaspoons (5ml), dessertspoons (10ml) and tablespoons (15ml) can also be used to measure liquids.

Measuring jug

Measuring spoons are used for small amounts, such as baking powder

Recipes mean a level spoon unless stated otherwise

Recipe modification

Modifying a recipe means changing it in some way.

Possible reasons to modify a recipe:
- To make the dish healthier
- To make it suitable for people with special dietary needs, such as vegetarians or coeliacs
- To increase or reduce the size of the dish
- To substitute an available ingredient for an unavailable one

Ways to modify a recipe for health reasons

To reduce fat
- Use low-fat milk, cheese, etc. in recipes.
- Use polyunsaturated fats, like Flora, instead of hard fats, such as margarine.
- Fry meat in its own fat in a non-stick pan (dry frying).
- Reduce the amount of meat in a recipe and increase the vegetable content.
- Don't use cream in desserts. Use low-fat yoghurt instead.
- Use low-fat cooking methods, such as steaming and baking, where possible.

To reduce sugar
- Use artificial sweeteners where possible.
- Avoid icing cakes, buns, etc.
- Serve fruit salad in orange juice instead of sugar syrup.

To reduce salt

- Flavour food with herbs instead of salt.
- Don't add salt to baked products, such as scones. Use salt substitutes if necessary.
- Avoid using commercial stock cubes, as they are high in salt.

To increase fibre

- Leave skins on fruit and vegetables where possible.
- Use brown rice, pasta, bread, etc.
- Add bran and/or seeds to bread and savoury scones.

Equipment

Equipment consists of:

- Utensils, such as cutlery and bowls
- Large appliances, such as the cooker and fridge
- Small appliances, such as a mixer and food processor

Utensils

Utensils are small pieces of equipment that need to be clean and well cared for.

Some common utensils

- Bowls
- Chopping board
- Cutlery
- Rolling pin
- Pie dishes
- Wooden spoons
- Saucepans
- Sharp knives
- Baking tins
- Potato peeler
- Frying pans
- Measuring jug
- Casserole dishes

Silicone bakeware is becoming very popular. It has many advantages: it is unbreakable, easy to clean, does not rust and is easily stored. Food does not stick to it easily and it can be used in the freezer, microwave and oven. Many different products are available, such as reusable bun cases, muffin tins, loaf tins and roasting tins.

Other utensils

| Balloon whisk | Fish slice | Garlic crush | Flour dredger | Pâté tin | Pot stand |
| Palette knife | Sieve | Pastry brush | Wok | Spatula | Grater |

Washing dishes and kitchen utensils

⚒ Soak dishes if necessary in cold water to loosen stubborn food.

⚒ Use hot water with a good-quality washing-up liquid.

⚒ Scrape dishes off completely before washing.

⚒ Stack all the dirty dishes to one side.

⚒ Wash using a clean dishcloth.

⚒ Drain dishes on the other side of the sink (on a tea towel if there is no double draining board).

⚒ Fill the sink with cold water.

⚒ Rinse all the dishes.

⚒ Dry thoroughly.

To wash metal utensils:

⚒ Never use abrasives, like Brillo pads, on metal utensils or non-stick surfaces such as a non-stick frying pan, or they will be destroyed.

⚒ Store saucepans when completely dry with the lids off.

To wash wooden utensils:

⚒ Scrub with the grain in warm soapy water.

⚒ Do not store away until completely dry or the wood will warp.

Large appliances

⚒ Cooker   ⚒ Fridge   ⚒ Microwave

⚒ Dishwasher   ⚒ Freezer

Using the cooker

Cookers can run on electricity, gas or solid fuel.

A cooker can consist of:

- A hob
- A grill (sometimes also a small top oven)
- An oven

Preheating: Ovens can take 10 minutes to heat up (gas ovens heat up more quickly). With electric ovens, a light usually goes off when the oven has reached the temperature it has been set at. You must preheat the oven for bread and cakes in particular.

Setting the oven: Oven temperature is written in degrees Celsius (°C) or gas mark 1 to 9. Some older ovens may be in degrees Fahrenheit (°F). Recipes will give an oven temperature and a cooking time.

Types of oven

There are basically two different types of oven:

- Conventional
- Fan (fan in oven at the back)

The temperature in a fan oven is the same on every shelf. In a conventional oven, the top shelf is hottest, the middle shelf is as you set it and the bottom shelf is coolest.

Arrange the shelves before you turn the oven on. Never place food on the floor of the oven, as it will burn.

Small appliances

- Liquidiser
- Hand-held electric mixer
- Food processor
- Electric knife

A conventional oven set at 200 °C

Small appliances

Liquidiser
Uses: To blend soups and smoothies, make breadcrumbs and purée cooked fruit and vegetables. No heavy-duty work.

Food mixer
Uses: To cream sugar and butter, whip cream and whisk egg whites. No heavy-duty work.

Food processor
Uses: Can do everything a liquidiser and mixer can do, plus shred, dice, chip raw vegetables and mix stiff doughs and cakes.

Caring for and cleaning small motorised appliances

Remove loose parts and wash in hot soapy water. Dry thoroughly and store without putting the appliance back together. Never put the motor in water – just wipe it with a damp cloth. Water and electricity are dangerous together.

Glossary of common cookery terms

You will frequently come across these terms in recipes. Read through and learn the list below before completing the crossword in your student activity pack.

Aerate: Introduce air to a mixture (sieving, rubbing in or whisking).
Al dente: Cook food (pasta, vegetables) so it still has a bite and is not too soft.
Au gratin: Food cooked in sauce, sprinkled with cheese or breadcrumbs, then browned under the grill or in the oven.
Bake blind: Bake a pastry case before filling it, such as for lemon meringue pie.
Baste: Spoon hot fat and meat juices over roasting meat to stop it from drying out.
Bind: Bring a mixture together, for example by adding beaten egg to minced meat to make burgers.
Blanch: Plunge foods into boiling water, then into cold. This removes skins (tomatoes and almonds) or destroys enzymes (vegetables) before freezing.
Blend: Gently add an ingredient to a mixture.
Bouquet garni: A bunch of herbs (or a commercial sachet) added to flavour soups and stews and later removed.
Brine: Salty water.
Coat: Cover with, for example, batter, breadcrumbs or sauce.

Consistency: The thickness of a mixture.

Cream: Beat foods together until they are soft and creamy.

Croutons: Small cubes of fried bread, used as a garnish for soups.

Dice: To cut into small cubes.

Dredge: To sprinkle sugar or flour, for example dredging a table with flour so that pastry does not stick to it while rolling it out.

Fold: Gently add an ingredient to a mixture.

Garnish: A decoration for a savoury dish.

Glaze: Brush over bread and cakes before baking to give them a shine when cooked.

Infuse: To give flavour to a liquid by gently heating flavouring ingredients in it, such as a vanilla pod in milk.

Knead: To work dough with your hands, such as when making bread.

Marinate: Steep foods in flavoured liquid before cooking.

Parboil: Partially cook by boiling (potatoes can be parboiled before oven roasting).

Poach: To cook in gently simmering water, for example eggs.

Purée: Mince up fruit or vegetables.

Raising agent: Produces gas in a mixture (such as bread dough) and causes it to rise.

Roux: A mixture of equal quantities of fat and flour, used to thicken many sauces.

Rub in: To crumble fat into flour using your fingertips – the mixture should resemble breadcrumbs.

Sauté: Fry gently for a short time in hot fat.

Season: Add salt, pepper, herbs or spices to food.

Shortening: Fat added to bread and cakes.

Simmer: Cook gently just below boiling point.

Texture: The feel of something: smooth, lumpy, coarse, crisp, soft, etc.

Whisk: Beat vigorously to introduce air, such as egg whites.

Rapid Revision

1. **Kitchen safety:** Never leave a frying pan or chip pan unattended. Don't touch anything electrical with wet hands. Use oven gloves. Curl your fingers inwards when chopping. Don't walk around the kitchen with knives or hot pans. Wipe up spills. Never run in the kitchen.

2. **Preparing to cook:** Know your recipe. Tie up or cover your hair. Wash your hands and remove jewellery. Gather all equipment and set the table. Preheat the oven.

3. **Measuring:** Solids are measured in grams (g) and liquids in millilitres (ml).

4. **Recipe modification:** Changing a recipe for health reasons:
   - To reduce fat, for example using low-fat cheese on a pizza
   - To reduce sugar, such as using artificial sweetener when stewing rhubarb
   - To reduce salt, such as flavouring with herbs instead
   - To increase fibre, for example by using brown rice

5. **Washing up:** Soak dishes if necessary. Use hot water and good-quality washing-up liquid. Scrape excess food off first. Stack to one side. Drain after washing. Fill the sink with cold water to rinse dishes. Dry thoroughly.

6. **Ovens:** Preheat electric ovens for 10 minutes before use. All shelves in a fan oven are at the set temperature, whereas in a conventional oven the top shelf is hottest and bottom is coolest. The middle shelf is as set.

7. **Cookery terms you need to know:** Aerate, al dente, au gratin, bake blind, baste, bind, blanch, blend, bouquet garni, brine, coat, consistency, cream, croutons, dice, dredge, fold, garnish, glaze, infuse, knead, marinate, parboil, poach, purée, raising agent, roux, rub in, sauté, season, shortening, simmer, texture, whisk.

Revision Questions

1. List eight kitchen safety guidelines.
2. Outline the work routine that should be followed in cookery class.
3. List six different pieces of information that a recipe gives.
4. In cookery, what unit is used to measure (a) solids and (b) liquids?
5. List four reasons why you may want to modify a recipe.
6. List three ways a recipe may be modified to reduce (a) its fat content (b) its sugar content (c) its salt content (d) to increase its fibre content.
7. Outline the procedure that you should follow while doing the washing-up by hand.
8. How should (a) metal utensils and (b) wooden utensils be cared for?
9. What does it mean to preheat the oven? How long should it be done for and why?
10. In a conventional oven, which area of the oven is hottest?
11. Name three small electrical appliances and state what each is commonly used for.
12. Outline how you should clean small appliances with a motor.
13. What do the following cookery terms mean?

(a)	Aerate	(f)	Blanch
(b)	Al dente	(g)	Bouquet garni
(c)	Au gratin	(h)	Marinate
(d)	Bake blind	(i)	Parboil
(e)	Baste	(j)	Roux

Test Yourself
eTest.ie

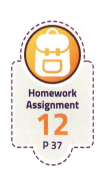

Homework Assignment
12
P 37

Cooking Food

 Teacher's CD

Slide presentation ▪ Student activity pack with revision crossword ▪ Class test ▪ Student learning contract

Key words

- ✓ Coagulate
- ✓ Conduction
- ✓ Convection
- ✓ Radiation
- ✓ Boiling/simmering
- ✓ Stewing and casseroling
- ✓ Poaching
- ✓ Steaming
- ✓ Pressure cooking
- ✓ Grilling
- ✓ Baking
- ✓ Frying
- ✓ Roasting
- ✓ Microwave cooking

Learning outcomes

After completing this chapter and the homework, assignments and activities that accompany it, you should:

- Know the three reasons why we cook food and the seven effects that cooking has on food.
- Understand the three main methods of heat transfer and be able to give examples of cooking methods using each one.
- Be able to describe the following moist cooking methods: boiling/simmering, stewing and casseroling, poaching, steaming and pressure cooking. Know what types of foods are suitable for each method and the advantages and disadvantages of each. Use these methods in practical classes.
- Be able to describe the following dry cooking methods: grilling, baking, frying, roasting and microwave cooking. Know what types of foods are suitable for each method and the advantages and disadvantages of each. Use these methods in practical classes.

Why food is cooked

- Cooking kills harmful bacteria, making food safe to eat. It also preserves food. For example, cooked chicken will last longer than raw chicken in the fridge.

- Cooking makes some foods easier to chew and digest, such as meat and starchy foods like potatoes.

- Cooking improves the colour and flavour of many foods.

Effects of cooking on food

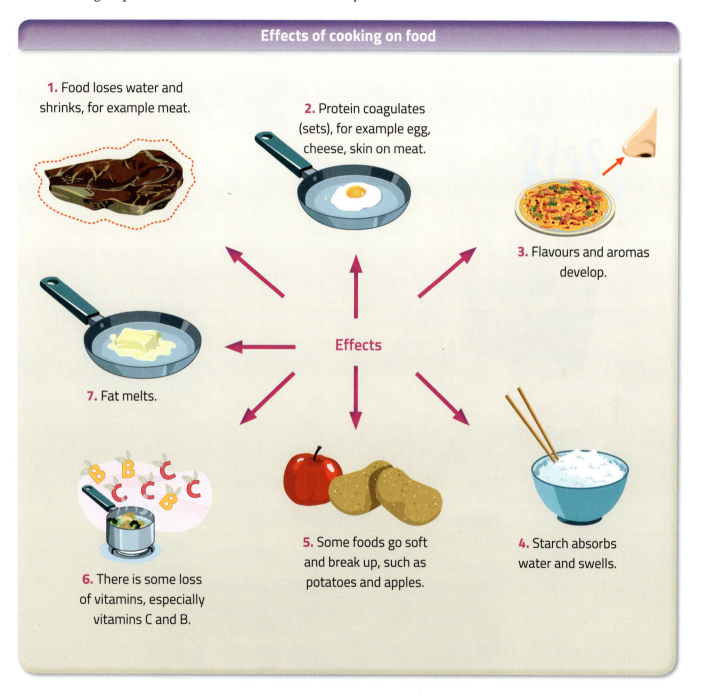

1. Food loses water and shrinks, for example meat.

2. Protein coagulates (sets), for example egg, cheese, skin on meat.

3. Flavours and aromas develop.

Effects

7. Fat melts.

6. There is some loss of vitamins, especially vitamins C and B.

5. Some foods go soft and break up, such as potatoes and apples.

4. Starch absorbs water and swells.

 How food is cooked: Methods of heat transfer

Conduction

Example: Frying

Heat travels from molecule to molecule along a solid object. For example, in frying, hot molecules in the cooker ring touch the molecules in the frying pan and cause them to get hot. They in turn touch the food and cause it to get hot, thus cooking it.

Heat travels from the cooker ring to the frying pan to the food by conduction

Convection

Examples: Boiling, deep-fat frying, baking

When liquid and gases are heated, they rise. They are then replaced by cooler gas or liquids. These movements are called convection currents. These currents heat and cook the food by convection.

Currents of circulating hot air cook food by convection

Radiation

Example: Grilling

Hot rays from a heat source hit food and heat its surface. The heat then travels into the middle of the food by conduction, thus cooking it through.

Heat travelling by radiation

Methods of cooking

1. **Moist methods:** Boiling and simmering, stewing, casseroling, poaching, steaming, pressure cooking.
2. **Dry methods:** Grilling, baking.
3. **Methods using fat:** Frying (shallow, deep and stir-frying), roasting.
4. **Other:** Microwave cooking.

Moist methods

Boiling/simmering

🍴 **Description:** Food is cooked in bubbling liquid (100°C). Usually the food is brought to the boil (bubbling rapidly) and then turned down for the rest of the cooking time (bubbling very gently). This is called simmering.

🍴 **Suitable foods:** Meat, vegetables, rice, pasta.

🍴 **Advantages:** Economical, needs little attention, safe for beginners.

🍴 **Disadvantages:** Nutrients are lost into the cooking liquid.

Tips:

🍴 Use a heavy saucepan with a tight lid.

🍴 Use cooking liquid for soups and sauces.

🍴 Once food is bubbling rapidly, reduce to a simmer (barely bubbling).

Saucepans should be heavy, with tight-fitting lids

Stewing and casseroling

🍴 **Description:** These are slow, moist cooking methods. Food is cooked in liquid in a heavy-lidded saucepan on the hob (stewing) or in a dish in the oven (casseroling). The food and the liquid it has been cooked in are usually both eaten.

🍴 **Suitable foods:** Tough cuts of meat, fruit.

🍴 **Advantages:** Economical – a whole meal can be cooked on one ring; tough, cheaper cuts of meat may be used; cooking liquid is consumed, so nutrients are not lost.

🍴 **Disadvantages:** Slow.

Tips:

🍴 Simmer (don't boil) stew.

🍴 Keep a tight-fitting lid on so that too much liquid does not evaporate.

🍴 Use stock as a cooking liquid instead of water, as it adds flavour.

Poaching

- **Description:** Food is cooked gently in water that is barely simmering. A shallow saucepan or poacher is used.
- **Suitable foods:** Eggs, fish.
- **Advantages:** Low-calorie method; food remains digestible (good method for invalid/convalescent cookery).
- **Disadvantages:** Foods can break up; constant attention is required.
- **Tip:** Do not let the water boil rapidly, or food will break up and be spoiled.

An egg poacher

If you do not have an egg poacher, place each egg in a small sandwich bag, tie a knot in the top and suspend the bag over the saucepan using a skewer or knitting needle

Steaming

- **Description:** Food is cooked in rising steam.
- **Suitable foods:** Vegetables, fish, puddings.
- **Advantages/disadvantages:** Steamed food can lack flavour, but is usually easily digestible.
- **Tip:** Flavour foods with herbs and spices, as steamed food can taste a little bland.

Electric steamers are relatively cheap to buy and allow you to cook more than one food at once, so they are very economical. Place foods that take the longest to cook on the bottom tier and then add the other tiers as required.

Electric steamers allow you to cook more than one food at once, so they are very economical

Pressure cooking

- 🍴 **Description:** Food is cooked quickly with steam under pressure.

- 🍴 **Suitable foods:** Vegetables, tough cuts of meat, puddings.

- 🍴 **Advantages:** Quick – pressurised steam is very hot and cooks food more quickly than boiling or steaming.

- 🍴 **Disadvantages:** Can be dangerous if the pressure cooker is not used correctly. Food can be easily overcooked.

- 🍴 **Tip:** Time cooking carefully – overcooking is common.

Dry methods

Grilling

- 🍴 **Description:** Food is cooked by rays from a hot gas or electric grill.

- 🍴 **Suitable foods:** Tender meat (steak), fish, some fruit and vegetables (tomatoes, grapefruit).

- 🍴 **Advantages:** Quick, not greasy, food has good texture.

- 🍴 **Disadvantages:** Only expensive meat can be used; needs constant attention.

- 🍴 **Tip:** Clean the grill pan after each use or old oil will smoke next time.

Baking

- 🍴 **Description:** Food is cooked by dry heat in an oven.

- 🍴 **Suitable foods:** Bread, cakes, tarts, pies, apples, potatoes, puddings, fish.

- 🍴 **Advantages:** Needs little attention, safe for beginners, adds flavour.

- 🍴 **Disadvantages:** Expensive if oven is used for one item.

Tips:
- 🍴 Batch-bake to make full use of the oven.
- 🍴 Always preheat the oven fully.
- 🍴 Adjust the shelves before the oven heats up.
- 🍴 Do not open the oven door, especially at the start of the cooking of cakes.

Pressure cooker

Methods using fat

Frying

🍴 **Description:** Food is cooked in hot fat by deep, shallow or stir-frying.

🍴 **Suitable foods:** Tender meat and chicken, fish, eggs, chips, onion rings, mushrooms.

🍴 **Advantages:** Quick, good flavour.

🍴 **Disadvantages:** Method adds kilocalories, dangerous, greasy, needs constant attention.

Tips:

🍴 Heat the fat fully before adding the food or it will soak up the fat and become soggy.

🍴 Fire is a risk with frying – do not leave a frying pan or wok unattended.

🍴 Do not use a chip pan – use a deep-fat fryer with a thermostat instead.

🍴 Drain fried food on kitchen paper to remove some greasiness.

A modern deep-fat fryer

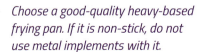

Choose a good-quality heavy-based frying pan. If it is non-stick, do not use metal implements with it.

A wok for stir-frying

Roasting

🍴 **Description:** Food is cooked in the oven and basted with hot fat (hot fat is spooned over).

🍴 **Suitable foods:** Meat, poultry (chicken, turkey, duck), potatoes and some vegetables, such as parsnips.

🍴 **Advantages:** Nice flavours, needs little attention, a number of foods can be cooked together, for example chicken and roast vegetables and potatoes.

🍴 **Disadvantages:** Basting adds kilocalories, food is dry if it is not basted.

🍴 **Tip:** Covering meat helps prevent drying – uncover 30 minutes before the end of the cooking time to give a brown colour.

Microwave cooking

- **Description:** Invisible microwaves bounce around the inside of the oven. The microwaves hit the food and cause the molecules in it to vibrate. This vibration produces heat, which cooks the food.

- **Suitable foods:** Reheats, thaws and cooks most foods.

- **Advantages:** Quick.

- **Disadvantages:** Does not brown food.

Tips:

- Do not put metal dishes or dishes with a metal rim in the microwave or sparks will fly!

- Foods with a skin, like tomatoes, will explode if you do not prick them with a fork first.

- Allow food to 'stand' after cooking and before eating it (standing time).

- Cover food when reheating to avoid it splattering and dirtying the oven.

Rapid Revision

1. **Cooking:** Cooking food destroys bacteria and makes it safe to eat. It makes some foods (meat) easier to chew and digest and it improves the colour and flavour of foods.

2. **Effects of cooking:** Protein coagulates. Flavour and aroma develop. Starchy foods absorb water, swell and soften. Some foods soften and will break up if overcooked (potatoes). There is some loss of vitamins (C and B). Fat melts. Some foods (meat) lose water and shrink.

3. **Methods of heat transfer:** Conduction (frying), convection (baking) and radiation (grilling).

4. **Methods of cooking:** Moist (boiling), dry (grilling), methods using fat (frying), other (microwave cooking).

5. **Moist methods:**
   - **Boiling/simmering:** Suitable foods are meat, vegetables, rice and pasta. Advantages/ disadvantages: Economical and safe, but nutrients can be lost into the cooking water. Do not boil food rapidly – simmer instead in a good-quality saucepan.
   - **Stewing and casseroling:** Suitable foods are tough cuts of meat, fruit. Advantages/ disadvantages: Economical, cheaper cuts of meat can be used and more than one food can be cooked at once, but it is a slow method. Use a saucepan or casserole dish with a tight-fitting lid to avoid too much liquid evaporating.
   - **Poaching:** Suitable foods are eggs and fish. Advantages/disadvantages: Low-calorie method, and food is easily digestible (invalids), but food can break up, so constant attention is required. Make sure water is just barely simmering.
   - **Steaming:** Suitable foods are vegetables, fish and puddings. Advantages/disadvantages: Can lack flavour, but is digestible and economical, as more than one food can be cooked at once if a tiered steamer is used.
   - **Pressure cooking:** Suitable foods are vegetables, tough cuts of meat, puddings. Advantages/disadvantages: Quick but can be dangerous and food can overcook easily.

6. **Dry methods:**
   - **Grilling:** Suitable foods are tender meats, tomatoes and grapefruits.
     Advantages/disadvantages: Quick, non-greasy, food retains texture, but only expensive cuts of meat can be used and needs constant attention.
   - **Baking:** Suitable foods are cakes, tarts and buns, potatoes, apples and fish.
     Advantages/disadvantages: Needs little attention, safe for beginners, but expensive if used for only one dish.

7. **Methods using fat:**
   - **Frying:** Food cooked in hot fat may be deep, shallow or stir-fried. Suitable foods are tender meat and chicken, fish, eggs, vegetables. Advantages/disadvantages: Quick and good flavour, but adds calories.
   - **Roasting:** Suitable foods are meat, poultry, potatoes and root vegetables. Advantages/disadvantages: Good flavour and needs little attention, but basting adds calories and food can dry out.

8. **Microwave cookery:** Reheats, thaws and cooks most foods.
   Advantages/disadvantages: Quick, but food does not brown.

Revision Questions

1. Give three reasons why food is cooked. Describe five effects of cooking on food
2. Name the three methods of heat transfer used in cookery and describe how each works.
3. Name (a) four moist cooking methods (b) three dry cooking methods and (c) two methods that use fat.
4. In relation to each of the following methods: (a) describe how the method works (b) list foods suited to this method (c) list its advantages and disadvantages (d) list any tips for using this method.
   - Stewing/casseroling
   - Poaching
   - Steaming
   - Pressure cooking
   - Grilling

Homework Assignment 13 P 40

Slide presentation • Student activity pack with revision crossword • Class test

Key words

- ✓ Task brief
- ✓ Task analysis
- ✓ Task investigation
- ✓ Task solutions
- ✓ Task evaluation
- ✓ Costings

Learning outcomes

After completing this chapter and the homework, assignments and activities that accompany it, you should:

- Know how much the practical examination is worth as part of your overall mark for Junior Certificate Home Economics.
- Understand the tasks you must complete before the day of the exam (in the two weeks coming up to it), during the 30-minute preparation time before the exam and during the 90-minute examination itself.
- Have read and understood the nine top tips for the practical exam outlined in this chapter.
- Have read and analysed the sample cookery examination folder presented in this chapter, picking up its strong points.
- Be able to use this sample folder as a guide to completing your own.

The practical cookery exam is worth 35% (Higher Level) or 45% (Ordinary Level) of your final Junior Certificate Home Economics mark. It is therefore very important that you prepare well and carry out the task given to you to the best of your ability.

Exam procedure

Approximately two weeks before the exam (exams are usually held in April), your Home Economics teacher will ask you to draw one task from a selection of six or seven different tasks. On the day of the exam, you will be given 30 minutes of preparation time and 90 minutes for the actual practical exam.

Sample task

Flour is an essential ingredient in home baking.
A. Name three different types of flour used in home baking.
B. Give a different example of the use of each type of flour when making scones and muffins.
C. Demonstrate your baking skills by preparing, baking and serving a batch of scones and a batch of muffins using at least two types of flour named.
D. Calculate the cost of the scones or muffins and compare the cost with a similar commercial product.

Before the day of the exam (two weeks)

Once you have drawn your task, you can then:

- Think about what exactly you have been asked to do.
- Come up with a number of dishes that would suit the task.
- Decide on the dish or dishes you are going to cook (solution).
- Practise your chosen dish or dishes.
- Complete the paperwork for the exam (see the sample).

During preparation time on the day of the exam (30 minutes):

- Collect equipment.
- Weigh ingredients.
- Wash vegetables, but do not peel them.
- Light the gas oven (if using) but do not set the temperature.
- Check that equipment, such as the electric mixer or food processor, is cleaning and working.

The examiner will check your preparation.

During the exam itself (90 minutes):

- Make the dish.
- Serve the dish (the examiner will taste it).
- Taste the dish yourself.
- Wash up (the examiner will check the dishes).
- Tidy up.
- Do your evaluation.

Top tips for the practical exam

When you have read each tip, tick the box.

1. Write your exam number:
    - On all your written work
    - On a sticker on your apron
    - On a large A4 sheet of paper taped to your table

    Example:

Exam number:	357146
Task number:	1
Dish:	Fruit scones and blueberry muffins

2. You must use fresh ingredients where possible. Marks will be lost if you use too many convenience foods, for example if you use a scone mix for the above task.

3. Make sure you wash your hands, cover cuts, tie back long hair, remove jewellery and have a clean apron on, or else marks will be taken away under 'hygiene'.

4. Take care doing written work for the cookery exam – use the sample below as a guide. Written work makes up 30% of your marks. You could get most of these marks before you even walk in the door, so don't lose out. Use the form provided in the Activity Packs on the Teacher's CD.

5. Do not waste anything: time, ingredients, water, gas or electricity.
    - **Time:** Know exactly what you have to do so that you can work quickly and efficiently. If you have to constantly look at your work plan or recipe to see what has to be done next, you are wasting valuable time and may not finish. (Marks will be taken off for this.)
    - **Ingredients:** When peeling vegetables, use a peeler – do not take large chunks of skin off with a knife. Try not to have more ingredients than you need. If you have extra, do not throw them out. Cover them and place in the fridge.
    - **Water:** Never leave a tap running. Do not wash anything under a running tap.
    - **Gas/electricity:** Turn off cooker rings or the oven immediately after you finish using them.

6. When serving food:
    - Clear the table before serving food. Serve all the food, not just a portion.
    - Garnish or decorate the food attractively.
    - Wipe any spills off serving dishes with kitchen paper.
    - Have clean cutlery, a side plate and a bowl of hot water ready for the examiner to taste your food.
    - Call the examiner immediately once your food is served.
    - You must taste a little food yourself so you can evaluate the taste of the dish.

7. Wash and dry dishes very carefully. Marks are taken off for badly washed dishes. Do not put your dishes away until the examiner has seen them (see the washing-up guidelines on page 65).

8. Do not throw out the contents of the bin until you have shown it to the examiner.

9. Evaluate both the dish and how you think you did in the exam (see the sample evaluation later in this chapter).

Case study

Luke Carroll has just finished his cookery exam. He was given the task from page 80 of this chapter. For his task he had to make a batch of both scones and muffins using two different types of flour. He also had to cost both dishes and compare them to similar commercial products. He decided to make fruit scones using plain flour (to which he added bread soda) and lemon drizzle muffins using self-raising flour. His examination went well except for the fact that he forgot to glaze the scones before putting them into the oven and they did not brown as nicely on top as he would have liked.

Sample cookery exam folder

Exam number: 5831563
Task number: 1

Flour is an essential ingredient in home baking. Name three different types of flour used in home baking. Give a different example of the use of each type of flour when making scones and muffins. Demonstrate your baking skills by preparing, baking and serving a batch of scones and a batch of muffins using at least two types of flour named. Calculate the cost of the scones or muffins and compare the cost with a similar commercial product.

Food and Culinary Skills Task, 2014

Analysis: What have you been asked to do?

I have been asked to name three different types of flour used in home baking. I then have to choose a different flour for a batch of scones and muffins. I must make them, cost them and then compare my costing to a similar commercial product.

Investigation: List three things that you must consider before deciding what to cook (two must be specific to the task with one general consideration).

1. I must find a recipe for homemade scones and muffins that each use a different type of flour (specific consideration).
2. I must be able to find similar commercial products to compare them to (specific consideration).
3. I must be able to make it in one hour (other half-hour for serving, washing up and evaluation) and it is best if I choose something I have made before and am confident making (general consideration).

List solutions and ideas

Types of flour used in home baking:

Strong flour (both wholemeal and plain)

Cream flour (no raising agent added)

Self-raising flour (has baking powder added)

Wholemeal, both coarse and less coarse (different amounts of bran and germ)

Muffin possibilities

Blueberry or lemon drizzle (both use plain flour and baking powder)

Chocolate (uses self-raising flour)

Bran and raisin (uses plain flour and bran)

Scone possibilities

Wholemeal breakfast (uses wholemeal flour, bread soda and buttermilk)

Fruit scones (uses self-raising flour, baking powder and buttermilk)

Note: Strong flour is not normally used for scones or muffins.

Decision: Choose one solution. Give two good reasons for your choice of dish(es).

I have chosen to make fruit scones and lemon drizzle muffins.

Reasons for choice:

1. They use two different types of flour and can be made in under an hour.
2. I have made both before in class, so I know they are good recipes and I feel confident that I can carry out this task well.

Planning and preparation: List all the ingredients and equipment you will need for the task. As you collect them during the half-hour preparation, tick them off the list.

List of ingredients

Scones (makes 9 large)	Cost	Muffins	Cost
600g self-raising flour	39c	275g plain flour	18c
100g butter or margarine	30c	225ml milk	19c
80g caster sugar	9c	100ml vegetable oil	
2 level teaspoons baking powder	6c	4 level teaspoons baking powder	12c
500ml buttermilk	39c	125g caster sugar	14c
100g raisins	24c	2 eggs	32c
		rind of 2 lemons	50c
		2 tablespoons poppy seeds	30c
		Topping	
		juice of 1 lemon	(priced above)
		225g icing sugar	49c
Electricity (approximately) for both: 20c			
Total	€1.57	Total	€2.24

Cost of 1 homemade scone: 17c
Cost of 1 commercial scone: 40c
Cost of 1 homemade muffin: 25c
Cost of 1 commercial muffin: 62c (mid-price range)

Conclusion: The home-baked products are much cheaper. The scone is 23c cheaper and the muffin is 37c cheaper.
Note: All prices are from Tesco.

List of equipment

Muffin tin with paper muffin cases	Wooden spoon	Knife	Cooling tray
Large baking tray	Measuring jug	Fork	Sieve
Large mixing bowl	Teaspoon	Oven gloves	Weighing scales
Small bowl	2 dessertspoons	Pastry brush	Grater
	Flour dredger	Rolling pin	

Preparation: List everything you are going to do during the half-hour preparation time before the exam.

1. I will collect and weigh my ingredients.
2. I will collect all the equipment I need and set my cookery table.
3. I will check the shelf positions and then light my gas oven but not set the temperature on it.
4. I will wash and dry my lemons with kitchen paper.

Work plan: List what you have to do during the exam in the correct order. Don't forget evaluation time at the end.

Step 1:   Set the gas oven to gas mark 6. Prepare the muffin tins and grease a tray for the scones.

Step 2:   Begin with the muffins. Zest the lemons and sieve the flour, caster sugar and baking powder into a bowl. Add the lemon rind and mix well. Beat the milk, oil and eggs in a small bowl. Add to the dry ingredients. Mix but do not beat.

Step 3:   Spoon into muffin cases. Bake for 30 minutes.

Step 4:   Wash up.

Step 5:   Begin the scones. Sieve the flour and baking powder into a bowl and rub in the butter or margarine. Add the caster sugar and raisins. Mix in the buttermilk until the dough comes together but is not wet.

Step 6:   Turn the dough out onto a lightly floured board. Knead lightly. Roll out (but not too thin). Cut out scones and place on the greased tray. Glaze with egg.

Step 7:   Place in the oven with the muffins (bake for 15–20 minutes, until golden brown).

Step 8:   Wash up.

Step 9:   Make the lemon drizzle. Remove the muffins and cool on a wire tray.

Step 10:   Remove the scones and cool on a wire tray. Decorate the muffins when cool.

Step 11:   Wash up, serve food and do evaluation.

Note: The evaluation is not a description of the dish.

Evaluation

Colour and presentation: How did you try to make the dish look good? Did you succeed?

The colour of my scones was not as good as I would have liked. I forgot to put the egg glaze on them and they turned out too pale, even though they were properly cooked. Apart from this, both my scones and muffins were presented very well. The lemon icing drizzled over the muffins looked very attractive and I presented both on a round plate with a doyley.

Texture and taste: Was there more than one texture (contrast)? Was the flavour strong enough/too strong? Would you add anything to improve the texture/flavour?

There was good contrast between the outside of the scones and the inside, which was very soft. I thought the scones were sweet enough (because of the raisins) but not too sweet. The muffins had a very nice lemon flavour. They were sweet, but at the same time the lemon in the icing gave them a nice sharp citrus taste. They had a good airy texture inside.

Cooked/doneness: Was your dish overcooked, undercooked or just right? How did you check if it was cooked properly?

My scones were cooked properly. I knew they were cooked because they were in for the correct amount of time at the correct oven temperature. The only problem was that I would have liked them to develop a better golden brown colour on top while they were cooking, but I forgot the egg glaze. I checked the bottom of the scones and they were light brown, which told me they were cooked. The muffins were properly cooked – they were crispy on the outside but with a light, airy texture inside.

Did you meet the brief? Did you do everything you were told to do for your task? Explain why you think you did/didn't.

I think I did meet the brief because I made scones and muffins using different types of flour and I also compared their cost with commercial varieties. I priced everything in one shop (Tesco) because I wanted to make sure I was comparing like with like.

Your overall performance: What did you do well/not so well?

I made the muffins very well. They were not too wet or too dry. I kept my workspace very tidy and worked very efficiently. The main problem

I encountered was that I forgot to glaze the scones. This meant that they were a little pale coming out of the oven. I realised I had forgotten to glaze them not long after they went into the oven when I was doing my wash up, so I probably could have taken them out again and glazed them. I was afraid, however, that if I took them out that it might affect how well they rose in the oven.

Are there any changes you would make?

Yes. I would have glazed the scones.

Top tip

It is a good idea to get accustomed to writing up your practical cookery assignments. There is a blank template available for you to use in the Activity Packs on the teacher's CD that comes with this book.

Revision Questions

1. What is the practical cookery exam worth in terms of marks at both Higher and Ordinary Levels? How soon before the exam should you draw your task? How much preparation time is there before the exam? How long is the practical cookery exam itself?
2. What should you do in the two weeks leading up to the practical cookery exam? Try to make five good points.
3. What kinds of things can you do during the half hour preparation before the exam?
4. What tasks do you need to complete during the exam itself?
5. Can you use convenience foods during the exam? Explain your answer.
6. How can you ensure you get good marks under 'hygiene'?
7. How can you ensure you do not waste (a) time (b) ingredients (c) water (d) fuel?
8. What points should you consider when serving food? Make six good points here.
9. Do you need to show your washed dishes and bin contents to the examiner?
10. What two things do you need to evaluate at the end of the exam?

Slide presentation ▪ Student activity pack with revision crossword ▪ Class test ▪ Student learning contract

Key words

- Food groups
- Offal
- Beef and veal
- Pork
- Mutton and lamb
- Composition of foods
- Nutritive value of foods
- Tenderise
- Meat alternatives: tofu, TVP, Quorn
- Pulse vegetables
- Poultry
- Fish fillets, cutlets and steaks
- Food processing
- Pasteurisation
- Homogenisation
- Rennet
- Curds and whey
- Bran, endosperm and germ
- Gluten
- Root and tuber vegetables
- Al dente
- In season
- Organically grown

Learning outcomes

After completing this chapter and the homework, assignments and activities that accompany it, you should know the following:

- **Four food groups:** Know the names of the four food groups, be able to list the foods that belong to each group and know how many servings from each group should be consumed daily. Understand the main reason each group is included in the diet.
- **Meat:** Know the different types of meat. Explain its composition, structure and nutritive value. Know which cuts of meat are toughest/most tender and be able to describe the ways meat can be tenderised. Be able to describe the rules for buying, storing, preparing and cooking meat. Understand the effects cooking has on meat. Use a variety of meat types in practical class.
- **Meat alternatives:** Know where the following meat alternatives come from and what each can be used for in cookery: tofu, textured vegetable protein (TVP), Quorn and pulse vegetables. Use at least one in a practical cookery class.

- **Poultry:** Know the different types of poultry commonly eaten in Ireland today (chicken, turkey, duck and goose). Be able to explain the nutritive value of chicken in the diet. Understand the rules for buying, storing and cooking both fresh and frozen poultry in order to prevent food poisoning.

- **Fish:** Be able to classify fish (both by shape and nutritive value) and give examples of each class. Be able to describe the composition and nutritive value of fish and explain why we should include more of it in our diet. Be able to explain and demonstrate the rules for buying, storing, preparing and cooking fresh and frozen fish. Know the different ways fish can be processed.

- **Eggs:** Be able to list the seven ways eggs can be used in cookery. Be able to describe the composition and nutritive value of eggs in the diet. Know what information should be found on an egg carton and what this information means for the consumer. Be able to check an egg for freshness. Be able to explain and demonstrate the rules for storing and cooking with eggs.

- **Milk and milk products:** Know why we include this group in our diet and how many servings are required daily. Be able to describe the composition and nutritive value of milk and cheese in the diet. Be able to list and describe the range of milks (both fresh and processed) and yoghurts on the market and the processes of pasteurisation and homogenisation. Know how to properly store dairy products. Be able to describe how cheese is made.

- **Cereal and potato group:** Be able to label a diagram of the structure of the wheat grain, describing the nutritive content of each part. Understand the effect that processing has on cereals. Be able to describe the average composition and nutritive value of cereals in the diet. List common cereals and their products. Understand the effects of cooking on cereals. Be able to describe how flour is processed and also describe the different types of flour, pasta and rice on the market today.

- **Fruit and vegetable group:** Be able to classify fruits and vegetables and outline their average composition and nutritive value in the diet. Be able to describe and in practical class physically prepare a range of fruits and vegetables for eating raw or cooking. Understand the effects that cooking has on fruit and vegetables and be able to describe all the ways fruit can be included in the diet. Be able to describe the ways vegetables may be cooked and how to prevent nutrient loss during preparation and cooking. Understand the guidelines for buying and storing fruit and vegetables.

Food groups

There are **four** food groups:

- Protein group
- Milk and milk products group
- Cereal and potato group
- Fruit and vegetable group

Questions on the food groups are frequently asked in section B, question 1 (both levels) in the Junior Certificate examination.

Protein group

This group is made up of meat, fish, eggs, meat alternatives and nuts. Eat two to three servings every day from this group (requirements vary – an adult requires less from this group than a teenager).

 Chapter 1, pages 4–5 – the sources and functions of protein in the diet

 Chapter 3, page 25 – the food pyramid

Meat

The term *meat* means the edible flesh and often internal organs of cattle, pigs, sheep, poultry (chicken and turkey) and game (wild animals and birds).

Offal is the name given to the edible internal organs, such as liver and kidneys. Offal is cheap, nutritious (it is particularly high in iron) and cooks quickly by grilling, baking or frying.

Red meat

Red meat refers to the meat from cattle, pigs and sheep. Red meat is given different names depending on the animal it has come from and whether it has been processed.

Types of red meat

| Beef, veal (calf) | Pork, bacon, ham and other products, such as sausages | Mutton (sheep), lamb, lamb's liver and kidneys |

Composition and nutritive value of red meat

Percentages are for Higher Level only.

Even though it is a great source of nutrients, especially **protein** (20–25%, for growth), **iron** (for healthy blood) and **vitamin B** (for a healthy nervous system and the control of energy release from food), red meat should not be eaten every day. This is because it contains large amounts of **saturated fat** (20%), which is linked to heart disease. Red meat does not contain any **carbohydrate** (0%), so it is usually eaten with a food high in carbohydrate, such as potatoes.

Under the microscope: The structure of meat

🔧 **Tough meat** has more tough connective tissue and comes from older animals or very active parts of the animal, such as the leg or neck.

🔧 **Tender meat** has less connective tissue and comes from younger animals or parts of the animal that do not move very much.

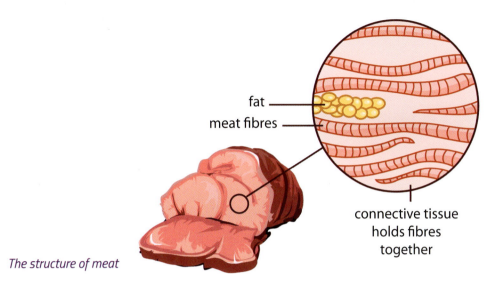

The structure of meat

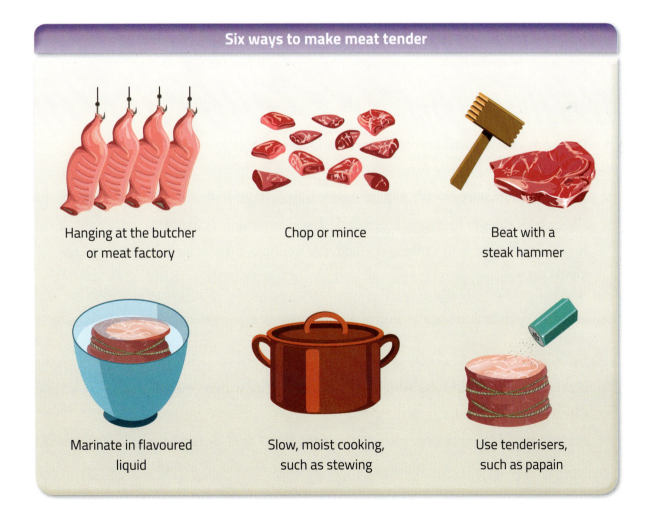

Six ways to make meat tender		
Hanging at the butcher or meat factory	Chop or mince	Beat with a steak hammer
Marinate in flavoured liquid	Slow, moist cooking, such as stewing	Use tenderisers, such as papain

For some cuts of meat, the more tender the cut, the more expensive it is.

Type of cut	Beef	Lamb	Pork
Tender (frying and grilling)	Fillet steak	Cutlets	Loin chops
Medium (roasting)	Rolled rib	Leg	Belly
Tough (stewing and mincing)	Topside	Gigot	

When buying meat

- Buy from a clean, reliable shop. Meat should be traceable to its farm of origin.
- Meat should have no bad smell.
- Do not buy fatty pieces – ask to have the fat trimmed off.
- Check both sides of the meat. If pre-packed, you are taking a chance.
- Buy a cut suited to your cooking method. For example, there is no point frying tough gigot chops.

Remember: Tough cuts are just as nutritious and tasty as expensive cuts if cooked correctly.

Safe storage of meat

- Meat is a high-protein food, which feeds bacteria – use within two days.
- Check best-before dates.
- Store in the fridge on a large plate so it cannot drip. Cover loosely with a clean tea towel.

Safe preparation and cooking of meat

- Never prepare or store raw meat and fish near cooked food or food that is eaten raw – food poisoning will result.
- Thaw meat fully before cooking it thoroughly.
- Never refreeze meat.

Effects of cooking on meat

- Fat melts.
- Meat shrinks.
- Colour changes from red to brown.
- Protein coagulates and the surface seals.
- Flavours develop.
- Bacteria are destroyed.

Meat alternatives

There are a number of different products on the market that can be used as high-protein alternatives to meat. The three most common are:

- Tofu
- Textured vegetable protein (TVP)
- Quorn (made from fungi)

Tofu

Tofu is a white, creamy, high-protein food made by separating soya milk into curds (tofu) and whey and then pressing the curds into cubes or blocks. Tofu can be used in the following ways:

- Tofu can be used much like cheese in vegan pizza or like chunks of chicken in a stir-fry.
- Thread cubes of firm tofu onto skewers with mushrooms, cherry tomatoes and onions. Marinate in soy sauce, brush with olive oil and grill to make tasty kebabs.
- Whizz tofu with strawberries and honey to make a dairy-free fruit smoothie. Tofu can also be used to make mousse, such as strawberry or chocolate.
- Mix with onion, garlic and herbs; form into burgers; coat in flour or egg and breadcrumbs; grill or fry.
- Cream tofu and add flavourings, such as garlic, to make tasty, nutritious dips.

A tofu stir-fry

TVP (textured vegetable protein)

This protein-rich food is made from soya beans. It is flavoured and shaped to resemble meat (chunks, mince and steaks). TVP is usually bought dried and once it has been reconstituted with water it can be used in a variety of dishes, such as lasagne, spaghetti Bolognese, burgers, stew or shepherd's pie. Some non-vegetarians use one-third TVP, two-thirds meat in dishes because it is healthier.

TVP burger

Lasagne made with Quorn

Quorn

Quorn is a leading brand of mycoprotein food products. Mycoprotein is a term for protein-rich foodstuffs made from processed edible fungi. Quorn is produced as both a cooking ingredient and as a range of ready meals. Quorn can be used for dishes such as pizza, lasagne and shepherd's pie.

Pulse vegetables

Pulse vegetables (peas, beans and lentils) and nuts are also used as meat substitutes because of their high protein content. Pulses often need to be soaked before use.

Meat

1. **Food groups:** There are four food groups, each with a main function in the body: protein group (growth and repair), milk and milk products (calcium for bone and teeth), cereal and potato group (carbohydrate for heat and energy) and fruit and vegetables (fibre for a healthy bowel and vitamins and minerals for general health).

2. **Meat:** Includes beef, veal, pork and pork products, mutton and lamb, offal, poultry and game.

3. **Nutritive value:** Excellent source of HBV protein, iron (healthy blood) and B vitamins (healthy nervous system, growth, regulation of energy release from food), but high in saturated fat (20%). Contains no carbohydrate.

4. **Structure:** Meat fibres are held together with connective tissue and fat is marbled between fibres. Cheap, tough cuts (topside) have more connective tissue, but are just as nutritious if cooked by slow, moist methods as more expensive tender cuts (fillet steak).

5. **Tenderising meat:** By hanging (in butcher shop or factory), chopping or mincing, beating (steak hammer), marinating in flavoured liquid, slow, moist cooking or by using tenderisers (papain).

6. **Buying meat:** Buy from a clean, reliable shop. Meat should have no bad smell. Ask for fat to be trimmed off. Avoid pre-packed meat. The cut chosen should match the cooking method. Cheap, tougher cuts are just as nutritious.

7. **Safety:** High-protein food, so bacteria love meat. Check best-before dates. Store in the fridge on large plate to avoid drips. Never prepare meat beside cooked food or food that is to be eaten raw. Thaw fully before cooking and never refreeze.

8. **Effects of cooking:** Fat melts. Meat shrinks, browns and the surface seals. Flavours develop and bacteria are destroyed.

9. **Meat alternatives:** High protein, low fat. Tofu (curds of soya milk), TVP (soya beans), Quorn (edible fungi) and pulse vegetables (peas, beans and lentils).

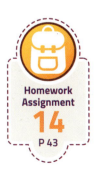

Homework
Assignment
14
P 43

Poultry: Chicken, turkey, duck, goose

Nutritive value of chicken

Chicken is high in protein yet low in saturated fat. It is lower in iron than red meat, but it can be served with iron-rich foods such as green vegetables. Chicken also contains vitamin B and small amounts of calcium. Chicken is an easily digested, high-protein food, so it is useful for all age groups.

Buying fresh poultry	Buying frozen poultry
• Buy from a clean shop. • Check the expiry date. • There should be no unpleasant smell. • Flesh should be firm and plump. • Flesh should not be discoloured.	• Poultry should be below the load line in the shop's cabinet. • Packaging should not be torn. • It should be frozen solid. • It should not be discoloured in any way.

Storing fresh and frozen poultry	Roasting poultry
Fresh • Remove the wrapper and giblets. • Place on a large plate, cover loosely with a clean tea towel and refrigerate. • Use within three days. **Frozen** • Place in your home freezer as soon as possible after buying it.	• Defrost completely. • Preheat the oven to 200°C /fan 190°C/gas 6. • Remove the giblets and pat the chicken dry with kitchen paper. • Season inside and out. • Cook for 20 minutes per 500g + 20 minutes extra. • To test if poultry is cooked, pierce the thickest part with a skewer – the juices should run clear.

Rapid Revision

Chicken

1. **Nutritive value:** High in protein, yet low in fat (if skin is not eaten) and easily digested. Not as high in iron as red meat, so serve with green vegetables. Small amounts of calcium and B vitamins.

2. **Buying:**
   - **Fresh:** Buy from a clean shop and check the expiry date. Chicken should have no unpleasant smell, the flesh should be firm and plump and there should be no discolouration.
   - **Frozen:** It should be below the load line. Packaging should be intact and it should be frozen solid.

3. **Storing:**
   - **Fresh:** Remove the wrapper and giblets and store on a large plate loosely covered in the fridge. Use within two or three days.
   - **Frozen:** Put into the freezer as soon as possible after purchase. Defrost completely before use.

4. **Cooking:** Whole poultry is usually cooked at 200°C/gas 6 for 20 minutes per 500g plus 20 minutes extra. Juices will run clear when fully cooked.
5. **Safety:** Thaw fully and cook thoroughly. Wash hands after handling. Avoid cross-contamination.

Homework
Assignment
15
P 47

Food safety

To reduce the dangers of food poisoning from harmful *Salmonella* bacteria, follow these simple rules:

- Thaw frozen, whole chicken properly: 24 hours in the fridge or eight hours at room temperature is necessary to defrost it properly.
- Make sure chicken is cooked right through to the bone. When the thickest part of the flesh is pierced with a skewer, the juices should run clear, not pink.
- After handling chicken, wash your hands and utensils in hot soapy water.
- Prepare and store raw chicken separately from cooked foods or foods to be eaten raw.

Fish

Irish people tend not to eat as much fish as other island nations. We should eat more fish, as it is an easily cooked, nutritious alternative to red meat.

Classification of fish

Fish can be classified according to its nutritive value:

- **White fish:** plaice, sole, cod, haddock, whiting
- **Oily fish:** mackerel, salmon, herring, trout, sardines
- **Shellfish:** crab, prawns, lobster, mussels

Unlike oily fish, which contains up to 20% fat (mostly unsaturated fat), white fish contains no fat. The fat of a white fish is stored in its liver, which is removed before cooking. Shellfish contain some fat (mostly unsaturated).

Fish can be described as either flat or round.

Flat fish – plaice

Round fish – herring

Percentages are for Higher Level only.

Composition and nutritive value of fish

- **Protein:** All fish is an excellent source of protein (17–20%). Unlike red meat, it does not contain saturated fat, so it will not raise cholesterol levels.
- **Fat:** White fish contains no fat (0%) and is therefore useful for those on weight-reducing diets. Oily fish (13%) and shellfish (2.5%) do contain fat, but it is unsaturated and therefore does not raise cholesterol.
- **Vitamins:** All fish is a good source of vitamin B. Oily fish also contains vitamins A and D.
- **Minerals:** All fish contain iodine. Canned fish also contains calcium if the bones are eaten.
- **Carbohydrate:** Fish contains no carbohydrate (0%) and may be served with a carbohydrate-rich food such as potatoes.
- Fish also lacks vitamin C and should therefore be served with a wedge of lemon.

Buying fish: Fresh	Buying fish: Frozen
Buy fish in season from a clean shop. Fish must be very fresh. Look for: • Moist, unbroken scales • Firm flesh, clear skin and markings • No bad smell or discolouration • Bulging, clear eyes • Gills should be red, not sticky	• Frozen solid • Stored below the load line in the freezer • Wrappings are not torn • Well within the expiry date • Put fish into your home freezer as soon as possible after buying it

Storing fish: Fresh	Storing fish: Frozen
• Remove wrapping and rinse in cold water. • Place in a deep container on crushed ice and cover with more ice if possible. • Cover to stop fish flavours from entering other foods. • Place in the refrigerator away from cooked foods. • Use within 24 hours.	• Store in the freezer as soon as possible. • Make sure that coverings are intact to prevent freezer burn. • Use by the expiry date shown on the packaging. • Follow the manufacturer's instructions for thawing and cooking.

How fish is sold

- **Whole:** Small fish, shellfish
- **Fillet:** Flat or round fish
- **Cutlets and steaks:** Large round fish – cutlet (taken from head end) or steaks (from tail end)

Preparing round fish

Round fish prepared like this can be stuffed and oven-baked. Round fish can also be filleted: two fillets are removed by paring them away from head to tail. Keep the knife as close as possible to the ribcage.

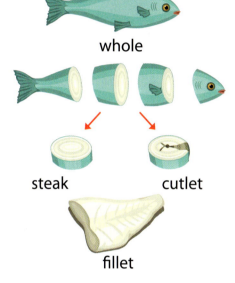

How fish is sold

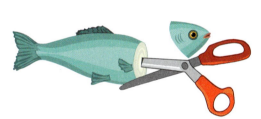

1. Remove the head and slit the underside open.

2. Remove gut.

3. Remove scales in the sink, working against the grain from head to tail.

4. Cut the fins off. Remove the black membrane inside the fish by rubbing with salt. Wash fish and dry with kitchen paper.

How to prepare round fish

Buying eggs

All the information you need to buy good-quality, fresh eggs must be written on the box they come in. Check that all eggs in the box are unbroken.

1. **Name of the producer:** This must be on the box.
2. **Class:** Eggs are graded A, B, C or Extra. Extra is the best, followed by A and so on.
3. **Size:** Eggs are now graded in four sizes: extra large (XL), large, medium and small. Most recipes require medium-sized eggs.
4. **Country of origin.**
5. **Expiry or best-before date:** This is usually three weeks from the day the eggs were laid. Eggs sold loose must have this stamped on each one.
6. **Week number:** Freshness can easily be judged by looking at this number. Eggs are given a number (1–52), week 1 being the first week in January.
7. **Caged or free-range:** Whether the eggs came from free-range or caged hens will be written on the box. If caged, then the print is usually very small. Free-range eggs tend to be more expensive.
8. In addition, the **Bord Bia Quality Assurance Scheme** requires each egg to be individually stamped.
   - The farming method: 0 = organic, 1 = free-range, 2 = barn, 3 = caged.
   - The country of origin. Ireland = IE.
   - The county (a letter) and farm code (a number).
   - Best-before date. For example, BB 6/12 = best before 6th December.

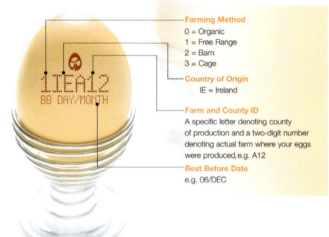

Farming Method
0 = Organic
1 = Free Range
2 = Barn
3 = Cage

Country of Origin
IE = Ireland

Farm and County ID
A specific letter denoting county of production and a two-digit number denoting actual farm where your eggs were produced, e.g. A12

Best Before Date
e.g. 06/DEC

Free-range hens

Battery hens

Storing fish: Fresh	Storing fish: Frozen
• Remove wrapping and rinse in cold water. • Place in a deep container on crushed ice and cover with more ice if possible. • Cover to stop fish flavours from entering other foods. • Place in the refrigerator away from cooked foods. • Use within 24 hours.	• Store in the freezer as soon as possible. • Make sure that coverings are intact to prevent freezer burn. • Use by the expiry date shown on the packaging. • Follow the manufacturer's instructions for thawing and cooking.

How fish is sold

🍴 **Whole:** Small fish, shellfish

🍴 **Fillet:** Flat or round fish

🍴 **Cutlets and steaks:** Large round fish – cutlet (taken from head end) or steaks (from tail end)

Preparing round fish

Round fish prepared like this can be stuffed and oven-baked. Round fish can also be filleted: two fillets are removed by paring them away from head to tail. Keep the knife as close as possible to the ribcage.

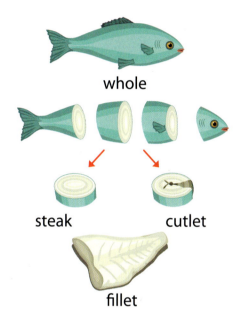

How fish is sold

1. Remove the head and slit the underside open.

2. Remove gut.

3. Remove scales in the sink, working against the grain from head to tail.

4. Cut the fins off. Remove the black membrane inside the fish by rubbing with salt. Wash fish and dry with kitchen paper.

How to prepare round fish

Preparing flat fish

1. Cut off fins. Make a slit slightly to one side of the back bone.

2. Slice around the head.

3. Using a flexible fish knife, peel off the first fillet, keeping as close to the ribcage as you can.

How to prepare flat fish

How to skin fish

A special flexible fish knife makes skinning fish easier.

1. Place fish skin side down, tail towards you on a chopping board.
2. Sprinkle salt on the tail end to give you grip.
3. Slide the knife between the skin and flesh, keeping the knife as close to the skin as possible.

How to skin a fish fillet

Cooking fish

Fish cooks very quickly. If overcooked, it breaks up. It loses its translucent (see-through) appearance and turns white. Micro-organisms are destroyed and some vitamins and minerals may dissolve into the cooking liquid.

Baked	May be stuffed or baked in a sauce.
Steamed	In a steamer or between two plates. Bland taste, so it needs a sauce.
Poached	Make sure liquid is not boiling or fish will break up. Bland taste, so it needs a sauce.
Grilled	Very quick method. Nutrients are retained.
Fried	Fried fish is often coated in batter or egg and crumbs. High in calories.

Once cooked, fish is usually garnished with a sauce (such as tartare sauce), parsley and a wedge of lemon.

Chapter 11, pages 136–138 – sauces; Chapter 5, page 49 – garnishes

Processed fish

Smoked

- ✎ Example: Smoked haddock fillets
- ✎ Smoking preserves fish

Smoked haddock

Frozen

- ✎ Nutrients are retained
- ✎ Expensive
- ✎ No waste
- ✎ Coated fish and ready-made dinners are available

Smoked salmon

Frozen fish

Canned/bottled

- ✎ In oil or brine
- ✎ Tuna, salmon, sardines and shellfish are often canned or bottled

Fish

1. **Classification:** By nutritive value or shape.
   - **Nutritive value:** White fish (e.g. plaice), oily fish (e.g. salmon), shellfish (e.g. crab).
   - **Shape:** Flat (e.g. plaice), round (e.g. salmon).

2. **Nutritive value:** High in protein (20%) and low in saturated fat (white fish has none unless processed) – good for those on low-cholesterol diets. Good source of vitamins B (all fish), A and D (oily fish). Source of iodine and calcium (canned fish). No carbohydrate or vitamin C.

3. **Buying:** Fish is sold whole or in fillets, cutlets or steaks.
   - **Fresh:** Buy in season from a clean, reliable shop. Fish should have moist, unbroken scales, firm flesh, clear markings, no smell or discolouration, bulging, clear eyes and red gills. It should not be sticky.
   - **Frozen:** Fish should be frozen solid. It should be below the load line and wrappings should be intact. Check the expiry date. Put in the freezer ASAP after purchase.

4. **Storing:**
   - **Fresh:** Remove the wrapping and rinse. Store in a deep container over crushed ice. Cover and keep away from cooked foods. Use within 24 hours.
   - **Frozen:** Store in the freezer ASAP after purchase. Make sure wrappings are intact (to avoid freezer burn). Use by the expiry date and follow instructions for thawing and cooking.

5. **Cooking:** Cooks quickly and will break up if overcooked. Can be baked, steamed, poached, grilled, fried or stewed (firm fish only, such as monkfish).

6. **Processing fish:** Smoking, freezing, canning or bottling in oil or brine.

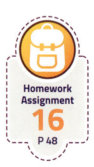

Homework
Assignment
16
P 48

Eggs

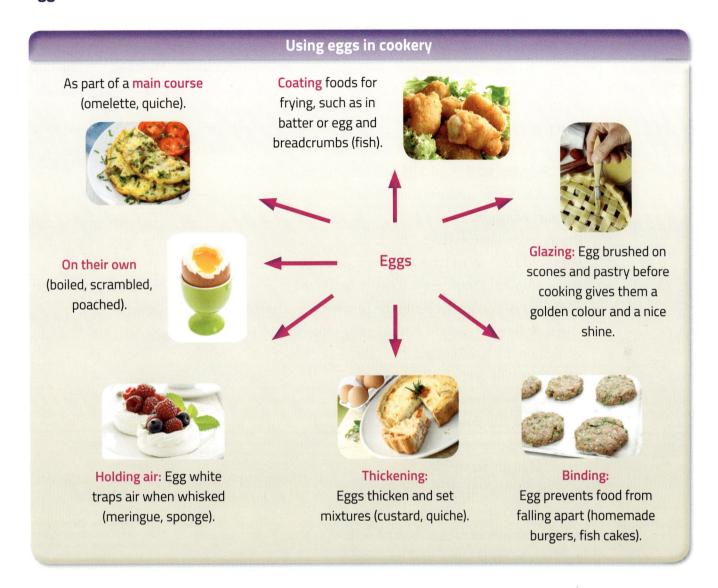

Using eggs in cookery

As part of a **main course** (omelette, quiche).

Coating foods for frying, such as in batter or egg and breadcrumbs (fish).

Glazing: Egg brushed on scones and pastry before cooking gives them a golden colour and a nice shine.

On their own (boiled, scrambled, poached).

Eggs

Holding air: Egg white traps air when whisked (meringue, sponge).

Thickening: Eggs thicken and set mixtures (custard, quiche).

Binding: Egg prevents food from falling apart (homemade burgers, fish cakes).

Composition and nutritive value of eggs

Eggs are a good source of protein (13%) but lack carbohydrate (0%), so they are often served with carbohydrate-rich foods, like boiled egg and toast. Fat (11%) in eggs is easily digested, and contrary to popular belief is mostly unsaturated. Eggs contain vitamins A, D and B and also the minerals calcium, iron and sulphur. Eggs lack vitamin C so they should be served with foods rich in vitamin C, such as an omelette served with a side salad, or a glass of orange juice served with a boiled egg in the morning.

In the past, people were advised not to eat more than two eggs per week because they contain fat (11%) and were thought to raise cholesterol levels. New research from the British Heart Foundation, however, has found that the fat in eggs does not contribute significantly to raising cholesterol levels (it is predominantly unsaturated – 56%) and therefore does not need to be as restricted in the diet.

Percentages are for Higher Level only.

Buying eggs

All the information you need to buy good-quality, fresh eggs must be written on the box they come in. Check that all eggs in the box are unbroken.

1. **Name of the producer:** This must be on the box.

2. **Class:** Eggs are graded A, B, C or Extra. Extra is the best, followed by A and so on.

3. **Size:** Eggs are now graded in four sizes: extra large (XL), large, medium and small. Most recipes require medium-sized eggs.

4. **Country of origin.**

5. **Expiry or best-before date:** This is usually three weeks from the day the eggs were laid. Eggs sold loose must have this stamped on each one.

6. **Week number:** Freshness can easily be judged by looking at this number. Eggs are given a number (1–52), week 1 being the first week in January.

7. **Caged or free-range:** Whether the eggs came from free-range or caged hens will be written on the box. If caged, then the print is usually very small. Free-range eggs tend to be more expensive.

8. In addition, the **Bord Bia Quality Assurance Scheme** requires each egg to be individually stamped.

    ● The farming method: 0 = organic, 1 = free-range, 2 = barn, 3 = caged.

    ● The country of origin. Ireland = IE.

    ● The county (a letter) and farm code (a number).

    ● Best-before date. For example, BB 6/12 = best before 6th December.

Farming Method
0 = Organic
1 = Free Range
2 = Barn
3 = Cage

Country of Origin
IE = Ireland

Farm and County ID
A specific letter denoting county of production and a two-digit number denoting actual farm where your eggs were produced, e.g. A12

Best Before Date
e.g. 06/DEC

Free-range hens

Battery hens

How to check if an egg is fresh

If eggs have been removed from their box and placed in the egg compartment of the fridge, the expiry date may be unclear. Eggs can be tested for freshness in other ways.

- As an egg gets stale, water evaporates out of the egg through the shell and air passes in. The air sac becomes larger and the egg lighter, so stale eggs float in salty water.
- Crack open an egg onto a saucer. It is fresh if the yolk is raised and the white around it is jelly-like.
- A stale egg has a flat yolk and a runny white.

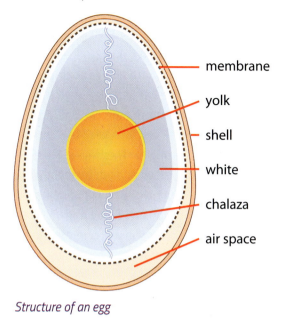

Structure of an egg

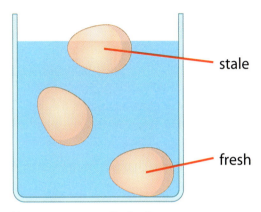

How to test an egg for freshness

Storing eggs

- Store in the fridge, pointed end down.
- Store away from strong-smelling foods.
- If storing yolks separately, place in a bowl of water in the fridge.
- Store whites in an airtight container in the fridge.

Using eggs in cookery

- Bring eggs to room temperature before using.
- Egg whites will not whisk properly if there is yolk present or if the bowl or whisk have even a trace of grease on them.
- To prevent curdling, do not overcook eggs. When adding egg to a hot liquid, such as milk for egg custard, cool the liquid somewhat and then add it to the egg, not the other way round.
- Raw or lightly cooked eggs should not be given to babies, toddlers, pregnant women, elderly people or invalids due to the risk of *Salmonella* poisoning.

Effects of cooking on eggs

- Protein coagulates (sets) – egg white changes from clear to white.
- If overcooked, eggs curdle and become less digestible.

Eggs

1. **Uses in cookery:** Coating, glazing, binding, thickening, holding air, eaten on their own, main course ingredient.

2. **Nutritive value:** Good source of HBV protein (13%) but no carbohydrate. 11% fat but mostly unsaturated. Eggs contain vitamins A, D and B plus some iron and sulphur. Eggs lack vitamin C, so serve with foods high in this vitamin.

3. **Information on carton:** Name of producer, class or grade, size, country of origin, expiry date, week egg was laid (1–52), will say free-range if it is.

4. **Testing for freshness:** Stale eggs are lighter and will float in salty water. If cracked, the yolk will be raised and white and it will be jelly-like, not watery.

5. **Structure of an egg:** Shell, membrane, white, chalaza, yolk, air space.

6. **Storing and using eggs:** Store pointed end down, away from strong-smelling foods. Yolks can be stored in water in the fridge. Whites can be stored in an airtight container. Bring eggs to room temperature before using. Egg white will not whisk if there is any yolk or grease present. If eggs are being added to hot liquid (custard), cool the liquid to prevent curdling. Raw or lightly cooked eggs are dangerous for babies, toddlers, pregnant women, the elderly or invalids.

7. **Effects of cooking:** Protein in eggs coagulates (sets) on cooking. Egg white changes from clear to white. Overcooked eggs curdle and become rubbery – difficult to digest.

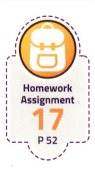

Homework
Assignment
17
P 52

Milk and milk products

This group includes milk, butter, cream, yoghurt and cheese. Eat three to five servings per day from this group, not including butter and cream.

 Chapter 1, page 12 – the sources and functions of calcium in the diet

 Chapter 3, page 25 – the food pyramid

Milk

Composition and nutritive value of milk

Milk contains 87% water, so it is good for keeping up daily fluid intake. Milk is a good source of digestible protein (3.5%) for growth and repair. It contains fat (4%) in an easily digested form. Milk is a good source of calcium in the diet – one 300ml glass provides 345mg. However, a survey conducted by the National Universities Nutrition Alliance in 2008 found that approximately 42% of teenage girls and 23% of teenage boys were not meeting their daily calcium requirements (1,300mg a day). Milk also contains vitamins A, B and D. Vitamin D works with calcium for strong bones and teeth. Milk lacks vitamin C and iron, so it should be served with foods rich in these. Milk contains carbohydrate (4.5%).

> Percentages are for Higher Level only.

Effects of heat on milk	Buying and storing milk
• Flavour changes. • Bacteria are destroyed. • Protein coagulates and a skin forms – steam then builds up under the skin and can boil over. • Vitamins C and B are lost.	• Check the expiry date. • Store in the fridge away from strong-smelling foods, such as onions. • Use in order of expiry dates. • Do not mix milks with different expiry dates.

Types of milk

- **Whole milk:** Ordinary milk with 4% fat. Recommended milk for children.
- **Low-fat milk:** Sometimes called semi-skimmed, this has less than half the fat of whole milk.
- **Skimmed:** All but a trace of fat is removed. The flavour is altered and vitamins A and D are also removed. Not suitable for children.
- **Fortified (for example, Supermilk):** A low-fat milk with vitamins A and D and calcium added.
- **Buttermilk:** Acidic, used in baking.
- **Protein milk:** a milk that is higher in protein (5%) yet low in fat (1%). It also has a higher calcium content, 495mg/100mls.

Processed milks

UHT (long-life): Heated to 132°C, UHT milk lasts for months if it is unopened. Available in cartons or small single portions, like in hotels.

Evaporated milk: Some water is removed and the milk is then canned. Long-lasting; used in desserts.

Condensed milk: Similar to evaporated milk but with sugar added.

Dried milk: All water is removed. The milk is made up by adding water. Taste is altered.

Soya milk: Made from soya beans. Suitable for vegans and those with dairy allergies.

Pasteurisation and homogenisation

Pasteurisation kills the bacteria in milk to make it safe without spoiling the taste of the milk. Milk is heated to 72°C for 15 seconds and then cooled quickly. All commercially sold milk is pasteurised.

Homogenisation spreads the cream, or fat, evenly throughout the milk. Most milk is treated in this way.

Using milk in the diet and in food preparation

- Milk as a drink is an excellent source of digestible protein and calcium.
- It can be added hot or cold to breakfast cereals, thereby improving their nutritive value.
- It is a main ingredient in many dishes (quiche), sauces (white sauce), pancakes and milk puddings (rice pudding).
- It can be added to soups to give a creamier taste and to improve its nutritive value (cream of mushroom soup).
- It is used in baking (buttermilk in bread making).

Milk products: Cream and butter

Please note that while cream and butter are milk products, they are not in the milk, yoghurt and cheese group. They belong at the top of the food pyramid and should be avoided or eaten sparingly.

Cream

Cream is the fat that rises to the top of milk and is then removed. Cream is very high in kilocalories.

Types of cream

Type	Description
Standard cream	Carton often states 'fresh cream'; 40% fat
Whipped cream	Standard cream that is whipped for convenience
Flavoured creams	Cream that is flavoured, for example with Baileys
Double cream	Used in dessert making; 48% fat
Low-fat cream	Reduced fat, though it still contains 30% fat
Sour cream or crème fraîche	Cream is treated with a lactic acid culture, which pleasantly sours and thickens it; used for dips, dressings, etc.
Aerosol	Keeps longer, quick and convenient

Butter

When cream is churned, the fat comes together as **butter**. The liquid that runs off is called **buttermilk**. Butter is usually salted. Butter is very high in fat (80%). **Low-fat** or 'light' butter has half this fat content. **Dairy spreads** such as Dairygold are a mixture of butter and vegetable oil. They contain roughly the same amount of fat but less cholesterol. **Polyunsaturated margarines** such as Flora are very low in cholesterol and are a much healthier option.

Yoghurt

Yoghurt is a milk product made by adding souring lactic acid bacteria (which are harmless) to milk. Yoghurt has all the nutrients of milk. Low-fat varieties are available, while others sometimes have sugar added.

Types of yoghurt

- **Natural yoghurt:** White, unflavoured yoghurt. A good base ingredient for savoury dips, etc.
- **Set yoghurt:** Petit Filous is one example.
- **Yoghurt drinks:** Milk and flavours are added to plain yoghurt, for example Yop.
- **Greek yoghurt:** A thick, creamy, unflavoured yoghurt.
- **Fruit yoghurt:** Either real fruit is added or just fruit juice if a smooth fruit-flavoured yoghurt is needed.

Uses of yoghurt

- Healthy alternative to cream
- Healthy dessert on its own
- In dips: natural or Greek with other ingredients added, such as chives
- In salad dressings: natural or Greek

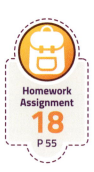

Homework
Assignment
18
P 55

Cheese

Classification of cheese

Cheese is classified into **hard**, **semi-hard**, **soft** or **processed**.

Hard cheese (Cheddar, Parmesan)

Semi-hard cheeses (Edam, Cashel Blue)

Soft cheeses (cream cheese, cottage cheese)

Processed cheese (cheese slices, cheese triangles, cheese strings, cheese spreads)

Composition and nutritive value of cheese

Hard cheese is an excellent source of both calcium (4%, or 720mg per 100g), for healthy bones and teeth, and protein (25%), for growth and repair. For this reason, cheese is ideal to include in the diets of children, teenagers, pregnant and breastfeeding women and vegetarians. Hard cheese is very high in fat (34%) and cholesterol, so it should be eaten in moderation, especially by those on low-fat diets or those with high cholesterol.

Percentages are for Higher Level only.

🍴 Cottage cheese is much lower in fat (4%), but it is not as good a source of either protein (14%) or calcium (1%).

🍴 Cheese lacks carbohydrate (0%), so it is generally served with carbohydrate-rich foods such as bread, pasta or crackers.

🍴 Cheese contains vitamins A, D and B and varying amounts of water depending on the type of cheese – hard cheeses contain less water than soft or semi-soft.

Using cheese in cookery

In main courses
(pizza, lasagne, quiche)

Desserts
(cheesecake)

Savoury dips and
fondues

On salads or in
salad dressings

Cheeseboard at
the end of a meal

On sandwiches, rolls,
crackers, panini

Effects of cooking on cheese

- **Eat raw** if possible, as cooked cheese is less digestible.
- **Protein coagulates** (sets) and cheese shrinks.
- **Fat melts**. If overcooked, fat separates from cheese and cheese becomes rubbery, oily and indigestible.
- **Mustard** helps make cheese more digestible.

The six stages of cheese making

1. A culture of harmless bacteria is added to pasteurised milk. This gives flavour.
2. Milk is warmed. Rennet is added, which clots the milk.
3. The milk separates into curds (solid) and whey (liquid).
4. Curds are chopped, pressed and salted. Whey is drained off.
5. Curds are put into moulds and pressed – firmly for hard cheeses.
6. Cheese is left to mature. Flavours develop over three to 12 months.

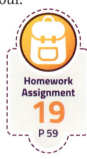

Homework
Assignment
19
P 59

Buying cheese	Storing cheese
• Buy in small quantities, as it will go off quickly once it is opened. • Check the expiry date.	• Cover with greaseproof paper, then foil. • Refrigerate. • Remove from the fridge one hour before use to let the flavours develop.

Milk and milk products

Milk

1. **Nutritive value:** 87% water, so it helps maintain daily fluid intake. Good source of easily digested protein (3.5%) for growth and repair. 4% fat – low-fat varieties should be included in low-cholesterol diets. Good source of calcium and vitamin D for healthy bones and teeth. Also contains vitamins A and B. Contains carbohydrate for heat and energy (4.5%) but lacks iron and vitamin C.

2. **Effects of heat:** Flavour changes. Bacteria are destroyed. Protein coagulates. Vitamins C and B are lost.

3. **Types:** Whole, low-fat, skimmed, fortified (Supermilk), buttermilk, protein milk. Processed milks: UHT, evaporated, condensed, dried, soya milk.

4. **Pasteurisation** kills bacteria (heated to 72°C for 15 seconds). **Homogenisation** spreads fat evenly throughout milk.

5. **Uses:** As a drink, on breakfast cereals, as a main ingredient in dishes (quiche) and added to soups. Buttermilk is used in baking.

Cream and butter

1. **Nutritive value:** Both are very high in saturated fat and cholesterol (butter 80%, standard cream 40%). Cream and butter are at the top of the food pyramid, so eat sparingly. It is better to eat polyunsaturated margarines (Flora).

2. **Types of cream:** Standard, double, low-fat, whipped, flavoured creams, crème fraîche, aerosol.

Yoghurt

1. **Manufacture:** Made by adding lactic acid bacteria to milk.

2. **Nutritive value:** Same nutrients as milk. Choose low-fat varieties with a low sugar content.

3. **Types:** Natural, set, drinks, Greek, fruit.

4. **Uses:** Healthy alternative to cream, handy dessert, dips, salad dressings.

Cheese

1. **Nutritive value:** Excellent source of protein (25%) and calcium (4%). Hard cheeses are high in fat (34%) and cholesterol, but lower-fat varieties are available (cottage cheese). Cheese lacks carbohydrate but contains vitamins A, D and B.

2. **Classification:** Hard, semi-hard, soft and processed.

3. **Uses:** Cheeseboard, sandwiches, on salads, in desserts, dips and fondues, as part of main courses (quiche).

4. **Effects of cooking:** Cooking makes cheese less digestible. Protein coagulates and fat melts. Cheese becomes rubbery if it is overcooked.

5. **Manufacture:** Bacteria culture is added to pasteurised milk. Milk is warmed. Rennet is added, which clots the milk. Milk separates into curd (solid) and whey (liquid). Whey is drained off. The cheese is salted, pressed and ripened.

6. **Storing dairy products:** Keep refrigerated and covered, away from strong-smelling foods. Check expiry dates.

Cereal and potato group

 Eat four to six servings per day, more if you are very active.

 Most of the food we eat should come from this food group. All over the world, cereals are eaten because they are cheap, nutritious, filling and easily prepared.

Potatoes are included in the section on vegetables.

🔗 Chapter 1, pages 7–8 – the sources and functions of carbohydrates and fibre in the diet

🔗 Chapter 3, page 25 – the food pyramid

Cereals

Structure of cereals

🍴 **The bran layer:** This part of the grain contains fibre, iron and vitamin B. It is removed during processing, for instance in making white flour.

🍴 **The endosperm:** Starch and gluten. This is the part of the grain that remains after processing.

🍴 **Germ:** This nutritious part of the grain is also removed during processing. It can be bought on its own as wheat germ. It contains protein, fat and vitamin B.

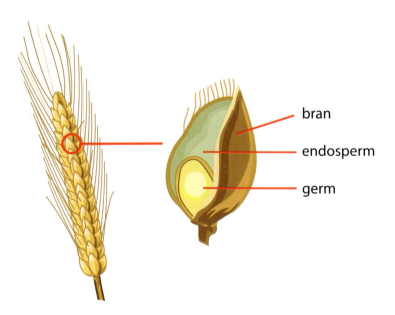

This is an illustration of a wheat grain. Other cereals have a similar structure.

Common cereals and some of their products

Cereal	Wheat	Rice	Maize	Oats	Rye	Barley
Products	Flour, bread, cakes, pasta, breakfast cereals (Weetabix), noodles and couscous	Brown and white rice, breakfast cereals (Rice Krispies), rice cakes, rice flour, ground rice	Corn on the cob, sweetcorn, breakfast cereals (cornflakes), cornflour, popcorn, corn oil	Breakfast cereals (porridge), muesli, Ready Brek	Rye bread (dark colour), rye flour, crispbread (Ryvita), rye whiskey	Whiskey, beer, pearl barley

Average composition and nutritive value of cereals

- **Carbohydrate** (70%) is the main nutrient in cereals. Cereals are therefore useful in the diet as a source of heat and energy. Those who lead active lives should eat plenty of carbohydrates (some very active individuals, like athletes, could eat up to 12 servings per day). Those with inactive lifestyles should be careful, though, as cereals such as bread are often accompanied by fatty foods and therefore can cause weight gain.

- Unprocessed cereals, such as brown bread and brown rice, contain fibre, which is essential for a healthy digestive system and should be chosen over processed cereals.

- Cereals also contain **low biological value protein** (13%). **Gluten** is a protein found in some cereals, such as wheat. While gluten gives bread dough its elastic quality and allows it to rise, people with coeliac disease cannot digest gluten and must not eat it.

- Cereals do contain a small amount of **fat** (2%), although it is usually what is put on the cereal, such as butter or cheese, that increases fat content.

- Cereals contain the minerals **calcium** and **iron** and some **B group vitamins**. If these are removed during processing, they are often put back in again. For example, you will see 'fortified with calcium and iron' written on such products.

> Percentages are for Higher Level only.

Effects of cooking on cereals

- Starch grains swell and burst, such as popcorn.
- Starch grains absorb liquid, such as rice.
- Starch becomes more digestible – compare eating a raw and cooked potato.

Effects of heat on cereals: starch grains swell, soften and absorb liquid

Flour

Although flour can be made from other cereals, such as corn, wheat flour is the most common in Ireland. The type of wheat flour produced depends on the type of wheat used and how much processing it undergoes.

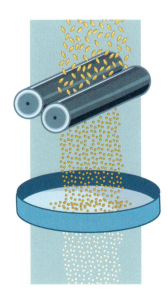

Processing flour

1. Grain is washed, dried and broken open between metal rollers. If processing stops here, wholemeal flour is produced.
2. Grain is sieved and rolled again and again until a refined white product is produced – white flour. Sometimes extra ingredients are added at this stage, such as calcium, or the flour may be bleached.

A **refined cereal product** is a processed product from which much of the bran and the germ have been removed. Examples of refined cereal products are white flour and white rice.

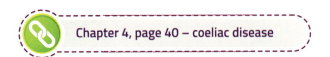

Types of flour

Strong flour: Wheat with a high concentration of gluten, used for making yeast bread	Brown: Similar to wholemeal, but with the coarsest bran and germ removed	Wholemeal: Coarse brown flour, contains the whole wheat grain	White or cream flour: Starchy endosperm only	Self-raising: Brown or white flour with a raising agent such as baking powder added

🔗 Chapter 4, page 40 – coeliac disease

If the gluten-free symbol appears on a product, it is suitable for coeliacs

Bread

Bread is one of our staple foods. Nowadays, breads from all over the world are available in our supermarkets. Some of these breads are pictured here.

Breads from around the world

Pasta

Special wheat called durum wheat is used to make pasta. Flour made from this wheat is mixed with water and egg to make a dough. Sometimes flavouring ingredients such as tomato or spinach are added at this stage. It is then shaped and dried. Fresh pasta is not totally dried and must be used within a few days. Dried pasta is fully dried and keeps for up to a year.

Fresh pasta

Rice

🍴 **Long-grain rice:** Served with savoury dishes, such as curry. Cooks in 25 minutes.

🍴 **Medium-grain rice:** Italian rice used for dishes where rice is mixed through, such as risotto.

🍴 **Short-grain rice:** Used in sweet puddings and desserts.

🍴 **Wholegrain/brown rice:** Brown long-grain rice is high in fibre, as the bran is not removed. It takes 40 minutes to cook.

🍴 **Convenience rice products:** Boil in the bag, non-stick, cooked frozen rice.

White and brown rice

Brown rice should be eaten instead of white rice, as it is higher in fibre, which helps to prevent constipation and other bowel disorders.

Homework
Assignment
20
P 62

Rapid Revision

Cereals

1. **Structure:** Bran layer, endosperm, germ.
2. **Common cereals:** Wheat, rice, maize (corn), oats, rye and barley.
3. **Nutritive value:** Carbohydrate is the main nutrient found in cereals (70%), which supplies heat and energy. The number of servings per day depends on activity levels – usually four to six, but it could be more. Unprocessed cereals (brown rice) contain fibre for a healthy bowel. They also contain LBV protein (13%) and some contain gluten (avoided by coeliacs). Small amounts of fat (although what is spread on cereal product may be high in fat). Fortified cereals contain calcium, iron and B vitamins.
4. **Effects of heat:** Grains may swell and burst (popcorn). Cereals absorb liquid (rice) and become more digestible.
5. **Flour:** The type produced depends on the grain used and the level of processing.
   - **Processing:** Grain is rolled and sieved if refined (white) flour is needed.
   - **Types:** Wholemeal, strong, white, self-raising, gluten-free.
6. **Pasta:** Made from durum wheat. Water and egg are added. May be dried (all water is removed) or fresh (less water is removed) – semi-perishable.
7. **Rice:** Long-grain (savoury dishes), medium-grain (risotto), short-grain (rice pudding), wholegrain/ brown (higher in fibre – savoury dishes), convenience (boil in the bag).

Fruit and vegetable group

Eat at least five servings of fruit and vegetables per day. Many nutritionists believe we should actually consume up to 10 servings (particularly vegetables) per day for maximum health.

 Chapter 1 – fibre (page 7), vitamins (page 8) and minerals (page 12)

 Chapter 3, page 25 – the food pyramid

Fruit

Classification of fruit

Citrus	Berries	Stone	Hard	Dried	Others
Grapefruit	Blackberries	Apricots	Apples	Apricots	Bananas
Lemons	Blackcurrants	Cherries	Pears	Currants	Melon
Limes	Gooseberries	Damsons		Dates	Pineapple
Oranges	Raspberries	Nectarines		Prunes	Rhubarb
Satsumas	Redcurrants	Peaches		Raisins	
Tangerines	Strawberries	Plums		Sultanas	

Average composition and nutritive value of fresh fruit

Fresh fruit is very important in the diet for three main reasons:

- Many fruits are high in vitamin C (up to 200mg per 100g for blackcurrants, followed by strawberries, with 77mg per 100g).
- Many fruits are high in fibre.
- Most fruits are low in kilocalories (fruit is up to 90% water).

In addition (although less importantly), some fruits contain a little iron and calcium. Highly coloured fruits such as peaches contain carotene, which the body changes into vitamin A. Fruit contains carbohydrate (5–20%) in the form of fruit sugar (fructose) and traces of protein. Fruit contains virtually no fat.

Percentages are for Higher Level only.

Preparing fruit

- Prepare just before cooking or eating to avoid loss of vitamin C.
- **Citrus fruits** (lemons): Wash in warm water if rind is to be grated and eaten.
- **Hard fruits** (apples): Remove core, leave skin on if possible, cut to required size for dish, toss in orange juice to prevent browning (avoid sugar syrup if possible).
- **Soft fruit** (strawberries): Remove damaged fruit, wash gently in a sieve, pat dry with kitchen paper.

Effects of cooking on fruit

- Texture softens.
- Vitamin C is reduced (up to 25%).
- Cellulose breaks down and fruit becomes more digestible.
- Moulds and other micro-organisms are destroyed.

Using fruit in the diet

Eaten raw

Drinks: orange and apple juice

Hot puddings: pies, tarts and flans

Cold desserts: yoghurt, trifle, mousse

Fruit in the diet

Preserves: jam, marmalade and chutney

Salads: fruit salad, Waldorf salad

Starters: melon

Sauces: cranberry and apple

Homework Assignment
21
P 67

Vegetables

Classification of vegetables

Roots/tubers	Green	Pulses	Fruits
Beetroot	Broccoli	Beans (green bean, broad bean, runner bean)	Aubergine
Carrot	Brussels sprouts	Dried peas, beans, lentils	Courgette
Onion (bulb)	Cabbage	Peas	Cucumber
Parsnip	Cauliflower		Pepper
Potato (tuber)	Curly kale		Pumpkin
Swede	Lettuce		Tomato
Turnip (tuber)	Spinach		

Average composition and nutritive value of vegetables

Vegetables are valuable in the diet for five main reasons:

- Pulse vegetables (peas, beans and lentils) are a good source of **vegetable protein** (up to 7%). For this reason they are very important in the diet, especially for vegetarians.

- Vegetables are **low in fat** and have a **high water content** (up to 95%). This means that they are **low in kilocalories**: good news for weight watchers and those at risk from heart disease.

- Vegetables are a good source of **vitamin C** (peppers have the highest, with 120mg per 100g). Vitamin C is vital for general health but is sometimes lacking in the Irish diet.

- Vegetables, especially green vegetables, are a good source of **iron**. Iron is vital for healthy blood and is another nutrient often lacking in the Irish diet.

- Vegetables (especially pulse vegetables) are a good source of **fibre** in the diet, which is needed to prevent constipation and other bowel problems.

Note: Vegetables also contain **vitamin A** in the form of **carotene**. Pulses also contain some **B group vitamins**.

Percentages are for Higher Level only.

Preparing vegetables for cooking

Type	Preparation
Roots/tubers	Scrub and peel if necessary. Cut off the ends, then slice, dice or cut into strips (julienne).
Greens	Remove wilted leaves, separate leaves and wash each leaf under cold running water. Chop if necessary with a sharp knife. Do not steep. Do not use bread soda in cooking (it was used to preserve colour, but it destroys vitamin C).
Pulses	Remove fresh pulses from their pod. Soak dried pulses overnight in water.
Fruits	Wash in cold water, then slice or dice with a sharp knife.

Cooking vegetables

Vegetables can be cooked in a variety of ways.

- **Boiling:** While not the best way to cook vegetables, it is traditional and is still one of the most common ways vegetables are cooked in Ireland. Greens, roots and tubers and pulses may be cooked this way.

- **Steaming:** This is an excellent way to cook vegetables. Because vegetables are not actually sitting in the cooking water, minerals and vitamins are not lost. It is suitable for all types of vegetables.

- **Stir-frying:** Chop vegetables for stir-frying just before cooking. Cook in the minimum amount of oil (use oil spray). Vegetables are cooked quickly, so nutrients are not lost. It is suitable for all types of vegetables.

- **Roasting:** Vegetables are best if they are par-boiled before roasting (boiled until half cooked). Put a little olive oil in the roasting tin and toss the vegetables in it before roasting in the oven. This method is best suited to roots, tubers and fruits, such as peppers.

- **Microwaving:** Prepare vegetables and chop into even-sized pieces. Cover and cook on high for up to 10 minutes (depends on the type of vegetable). Allow vegetables to 'stand' for two to three minutes before serving. Suitable for all types of vegetables.

- **Grilling:** Used for tomatoes and peppers – sometimes food is brushed with oil.

- Vegetables (mainly roots and tubers) are also cooked in **stews** and **casseroles**.

Effects of cooking on vegetables

- Al dente means cooking vegetables until they are soft.
- Vitamins and minerals dissolve into the cooking liquid.
- Vitamin C is destroyed.
- Fibre softens.
- Starch becomes more digestible (potatoes).
- Flavour, texture and colour may be lost, especially if overcooked.

> **Al dente** means cooking vegetables until they are soft right through but still have bite.

How to prevent nutrient loss when preparing and cooking vegetables

1. Buy good-quality fruit and vegetables in season. Eat them raw where possible.

2. Do not use bread soda when cooking cabbage because it destroys vitamin C.

3. Use a small amount of water and keep saucepan lids on. Don't overcook – cook until they are just al dente.

4. Do not soak vegetables.

5. Chop with a sharp knife.

6. Cook with the skins on if possible. If peeling, use a vegetable peeler, as a knife peels too thickly.

Buying fruit and vegetables

- Buy fruit and vegetables in season, when they are the freshest and at their best.
- Buy undamaged fruit and vegetables that feel heavy for their size.
- Buy medium-sized fruits and vegetables, as large ones lack flavour.
- Avoid pre-packed fruit and vegetables, as any damage may not be visible.
- Buy in small quantities, as they go off quickly.

- **In season:** Most fruit and vegetables grow at a certain time of year. This is when they are in season and at their best. Fruit and vegetables must be imported when they are out of season and are usually expensive, such as strawberries at Christmastime.
- **Organically grown** fruit and vegetables are grown naturally, without the use of artificial fertilizers. They are more expensive.

EU grading and regulations

Fruit and vegetables must be:

- Sound and free from chemicals
- Graded according to size
- Marked with the country of origin, variety and class

Classes

- Extra: Excellent quality
- Class I: Good quality
- Class II: Marketable but with defects of shape or colour
- Class III: Marketable but inferior

Storing fresh fruit and vegetables

- Use as soon as possible after you buy them.
- Remove plastic wrappings or bags.
- Store fruits and green vegetables in the fridge if possible.
- Store roots and tubers in a cool, dark, ventilated place on a vegetable rack or basket.
- Bananas should not be stored in the fridge, as they will blacken.

Processed fruit and vegetables

Fruit and vegetables are generally processed to prolong their shelf life.

Frozen

- No loss of goodness, but can go soft when they thaw.

Canned

- Canning involves high temperatures, which destroys vitamins C and B.
- Fruit canned in syrup has a high sugar content.

Dried

- Vitamins C and B are lost.

Frozen vegetables

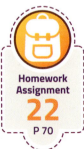

Homework
Assignment
22
P 70

Fruit

1. **Classification:** Citrus (oranges), berries (strawberries), stone (peaches), hard (apples), dried (raisins) and others (pineapples).
2. **Nutritive value:** Five or more per day (including vegetables). Some (strawberries and citrus) are high in vitamin C (healthy skin and gums, healing, iron absorption), some are high in fibre (healthy bowel) and most are low in calories. Fruit contains carbohydrate (fruit sugar).
3. **Effects of cooking:** Fibre softens, some vitamin C is lost and micro-organisms are killed.
4. **Uses:** Eaten raw, in hot puddings/tarts, jams, sauces (cranberry), starters (melon), salads (Waldorf), fruit yoghurts and drinks (orange juice, smoothies).

Vegetables

1. **Classification:** Roots/tubers (carrots), green (cabbage), pulses (peas), fruits (tomatoes).
2. **Nutritive value:** Pulses contain some vitamin B and are a good source of LBV protein (growth and repair). Low in fat, high water content (good for weight watchers), some have vitamin C (peppers). Green vegetables have iron (healthy blood) and are a good source of fibre (healthy bowel). Some highly coloured vegetables contain carotene (vitamin A).
3. **Cooking methods:** Boiling, steaming, stir-frying, roasting, microwaving, grilling, in stews and casseroles (roots and tubers).
4. **Effects of cooking:** Vitamins and minerals dissolve into cooking liquid if boiled. Vitamin C is destroyed. Fibre softens. Starch (potatoes) becomes digestible. If overcooked, texture, flavour and colour will be lost.
5. **Preventing nutrient loss:** Buy good-quality vegetables and eat raw if possible. Do not use bread soda when cooking and do not soak. Steaming is better than boiling. Use a sharp knife and peel thinly if necessary.
6. **Buying:** Buy fruit and vegetables in season. They should be undamaged and medium sized. Avoid pre-packed fruit and vegetables. Buy in small quantities.
7. **Organic:** Grown without using artificial chemicals.

1. What foods make up the protein group?
2. What is (a) offal (b) beef (c) veal (d) mutton and (e) pork?
3. Outline the composition and nutritive value of red meat.
4. What factors make meat either tough or tender? List six ways meat can be tenderised.
5. List the guidelines for buying, storing and cooking meat. List four effects of cooking on meat.
6. Suggest two uses for each of the following meat alternatives: (a) tofu (b) Quorn and (c) TVP.
7. What are pulse vegetables? Why should they be included in the diet?
8. Outline the nutritive value of chicken.
9. List the guidelines for buying, storing and cooking both fresh and frozen chicken.
10. Chicken is sometimes a source of food poisoning. List four food safety guidelines for preparing and cooking chicken.
11. Classify fish according to its nutritive value and give an example in each class.

12. Outline the composition and nutritive value of fish. Make six good points.
13. List the guidelines for buying, storing and cooking both fresh and frozen fish.
14. Name three ways fish can be processed.
15. List five uses for eggs in cookery. Outline the composition and nutritive value of eggs in the diet.
16. List five items of information you would expect to find on an egg box. Draw a labelled diagram of an egg.
17. Explain two ways that eggs can be tested for freshness. List four guidelines for storing eggs.
18. Explain how cooking affects eggs. List four guidelines for using eggs in cookery.
19. Outline the composition and nutritive value of milk. State how many servings from the calcium group should be consumed daily.
20. Explain the effects that heat has on milk. List the guidelines for buying and storing milk.
21. Explain the characteristics and uses of the following forms of milk: (a) whole milk (b) skimmed milk (c) fortified milk (d) UHT milk (e) condensed (f) evaporated milk.
22. Describe the process of both homogenisation and pasteurisation. Why is each process carried out?
23. How much fat is in butter? How are dairy spreads made? Suggest one healthier alternative to butter.
24. How is yoghurt made? Name five different types of yoghurt. List four different uses for yoghurt.
25. Classify cheese and give two examples in each class.
26. Outline the composition and nutritive value of cheese. List six uses of cheese in cookery. Describe how heat affects cheese.
27. Describe the six stages in cheese making.
28. List guidelines for buying and storing cheese.
29. On average, how many servings from the cereal and potato group should be eaten daily? Why would some groups of people need to eat larger numbers of servings from this group?
30. Name each part of the wheat grain pictured here and outline what nutrients are contained in each part named.
31. List four different cereals.
32. Outline the average composition and nutritive value of cereals. List three effects of cooking on cereals.
33. Describe how flour is processed. Describe five different types of flour.
34. What type of wheat is used to make pasta? Name three different types of pasta.
35. Name five different types of rice/rice products. Explain why brown rice should be eaten instead of white.
36. How many servings per day should be eaten from the fruit and vegetable group?

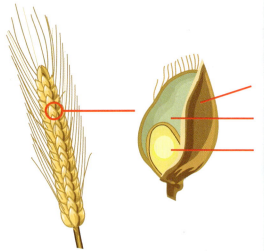

37. Classify fruits, giving two examples from each class.
38. Outline the average composition and nutritive value of fruit.
39. Outline how the following classes of fruits may be prepared, cooked (if appropriate) and served: (a) citrus fruits (b) berries (c) hard fruits. List the effects of cooking on fruit.
40. Classify vegetables, giving two examples from each class.
41. Outline the average composition and nutritive value of vegetables.

42. How should the following vegetables be prepared for cooking: (a) roots and tubers (b) greens (c) pulses? List and describe six methods of cooking vegetables. What are the effects of cooking on vegetables? Describe six ways nutrient loss can be prevented during preparation and cooking.

43. Describe the EU grading system for fruit and vegetables. How should fruit and vegetables be stored? Name three ways vegetables may be processed.

The examination

As part of section B, question 1 on both the Higher and Ordinary Level paper, you are usually asked to evaluate the nutritive value of a particular food product. Sometimes the product is a single food product, such as milk or porridge oats, but other times it is a product that contains a number of the food groups, such as a pizza. Below is a sample examination question and answer (the question is from section B, question 1, Higher Level 2012).

Sample question

The following information is displayed on the label of a Fruit Smoothie Drink.

FRUIT SMOOTHIE DRINK
Apples and Berries

NUTRITIONAL INFORMATION
GDA for a typical adult
Typical value per 100ml serving

Energy	56kcal	2000kcal
Protein	0.4g	
Carbohydrate	14.0g	90g
Fat	3.0g	70g
Fibre	0.6g	35g
Vitamin C	40.0mg	

INGREDIENTS
Pasteurised whole milk, apples, raspberries, strawberries, blueberries.

One of your **5** a day

Use within 2 days of opening

(a) Evaluate the nutritive value of the Fruit Smoothie Drink.

(b) (i) What is meant by the term *whole milk*?

 (ii) Why is milk pasteurised?

(c) Explain the term *GDA*.

(d) This drink contains 'one of your 5 a day'. Suggest ways in which an adult can make up the recommended five a day.

(e) Name **two** milk products, other than smoothies, that are available in supermarkets.

(f) Give **two** uses of milk and **two** uses of fruit in food preparation.

Sample answer

(a) *Nutritive value:* This smoothie contains a number of different nutrients that are useful in the diet. It is a relatively low-calorie food. 100ml is a small serving, so it is likely that more than that would be consumed. Even so, it is still a low-fat, low-calorie drink. The smoothie contains very little protein and very little fibre, which surprised me. Fibre is required for a healthy bowel. The smoothie contains a lot of vitamin C, which is essential for general health, healthy skin and gums. It also helps wounds heal and is needed to fully absorb iron from food. This is probably the best thing nutritionally about this product.

(b) (i) Whole milk is milk that has not had any fat removed.

   (ii) Milk is pasteurised to kill bacteria in the milk, making it safe to drink without altering its taste.

(c) The term GDA stands for guided daily amount. It tells you how much a person needs to take daily of a nutrient.

(d) Adults can make up their recommended five a day by eating fruit at breakfast and for healthy snacks during the day. Lunch and dinner can include fruit and vegetables as part of a meal, such as salads and soups. Vegetables can also be included as an accompaniment, such as vegetables with meat and potatoes.

(e) Yoghurts and cheese are milk products found in supermarkets.

(f) Milk can be used as a main ingredient in some dishes, such as quiche. It can also be used in baking, such as buttermilk. Fruit can be used in puddings and tarts (apple tart) or as part of salads (fruit salad).

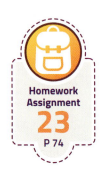

Homework
Assignment
23
P 74

Unit 1 Food

CHAPTER 11

Breakfasts, Packed Meals, Soups and Sauces

Teacher's CD

Slide presentation ▪ Student activity pack with revision crossword ▪ Class test ▪ Student learning contract

Key words

- ✓ Polyunsaturated spreads
- ✓ Thick soups
- ✓ Thin soups
- ✓ Convenience soups
- ✓ Garnish
- ✓ Roux
- ✓ Fruit coulis
- ✓ Convenience sauces
- ✓ Herbs
- ✓ Spices

Learning outcomes

After completing this chapter and the homework, assignments and activities that accompany it, you should:

- Be able to plan, cook (where necessary) and serve a healthy breakfast that includes the four food groups.
- Be able to plan and pack a healthy lunch that includes the four food groups.
- Know the different types of sandwiches that can be made and make a selection of them in practical class.
- Be able to classify soups and know the characteristics of a good soup. Know the ways in which soups can be thickened. Prepare, cook and serve a range of nutritious soups in practical class.
- Be able to list the main types of convenience soups on the market today and be aware of their advantages and disadvantages.
- Be able to classify sauces. Be able to make a roux sauce in practical class suited to its use. Be able to give examples of ingredients that can be added to roux sauces to improve their flavour. Be able to list the correct sauce for serving with beef, pork, lamb, turkey, goose and duck.
- Be aware of the range of convenience sauces on the market today together with their advantages and disadvantages.
- Be able to name a variety of herbs and spices and what dishes they are commonly used in.

Breakfasts

A healthy breakfast is an essential start to the day. When you wake up, your blood sugar is low after fasting all night. If you do not eat breakfast, it remains low. Because of this you will be less able to concentrate at school or at work and more likely to eat high-calorie mid-morning snacks such as crisps and fizzy drinks.

Planning a healthy breakfast

- Get up early and do not rush – sit down and enjoy your breakfast.
- Include food from all four food groups: protein group, cereal group, milk, cheese and yoghurt group and fruit and vegetable group.
- It is important to include fluids, such as juice, after being without fluids all night.
- Choose high-fibre breakfast cereals. Avoid those high in sugar.
- Use polyunsaturated spreads such as Flora instead of butter on bread.
- Grill instead of fry.

Choose foods from each group for a healthy breakfast.

1. Fruit and vegetable group

- Fruit juice (orange, grapefruit, cranberry)
- Fruit salad
- Grilled grapefruit
- Fruit segments or whole fruit
- Stewed fruit, such as prunes
- Grilled mushrooms or tomatoes
- Fruit smoothies

2. Cereal and bread group

- Healthy breakfast cereals include muesli, porridge with a sprinkle of All-Bran, cornflakes, bran flakes, Weetabix, Shredded Wheat and Fruit 'n' Fibre.
- Bread (brown, toast, scones, croissants, bagels).

3. **Protein group**

🍴 Eggs (poached, scrambled, boiled, omelettes)

🍴 Grilled bacon, sausage, pudding, kidney, liver

🍴 Cold meats, such as ham

4. **Milk, cheese and yoghurt group**

🍴 Milk on cereal or alone

🍴 Yoghurt, cheese

🍴 Yoghurt in smoothies

Example of a healthy breakfast: Orange juice, muesli with low-fat milk, boiled egg and toasted brown bread.

Setting a breakfast tray

1. Collect all tableware (it should be spotless).

2. Set the tray as shown in the diagram.

3. Cover the cooked main course with another plate to keep it warm.

A breakfast tray

Packed meals, lunches and picnics
Guidelines for a packed meal

🍴 Consider personal likes and dislikes. Perhaps the individual is on a special diet, such as gluten-free.

🍴 As the individual will usually have had nothing since breakfast and nothing again until evening, it is important that packed meals are both filling and nutritious.

🍴 Try to include all four food groups.

🍴 Try to have variety – the same lunch every day can become boring.

- Avoid empty-calorie foods such as chocolate and include healthier treats such as homemade scones or buns.
- Spread bread thinly with polyunsaturated margarine (Flora) and use low-fat mayonnaise. A spread provides a waterproof seal on the bread, preventing the sandwich ingredients from soaking into it and making it soggy.
- Use suitable packing materials, such as securely sealed plastic boxes and bottles, Thermos flasks, foil, lunch bags and cling film.
- Pack heavy items at the bottom of the box, such as cartons of juice.
- Include a drink high in vitamin C, like orange juice.
- Do not pack foods that spoil too easily, for example banana sandwiches.
- Sometimes it is better to pack ingredients for sandwiches (buttered bread and filling) separately so that they can be easily made up fresh before eating.

Designing a healthy packed meal

Choose foods from each group for a healthy packed meal.

Fruit and vegetable group

Apples, oranges, kiwi fruit, grapes, salads, fruit juices and smoothies, sticks of carrot, celery and cucumber, Branston pickle.

Milk, cheese and yoghurt group

Milk, milkshakes, yoghurt and yoghurt drinks, cheese alone, in crackers or in sandwiches.

Protein group

Sliced cold meats (chicken, ham, beef, turkey), nuts, sausage rolls, chicken drumsticks, prawn cocktail, tuna, salmon.

Cereal and potato group

Bread (rolls, baps, sliced white or wholemeal, tortilla wraps, bagels, panini, croissants), rice, potato and pasta salad, popcorn.

Sample packed meal

Orange juice
Spiced chicken salad wrap
Low-fat strawberry yoghurt

Sandwiches

Sandwiches need not be boring. They consist of three parts – bread, spread and filling – each of which can be varied. Make sure to use plenty of filling and that it is not too dry.

Sandwich ingredients

Breads	Spreads	Fillings
Wholemeal, soda, brown sliced, white sliced, rolls, baps, pita pockets, bagels, tortilla wraps, panini	Polyunsaturated margarine, low-fat spreads, spreadable butter, low-fat mayonnaise, salad cream, mustard, ketchup, Branston pickle, low-fat cream cheese, chutney	Ham, chicken, beef, turkey, luncheon meats, corned beef, cheese, tuna, salmon, sardines, prawns, eggs, tomatoes, lettuce, scallions, onion, grated carrot, cucumber, peppers, bean sprouts, cress

Types of sandwich

Single
Two slices of bread with spread and filling(s).

Toasted
Toasted in a sandwich toaster or under the grill – no lettuce.

Rolled
Thinly sliced crustless bread with a filling, such as ham, salmon, cream cheese, rolled and fastened with a cocktail stick – for parties.

Pita pockets
Split on one side and filled, for example with bacon, lettuce, tomato and garlic mayonnaise.

Panini
Stick of bread, often ciabatta, filled and toasted on a contact grill (a George Foreman grill).

Wrap
Tortilla with spread and filling, wrapped tightly and cut in half for eating.

Double/club
Three slices of bread with fillings in between.

Open
Firm bread with a spread and a variety of fillings on top.

Rolls
French stick with a spread and fillings.

BLT
Bacon, lettuce, tomato and mayonnaise – usually toasted.

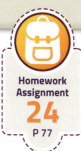

Homework Assignment
24
P 77

Soups

A good soup:

- Is made from a fresh, well-flavoured stock. Soup should be seasoned with pepper and herbs. Do not add too much salt – use a salt substitute.

- Tastes of its main ingredient. For example, tomato soup should have a strong tomato flavour.

- Is piping hot and has no grease floating on the top (note: some soups are meant to be served cold).

- Has a good colour.

- A thick soup should not be too thick and should not have starchy lumps.

Soups can be classified into thick soups and thin soups.

Thick soups

- **Puréed:** Thickened by blending the soup's own ingredients using a sieve, liquidiser or food processor, such as thick farmhouse vegetable soup.

- **Thickened:** By adding a starch, such as flour, cornflour, pasta or potato.

Thick soup   *Thin soup*

Thin soups

- **Clear soup:** Thin soup made with well-flavoured stock, such as consommé.

- **Broth:** Thin, clear soup with finely chopped meat, vegetables and a starch such as barley floating in it. For example, chicken broth is made from a thin, clear stock, with chicken pieces, vegetables and perhaps barley.

Four ways to thicken a soup

🍴 Blend 25g of cornflour with cold water. Stir this mixture into the soup just before the end of the cooking time. Bring the soup back to the boil and boil for approximately 5 minutes, stirring all the time. Garnish and serve.

🍴 Begin by gently frying (sautéing) the soup ingredients, such as vegetables, in 25g of fat or oil. Add 25g of flour and cook for a few minutes. Gradually add the stock. The soup will thicken once it comes to the boil.

🍴 Add barley, rice or pasta to the soup 20 minutes before the end of the cooking time.

🍴 Purée the soup ingredients after cooking – this will thicken it.

How to garnish a soup

Herbs, such as parsley

Croutons (cubes of bread fried in oil – use a polyunsaturated fat)

Swirl of cream, for example in a cream of vegetable soup

Convenience soups

🍴 Instant soups, such as Cup-a-Soup, are cheap but are not very nutritious. They sometimes contain a lot of salt and flavour enhancers, such as monosodium glutamate (MSG).

🍴 Canned soups just need heating up, so they are convenient. However, sometimes they taste very artificial, some can be high in salt and some contain flavour enhancers such as MSG.

🍴 Cartons of fresh soup are expensive but convenient, tasty and nutritious. Store in the fridge.

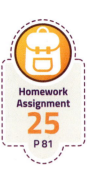

Homework
Assignment
25
P 81

Dried packet soup

Canned soup

Fresh soup

Sauces

Sauces are well-flavoured liquids and can take many forms. They can be sweet or savoury, hot or cold. Sauces can be used as a garnish or can be part of the dish itself. For instance, cheese sauce is part of a lasagne dish. Sauces can also bind or coat foods and generally add colour and flavour to a dish.

Classification

Type of sauce	Examples
Roux based	White sauce, cheese sauce
Fruit purée	Apple, raspberry coulis, cranberry
Egg based	Egg custard
Cold	Mint sauce
Other	Peppercorn, chocolate, butterscotch, barbecue

Roux-based sauces

✎ A roux-based sauce is made from equal amounts of fat and flour. Different flavourings and amounts of liquid are added to vary the basic sauce.

✎ There are four basic thicknesses of roux sauces. The amounts of fat and flour stay the same for each one – it is the amount of liquid that changes.

Note: If a recipe says, for example, '500ml of coating sauce', it is the amount of liquid that is meant. Thus, the ingredients for 500ml of coating sauce are 50g fat, 50g flour and 500ml liquid.

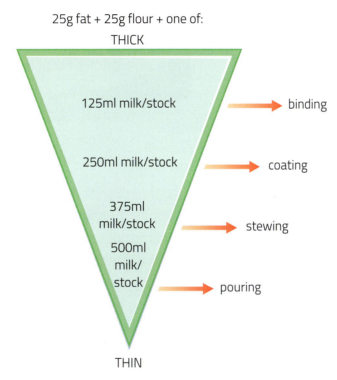

25g fat + 25g flour + one of:

THICK

125ml milk/stock → binding

250ml milk/stock → coating

375ml milk/stock → stewing

500ml milk/stock → pouring

THIN

How to make a basic white roux sauce

1. Melt the fat. Add the flour and seasoning and cook for 1 minute. Do not allow to burn.
2. Take off the heat. Add the milk gradually, stirring all the time.
3. Return to the heat. Keep stirring to prevent lumping.
4. Bring to the boil, simmer for 5 minutes, then serve.

Variations on basic pouring sauce (500ml)

Sauce	Extra ingredients	Goes well with
Parsley	Add 2 teaspoons chopped fresh parsley.	Bacon, fish
Mustard	Add 1 teaspoon made mustard and 2 teaspoons vinegar.	Fish
Cheese	Add ¼ teaspoon mustard to the roux. Add 50g grated cheese at the end and allow to melt. Do not return to the heat.	Fish, cauliflower
Mushroom	Add 50g sautéed mushrooms after the liquid has been added and then simmer for 5 minutes.	Steak, roast beef

Other traditional sauces

Food	Sauce(s) that goes well with food
Beef	Pepper (steaks), horseradish (roast beef)
Pork	Apple
Lamb	Mint
Turkey	Bread sauce or cranberry
Goose	Apple
Duck	Orange

Fruit coulis

Desserts look good if you decorate them with a fruit coulis. To make a coulis, simply purée highly coloured fruits such as strawberries or raspberries, pass through a sieve to remove the seeds, add a little icing sugar and then pour to the side of the dish.

Convenience sauces

Convenience sauces are available in many different forms: canned, bottled, dried, frozen or in cartons. **Advantages** are that they speed up the preparation and cooking time of some dishes, for example buying ready-made sauces for pasta dishes. They are also useful for people with poor cooking skills because it allows them to cook a greater variety of dishes. **Disadvantages** of convenience sauces are that they can be high in sugar, salt and other additives. They can also sometimes be expensive and often lack flavour.

Herbs and spices

Herbs and spices are used in cookery to add flavour to foods and sometimes to make the food look more appetising. Below is an alphabetical list of common herbs and spices and their uses.

Herb or spice	Uses
Bay leaves	Bouquet garni in soups and stocks
Basil	Added to tomato-based sauces (Bolognese, pizza)
Caraway (seed)	Bread and biscuits as well as cheese dishes, salads and soups
Cayenne pepper	Add a little to meat, fish, vegetable, egg or cheese dishes
Chives	Salads and dressings, chopped through mashed potatoes, garnish
Cinnamon	Cakes, tarts, biscuits, pickles and chutneys
Cloves	Apple tarts, Christmas puddings, mince pies, with ham and pork
Fennel	Fish dishes, soups and sauces
Garlic	Many savoury dishes
Ginger	Biscuits and cakes, Chinese cookery, chutneys
Mint	In a sauce with lamb, as a garnish or decoration
Mustard	Many savoury dishes, cheese sauce, with ham and bacon
Nutmeg	Chicken, vegetables, cheese dishes, cakes, custard and milk puddings
Oregano	Italian dishes (Bolognese, pizza)
Paprika	In beef goulash and to garnish meat, fish, cheese and egg dishes
Parsley	Used in sauces, most savoury dishes, as a garnish
Pepper	All savoury dishes
Rosemary	Meat (especially lamb), fish and poultry dishes
Sage	Stuffing and casseroles
Thyme	Stuffing, beef, lamb and poultry dishes

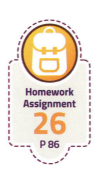

Homework Assignment **26** P 86

139

1. **Breakfasts:** Don't rush. Include foods from all four food groups. Avoid sugary cereals. Use polyunsaturated spreads and grill instead of frying.

2. **Packed lunches:** Consider likes/dislikes and dietary considerations (diabetes, gluten-free). Try to include all food groups and have variety. Avoid empty-calorie foods (chocolate). Use polyunsaturated spreads. Use suitable packing material. Pack heavy items at the bottom. Include a healthy drink. Do not pack foods that spoil easily (banana sandwiches).

3. **Sandwich types:** Single, double decker/club, open, rolls, toasted, pita pockets, rolled, panini, wrap, BLT.

4. **A good soup** is made from a fresh, well-flavoured stock, is seasoned well, tastes of its main ingredient, is piping hot, has a good colour and is not too thick.

5. **Soup classification:** Thick (puréed, thickened), thin (clear, broth).

6. **Thickening soup:** Add cornflour blended with water, add flour while the vegetables are sautéing, add rice, pasta or barley or purée the soup.

7. **Garnishing soup:** Croutons, herbs, swirl of cream.

8. **Convenience soups:** Dried, canned, carton (fresh soup).

9. **Sauce classification:** Roux based, fruit purée, egg based, cold, other.

10. **Roux-based sauces:** Vary in thickness: binding (thickest), coating, stewing and pouring. There is the same amount of fat and flour in all, but different amounts of liquid. Flavouring ingredients are often added: parsley, cheese, mustard, mushroom.

11. **Other traditional sauces:** Peppercorn and horseradish (beef), apple (pork and goose), mint (lamb), bread sauce and cranberry (turkey).

12. **Convenience sauces:** They speed up preparation and cooking time, but can be high in salt, sugar and other additives. May also be expensive and lack flavour.

13. **Herbs and spices:** An excellent and healthy way to add flavour to foods, reducing the need to add salt.

Revision Questions

1. List five guidelines for planning a healthy breakfast. Give an example of a healthy breakfast to include all four food groups.
2. List six guidelines for planning a healthy packed meal. Give an example of a healthy packed meal to include all four food groups.
3. Name and describe four different types of sandwich.
4. How are soups classified? Name two examples of each class.
5. List five characteristics of a good soup.
6. Suggest three ways a soup may be (a) thickened and (b) garnished.
7. Name three different types of convenience soup. Give the advantages and disadvantages of each type.
8. Suggest three different purposes of sauces in cookery. List five different classes of sauces and give one example from each class.
9. Roux-based sauces have four basic thicknesses. What are they? Describe how you would make a basic roux sauce. The basic roux sauce can be varied by adding extra ingredients. Describe three variations on the basic roux sauce.
10. What sauce(s) would best accompany each of the following meats: (a) beef (b) pork (c) lamb (d) turkey (e) goose?
11. What is a fruit coulis and how is it made?
12. How are convenience sauces sold? List the advantages and disadvantages of convenience sauces.
13. Why are herbs and spices used in cookery? Give one use for each of the following herbs and spices: (a) bay leaves (b) cinnamon (c) chives (d) cloves (e) garlic (f) oregano (g) rosemary (h) sage.

Test Yourself
eTest.ie

Food Processing and Leftovers

Teacher's CD · Slide presentation · Student activity pack with revision crossword · Class test · Student learning contract

Key words

- Food processing
- Food preservation
- Blanching
- Open freezing
- Blast freezing
- Expiry date
- Food labelling
- Food additives
- E numbers
- Cocktail effect (additives)
- Convenience foods
- Cook-chill foods
- Leftovers

Learning outcomes

After completing this chapter and the homework, assignments and activities that accompany it, you should:

- Understand what food processing is and what its advantages and disadvantages are.
- Be able to list and understand the six conditions that micro-organisms need to grow. Be able to describe how this relates to each method of food preservation: freezing, applying heat, drying, canning and bottling, adding chemicals, irradiation.
- Understand the guidelines for successfully freezing food and put this information into practice in practical class or at home.
- Know what blanching is and why it is done before freezing vegetables.
- Know why and how some foods are open frozen and put this information into practice in practical class or at home. Understand the term *blast freezing*.
- Understand the rules for buying, thawing and packing frozen foods and put this information into practice.
- Know what information food packaging should carry by law.
- Understand what the E number system of coding food additives is and the facts about E numbers. Be able to name a range of additives used in food and describe the advantages and disadvantages of additives.
- Be able to list a range of convenience foods on the market today and describe their advantages and disadvantages. Know what cook-chill foods are and the dangers that can be associated with them.
- Understand and be able to describe the guidelines for using leftovers. Be able to name some dishes that can be made using leftovers.

Food processing

Food processing means treating foods in some way to make them easier to use. Most foods nowadays undergo some degree of processing.

Advantages of food processing

- Processed foods usually last longer than unprocessed foods.
- Processed foods require less preparation – saves time and effort.
- Processed foods are easier to transport – compare transporting fresh peas with tinned peas.
- Processed foods are easier to store in shops and at home.
- Seasonal foods are available all year round.

Disadvantages of food processing

- Processed food is expensive.
- Processed food is frequently not as tasty as fresh foods.
- Nutritional value is often reduced, such as the fibre content.
- Packaging is bad for the environment.

Before processing	After processing
Wheat grains	Flour
Unpasteurised milk	Pasteurised milk
Milk	Cheese
Raw chicken	Chicken curry, TV dinner
Pork	Frozen sausage rolls
Fresh vegetables	Packet of frozen vegetables
Mandarin oranges	Tinned mandarin oranges
Potatoes	Oven chips

Food preservation

Food preservation is a form of food processing that slows down food spoilage (food going bad). Food spoilage is caused by **enzymes, moulds, yeast** or **bacteria** attacking food. Spoilage of some foods, such as butter, may be caused by oxygen in the air.

Enzymes, moulds, yeast and bacteria need **six conditions** to grow:

- Food
- Moisture
- Oxygen (most)
- Warmth
- Time
- Correct pH

Take one or more of these conditions away or add a chemical preservative, such as vinegar (which is acidic and thus alters pH), and the food is preserved.

Advantages of preservation

- 🍴 Preservation prevents waste, so it saves money.
- 🍴 Seasonal foods are available all year round (e.g. strawberries).
- 🍴 Preserved foods add variety to the diet.
- 🍴 Many preserved foods are easy to prepare (e.g. frozen vegetables).

Methods of preservation

Freezing and refrigeration = removing warmth

Pasteurisation, canning and bottling = applying strong heat

Drying = removing moisture

Canning and bottling = removing air

Adding chemical preservatives, such as sugar, vinegar, smoke, salt or other E numbers

Irradiation = passing rays through foods (usually fruit and vegetables). Rays destroy enzymes and bacteria, so food keeps longer. Some scientists question the safety of this method.

Freezing

Food is brought to a temperature of –18°C or below. Enzymes and micro-organisms are not killed at this temperature, but become inactive (sleep). Once food is **thawed**, enzymes and micro-organisms become active again.

Guidelines for successful freezing

If frozen properly, frozen food is almost as nutritious as fresh food. Because food is usually frozen while at its freshest and most nutritious, it is actually more nutritious than fresh food that has been lying around for a few days.

🍴 The first rule of freezing is to turn the freezer to its coldest setting two to three hours before freezing and freeze food *quickly*.

🍴 Freeze food at its freshest.

🍴 Do not freeze too much at a time.

🍴 Cool food before freezing it.

🍴 Choose suitable packaging, such as plastic freezer bags or plastic tubs.

🍴 Freeze in useable amounts.

🍴 If there is a 'fast freeze' cabinet, use it to freeze foods.

🍴 Label foods clearly.

Blanching

Blanching destroys enzymes that can reduce the quality of frozen vegetables.

Blanching times	
1 minute	Mushrooms, peas
3 minutes	Beans, broccoli, cauliflower, parsnips, turnips
4 minutes	Brussels sprouts, carrots

Plunge prepared vegetables into boiling water for 1–4 minutes. 100°C → 0°C Plunge into ice-cold water.

Freezing

Quick freezing: Small ice crystals are formed. On thawing, the cell walls of food are unbroken, food stays firm and keeps its shape.

Slow freezing: Large ice crystals are formed. On thawing, food loses its shape and nutrients and becomes soft and mushy.

Open freezing

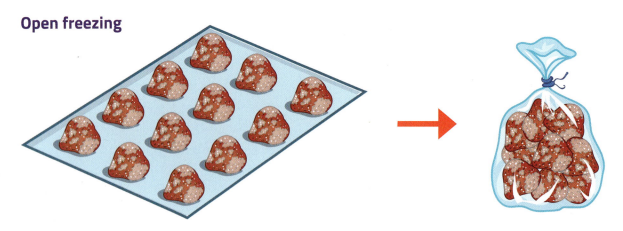

Open freezing: Fruit and vegetables that are likely to stick together (berries or peas) are open frozen as above and then packed into bags.

Blast freezing

This is a commercial method of freezing. Very cold air (−35°C) is blown over food to freeze it quickly.

Buying frozen foods	Thawing frozen foods
• Packaging should not be torn. • Food should be frozen solid. • The shop's freezer should read −18°C or less. • Check that food is below the load line in open freezers.	• Some foods can be cooked from frozen (burgers, chips) – read the packet instructions. • Thaw meat completely, especially chicken. • Food can be thawed in the microwave or in the fridge overnight. • Never refreeze thawed food.

Packaging suitable for freezing

Polythene bags (freezer bags), polythene (plastic) boxes, aluminium foil and containers, waxed cartons with lids. Care should be taken to seal containers well or else **freezer burn** will result and food will be inedible.

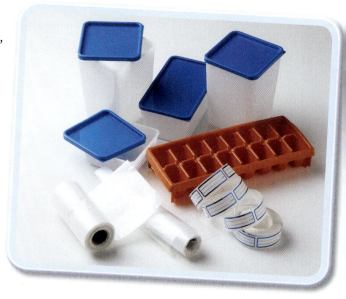

Foods not suitable for freezing

🍴 Vegetables with a high water content, such as cucumber or lettuce

🍴 Bananas and avocados – they go black

🍴 Whole eggs – they crack (although egg white and yolk can be frozen separately)

🍴 Milk, cream and mayonnaise (the fat and water separate)

Other methods of preservation

Drying	Chemical preservation	Canning and bottling
• Enzymes and micro-organisms need moisture (water) to survive. • Dehydration or drying removes moisture and so preserves the food. • Examples: Breakfast cereals, pasta, rice, raisins (dried grapes), soups.	• Certain chemicals preserve food. Many of them are natural and have been used for centuries. • Sugar (jam). • Vinegar (pickles). • Salt (canned fish). • Smoke (smoked fish). • There are also many artificial preservatives.	• Food is heated to a high temperature (this kills enzymes and micro-organisms). • Food is then sealed in sterile containers. • Food keeps for years. • Vitamins B and C are lost. • Do not buy damaged or bulging cans – they may contain food-poisoning bacteria.

Food labelling

Under EU law, all packaged food must have certain information on the label:

- Name of food
- List of ingredients: the product's main ingredient (by weight) listed first, etc.
- Net quantity
- Use-by/best-before/sell-by date

- Storage instructions
- Name and address of manufacturer
- Country of origin
- Instructions for use
  (if necessary)
- Nutritional information (if product is making health claims)

Food additives

In 1984, the EU decided to make it the law for food manufacturers to display lists of ingredients (including all additives) on food packaging. A system of coding for additives was also developed and many additives were given an E number. There has been much public debate and misunderstanding about E numbers since then. Many people believe that all E numbers are a health risk, causing hyperactivity and allergic reactions. It is because of this bad press that most food labels now list additives by their full names instead of by their E numbers.

What are the facts?

Additives thought to be safe by the EU's scientific committee for food are given an E number. Many E numbers are natural, healthy substances. For example, vitamin C is E300 and vinegar is E260. However, there are questions about the safety of some additives still being passed off as safe under EU regulations. Another important issue is that of the '**cocktail effect**'. This means that while individual additives may be quite safe on their own, they may not be when mixed with others.

Advantages of additives

- They preserve food so that it lasts longer, thus reducing waste.
- They reduce the chance of food poisoning.
- They allow for a wider choice of foods.
- They improve the appearance, texture and flavour of foods.

Disadvantages of additives

- Some people suffer side effects from additives (rashes, hyperactivity, migraine).
- People get used to the taste of foods containing additives, especially monosodium glutamate (MSG), and may then find fresh, healthy, additive-free foods tasteless.
- While individual additives may be safe on their own, it is still unknown what the 'cocktail effect' will be on the body.
- Additives such as colouring can deceive consumers about food quality.

Functions of food additives

Type of additive	What it does
Colourings (E100–E199)	Make food look more appetising.
Preservatives (E200–E299)	Prevent food from going off. For example, vinegar preserves pickled onions.
Antioxidants (E300–E399)	These prevent fats, such as butter, from reacting with the air and going rancid (off).
Emulsifiers, stabilisers and thickening agents (E400–E499)	Emulsifiers allow oil and water to mix. Stabilisers keep mixtures from separating (mayonnaise). Thickening agents are used to thicken foods (sauces) without altering the taste of the product. Starch is an example of a thickening agent.
Flavourings (no E number)	Add to the flavour of food, such as vanilla essence.
Flavour enhancers (E600+)	Strengthen the flavour of food, such as MSG or saccharin.
Nutritional additives (no E number)	These improve the nutritional quality of food or replace nutrients lost in processing.

Convenience foods

Convenience foods are foods that have been processed in some way to make them easier and quicker to use. There are a number of different types of convenience foods:

- **Foods in cans, bottles and jars**: Soups, vegetables, fruits and sauces (Bolognese sauce)

- **Frozen food**: Vegetables, fish, meat products, ready meals, pizza

- **Dried foods**: Soups, noodles, sauces, dried fruit

- **Ready-to-cook foods** (foods are prepared for cooking but are not cooked): Chicken Kiev, stuffed pork, chicken stir-fry

- **Cook-chill foods** (prepared, cooked and chilled – just need reheating): Lasagne, spaghetti Bolognese, shepherd's pie, mashed potato

Cook-chill food

Advantages of convenience foods

- They are quick and easy to use, especially for those with busy lifestyles or limited cooking skills.

- They are easy to store.

- Some convenience foods, such as frozen vegetables, are very nutritious.

- Many last longer and so reduce waste.
- Cook-chill foods often come in individual portion sizes so they are useful for people living alone, such as the elderly.

Disadvantages of convenience foods

- Some convenience foods are expensive.
- They may contain additives.
- Nutritive value may be reduced during processing (canned fruit).
- Portion sizes may be very small.
- Cook-chill foods can be a source of food poisoning if not stored properly or reheated thoroughly.

The dangers of cook-chill foods

Because they are only reheated and not cooked again at home, cook-chill foods can be a source of food poisoning. These foods are safe if they are stored in a fridge or freezer below 4°C and are reheated thoroughly. If a microwave is used to reheat the food, it must be stirred so that all parts of the food reach a high enough temperature.

Leftovers

Good meal planning should ensure that too much food is not cooked for meals. At times, however, there will be food left over. Leftovers may be eaten cold, such as roast chicken made into sandwiches, or reheated (réchauffé).

Guidelines for using leftovers

- When food is reheated its food value decreases, so try to serve leftovers with fresh foods, such as leftover chicken with a fresh salad and brown bread.
- Cool leftovers quickly, cover and store in the fridge.
- Use leftovers within two days.
- Reheat leftovers thoroughly (especially if they contain protein, such as meats), as they are a likely source of food poisoning.
- Never reheat leftovers twice.

Dishes using leftovers

- Chicken: Curry, sandwiches, salads
- Beef: Curry, sandwiches
- Eggs: Yolks can be used to make mayonnaise or in baking; whites can be used to make meringues; whole eggs can be used for bread and butter pudding
- Potatoes: Potato salad, shepherd's pie, cheese and potato pie
- Bread: Stuffing, French toast, bread and butter pudding

Food processing

1. **Definition:** Treating foods in some way to make them easier to use.
2. **Advantages:** Processed food lasts longer and needs less preparation. It is easy to transport and store. Seasonal food is available all year round.
3. **Disadvantages:** Processed food is expensive. It can lack flavour and can have poorer nutritional value. Packaging is bad for the environment.

Food preservation

1. **Definition:** A form of food processing that slows down food spoilage by disrupting the conditions needed for the growth of enzymes and micro-organisms.
2. **Conditions for growth:** Food, warmth, moisture, time, oxygen (most), correct pH.
3. **Advantages:** Prevents waste. Seasonal foods are available all year round. Adds variety to the diet. Foods are easy to prepare.
4. **Methods:** Freezing, pasteurisation, canning, bottling, drying, adding chemicals, irradiation.

Freezing

1. **Definition:** Freezing is a method of food processing that brings food as quickly as possible to −18°C or below, which causes enzymes and micro-organisms to become inactive.
2. **Guidelines:** Freeze fresh food only. Don't freeze too much at once. Freeze in usable amounts. Cool before freezing. Freeze quickly. Use suitable packaging and label clearly.
3. **Blanching:** Destroys enzymes that spoil vegetables. Plunge into boiling water for 1–4 minutes, then into ice-cold water.
4. **Open freezing and blast freezing:** Open freeze foods that are likely to stick together. Blast freezing is used for commercial foods (−35°C).
5. **Buying and thawing:** Packaging should be intact. Food should be frozen solid and below the load line (−18°C or less). Some foods can be cooked from frozen. Read packet instructions. Thaw meat completely and never refreeze.

Other methods

1. **Drying:** Removes moisture (breakfast cereals, rice, pasta, raisins, soups).
2. **Chemical: Adding sugar, vinegar, salt, smoking and artificial preservatives.**
3. **Canning/bottling:** Food is heated to a high temperature and stored in airtight, sterile containers. Vitamins B and C are lost. Canned or bottled food keeps for years. Do not buy damaged or bulging cans.

Food labelling and additives

1. **Labels:** By law, labels must include the name of the food, ingredients, net quantity, expiry date, storage instructions, manufacturer, country of origin, instructions for use and nutritional information.
2. **Additives:** Many are given an E number. The EU gives an E number to additives thought to be safe, cocktail effect.
    *   **Advantages:** Preserve food, reduce chance of food poisoning, allow for wider choice and improve appearance, texture and flavour.
    *   **Disadvantages:** Side effects, people become accustomed to flavour enhancers (MSG) and think fresh food tastes bland, cocktail effect (unknown), can deceive consumer.

Convenience foods

1. **Definition:** Food is processed to make it easier to use. Includes food in cans, bottles, jars, frozen foods, dried foods, ready-to-cook foods and cook-chill foods.
2. **Advantages:** Quick and easy to store. Some are nutritious (frozen vegetables). Reduces waste. Cook-chill individual portions are useful for those living alone.
3. **Disadvantages:** Expensive. May contain additives. Nutrients are lost. Portion sizes are small. There is a risk of food poisoning with cook-chill foods.

Leftovers

1. **Guidelines:** Cool quickly and store in the fridge. Serve leftovers with fresh foods. Use within two days. Reheat thoroughly and never reheat twice.

Revision Questions

1. What is meant by food processing? List four advantages and three disadvantages of food processing. Give one example of how each of the following foods are processed: (a) wheat grains (b) milk (c) raw chicken (d) pork (e) potatoes.
2. What is food preservation? List six conditions micro-organisms need to grow. List four advantages of food preservation. List six methods of preserving food.
3. Outline six guidelines for successful freezing. What is the purpose of blanching foods before freezing? Describe how it is done. Why is it important to freeze foods quickly? What is open freezing? Why and how is it carried out? What is blast freezing?
4. Suggest four guidelines for buying frozen foods and suggest four guidelines for thawing frozen foods. Name three different types of packaging suitable for freezing. Name four foods that are not suitable for freezing.
5. List and briefly describe three other methods of preserving food.
6. List nine items of information that must appear on a food label under EU law. What are E numbers? What is meant by the 'cocktail effect' in relation to food additives? List four advantages and four disadvantages of food additives.
7. What is the purpose of each of the following: (a) colourings (b) preservatives (c) antioxidants (d) emulsifiers (e) flavour enhancers?
8. Describe four different types of convenience foods. How can you ensure cook-chill foods are safe to eat? Outline four guidelines for using leftovers.
9. Name one leftover dish that could be made with each of the following: (a) chicken (b) eggs (c) bread.

Test Yourself
eTest.ie

Homework Assignment
27
P 90

Teacher's CD

Slide presentation ▪ Student activity pack with revision crossword ▪ Class test ▪ Student learning contract

Key words

- ✓ Raising agent
- ✓ Bread soda
- ✓ Baking powder
- ✓ Yeast
- ✓ Gluten
- ✓ Rubbing-in method
- ✓ Creaming method
- ✓ Whisking method
- ✓ Melting method
- ✓ All-in-one method
- ✓ Shortcrust pastry
- ✓ Rich shortcrust
- ✓ Cheese pastry
- ✓ Choux pastry
- ✓ Flaky pastry
- ✓ Rough puff pastry
- ✓ Filo pastry

Learning outcomes

After completing this chapter and the homework, assignments and activities that accompany it, you should:

- Know and understand the guidelines for home baking and apply them while cooking at home or in practical class.
- Know the different types of raising agents that are commonly used in baking and understand how each one works.
- Know and understand the following methods of making bread and cakes and have used each method at home or in practical class: rubbing in, creaming, whisking, melting and all-in-one.
- Be able to line a round, square and Swiss roll tin properly.
- Know the different types of pastry available and know what dishes each is suitable for. Follow the guidelines for pastry making while making pastry dishes at home and in practical class.
- Know the advantages and disadvantages of using commercial cake mixes.

The main advantage of baking your own bread, cakes and biscuits is that you can control exactly what goes into them. Many commercially produced cakes and buns contain a lot of fat and sugar. It is possible to bake at home using less fat or unsaturated fat and less sugar too.

Guidelines for home baking

- Collect all the ingredients. Make sure they are fresh (check expiry dates) and weigh them accurately.

- Collect all the equipment and prepare the tins (see page 157).

- Arrange the oven shelves, then set the oven temperature accurately and preheat fully (electric ovens: until the light goes off).

- Follow the recipe step by step and take care when adding the liquid to the dry ingredients. Do not over-handle dough and pastry.

- Time cooking accurately and know how to test baked products to see if they are cooked.

- Do not open the oven door unnecessarily.

- Baked products are usually cooled on a wire rack.

- Wash and dry equipment and work surfaces thoroughly. If any food remains on them, they will grow mould or rust if they are metal and attract vermin to the kitchen.

Raising agents

A raising agent is something that makes bread and cakes rise. There are four raising agents:

- Air
- Bread soda
- Baking powder
- Yeast

Fresh and dried yeast

Air

Air is introduced into the mixture by sieving, rubbing in, creaming or whisking.

Once the mixture is heated, the hot air in the mixture rises, pushing the mixture up. A crust forms on top, which stops the mixture from collapsing when cool.

Bread soda and baking powder

These two raising agents cause a chemical reaction in the mixture.

- **Bread soda** is an alkali. When it is mixed with an acid liquid, such as buttermilk, it produces CO_2.
- **Baking powder** contains both an acid and an alkali. When liquid is added, for example when you add egg, CO_2 is produced.

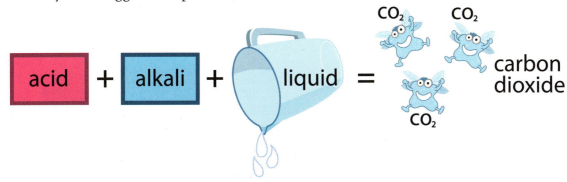

The CO_2 produced works much like the air described above – it pushes the mixture up. A crust forms in the oven, which keeps the mixture risen.

Note: Once the acid and the alkali get wet, they begin producing CO_2. It is important to get the mixture into the oven quickly or the CO_2 will escape before the crust forms and the mixture will not rise properly.

Yeast

Yeast are living organisms used in bread making. When they are warm and moist (in bread dough), they produce CO_2. Yeast dough rises before it goes into the oven. A crust then forms in the oven, keeping it in its risen state.

Gluten – its function in bread and cake making

Gluten is a protein found in wheat and other cereals. It has an important role in bread and cake making, although gluten-free products can also be made. When gluten is moistened, it becomes stretchy and elastic. This allows the bread to rise well. In the oven, the gluten sets when heated, forming a crust and keeping the bread risen.

Methods of making bread and cakes

Rubbing in

Fat is rubbed into the flour with your fingertips until it looks like breadcrumbs. Liquid is then added. Example: Scones.

Rubbing in

Creaming

Creaming

Fat and sugar are beaten together until white and creamy. Egg, flour and a raising agent are then added. Example: Queen cakes.

Whisking

Eggs and sugar are whisked until thick and creamy. Flour is then gently folded in. Example: Sponge cake.

Melting

All ingredients that melt are melted together, such as fat, sugar and/or syrup. This mixture is then added to the flour and the other dry ingredients. Example: Gingerbread.

Melting

All-in-one

All ingredients are added at once. They are often mixed in a food processor. Example: All-in-one Madeira mix.

All-in-one method

Tin preparation

Food	How to prepare the tin
Bread, plain scones (no sugar)	Dust lightly with flour.
Pastry, small cakes and buns, such as coconut buns	Grease lightly.
Fatless sponge	Grease lightly and dust with a mixture of caster sugar and flour.
Light cakes, such as Madeira	Line the base only. Grease the sides.
Richer cakes	Line with greaseproof paper (see illustrations below). Dabbing some oil on the tin itself will make the greaseproof paper fit better.

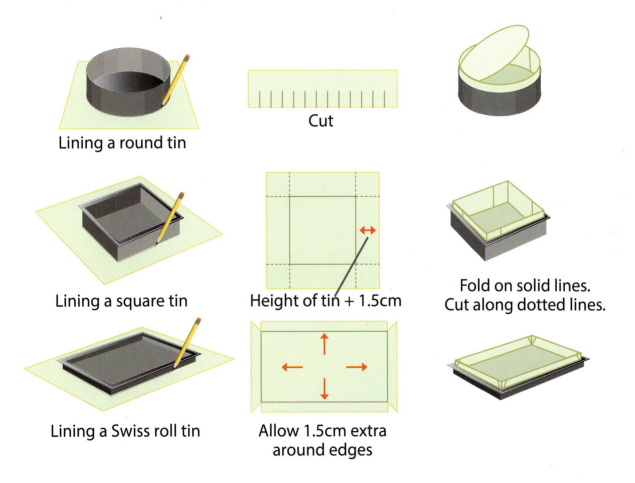

Lining a round tin

Cut

Lining a square tin

Height of tin + 1.5cm

Fold on solid lines. Cut along dotted lines.

Lining a Swiss roll tin

Allow 1.5cm extra around edges

Pastry
Types of pastry and their uses

Type	Uses	Description
Shortcrust and wholemeal shortcrust	Tarts, pies, quiche, sausage rolls	Half the amount of fat to flour – just add water. Add wholemeal flour to make wholemeal pastry. Increases fibre content.
Rich shortcrust	Mince pies, sweet flans, pies, such as lemon meringue pie	Shortcrust pastry is made rich by adding icing sugar and eggs.
Cheese pastry	Quiche	Add grated cheese to shortcrust pastry.
Choux pastry	Éclairs and profiteroles	Melt fat in water, add flour and cook for a few minutes, then gradually beat in egg. Spoon or pipe onto tin.
Flaky, puff and rough puff	Vol-au-vents, sausage rolls	Special rolling and folding techniques are used to introduce air into the pastry. High in fat. Very time consuming to make.
Filo	Spring rolls	Very thin Greek pastry.

Pastry-making guidelines

Weigh all the ingredients accurately.

Keep everything cold.

Introduce air by sieving, rubbing in, rolling and folding.

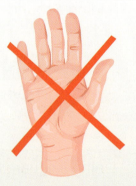

Handle pastry as little as possible.

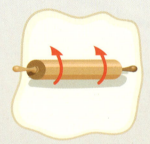

Roll lightly in one direction only on a lightly floured board. Turn the pastry to prevent sticking. Do not stretch pastry.

Allow pastry to relax in the fridge before rolling.

Bake first in a hot preheated oven (220°C/gas 7), then reduce the heat to finish baking.

Commercial cake mixes

Commercial cake mixes contain all the dry ingredients needed to make a cake. To make them up, you usually just have to add the wet ingredients (egg, milk or water). Follow the instructions on the packet.

Advantages

- Quick and easy to use
- Useful for beginners
- No waste

Disadvantages

- Expensive
- Usually do not taste as good as products made from scratch
- Photo on the front can be deceptive
- Often high in sugar and salt and low in fibre
- May contain additives

Rapid Revision

1. **Baking guidelines:** Collect and weigh all the ingredients. Make sure they are fresh. Collect equipment, prepare tins and arrange oven shelves when the oven is still cool. Preheat the oven. Follow the recipe closely. Don't over-handle pastry. Time the cooking and test for doneness. Don't open the oven door unnecessarily. Cool on a wire rack. Wash and dry equipment and surfaces thoroughly.

2. **Raising agents:** Make bread and cakes rise. Raising agents include air, bread soda and buttermilk, baking powder, yeast.

3. **Gluten:** Gluten is a protein found in wheat and other cereals. When wet it becomes elastic, allowing bread and cakes to rise. Gluten sets on top, forming a crust.

4. **Methods:** Rubbing in (scones and bread), creaming (queen cakes), whisking (sponge cake), melting (gingerbread), all-in-one (Madeira mix).

5. **Types of pastry:** Shortcrust, rich shortcrust, cheese, choux, flaky, puff, rough puff, filo.

6. **Pastry-making guidelines:** Weigh accurately. Everything should be cold. Introduce air. Handle as little as possible. Flour the board lightly. Roll in one direction only and turn the pastry. Relax the pastry in the fridge. Bake in a preheated oven.

7. **Commercial cake mixes:** Contain all dry ingredients – just add egg and liquid. Advantages: Quick, useful for beginners, no waste. Disadvantages: Expensive, inferior taste, photo on front can be deceptive, often high in sugar and salt and low in fibre, may contain additives.

1. What are the main advantages of home baking? Outline six guidelines for home baking.
2. Name four types of raising agent used in home baking and describe how each one works.
3. What is gluten? Why is it important in home baking?
4. Describe five methods of making bread and cakes.
5. How would you prepare the tin for each of the following? (a) Bread (b) Pastry (c) A rich fruit cake
6. List four types of pastry and suggest one use for each.
7. Outline seven pastry-making guidelines.
8. List three advantages and three disadvantages of commercial cake and bread mixes.

Test Yourself
eTest.ie

Homework Assignment
28
P 95

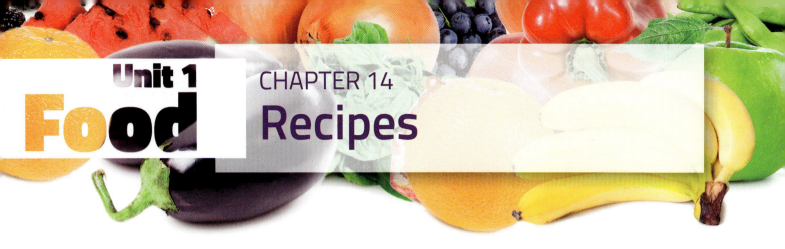

Recipe index

 * Demonstration videos available for these recipes in the eBook, on the Teacher's CD-ROM and online at gilldigital.ie

* Demonstration videos available for these recipes in the eBook, on the Teacher's CD-ROM and online at gilldigital.ie

Breakfasts

Summer berry smoothie

Makes 2 large smoothies

Ingredients
300g frozen fruit mix (strawberries, raspberries, blackberries)
1 banana
500ml cranberry juice
200ml low-fat fruit yoghurt

Method
1. Whizz all the ingredients in a food processor until smooth.
2. Serve in a large glass.

Scrambled eggs with cheese and bacon

Serves 2

Ingredients
2 large back rashers
4 large eggs
2 tablespoons milk
salt and pepper
knob of butter or margarine
25g cheese, grated
chopped fresh parsley, to garnish
toast, to serve

Method
1. Chop the rashers into very small pieces and dry fry in a saucepan until brown and a little crispy (do not wash the saucepan, as the oil remaining in it will be used again). Remove from the pan.
2. Beat the eggs, milk and some salt and pepper lightly in a bowl. Mix in the knob of butter and the rashers.
3. Make the toast.
4. Heat the oil remaining in the saucepan from the rashers. Add the egg mixture and cook the eggs over a low heat, stirring with a wooden spoon until they scramble. Be careful not to overcook them – scrambled eggs should be thick and creamy, not crumbly and rubbery.
5. Serve on warm toast. Sprinkle the grated cheese on top and allow it to melt in. Garnish with parsley.

Granola

Ingredients

125ml maple syrup

2 tablespoons honey

2 tablespoons vegetable oil

1 teaspoon ground cinnamon (if adding apple)

1 teaspoon vanilla essence (if adding fresh berries)

300g rolled oats

100g seeds (sunflower, sesame, pumpkin)

100g flaked almonds

100g dried fruit (raisins, chopped apricots)

50g desiccated coconut

1 large Granny Smith apple or a selection of fresh berries, to serve

cold milk or yoghurt, to serve

Method

1. Heat the oven to 150°C/fan 130°C/gas 2.
2. Mix the maple syrup, honey, oil and cinnamon or vanilla in a large bowl. Add in the oats, seeds and flaked almonds and mix well.
3. Tip the granola onto 2 baking sheets and spread it out evenly. Bake for 15 minutes, then mix in the dried fruit and coconut and bake for 10–15 minutes more. Remove from the oven and allow to cool.
4. Chop a Granny Smith apple into small pieces or wash and pat dry a selection of summer berries. Sprinkle some apples or berries over each serving of granola and add cold milk or yoghurt.
5. The granola (minus the apple and berries) can be stored in an airtight container for up to 1 month.

Starters

Chilled melon and summer fruits

Serves 2

Ingredients

1 small cantaloupe melon

150g summer fruits (strawberries, raspberries, blueberries, blackberries)

Method

1. Cut the melon along the equator. Remove the seeds.
2. Using a melon baller, scoop out the flesh.
3. Wash and slice the strawberries (if using). Leave the other berries whole.
4. Place the fruit carefully in a glass serving bowl, chill and then serve the glass on a small plate with a doyley.

A melon baller

Apple and walnut stuffed avocado

Serves 4

Ingredients

2 ripe avocados
lemon juice
1 red eating apple
50g walnuts
2 tablespoons low-fat
mayonnaise
walnut halves, to garnish
lettuce, cherry tomatoes and
cucumber slices, to serve

Method

1. Wash and cut into the avocados all round until you reach the stone. Take half of the avocado in each hand and twist to separate. Remove the stone by piercing with a knife and twisting. Remove the flesh from the skin in one piece with a dessertspoon (keep the skins). Chop into even-sized pieces. Sprinkle with a little lemon juice to prevent browning.
2. Wash, core and chop the apple. Chop the walnuts.
3. Mix the chopped avocados, apple and walnuts with the mayonnaise.
4. Fill the avocado shells with the mixture and garnish with walnut halves.
5. Serve with lettuce leaves, cherry tomatoes and cucumber slices.

To make a cucumber look nice, before you slice it, cut into the cucumber by dragging a fork along its length or making little trenches in it with a knife. When you slice it, you will get a nice serrated edge.

Prawn cocktail

Serves 4

Ingredients

1 tablespoon salt
1 litre boiling water
32 large prawns (double this number if
   they are small)

Marie rose sauce:

8 dessertspoons mayonnaise
1–1½ dessertspoons ketchup
1 dessertspoon lemon juice

Salad:

16 cherry tomatoes or 8 sun-dried
   tomatoes
4 scallions
1 red pepper, deseeded
bag of mixed baby leaf lettuce, washed

paprika, 4 lemon wedges and 4 small
   parsley sprigs, to garnish
homemade brown bread (page 199), to
   serve

Note: You can buy some prawns pre-
cooked; these just have to be defrosted.

Method

1. Add the salt to the water and bring to a fast boil.
2. Rinse the prawns and add to the fast-boiling salted water. Prawns do not take long to cook – just 1–2 minutes after the water has returned to the boil after adding the prawns. They should be firm and white but not opaque (undercooked) or crumbly (overcooked). Strain off the water through a sieve or colander. Allow the prawns to cool.
3. To make the marie rose sauce, mix the mayonnaise, ketchup and lemon juice together in a small bowl.
4. To make the salad, halve the cherry tomatoes or chop the sun-dried tomatoes into small pieces. Chop the scallions and finely slice the deseeded red pepper. Divide the baby leaf lettuce between 4 individual plates, then scatter the vegetables on top of the lettuce.
5. Place one-quarter of the prawns on each plate and spoon over one-quarter of the marie rose sauce. Sprinkle a little paprika on top.
6. Garnish each plate with a lemon wedge and a sprig of parsley. Serve with homemade brown bread.

Bruschetta with olive tapenade and goat's cheese

Serves 4

Ingredients

4 large, thick slices of French bread or ciabatta

100–150g strongly flavoured semi-soft cheese,
    such as goat's cheese or Brie, sliced

dressed green salad (page 173), to serve

Olive tapenade (paste):

100g stoned black olives

1 × 30g tin anchovy fillets

3 tablespoons extra virgin olive oil

1 tablespoon capers

1 teaspoon Dijon mustard

1 teaspoon freshly squeezed lemon juice

salt and pepper

Tomato mix:

olive oil, to fry

1 small onion, finely chopped

1 clove garlic, crushed

4 tomatoes, skinned and chopped

1 dessertspoon tomato purée

1 teaspoon chopped fresh marjoram
    or oregano

Ciabatta

Method

1. Preheat the oven to 200°C/fan 190°C/gas 6.
2. Liquidise all the ingredients for the olive tapenade (paste). It can be left smooth or coarse, according to taste. Set aside.
3. For the tomato mix, heat the olive oil in a small saucepan over a medium heat. Fry the onion and garlic until softened but not browned. Add the chopped tomatoes, tomato purée and the marjoram or oregano. Simmer for 5 minutes, until the mixture reduces and becomes fairly thick.
4. Spread each slice of bread thickly, first with the olive tapenade, then with the tomato mix. Place on a baking tray. Lastly, place 1 or 2 slices of cheese (depending on size) on top.
5. Bake for 10 minutes, until the cheese has melted and has started to brown slightly.
6. Serve with a dressed green salad (see page 173).

Garlic bread

Makes about 8 large slices

Ingredients

4 cloves garlic
100g butter or low-fat spread,
    softened
1 teaspoon dried oregano or basil
1 large plain bloomer (see photo)

Bloomer bread

Method

1. Preheat the grill or set oven to 200°C/fan 190°C/gas 6.
2. Peel and crush the garlic. Mix with the butter and herbs.
3. Slice the bread thickly and butter each slice.
4. Grill until the butter has melted and the bread is beginning to brown. Serve hot.

Soups

Farmhouse vegetable soup

Serves 4

Ingredients

3 medium carrots
1 medium potato
1 parsnip
2 sticks celery
1 medium leek
1 onion
1 tablespoon olive oil
1.5 litres vegetable stock (use 2 stock cubes
    or stock pots)
salt and pepper
cream and chopped fresh parsley (optional),
    to garnish

Method

1. Wash, peel and dice the carrots, potato and parsnip. Wash and chop the celery, leek and onion. (**Note:** The vegetables will have to be finely and evenly diced or chopped if you do not blend the soup at the end.)
2. Heat the oil in a large, heavy saucepan over a medium heat. Gently fry the onion and the leek.
3. Add the carrots, potatoes, parsnips and celery. Continue to fry gently for a few minutes.
4. Add the stock and some salt and pepper. Bring to the boil. Once boiling, reduce the heat, cover and simmer for 25 minutes. Purée in a blender or food processor if you wish.
5. Serve piping hot in warm bowls. Garnish with a swirl of cream and some chopped fresh parsley.

Cream of roast Mediterranean vegetable soup

Serves 4

Ingredients

6 shallots, peeled (or 1 onion, peeled and cut into quarters, if shallots are not available)
1 red pepper, deseeded and cut into quarters
1 yellow pepper, deseeded and cut into quarters
1 courgette, sliced
½ aubergine, cut into cubes
2 cloves garlic, roughly chopped
1 tablespoon olive oil
1 x 400g tin chopped tomatoes
2 dessertspoons tomato purée
500ml vegetable stock
2 dessertspoons chopped fresh basil or 1 dessertspoon dried basil
salt and pepper
100ml fresh cream
fresh chopped basil, to garnish

Method

1. Preheat the oven to 200°C/fan 190°C/gas 6.
2. Toss the shallots, peppers, courgette, aubergine and garlic in the olive oil on a baking tray. Roast for 15–20 minutes. Halfway through, take the tray out and shake the vegetables so that they roast evenly and brown a little.
3. Transfer to a medium or large saucepan and add the tinned tomatoes, tomato purée, stock and basil. Season with salt and pepper.
4. Bring to the boil and simmer for 5 minutes. Blend in a food processor. Return to the saucepan.
5. If serving straight away, stir in the cream and serve in warmed soup bowls, garnished with a little chopped fresh basil.

Croutons

Ingredients

2 thick slices of bread, cubed
1 clove garlic, crushed
1 tablespoon olive oil
¼ teaspoon sea salt

Method

1. Preheat the oven to 180°C/fan 170°C/gas 4.
2. Toss the bread cubes, garlic, oil and salt in a plastic freezer bag.
3. Spread out on a baking tray and bake for 15 minutes.

Top tip: Use bread that is not too fresh.

Snacks

Spicy chicken wrap

Serves 2

Ingredients

2 chicken breasts
2 dessertspoons olive oil
2 teaspoons Cajun spice
2 large soft flour tortilla wraps
2 dessertspoons low-fat
    mayonnaise
2 dessertspoons Ballymaloe
    Country Relish (or similar
    brand)
baby leaf lettuce
6 cherry tomatoes, halved
6 thin cucumber slices
2 scallions, chopped
25g smoked Cheddar cheese,
    grated

Method

1. Toss the chicken breasts in the olive oil and then in the Cajun spices. Grill the chicken on a preheated contact grill, such as a George Foreman grill, for 8–10 minutes, until the chicken is cooked through. If no contact grill is available, cook under a normal grill for 15–20 minutes, turning regularly until the chicken is cooked through. Cut into bite-sized pieces or strips.

2. Dampen the 2 tortilla wraps and heat in the microwave for approximately 20 seconds (depending on the wattage of the microwave). If no microwave is available, then tortillas can be dampened, wrapped in tin foil and heated at 200°C/ fan 190°C/gas 6 for 3–5 minutes in the oven.

3. Spread the mayonnaise and relish on each heated wrap. Place the chicken, salad ingredients and grated cheese on top. Wrap the tortilla as shown in the illustration. Cut in half and serve.

How to wrap up a tortilla

French bread pizza

Serves 2

Ingredients

olive oil, for frying

1 small onion, finely chopped

1 large clove garlic, crushed

450g very ripe, fresh tomatoes, skinned and chopped, or 1 x 400g tin chopped tomatoes

1 dessertspoon chopped fresh marjoram or 1 teaspoon dried

pinch of black pepper

1 French stick

extra toppings can be added, such as fried mushrooms, cooked ham, pineapple, etc.

100g mozzarella cheese, grated

1 dessertspoon finely grated Parmesan

coleslaw (page 173) and green salad (page 173), to serve

Method

1. Preheat the oven to 200°C/fan 190°C/gas 6.

2. To make the tomato sauce, heat the olive oil in a medium saucepan over a medium heat. Sauté the onion and garlic. Add the tomatoes, marjoram and black pepper. Simmer for 5–10 minutes, until the mixture has thickened down to a paste. Purée using a sieve or liquidiser.

3. Cut the French stick in half, then cut each piece in half again along the middle. Spread with the tomato sauce and your chosen toppings. Place on a baking tray, then sprinkle with the mozzarella and Parmesan.

4. Bake for 5–10 minutes, until the cheese has fully melted.

5. Serve with coleslaw and a green salad.

Roast Mediterranean vegetable and cheese panini

Makes 4

Ingredients

4 medium part-cooked French sticks
   or ciabatta
100g mozzarella cheese, sliced

Pesto:

50g fresh basil leaves
50ml extra virgin olive oil
1 dessertspoon pine nuts
1 large clove garlic
25g fresh Parmesan, finely grated

Mediterranean vegetables:

1 red onion, peeled and sliced
1 red pepper, deseeded and sliced
1 yellow pepper, deseeded and sliced
8 mushrooms, washed and sliced
1 clove garlic, crushed
olive oil

green salad (page 173), to serve

Method

1. Preheat the oven to 200°C/fan 190°C/gas 6.
2. To make the pesto, whizz all the ingredients except the Parmesan in the food processor or crush with a pestle and mortar. Stir in the grated Parmesan.
3. To make the Mediterranean vegetables, toss the prepared vegetables and garlic in a small baking tin with the olive oil. Roast in the oven for 10–15 minutes, until softened and slightly browned.
4. To assemble the panini, cut the bread in half lengthwise. Spread the pesto on the bread first, followed by the vegetables and mozzarella. Try not to have the cheese too close to the outside edge.
5. Cook the panini on a contact grill or sandwich toaster for approximately 5 minutes, until it has browned and the cheese has melted.
6. Serve with a green salad.

Salads

Green salad

Serves 4

Ingredients
1 small bag baby leaf lettuce, washed
½ cucumber, peeled and thinly sliced
3 scallions, chopped
1 green pepper, deseeded and chopped

Method
1. Mix all the ingredients together in a large bowl. Toss in vinaigrette or balsamic dressing.

Coleslaw

Serves 4

Ingredients
¼ head white cabbage, roughly grated
1 small carrot, peeled and roughly grated
1 small onion, finely grated
3 dessertspoons mayonnaise
1 dessertspoon finely chopped fresh parsley
freshly ground black pepper

Method
1. Mix all the ingredients together in a large bowl, tossing well to combine.

Waldorf salad

Serves 4

Ingredients
1 Pink Lady apple, cored and diced
1 Granny Smith apple, cored and diced
2 sticks celery, sliced thinly
50g raisins
25g coarsely chopped walnuts
3 dessertspoons mayonnaise
1 dessertspoon lemon juice

Method
1. Mix all the ingredients together in a large bowl, tossing well to combine.

Couscous salad

Serves 4

Ingredients

225ml vegetable stock

50g raisins

3 dessertspoons extra virgin olive oil

150g couscous

1 small onion, finely chopped

1 small red pepper, deseeded and chopped

1 large clove garlic

25g pine nuts, lightly toasted

2 dessertspoons red wine vinegar

1 dessertspoon finely chopped fresh parsley

sea salt and freshly ground black pepper

Method

1. Boil the stock, raisins and 1 dessertspoon of the olive oil in a saucepan. Stir in the couscous and allow to stand for 5 minutes. Transfer to a large bowl and fluff up the couscous with a fork.

2. Heat 1 dessertspoon of the olive oil in a saucepan over a medium heat. Sauté the onion, red pepper and garlic until soft but the onion is still pale.

3. Stir the remaining 1 dessertspoon of olive oil into the couscous along with the pine nuts, vinegar, onions and peppers and chopped parsley. Season with salt and pepper.

 ## Chicken Caesar salad with bacon bits

Serves 4

Ingredients

3 smoked back rashers

2 chicken breasts

olive oil, to fry

1 large head of Cos (Romaine) lettuce, roughly torn

sliced hardboiled egg (optional)

1 batch of homemade croutons (page 169)

50g freshly grated Parmesan

Dressing:

1 x 30g tin anchovies, drained

2 egg yolks

1 clove garlic, crushed

juice of ½ lemon

¼ teaspoon English mustard powder

1 dessertspoon Worcestershire sauce

1 dessertspoon Tabasco sauce

150ml sunflower oil

50ml extra virgin olive oil

50ml cold water

Method

1. To make the dressing, whizz all the ingredients except the oils and water in a food processor until smooth. Slowly pour in first the oils and then the water, keeping the food processor going all the time.
2. Grill or fry the rashers until crispy. Cut them up small.
3. Toss the chicken in a little olive oil and then grill on a preheated contact grill, such as a George Foreman grill, for 8–10 minutes, until the chicken is cooked through. If no contact grill is available, cook on a traditional grill until cooked through, 15–20 minutes. Cut the chicken into chunks or strips.
4. Pour 1 tablespoon of the dressing per person into a bowl. Toss the lettuce, half the croutons and half the Parmesan in it. Divide into 4 large, deep serving bowls. Spread the remainder of the croutons, chicken and bacon pieces on top along with the sliced hardboiled egg, if using. Sprinkle with the remaining Parmesan. (Leftover dressing can be covered and stored in the fridge for 3–4 days.)

Main courses: Beef, pork and lamb

Spaghetti Bolognese

Serves 4

Ingredients

olive oil
2 streaky rashers, chopped into
    small pieces
1 onion, chopped
6 medium mushrooms, sliced
1 stick celery, sliced
2 cloves garlic, crushed
300g lean minced beef
1 x 400g tin chopped tomatoes
    or 2 fresh ripe tomatoes, sliced
2 tablespoons tomato purée
1 beef stock pot
1 teaspoon dried oregano
1 teaspoon dried rosemary
1 teaspoon ground chilli flakes

salt and pepper
200g spaghetti
freshly grated Parmesan cheese and garlic
    bread (page 168), to serve

Method

1. To make the Bolognese sauce, heat 1 tablespoon of olive oil in a medium-sized saucepan over a medium heat. Gently fry the rashers, onion, mushrooms, celery and garlic for 5 minutes.
2. Add the mince and fry until it has lost its red colour.
3. Add the tomatoes, tomato purée, beef stock pot, oregano, rosemary, chilli flakes and some salt and pepper. Bring to the boil. Turn down the heat and simmer for 20–25 minutes.
4. To cook the spaghetti, boil 2 litres of water in a large saucepan. Add 1 dessertspoon of olive oil.
5. When the water is boiling, ease the spaghetti into it. Boil for 10–12 minutes, or until the spaghetti is al dente (this means it is cooked but still has a bite). Fresh spaghetti takes less time to cook and has a better flavour, so use this if available. Drain the spaghetti in a sieve or colander. Rinse with hot water to remove excess starch.
6. Mix the drained spaghetti into the Bolognese sauce. Serve with freshly grated Parmesan cheese and garlic bread (see page 168).

Lasagne

Serves 4

Ingredients

1 quantity of Bolognese sauce
   (see recipe above)
9 lasagne sheets
fresh parsley, to garnish
garlic bread (page 168) and green salad
   (page 173), to serve

Cheese sauce:

750ml milk
50g butter or margarine
50g plain flour
½ teaspoon dry mustard
salt and pepper
150g Cheddar cheese, grated

Method

1. Preheat the oven to 190°C/fan 180°C/gas 5.
2. Make the Bolognese sauce as described for the spaghetti Bolognese recipe (see above).
3. Grease a large rectangular pie dish.
4. Make the cheese sauce by whisking the milk, butter or margarine, flour, mustard and some salt and pepper in a saucepan. Heat until it boils and thickens, stirring with a balloon whisk. Alternatively, make a roux sauce in the traditional way (see page 137).
5. Add 100g of the grated cheese to the sauce. Set the other 50g aside.
6. Layer the meat sauce, lasagne sheets and cheese sauce in the dish. Finish with a layer of cheese sauce. Sprinkle the remaining cheese on top.
7. Bake for 30 minutes or until lasagne sheets have softened.
8. Garnish with parsley. Serve with garlic bread and a green salad.

Beef or lamb curry

Serves 4

Ingredients

500g stewing beef or lamb
1 dessertspoon olive oil
1 large onion, chopped
1 clove garlic, crushed
25g flour
2 dessertspoons curry powder (or to taste)
750mls beef stock (use 2 beef stock cubes
    or stock pots)
1 large cooking apple, peeled and chopped
rice, to serve
fresh parsley, to garnish

Note: Do not add any extra salt, as there is plenty in stock cubes/stock pots.

Method

1. Remove any fat from the meat. Cut the meat into small pieces.
2. Heat the olive oil in a medium-sized saucepan over a medium heat. Fry the meat, onion and garlic until the meat is brown on all sides.
3. Add the flour and curry powder. Cook for 2–3 minutes.
4. Gradually stir in the stock. Add the chopped apple.
5. Bring to the boil, reduce the heat and simmer for 1–1½ hours, until the meat is tender.
6. Serve on a bed of rice and garnish with parsley.

Carbonnade of pork with mushrooms

Serves 3–4

Ingredients

olive or sunflower oil, for frying
450g pork fillet, cut into very thin strips
1 onion, finely chopped
100ml chicken stock
100g mushrooms, sliced
50g flour
150ml light cream
1 dessertspoon lemon juice
1 dessertspoon chopped fresh parsley
salt and freshly ground pepper
300g uncooked rice (400g cooked)
croutons (page 169) and fresh parsley,
    to garnish

Method

1. Heat a little oil in a saucepan or frying pan over a medium heat. Sauté the pork strips a few at a time until they are brown on all sides. Remove to a plate and keep warm. Do not clean the pan.
2. Heat a little more oil in the pan if necessary and sauté the onion until it is soft and golden. Add the stock and boil until the mixture reduces by one-quarter. Pour into a jug. Wipe the pan dry.
3. Heat a little more oil in the pan and sauté the mushrooms. Return the pork to the pan. Add the flour and cook for 1–2 minutes. Add the cream, lemon juice, most of the chopped parsley and some salt and pepper. Bring to the boil and simmer for a few minutes, especially if the sauce is not thick enough.
4. Serve on a bed of rice. Garnish with croutons and fresh parsley.

Homemade burgers

Serves 4

Ingredients

450g lean minced beef
1 small onion, very finely chopped
2 tablespoons wholemeal
    breadcrumbs
pinch of mixed dried herbs
salt and pepper
1 egg, beaten
a little flour
olive oil
burger buns, lettuce, tomato slices,
    ketchup and mayonnaise, to serve

A burger press

Method

1. Mix the mince, onion, breadcrumbs, herbs, salt and pepper in a bowl. Bind the mix together with the beaten egg.
2. Divide the mixture into burgers. Shape on a floured board or use a burger press like the one pictured.
3. Brush each burger with a little olive oil.
4. Place the burgers under a preheated hot grill for about 6 minutes on each side, until the burgers are cooked through.
5. Serve on a toasted burger bun with lettuce, tomato slices and ketchup or mayonnaise.

Main courses: Chicken

Chicken curry

Serves 4

Ingredients

2 tablespoons sunflower oil
4 chicken breast fillets, cut in large dice –
    6–8 per fillet
2 large onions, sliced
3 cloves garlic, crushed
3 tablespoons curry powder
1 tablespoon Chinese 5 spice mix

500ml chicken stock
pinch of sugar, salt and black pepper
1½ tablespoons cornflour
1 tablespoon water
1 tablespoon chopped fresh coriander
rice, to serve

Method

1. Heat 1 tablespoon of the sunflower oil in a pan over a medium heat and quickly brown the diced chicken. Remove from the pan and set aside.
2. Add another tablespoon of oil to the pan and sauté the onion and garlic until soft, but do not let them colour.
3. Add the curry powder and Chinese 5 spice mix and cook for 1–2 minutes, then gradually add in the stock. Bring to the boil. Season with a pinch of sugar, salt and pepper.
4. Soften the cornflour with 1 tablespoon of water in a small bowl. Thicken the sauce with the cornflour mixture, adding it bit by bit.
5. Add the chicken to the sauce and simmer for 20 minutes. This will ensure the chicken is cooked through but still moist. Add the coriander and serve on a bed of rice.

Top tips:

- Some reduced-fat coconut milk could also be added for extra depth of flavour.
- Curries are best eaten the day after they are made, when the flavours have had a chance to develop.

Chicken and bacon risotto

Serves 4

Ingredients

2 tablespoons olive oil
3 streaky rashers, cut into bite-sized pieces
1 medium onion, chopped
6 mushrooms, sliced
1 green pepper, deseeded and chopped
1 red pepper, deseeded and chopped
1 clove garlic, crushed
2 chicken breasts, cut into bite-sized pieces
300g uncooked Arborio rice
salt and black pepper
approx. 1 litre chicken stock
fresh parsley, to garnish

Method

1. Heat 1 tablespoon of oil in a large, heavy saucepan over a medium heat. Fry the rashers and onions until the onions soften and the rashers begin to brown.
2. Add the mushrooms, peppers and garlic. Fry gently for another minute. Remove the rashers and vegetables to a plate.
3. Heat 1 tablespoon of oil in the saucepan. Fry the chicken for 3 minutes. Add the rice and fry for another minute. Add some salt and pepper. Return the rashers and vegetables to the saucepan.
4. Add 250ml of the stock, stirring the mixture continuously until the rice has absorbed it. Add another 250ml of stock and stir again. Repeat this process until all the stock has been absorbed and the rice is al dente.
5. Serve on a warm oval plate. Garnish with parsley.

Sweet and sour chicken or pork

Serves 4

Ingredients

2 chicken breasts or 3 pork chops
1 tablespoon olive oil
1 onion, chopped
1 clove garlic, crushed
1 carrot, peeled and cut into strips
1 green pepper, deseeded and diced
½ x 400g can of pineapple in own juice
1 dessertspoon cornflour
1 tablespoon vinegar
1 tablespoon soy sauce
1 teaspoon brown sugar
1 teaspoon tomato purée
salt and black pepper
fresh parsley, to garnish
300g uncooked rice (400g cooked),
  to serve

Method

1. Wipe the meat, trim the fat and cut into bite-sized pieces.
2. Heat the oil in a medium-sized heavy saucepan over a medium heat. Fry the meat quickly to seal it. Remove the meat from the pan and set aside on a plate.
3. Sauté the onion, garlic, carrot and pepper for 2–3 minutes. Return the meat to the pan.
4. Measure the pineapple juice and make it up to 400ml with water. In a separate small bowl, blend the cornflour with a little of this juice.
5. Add the pineapple juice, the blended cornflour and all the other ingredients except the parsley and rice to the saucepan.
6. Bring to the boil, turn down the heat and simmer with the lid on for 30 minutes.
7. Serve on a bed of rice and garnish with fresh parsley.

Main courses: Fish

 ## Baked salmon with tartare sauce, steamed vegetables and baby potatoes

Serves 4

Ingredients

4 medium carrots, washed, peeled and
  sliced or julienned
20 baby potatoes, washed
4 salmon fillets, patted dry with
  kitchen paper
1 head of broccoli, washed and broken
  into florets
8 cauliflower florets, washed
lemon wedges, to garnish

Tartare sauce:

4 tablespoons low-fat mayonnaise
1 tablespoon chopped gherkins
1 tablespoon chopped capers
1 tablespoon chopped fresh chives
1 tablespoon chopped fresh parsley
1 teaspoon dried tarragon
juice of ½ lemon

Method

1. Preheat the oven to 200°C/fan 190°C/gas 6.
2. Using a tiered steamer, put the carrots and baby potatoes on to cook. They will take about 25 minutes (although appliances vary).
3. Place the salmon on a lightly greased tray and put in the oven to bake for about 20 minutes, until cooked through.
4. Make the tartare sauce by mixing all the ingredients together in a bowl. Transfer to a serving dish and refrigerate.
5. About 10 minutes before the end of the cooking time, put the broccoli and cauliflower on to cook in the next tier of the steamer.
6. Plate the dish and serve with the tartare sauce and a wedge of lemon on each plate.

Salmon fishcakes

Makes 8 fishcakes

Ingredients

450g salmon
4–6 potatoes, depending on size,
     cooked and mashed
2 eggs
2 dessertspoons chopped
     fresh parsley
25g butter, melted
salt and black pepper
50g plain flour, for dusting
75g breadcrumbs (3 slices of bread)
olive oil, for frying
fresh vegetables, to serve

Method

1. Preheat the oven to 200°C/fan 190°C/gas 6.
2. To cook the salmon, wrap it in tinfoil and bake in the oven for 20 minutes. Set aside to cool, then flake with a fork.
3. Mix the flaked fish, mashed potatoes, 1 beaten egg, the chopped parsley, melted butter and some salt and pepper in a bowl. Leave in the fridge for 30 minutes.
4. Remove from the fridge and roll into a long snake shape on a floured board. Cut into 8 even-sized pieces. Flatten each piece into a round cake.
5. Beat the remaining egg in a shallow bowl. Put the breadcrumbs in a second shallow bowl. Dip each cake first in the beaten egg and then in the breadcrumbs.
6. Fry or grill the cakes (grilling is healthier) for 5 minutes on each side, until golden brown and the cake is heated through. Serve with fresh vegetables.

Top tip: In a hurry? Use tinned salmon or tuna.

Smoked salmon and bacon carbonara

Serves 4

Ingredients

2 tablespoons olive oil
300g uncooked tagliatelle (400g cooked)
150g smoked bacon lardons (small cubes of
     bacon)
1 small onion, finely chopped
2 cloves garlic, crushed

400ml cream
1 tablespoon finely chopped fresh herbs
     (basil, oregano or marjoram)
pinch of sea salt
freshly ground black pepper
200g smoked salmon, cut into strips
chopped fresh parsley, to garnish

Method

1. Bring a large saucepan of water to the boil and stir in 1 tablespoon of the olive oil. Add the tagliatelle and cook until al dente, 10–12 minutes. Drain in a sieve or colander and rinse with hot water.
2. While the tagliatelle is cooking heat 1 tablespoon of olive oil in a saucepan or deep frying pan over a medium heat. Fry the bacon lardons until they are lightly browned. Add the onion and garlic and sauté gently for a few minutes, until the onion has softened but has not browned. Drain off any excess grease.
3. Add the cream, herbs and some salt and pepper. Bring to the boil and simmer, stirring all the time, until the sauce has reduced and thickened a little.
4. Add the smoked salmon and heat right through (smoked salmon is already cooked).
5. Divide the drained pasta among 4 deep serving plates. Ladle the sauce evenly over each portion. Garnish with chopped fresh parsley.

Milk, eggs and cheese

Quiche Lorraine

Serves 4

Ingredients

Shortcrust pastry:
150g plain flour
pinch of salt
75g cold butter or margarine, diced
cold water

Filling:
4 back rashers
olive oil, for frying
150g grated Cheddar cheese
1 small onion, finely chopped
3 large eggs
200ml milk
100ml cream
salt and pepper

tomato slices and fresh parsley, to garnish
green salad (page 173), and coleslaw (page 173) to serve

Method

1. Preheat the oven to 190°C/fan 180°C/gas 5.
2. To make the pastry, sieve the flour and salt into a bowl. Rub in the diced butter or margarine until it looks like breadcrumbs. Add the water little by little with a spoon. Stir with a knife until you have a stiff dough. Roll out on a lightly floured work surface and use to line a 20cm flan tin.
3. Fry the rashers in a pan with a little olive oil over a medium heat, then chop them up. Place them in the lined tin with three quarters of the grated cheese. Sauté the onion in the remaining fat after frying the rashers, until soft but not browned. Spread these on the base as well.
4. Mix together the eggs, milk, cream and some salt and pepper. Pour over the rashers. Sprinkle the remaining cheese on top.
5. Bake for 40–45 minutes, until set.
6. Garnish with tomato slices and parsley. Serve with a green salad.

Top tip: Fillings can be varied. Try adding 100g mushrooms: grill or fry the mushrooms, allow to cool, slice and arrange on a flan tin with rashers, onion and grated cheese; continue as stated in recipe.

French savoury omelette

Serves 1

Ingredients

2 large eggs
15g butter or margarine
1 tablespoon water
salt and pepper
mixed chopped fresh herbs
oil, for frying
fresh parsley, to garnish
toast, to serve

Fillings:

Choose the cheese plus one or
  two of the following:
25g grated cheese
2 cherry tomatoes, quartered
1 grilled rasher, chopped
1 slice of ham, chopped
50g sautéed mushrooms

Method

1. Lightly beat the eggs, butter, water, seasoning, herbs and filling(s) in a bowl (but not the cheese).
2. Heat a little oil in a small pan over a low heat. Pour the egg mixture in. As the egg sets, pull it gently towards the middle of the pan with a palette knife. Tilt the pan and run the uncooked egg into the edge of the pan. Continue until all the egg is just set.
3. Tip the omelette onto a warmed plate. Sprinkle the grated cheese on top and fold the omelette over using a palette knife.
4. Garnish with parsley and serve with toast.

Calzone

Makes 1 calzone

Ingredients

Dough:

100g plain flour

pinch of salt

25g butter or margarine, diced

1 egg, beaten (keep some back for glazing)

a little milk

Filling:

150g mozzarella, roughly grated

50g cooked ham or crispy bacon

2 tablespoons pesto (page 172) or tapenade (page 167)

1 teaspoon chopped fresh parsley

1 teaspoon dried marjoram

green salad (page 173) and coleslaw (page 173), to serve

Method

1. Preheat the oven to 190°C/fan 180°C/gas 5.
2. To make the base, sieve the flour and salt into a bowl. Rub in the diced butter or margarine until the mixture looks like breadcrumbs. Add most of the beaten egg and enough milk to make a stiff dough. On a lightly floured work surface, roll the dough out into a large, thin circle. Place on a greased tin.
3. Mix all the filling ingredients together and place on half of the base. Do not go too close to the edges or the filling will spill out in the oven.
4. Wet the edges all round and fold the base over on itself. Press sealed with floured fingers. Pierce a few holes in the top with a fork. Glaze with a little beaten egg.
5. Bake in the oven for 25–30 minutes.
6. Serve with a green salad and homemade coleslaw.

Vegetarian

Vegetable stir-fry with rice

Serves 4

Ingredients
300g uncooked rice
1 dessertspoon olive oil

Stir-fry:
8 baby sweetcorn
8 mushrooms, sliced
1 carrot, peeled and cut into
   thin batons
1 red pepper, deseeded and sliced
1 small courgette, sliced
½ red onion, chopped
1 clove garlic, crushed
1 tablespoon olive oil
1 teaspoon cornflour
1 teaspoon Cajun spices
50g pine nuts
2 tablespoons soy sauce

Method
1. Put the rice on to cook in a saucepan of boiling water to which you have added 1 dessertspoon of olive oil. Cook for 15–20 minutes or according to the packet instructions.
2. Mix all the vegetables together in a bowl.
3. Heat 1 tablespoon of oil in a wok or frying pan over a high heat. Add the vegetables and stir-fry.
4. Add the cornflour and Cajun spices and stir through. Add the pine nuts and soy sauce. Continue stir-frying for approximately 5 minutes, until the vegetables are cooked but still have bite. Serve with the boiled rice.

Vegetable curry

Serves 4

Ingredients
Rice:
300g uncooked rice (400g cooked)
1 dessertspoon olive oil

Curry sauce:
1 dessertspoon olive oil
1 onion, chopped
3 dessertspoons curry powder
1 dessertspoon plain flour
500ml vegetable stock

Vegetables:
8 mushrooms, sliced
6 cauliflower florets, broken into
   bite-sized pieces
6 broccoli florets, broken into
   bite-sized pieces
2 sticks celery, sliced
1 carrot, peeled and sliced
1 small courgette, sliced
1 green or red pepper, deseeded and sliced
1 cooking apple, peeled, cored and chopped
50g sultanas
½ x 400g tin pineapple chunks, drained
1 dessertspoon desiccated coconut
1 teaspoon lemon juice
1 teaspoon brown sugar
salt and pepper
fresh parsley, to garnish

Method
1. To make the curry sauce, heat the olive oil in a small saucepan over a medium heat. Fry the onion gently for 2–3 minutes. Add the curry powder and flour and gradually stir in 100ml of the stock.
2. Put all of the vegetables, fruit, coconut, lemon juice and brown sugar into a large saucepan. Add the remaining 400ml of stock and season with salt and pepper. Bring to the boil, reduce the heat and simmer with the lid on for 10 minutes.
3. Put the rice on to cook in a medium saucepan of boiling water to which you have added 1 dessertspoon of olive oil. Cook until soft but still al dente (15–20 minutes).
4. Add the onions to the large saucepan. Bring to the boil again, reduce the heat and simmer for a further 10–15 minutes.
5. Serve on a bed of rice and garnish with parsley.

Cheesy vegetable and pasta bake

Serves 4

Ingredients

Vegetable mix:
1 dessertspoon olive oil
1 onion, chopped
1 green pepper, deseeded
    and chopped
8 mushrooms, sliced
1 clove garlic, crushed
1 x 400g tin chopped tomatoes
1 teaspoon dried basil

Pasta:
200g pasta shapes (fresh pasta
    if possible)
1 dessertspoon olive oil

Cheese sauce:
25g butter or margarine
25g plain flour
500ml milk
50g grated Cheddar cheese

Topping:
50g brown breadcrumbs
25g grated Cheddar cheese

garlic bread (page 168), to serve
fresh parsley, to garnish

Method

1. Preheat the oven to 200°C/fan 190°C/gas 6.
2. Heat the oil in a medium-sized saucepan over a medium heat. Gently fry the onion, green pepper, mushrooms and garlic for 2–3 minutes. Add the tomatoes and basil and bring to the boil. Reduce the heat and simmer with the lid on for 20 minutes.
3. Meanwhile, cook the pasta shapes in boiling water to which 1 dessertspoon of oil has been added for 12–15 minutes. Drain and add to the vegetables.
4. To make the cheese sauce, melt the butter or margarine in a small saucepan, then add the flour. Cook this roux for 1 minute, stirring all the time. Remove from the heat and cool slightly. Add the milk bit by bit, stirring all the time. Return to the heat and bring to the boil. Reduce the heat and cook for 3 minutes. Remove from the heat and stir in the grated cheese. Set aside.
5. Put the vegetables and pasta in a casserole dish and pour on the cheese sauce.
6. Mix the breadcrumbs and grated Cheddar together, then sprinkle over the pasta in the casserole dish.
7. Bake for 15 minutes. Serve hot with garlic bread and garnish with parsley.

Pasta with creamy vegetable sauce

Serves 2

Ingredients

150g uncooked pasta shells
  (fresh pasta is best)
2 tablespoons olive oil
1 small onion, finely chopped
8 mushrooms, sliced
2 cloves garlic, crushed
1 red pepper, deseeded and
  sliced
1 yellow pepper, deseeded and
  sliced
1 x 400g tin plum tomatoes
100ml cream
50g Cheddar cheese, grated
1 tablespoon chopped fresh
  parsley
garlic bread (page 168), to serve

Method

1. Put the pasta on to cook in a large saucepan of boiling water to which 1 tablespoon of the oil has been added. Cook until al dente, approximately 10–12 minutes. Rinse in hot water and drain.

2. Meanwhile, heat 1 tablespoon of olive oil in a large saucepan over a medium heat. Gently sauté the onion, mushrooms and garlic until soft but not brown. Add the peppers and continue to fry gently, stirring constantly with a wooden spoon. Add the plum tomatoes with their juice. Break up the tomatoes roughly with a wooden spoon.

3. Bring to the boil and simmer until all the vegetables are softened but not mushy. Remove from the heat and stir in the cream.

4. Divide the pasta between 2 deep serving plates. Spoon over the vegetable stew. Sprinkle each portion with grated cheese and chopped fresh parsley.

5. Serve with garlic bread.

Desserts

Fresh fruit salad

Serves 4

Ingredients

1 apple
1 pear
1 orange
6 green seedless grapes
6 black seedless grapes
6 strawberries
2 kiwi fruit
1 banana
200ml orange juice
low-fat cream, ice cream or yoghurt,
  to serve

Method

1. Prepare the fruit: core and cut the apple and pear into bite-sized pieces. Remove the pith and skin from the orange. Divide into segments and cut each segment in two. Halve the grapes and strawberries. Peel and slice the kiwi and banana.
2. Arrange the fruit in a bowl. Pour the orange juice over.
3. Serve with low-fat ice cream, cream or natural yogurt (healthier option).

> **Top tip:** Orange juice is a healthy alternative to sugar syrup.
> It also prevents apples, pears and bananas from browning.

Strawberry and rhubarb crumble

Serves 4

Ingredients
250g rhubarb, sliced
1 x 400g tin strawberries, drained
50g caster sugar

Crumble:
150g plain flour
75g butter or margarine, diced
50g brown sugar
1 teaspoon ground cinnamon
low-fat cream, ice cream or yoghurt,
   to serve

Method

1. Preheat the oven to 190°C/fan 180°C/gas 5.
2. Place the rhubarb and strawberries in a large greased ovenproof dish or 4 individual ovenproof dishes. Sprinkle the sugar evenly over the top.
3. To make the crumble, sieve the flour into a large bowl. Rub in the diced butter or margarine until the mixture looks like breadcrumbs. Add the brown sugar and cinnamon.
4. Spread the crumble evenly over the fruit.
5. Bake for 30 minutes, until the topping is golden and the fruit is soft.
6. Serve with low-fat cream, ice cream or natural yoghurt (healthier option).

Bread and butter pudding

Serves 4

Ingredients

8 slices of bread
50g butter, softened
50g sultanas
pinch of ground nutmeg
300ml milk
25g caster sugar
¼ teaspoon vanilla essence
2 eggs
low-fat cream, ice cream or yoghurt,
　to serve

Method

1. Preheat the oven to 190°C/fan 180°C/gas 5.
2. Lightly butter the bread and remove black crusts only. Cut 6 slices into fingers. Cut the remaining 2 slices into triangles.
3. Line the bottom of an ovenproof dish with the bread fingers, butter side down. Sprinkle with the sultanas and a little nutmeg.
4. Repeat until all the bread is used, finishing with a layer of triangular-shaped bread, butter side up.
5. In a saucepan, heat the milk, sugar and vanilla essence until hot – not boiling.
6. Beat the eggs in a bowl. Gradually add the milk to the eggs, stirring constantly.
7. Pour the milk and egg mixture over the bread and sultanas. Sprinkle with nutmeg and a little sugar.
8. Place the dish on a roasting tin. Put some water in the roasting tin: this helps keep the pudding moist.
9. Bake for 30–35 minutes. Serve with low-fat cream, ice cream or natural yoghurt (healthier option).

Top tip: Bread and butter pudding can be made in small individual ramekin dishes (grease the ramekin dishes lightly). Tip each one out upside down on a dessert plate. Serve surrounded with hot custard.

Delicious filled crêpes

Makes 6 crêpes

Ingredients
Crêpes:
100g self-raising flour
pinch of salt
1 egg
250ml milk
sunflower oil, for frying

Fillings (pick one):
ice cream and bananas
   with butterscotch sauce
   (see below)
strawberries and whipped cream
stewed apple with cinnamon

Method

1. Sieve the flour and salt into a bowl. Make a well in the centre.
2. Drop the egg and half the milk into the well. Using a whisk, beat from the centre out until the mixture is smooth.
3. Add the rest of the milk. Beat for 5 minutes to introduce air.
4. Pour into a jug. Allow to stand in the fridge for 20 minutes if you have time.
5. Heat a little oil in a frying pan over a medium heat. Pour in some batter and tilt to cover the base. Cook until the edges begin to brown. Shake the pan to loosen the crêpe.
6. Turn the crêpe over using a fish slice or palette knife. Repeat with the rest of the batter. Keep cooked crêpes warm between 2 plates over a saucepan of simmering water.
7. Serve 2 crêpes per person on a dessert plate.

To prepare the fillings:

- **Ice cream and bananas with butterscotch sauce:** Fill crêpes with 1 scoop of ice cream and half a sliced banana. Drizzle butterscotch sauce over.

- **Strawberry or apple:** Fill with 4 sliced strawberries or 1 dessertspoon of apple stewed with cinnamon. Fold over and serve with whipped cream. Dredge with icing sugar.

Butterscotch sauce

Ingredients
75g brown sugar
50g granulated sugar
50g butter
4 dessertspoons golden syrup
100ml double cream
½ teaspoon vanilla essence

Method

1. Put the sugars, butter and golden syrup into a heavy saucepan. Melt on a low heat. Simmer for 3–5 minutes, stirring all the time.
2. Remove from the heat and gradually stir in the cream and vanilla essence. Return to the heat for 2 minutes.

Top tip: This sauce is very high in calories – serve only occasionally.

Fruit coulis

Ingredients

100g raspberries (fresh, frozen
or tinned)
100g strawberries (fresh, frozen
or tinned)
1 tablespoon lemon juice
1 tablespoon icing sugar

Method

1. Wash the fruit. Put all the ingredients in a food processor or liquidiser. Blend until smooth.
2. Press the mixture through a sieve to remove any seeds.

Top tip: A fruit coulis can be served with almost any dessert: rice pudding, ice cream, bread and butter pudding, pancakes, etc.

Pastry

Shortcrust pastry

Ingredients

200g plain flour
pinch of salt
100g butter or margarine, diced
cold water

Method

1. Sieve the flour and salt into a bowl.
2. Rub the diced butter or margarine into the flour with your fingertips until the mixture looks like breadcrumbs.
3. Add the water with a spoon. Mix with a knife until the pastry comes together in a ball. Do not make it too wet.
4. Wrap in clingfilm and leave to relax in the fridge until needed.

Top tip: Do not handle pastry too much and keep it as cool as possible.

Variations for savoury dishes, such as quiche:

 Wholemeal pastry: Rich in fibre. Use half wholemeal flour and half plain flour.

 Cheese pastry: Add 75g grated cheese and ¼ teaspoon mustard to the basic shortcrust pastry recipe (add before the water).

Rich shortcrust pastry

Ingredients
200g plain flour
pinch of salt
100g butter or margarine, diced
50g icing sugar, sieved
1 egg, beaten
2 dessertspoons cold water
   (approximately)

Method
1. Sieve the flour and salt into a bowl.
2. Rub the diced butter or margarine into the flour with your fingertips until the mixture looks like breadcrumbs. Add the icing sugar.
3. Add the egg and water with a spoon (you may not need all of the water). Mix with a knife until the pastry comes together in a ball. Do not make it too wet – you want a firm dough.
4. Wrap in cling film and leave to relax in the fridge until needed.

Mince pies

Makes 12 pies

Ingredients
200g rich shortcrust pastry (above)
150g mincemeat
1 egg, beaten
icing sugar, to decorate
whipped cream and brandy butter, to serve

Method
1. Preheat the oven to 230°C/fan 220°C/gas 8.
2. Make the rich shortcrust pastry.
3. Roll out two-thirds of the pastry thinly. Cut out 12 circles using a large (6cm) cutter. Place each pastry circle in a lightly greased patty tin. Dampen the edges of the pastry with water.
4. Put 1 teaspoon of mincemeat in each circle (do not put too much in or it will spill out during cooking).
5. Roll out the rest of the pastry. Use a smaller cutter (5cm) to cut out 12 lids. Put a lid on each pie. Seal the edges with your fingers. If the pies are for Christmas, cut out star shapes or holly shapes and place on top.
6. Glaze with the beaten egg.
7. Bake for 8–10 minutes, then reduce the heat to 190°C/fan 180°C/gas 5 and cook for a further 10 minutes.
8. To decorate, sprinkle icing sugar over the pies through a sieve.
9. Place on a round plate with a doyley. Serve with whipped cream or brandy butter.

Top tips:
- If a recipe calls for 200g of pastry, this refers to the amount of flour in the recipe.
- When rolling out pastry, roll lightly in one direction only. Keep turning the pastry to stop it from sticking to the table.

Apple tart

Serves 6

Ingredients

200g shortcrust or rich shortcrust pastry (page 192)

3 medium cooking apples, peeled, cored and sliced

3–4 tablespoons granulated sugar

4–5 cloves or 1 heaped teaspoon ground cinnamon, whichever you prefer

1 egg, beaten

ice cream, whipped cream or custard, to serve

Method

1. Preheat the oven to 230°C/fan 220°C/gas 8.
2. Make the pastry.
3. Divide the pastry in two. Return one half to the fridge while you roll out the other half to fit a greased deep plate or dish. Trim off any excess pastry, cutting away from you all the time.
4. Place the apple slices on top and sprinkle with sugar and cinnamon or cloves. Wet the edges of the pastry with water.
5. Roll out the other pastry half and place on top of the apples. Trim off any excess. Press the pastry firmly together to seal the edges.
6. Brush with the beaten egg and prick a few fork holes on top.
7. Bake for 10 minutes, then reduce the heat to 190°C/fan 180°C/gas 5 for the rest of the cooking time (approximately 30 minutes).
8. Serve with ice cream, whipped cream or custard.

Bread and cakes

Rubbing-in method

White fruit scones

Makes about 9 large scones

Ingredients

600g self-raising flour

2 teaspoons baking powder

110g butter or margarine, diced

80g caster sugar

150g raisins

350ml buttermilk (approximately)

1 egg, beaten for mixture, and a small quantity to glaze

butter and jam, to serve

Method

1. Preheat the oven to 200°C/fan 190°C/gas 6.
2. Sieve the flour and baking powder into a bowl. Rub in the butter or margarine with your fingertips until the mixture looks like breadcrumbs. Add the sugar and raisins.
3. Mix in the beaten egg and buttermilk until you have a soft dough (but not sticky – add more if you have to).
4. Turn the dough out onto a lightly floured board and knead lightly. Roll or flatten out the dough a little until it is about 4cm thick. Do not roll it out too thinly. Using a large scone cutter, cut out 12 or so scones.
5. Place the scones on a lightly greased baking tray. Brush a little beaten egg over the scones to glaze.
6. Bake for 15–20 minutes, until baked through (check that the bottom has browned a little) and golden on top.
7. Cool on a wire rack. Serve warm or cold with butter and jam.

Coconut buns

Makes 10 buns

Ingredients

200g plain flour
1 teaspoon baking powder
pinch of salt
50g butter or margarine, diced
50g caster sugar
50g desiccated coconut
1 egg, beaten
a little milk
2 tablespoons jam, to decorate
2 heaped tablespoons desiccated coconut, to decorate

Method

1. Preheat the oven to 200°C/fan 190°C/gas 6.
2. Sieve the flour, baking powder and salt into a bowl.
3. Rub in the diced butter or margarine with your fingertips until the mixture looks like breadcrumbs. Add the sugar and coconut.
4. Add the egg and enough milk to make a stiff dough.
5. Using a spoon and a fork, pile the mixture into 10 heaps on a greased baking tray.
6. Bake for 20 minutes.
7. To decorate, beat the jam in a small bowl to make it soft. Put the coconut onto a plate. Dip the buns first in jam and then in coconut.

Top tip: Never put tins or dishes on the floor of the oven, as the bottom of the food will burn.

Rock buns

Makes 8–10 buns

Ingredients

200g plain flour

pinch of salt

50g butter or margarine, diced

50g dried fruit

25g mixed peel

25g caster sugar

½ teaspoon mixed spice

1 egg, beaten

a little milk

granulated sugar, to decorate

Method

1. Preheat the oven to 200°C/fan 190°C/gas 6. Grease a patty tin.
2. Sieve the flour and salt into a bowl. Rub in the butter or margarine until the mixture looks like breadcrumbs.
3. Add the dried fruit, mixed peel, caster sugar and mixed spice. Mix well.
4. Add the egg and enough milk to make a stiff dough.
5. Pile into the prepared patty tin. The mixture should make 8–10 cakes.
6. Sprinkle each cake with a little granulated sugar.
7. Bake for 20–25 minutes, until golden. Cool on a wire rack.

Creaming method

Chocolate orange cupcakes (queen cakes)

Ingredients

Cupcakes:

100g caster sugar

100g butter or margarine, softened

2 medium eggs, beaten

zest of 1 large orange and juice of ½ orange

150g self-raising flour (or plain flour with 1 level teaspoon baking powder added)

1 dessertspoon cocoa powder

1 dessertspoon drinking chocolate

Chocolate orange butter icing:

100g icing sugar

zest of 1 large orange

1 dessertspoon drinking chocolate

1 tablespoon orange juice

1 heaped teaspoon cocoa powder

Top tip: Plain queen cakes can be made by leaving out the orange zest, juice, drinking chocolate and cocoa. Add 1 tablespoon of milk and a few drops of vanilla essence instead.

Method

1. Preheat the oven to 200°C/fan 190°C/ gas 6. Line a patty tin with bun cases.

2. Beat the sugar and butter or margarine until it is white and creamy.

3. Add the eggs and orange zest a little at a time, beating well between additions.

4. In a separate bowl, sieve the flour, cocoa and drinking chocolate together. Add to the sugar mixture. Gently stir in the orange juice.

5. Spoon into the bun cases. Bake for about 15 minutes, until golden. To test if the cupcakes are cooked, check the top and bottom of the cake: both should be light brown. Cool on a wire rack.

6. To make the chocolate orange butter icing, put all the ingredients in a bowl and beat until smooth. Icing can be piped onto the top of the cupcakes.

Top tip: A little flour can be added with the egg to stop the egg from curdling.

Note: This mixture can also be made using the all-in one method whereby all ingredients are put in a food processor and mixed at once.

Welsh cheese cakes

Makes 10–12 cakes

Ingredients

Pastry:
100g plain flour
pinch of salt
50g butter or margarine, diced
cold water

Filling:
1–2 tablespoons jam

Madeira mix:
50g caster sugar
50g butter or margarine, softened
1 egg, beaten
75g flour, sieved
1 tablespoon milk
1 drop vanilla essence

Banana bread

Makes 1 loaf

Ingredients
250g plain flour
185g soft brown sugar
150g unsalted butter, softened
2 eggs
2 ripe medium-sized bananas, mashed
2 teaspoons baking powder
1 teaspoon mixed spice

Method
1. Preheat the oven to 190°C/fan 180°C/gas 5. Line a 1lb loaf tin (if you use a silicone tin, you only have to line the bottom).
2. Mix all the ingredients together in a food processor. Pour into the loaf tin. Cover loosely with tin foil.
3. Bake for 45–55 minutes, until golden on top and a skewer pushed into the middle of the cake comes out relatively clean.

Gingerbread men

Makes 20

Ingredients
350g plain flour, plus extra for rolling out
2 teaspoons ground ginger
1 teaspoon ground cinnamon
1 teaspoon bicarbonate of soda
125g butter or margarine
175g light soft brown sugar
1 egg
4 tablespoons golden syrup

To decorate:
glaze icing
cake decorations

Method
1. Sieve together the flour, ginger, cinnamon and bicarbonate of soda and pour into the bowl of a food processor. Add the butter and blend until the mix looks like breadcrumbs. Stir in the sugar.
2. Lightly beat the egg and golden syrup together, add to the food processor and pulse until the mixture clumps together. Tip the dough out, knead briefly until smooth, wrap in cling film and leave to chill in the fridge for 15 minutes.
3. Preheat the oven to 180°C/fan 170°C/gas 4. Line 2 baking trays with greaseproof paper.
4. Roll the dough out to a 0.5cm thickness on a lightly floured surface. Using cookie cutters, cut out the gingerbread men shapes and place on the baking tray, leaving a gap between them.
5. Bake for 12–15 minutes, or until lightly golden brown. Leave on the tray for 10 minutes and then move to a wire rack to finish cooling.
6. When cooled, decorate with the glaze icing and cake decorations.

Method

1. Preheat the oven to 200°C/fan 190°C/ gas 6. Line a patty tin with bun cases.
2. Beat the sugar and butter or margarine until it is white and creamy.
3. Add the eggs and orange zest a little at a time, beating well between additions.
4. In a separate bowl, sieve the flour, cocoa and drinking chocolate together. Add to the sugar mixture. Gently stir in the orange juice.
5. Spoon into the bun cases. Bake for about 15 minutes, until golden. To test if the cupcakes are cooked, check the top and bottom of the cake: both should be light brown. Cool on a wire rack.
6. To make the chocolate orange butter icing, put all the ingredients in a bowl and beat until smooth. Icing can be piped onto the top of the cupcakes.

Top tip: A little flour can be added with the egg to stop the egg from curdling.

Note: This mixture can also be made using the all-in one method whereby all ingredients are put in a food processor and mixed at once.

Welsh cheese cakes

Makes 10–12 cakes

Ingredients
Pastry:
100g plain flour
pinch of salt
50g butter or margarine, diced
cold water

Filling:
1–2 tablespoons jam

Madeira mix:
50g caster sugar
50g butter or margarine, softened
1 egg, beaten
75g flour, sieved
1 tablespoon milk
1 drop vanilla essence

Method

1. Preheat the oven to 200°C/fan 190°C/gas 6. Grease a patty tin.
2. Make the shortcrust pastry as per the instructions on page 192.
3. Roll out the pastry thinly. Cut into 10–12 circles and place them in the greased tin. Put a small amount of jam on each circle.
4. To make the Madeira, beat the sugar and butter or margarine until it is white and creamy.
5. Add the egg a little at a time, beating well between additions.
6. Gently fold in the sieved flour. Mix in the milk and vanilla.
7. Pile 1 large teaspoon of the mix on top of the jam in the patty tin. Smooth with a wet knife to seal the jam in.
8. Roll out the pastry scraps and cut into thin strips. Lay on top of the Madeira mix in a cross shape.
9. Bake for about 15 minutes. Cool on a wire rack.

All-in-one method

All-in-one chocolate cake

Serves 6

Ingredients

175g butter or margarine, softened
175g self-raising flour
175g caster sugar
3 eggs
2 tablespoons drinking chocolate
1 tablespoon boiling water
chocolate butter icing (page 199)

Method

1. Preheat the oven to 180°C/fan 170°C/gas 4.
2. Grease 2 x 18cm sandwich tins. Line the bottom of each with circles of greaseproof paper (or use silicone bakeware).
3. Place all the ingredients in a food processor or bowl and beat until smooth.
4. Divide the mixture between the lined sandwich tins.
5. Bake for 25–30 minutes. Cool on a wire rack.
6. To decorate, sandwich 2 cakes together with chocolate icing. Spread icing on top of the cake. Score the top of the cake with a fork or pipe roses of icing around the edges.

Chocolate butter icing

Ingredients

150g icing sugar, sieved

75g butter or margarine, softened

1 tablespoon drinking chocolate

1 dessertspoon milk

1 teaspoon cocoa

Method

1. Beat all the ingredients together in a bowl until completely smooth.

Simple carrot cake

Serves 6

Ingredients

225g self-raising flour

150g light brown sugar

100g grated carrot

50g walnut pieces

2 ripe bananas, mashed

2 eggs, beaten

150ml sunflower oil

2 teaspoons baking powder

Topping:

100g cream cheese

50g icing sugar, sieved

3 drops vanilla essence

walnut halves, to decorate

Method

1. Preheat the oven to 190°C/fan 180°C/gas 5. Line the bottom of a 1lb loaf tin with a rectangle of greaseproof paper or use silicone bakeware.
2. Mix all the ingredients for the cake together thoroughly. Pour into the tin. Cover loosely with tin foil so that the top doesn't get too crusty.
3. Bake for 50–60 minutes. Cool on a wire rack before decorating.
4. To make the topping, cream the cream cheese, sieved icing sugar and vanilla essence until very smooth. Spread onto the cake. Make lines in it with a fork. Decorate with walnut halves.

Brown bread (wet mix)

Makes 1 loaf

Ingredients

300g plain flour

300g coarse brown flour

2 teaspoons bread soda

500ml buttermilk (approximately)

Method

1. Preheat the oven to 210°C/fan 200°C/gas 6. Grease a 1lb loaf tin or use silicone bakeware.
2. Mix the flours with the bread soda in a large bowl. Add enough buttermilk to make a wet, sticky dough.
3. Pile into the greased loaf tin. Cover loosely with tin foil so that the top doesn't get too crusty.
4. Bake for 1 hour. Wrap the bread in a clean tea towel and allow to cool.

Top tip: Silicone loaf pans are excellent in that they require no greasing and bread will not stick to it.

Banana bread

Makes 1 loaf

Ingredients

250g plain flour
185g soft brown sugar
150g unsalted butter, softened
2 eggs
2 ripe medium-sized bananas, mashed
2 teaspoons baking powder
1 teaspoon mixed spice

Method

1. Preheat the oven to 190°C/fan 180°C/gas 5. Line a 1lb loaf tin (if you use a silicone tin, you only have to line the bottom).
2. Mix all the ingredients together in a food processor. Pour into the loaf tin. Cover loosely with tin foil.
3. Bake for 45–55 minutes, until golden on top and a skewer pushed into the middle of the cake comes out relatively clean.

Gingerbread men

Makes 20

Ingredients

350g plain flour, plus extra for rolling out
2 teaspoons ground ginger
1 teaspoon ground cinnamon
1 teaspoon bicarbonate of soda
125g butter or margarine
175g light soft brown sugar
1 egg
4 tablespoons golden syrup

To decorate:

glaze icing
cake decorations

Method

1. Sieve together the flour, ginger, cinnamon and bicarbonate of soda and pour into the bowl of a food processor. Add the butter and blend until the mix looks like breadcrumbs. Stir in the sugar.
2. Lightly beat the egg and golden syrup together, add to the food processor and pulse until the mixture clumps together. Tip the dough out, knead briefly until smooth, wrap in cling film and leave to chill in the fridge for 15 minutes.
3. Preheat the oven to 180°C/fan 170°C/gas 4. Line 2 baking trays with greaseproof paper.
4. Roll the dough out to a 0.5cm thickness on a lightly floured surface. Using cookie cutters, cut out the gingerbread men shapes and place on the baking tray, leaving a gap between them.
5. Bake for 12–15 minutes, or until lightly golden brown. Leave on the tray for 10 minutes and then move to a wire rack to finish cooling.
6. When cooled, decorate with the glaze icing and cake decorations.

Whisking method

Fresh strawberry sponge cake

Serves 6

Ingredients
4 eggs
100g caster sugar
100g self-raising flour, sieved
1 tablespoon strawberry jam
125ml whipped cream
8 strawberries, sliced

Method

1. Preheat the oven to 190°C/fan 180°C/gas 5. Grease 2 x 18cm sandwich tins. Dust with a mix of caster sugar and flour.
2. Whisk the eggs and sugar until thick and creamy.
3. Gently fold half of the sieved flour into the mixture, then fold in the other half.
4. Divide between the 2 greased tins and bake for 15–20 minutes (see Top tips below). Cool on a wire rack. Fill with the jam, whipped cream and sliced strawberries.

Note: Place a doyley on top of the cake and sprinkle over some icing sugar through a sieve to make a nice pattern.

Top tips:

- If whisking the egg and sugar by hand, place the bowl over a saucepan of hot water – the mixture will whisk more easily.
- To check if a sponge is done, press on it – if it springs back, it is cooked.

Melting method

Ginger snaps

Makes 12–15

Ingredients
100g self-raising flour
1 heaped teaspoon ground ginger
50g butter or margarine
50g granulated sugar
3 dessertspoons golden syrup

Method

1. Preheat the oven to 180°C/fan 170°C/gas 4. Grease a baking tray.
2. Sieve the flour and ginger into a bowl.
3. Gently melt the butter or margarine, sugar and golden syrup in a saucepan. Do not boil. Mix into the flour.
4. Make 12–15 balls of dough. Flatten into biscuit shapes on the greased tray.
5. Bake for 15 minutes. Cool on the tray.

Gingerbread

Makes 24 squares

Ingredients

100g butter or margarine

50g brown sugar

3 tablespoons treacle

150g plain flour

2 heaped teaspoons ground ginger

½ teaspoon mixed spice

½ teaspoon baking powder

1 egg, beaten

100g stewed apple

Method

1. Preheat the oven to 180°C/fan 170°C/gas 4. Grease a large baking tray. Line the bottom with greaseproof paper.
2. Gently melt the butter or margarine, sugar and treacle in a saucepan.
3. Sieve the flour, ginger, mixed spice and baking powder into a bowl. Add the melted ingredients and then stir in the beaten egg and apple.
4. Pour the mixture into the greased baking tray. Bake for 15 minutes.
5. Cut into 24 squares. Remove from the tin and allow to cool on a wire rack.

Brownies

Ingredients

175g butter or margarine

350g caster sugar

2 eggs

1 teaspoon vanilla essence

125g plain flour

50g cocoa

1 level teaspoon baking powder

150g milk chocolate chips

icing sugar, for dusting

cream or ice cream, to serve

Method

1. Preheat the oven to 150°C/140°C fan/gas 2.
2. Melt the butter or margarine in the microwave. Leave it in only for as long as it takes to melt – it is best if it is not too hot. Allow to cool if it is hot.
3. Beat in the sugar, eggs and vanilla essence.
4. Sieve the flour, cocoa and baking powder together in a separate bowl, then mix through. Add the chocolate chips and mix once more.
5. Add the melted margarine, egg and vanilla essence mix through.
6. Transfer the mixture to a square silicone tin or a lined metal tin. The tin should be approximately 23cm x 23cm and about 4cm deep.
7. Bake for 30–35 minutes, until a crust has formed on the top but the centre is still moist.
8. Remove from the oven and allow to stand in the tin for 15 minutes. While still warm, sprinkle with icing sugar and cut into squares.
9. Remove from the baking tin and cool fully on a wire rack, or eat warm with cream or ice cream.

Chocolate chip cookies

Ingredients

100g self-raising flour
50g plain flour
150g milk chocolate chips
100g butter or margarine
100g brown sugar
50g caster sugar
1 egg, beaten
1 teaspoon vanilla essence

Method

1. Set the oven to 160°C/fan 150°C/gas 4. Grease 2 large flat Swiss roll tins.
2. Sieve the flours into a bowl. Add the chocolate chips.
3. Melt the butter or margarine in the microwave or in a bowl set over a saucepan of simmering water (heat it only enough to melt it). Add the sugars, egg and vanilla essence.
4. Add the butter or margarine mix to the flour and chocolate chips. Mix well.
5. Take dessertspoonfuls of the mixture and roll them into balls. Place each ball on the greased tin. Space them out well, as they will flatten out in the oven.
6. Bake for 10–15 minutes. Allow to cool somewhat on the tray, until they firm up a little. Scoop the cookies off the tray using a fish slice. Cool fully on a wire rack.

Unit 2
Consumer Studies

CHAPTER 15
Consumers and Shopping

Key words

- ✓ Goods
- ✓ Services
- ✓ Needs
- ✓ Wants
- ✓ Merchandising
- ✓ Impulse buying
- ✓ Buyer's remorse
- ✓ Environmental impact
- ✓ After-sales service
- ✓ Multiple chain stores
- ✓ Voluntary chain stores
- ✓ Department stores
- ✓ Barcodes
- ✓ Customer loyalty cards
- ✓ Debit card
- ✓ Credit card
- ✓ Loss leader
- ✓ Bulk buying
- ✓ Unit pricing
- ✓ Own brands
- ✓ Branded goods

Learning outcomes

After completing this chapter and the homework, assignments and activities that accompany it, you should:

- Be able to define the word *consumer* and know what goods and services are.
- Be able to differentiate between needs and wants.
- Understand the factors that influence consumer decisions.
- Understand what the terms *impulse buying* and *buyer's remorse* mean.
- Know what factors should be considered when buying a product.
- Be able to list the main sources of consumer information.
- Be able to describe modern shopping trends.
- Be able to list and give examples of the different types of shops.
- Describe guidelines for grocery shopping that can help prevent overspending.
- Know what barcodes and customer loyalty cards are and the advantages and disadvantages of them for you and for the retailer.
- Be able to describe the different ways we can pay for goods and services and the advantages and disadvantages of each.
- Know what the following retail terms mean: *loss leader*, *bulk buying*, *unit pricing* and *own brands*.
- Be able to describe and understand the methods used by supermarkets to encourage you to spend more.

What is a consumer?

A consumer is someone who buys or uses goods and services.

Goods and services

Goods: Things

Books, CDs, cigarettes, clothes, computer games, drinks, food, heating, lighting, mobile phones, sweets, toiletries (such as shampoo).

Services: People who do something for you

Bin collection, dentists, doctors, education, gardaí, hairdressers, postal services, public parks, public transport, roads, street lighting, taxis.

Many services provided by the state, such as education and the gardaí, are paid for indirectly through taxation.

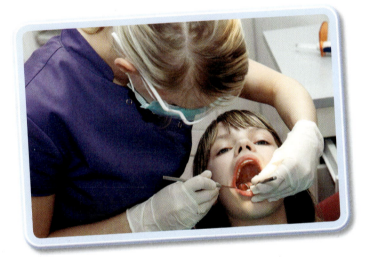

Needs and wants

Needs are *essential* goods and services. Examples of needs are food, clothes, shelter, doctors and dentists.

Wants are *non-essential* goods and services. Examples of wants are takeaways, cars, designer clothes, jewellery, beauticians and hairdressers.

Nowadays, the line between what is a need and what is a want has become blurred. For example, many people would consider having a car to be a need, yet 40 years ago, very few people had cars. In developing countries today, a car is most definitely a want.

Whether something is considered a need or a want will depend on the consumer's age, their circumstances (how well off they are) and their values (what is important to them).

In a family where money is tight, debts build up when wants are bought before needs are paid for, for example buying a wide-screen TV (non-essential) when the electricity bill (essential) has not been paid or spending money on alcohol and cigarettes (non-essential) when there is no food (essential) in the house.

Shopping

Shopping is part of our lives, something we do to meet our basic needs and wants. What exactly we buy, however, will depend on a number of factors.

Factors that influence consumer decisions

- **Resources (time and money):** During the Celtic Tiger years, Ireland saw a massive increase in consumer spending due to increased money in the economy. People did not spend much time making consumer decisions because many were cash rich and time poor. More recent times have seen a reversal of this trend – people have less money and more time, so we are once again thinking more before we buy something.

- **Peer pressure:** You want what other people your age have.

- **Fashion trends:** For example, Converse runners have been fashionable over the past number of years. 30 years ago Converse runners were on the market but were cheap and not considered at all fashionable.

- **Advertising:** Advertisements try to make us feel that if we have this product, our life will be better in some way.

- **Personal values:** A golfer who spends €650 on one golf club may be thought of as mad by non-golfers, for example.

- **Culture:** We buy certain things at particular times of year, like a Christmas tree in December.

- **Merchandising:** Retailers have to come up with ways to encourage you to buy, especially when money is tight, such as interest-free credit or discounts – this is merchandising.

Making wise consumer decisions

When we buy things on the spur of the moment without thinking, it is called **impulse buying**. Goods and services bought in this way are often bad buys and ones we often regret. This regret is called **buyer's remorse**. When buying goods and services, it is better to think carefully before we buy. Below are some of the factors that should be considered.

Factors to be considered when choosing a product

- **Money:** Can I afford it?
- **Value:** Shop around and compare similar products in different shops.
- **Quality:** Is the product made from good-quality materials? Does it have any quality symbols on it?
- **Suitability:** Will it do the job you want it to? For example, hill-walking boots need to be waterproof.
- **Durability:** Will it last (for example, carpets, shoes)?
- **Design:** Is it nice to look at and well finished?
- **Safety:** Look for safety symbols, especially on children's toys and electrical goods.
- **Brand name:** It is often safer to buy well-known, reliable brands, for example washing machines.
- **Environmental impact:** Is the product environmentally friendly?

🛒 **After-sales service:** Will the shop fix the product if it breaks?

🛒 **Maintenance:** Is the product easy to look after and keep clean?

🛒 **Size and comfort:** Are goods such as clothes and shoes well-fitting and comfortable?

Sources of consumer information

Sometimes when we buy particular goods or services we are asked where we heard about them. Below are common sources of consumer information about goods and services.

🛒 Newspaper and magazine articles

🛒 Advertisements

🛒 Word of mouth

🛒 Manufacturers' brochures and leaflets

🛒 In the shop (salespeople inform us) or we get information about products by looking at them ourselves

🛒 Text alerts

🛒 Internet

Shopping trends

How we shop has changed dramatically over the past 20 years. There has been:

🛒 A decrease in the number of counter service shopping (corner shops)

🛒 An increase in self-service shopping (supermarkets)

🛒 An increase in the number of shopping centres

🛒 Increased late opening and Sunday shopping (some shops are open 24 hours)

🛒 Better facilities for shoppers (crèche, parking, cafés)

🛒 An increase in online shopping

Self-service vs. counter service

Self-service

Advantages	Disadvantages
• Quick • Products are cheaper, especially own brands, such as Euroshopper and St Bernard • Good choice • High turnover means goods are fresh • Time is available to study and compare goods to make informed decisions	• Less personal • Impulse buying is more likely • Sometimes crowded, with long queues at checkouts • Often on the outskirts of town, so a car is needed

Counter service

Advantages	Disadvantages
● Personal, friendly service. This is particularly important for those living alone, such as the elderly. ● Nearby – great for those without a car or if you need to pop out for something, like milk ● Some pack and deliver groceries ● Some give credit	● Can be slow ● Less choice ● Slower turnover so goods may not be as fresh as supermarket products ● More expensive

Types of shops

Multiple chain stores

These are large self-service shops. Branches are all owned by the same company. Examples include Hollister, Abercrombie & Fitch, Superdry, Dunnes Stores, Penneys, Marks & Spencer, Tesco, Next and A-Wear.

Voluntary chain stores

An individual shop owner can apply and pay to be part of a voluntary chain, such as Spar, Centra, Londis, Valuland or SuperValu.

Independent shops

Traditionally family-run shops, usually open till late and on Sundays. Limited choice of goods, but personal service.

Specialist shops

Usually sell only one type of product, such as shoes or cameras. A boutique specialises in expensive clothes.

Department stores

Very large shops divided into different departments (household, ladies' fashions, gifts, sportswear). Each department has its own sales staff with good product knowledge. Examples of department stores are Clerys, Arnotts, Brown Thomas and House of Fraser.

Other

● Shopping online
● Discount stores – these may also be voluntary chains, such as Valuland
● Mail order shopping, such as Family Album
● Markets
● Auctions

Grocery shopping guidelines

1. Make a list:
   - Check what is in the house already.
   - Plan meals for the week.
   - Write up a list and be as accurate as possible. For example, write '4 tomatoes' rather than just 'tomatoes'.
   - Group similar items together. For example, list all fruit and vegetables together, as these are found together in the supermarket.
2. Stick to the list and avoid impulse buying.
3. Shop around for good value.
4. Try not to shop too often, as you will end up spending more.
5. Bulk buy for items such as washing powder, toilet rolls, etc. because it is cheaper.
6. Check expiry dates for freshness.
7. Avoid shopping when you are tired or hungry.
8. Bring shopping bags.

Shopping technology

Supermarkets today use various types of technology to make their service quicker and more efficient. For example:

- Self-service weighing scales that print the product label
- Computerised checkouts that scan **barcodes** and then print **itemised receipts**
- Self-service checkouts

Self-service checkout

Barcodes

A barcode is a series of lines and spaces that are read by a scanner attached to a computerised cash register.

ISBN 978-0-7171-4671-0

Advantages and disadvantages of barcodes

- An itemised receipt allows customers to see exactly what was bought.
- Quick stock control – once an item is scanned, a central stock control computer records that there is one less of that item on the shelves. When stocks of the item get to a certain level, the computer reorders the product automatically.
- Goods are not individually priced.

Customer loyalty cards

Some large chains offer **customer loyalty cards**, such as the Tesco Clubcard or the SuperValu Real Rewards card. The card is swiped every time you shop and you build up points towards various 'gifts'.

The advantage for the shop is that they have your name and address together with a complete record of everything you have ever bought in the store. This information can then be used for marketing purposes.

For example, say a supermarket has a consignment of a particular brand of Bolognese sauce that is not selling well. They see that you buy Bolognese sauce weekly and they send you money-off coupons to encourage you to buy the brand they want to get rid of instead of your normal brand.

Methods of payment
Cash

Cash is still the most common method of payment today. Some large supermarkets have ATM machines in-store for customers to withdraw cash. PASS and BankLink are examples of ATM cards. The main advantage of using cash is that you are less likely to overspend and get into debt. Carrying cash is not very secure, however. If it is lost or stolen, there is nothing you can do about it.

Cheque and cheque card

Customers can write a cheque if they have a cheque guarantee card (which is normally combined with a debit card). The card guarantees the retailer that the cheque will not bounce. Cheque cards usually cover cheques up to €130. This is a secure payment method, but there is a risk of overspending. This is no longer a commonly used method of payment. Banks have a charge per cheque cashed.

SuperValu
Real Food, Real People

LUCAN
Telephone – 01 6240277
Manager
Ian Smith
Served by Bronagh

100% WHOLEMEAL	€1.99
* CAJUN SALMON	€4.99
* CARROT BAG	€0.99
HADDOCK FILLETS	€4.49
* HONEY RST HAM	€3.49
K/MAID D/SPRD	€2.09
KELLOGGS BARS	€2.00
LOOSE CUCUMBER	
2 pc at €0.69 each	€1.38
* MED WHT CHEESE	€3.00
NY BAGELS	€1.90
PHILADELPHIA REG	€1.50
* POTATOES	€2.38
PUNNET PEAR	
2 pc at €1.99 each	€3.98
* SQUINN SAUSAGE	€2.99
* SUPERVALU LIGHT MILK	€2.19
SV APPLE TRAY	€1.99
* SV BUTTON MSHR	€1.19
SV GREEN BEANS	€1.79
* SV TURKEY BREAST	€3.00
Base promo	
>>>>>>>>>>>>>	73 Points

SUB-TOTAL   €48.12

####################################
TODAY YOU EARNED   73 POINTS
####################################

Reward Card
Offering more Rewards

####################################

SUB-TOTAL	€48.12
CRM Voucher	€11.00
EURO CASH	€70.00
CHANGE	€32.88
HOUSEHOLD	
Reward Number	1234567
PREVIOUS BALANCE	506
New Points Balance	579
Promotion Value	

SuperValu Promotions this week
Saved you €2.16

Number of items	22
Value of Irish Purchases	€24.22

6804 0014/004/191   05.03.15 17:08 AC-04
THIS WEEK'S BEEF FARMER IN LUCAN

#########################

DAVID MURPHY
GOULACULLIN, DUNAWAY,
CO. CORK

#########################

An itemised receipt

Debit card (Laser)

The card is swiped or inserted into the card terminal and the amount is entered. The consumer checks the amount and enters their PIN number. The amount is processed and taken from the cardholder's bank account within a number of days. It is possible to get cash back. Laser cards are secure and convenient, but it is easy to overspend because you are not physically handing over cash.

Credit card (Visa, MasterCard)

The card is swiped or inserted into the card terminal and the amount is entered. The consumer checks the amount and enters their PIN number. The amount is processed and it goes onto a bill. The bill can be paid in part or in full every month. No interest is charged if the bill is paid in full. As with debit cards, credit cards are secure and convenient and they can be used for online or over-the-phone purchases. However, it is easy to overspend because you are not handling cash – you can forget how much you have put on a bill and get a nasty surprise at the end of the month.

Shopping terms

- **Bulk buying:** Buying a product in large quantities. This is cheaper as long as you use it all.

- **Loss leader:** These are goods sold off cheaply by the retailer. It is hoped that these will lead you into the shop, where you will then buy more.

- **Own brands:** Own brands are plainly packaged products, for example St Bernard, Euroshopper. They are often good quality and much cheaper than branded products, such as Lyons Tea.

- **Unit pricing:** Goods are priced per unit, for example per kilogram. Meat, fruit and vegetables are often priced in this way. Sometimes the tags on shelves show the unit price of goods, such as the price of flour, sugar, etc., so that consumers can compare the actual prices of products.

Ways supermarkets encourage you to buy

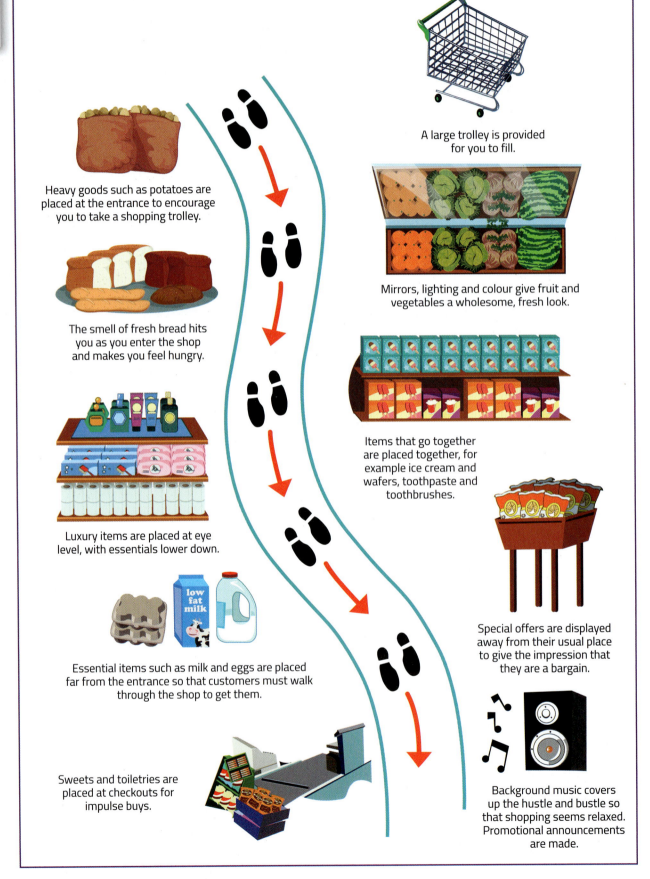

A large trolley is provided for you to fill.

Heavy goods such as potatoes are placed at the entrance to encourage you to take a shopping trolley.

The smell of fresh bread hits you as you enter the shop and makes you feel hungry.

Mirrors, lighting and colour give fruit and vegetables a wholesome, fresh look.

Luxury items are placed at eye level, with essentials lower down.

Items that go together are placed together, for example ice cream and wafers, toothpaste and toothbrushes.

Essential items such as milk and eggs are placed far from the entrance so that customers must walk through the shop to get them.

Special offers are displayed away from their usual place to give the impression that they are a bargain.

Sweets and toiletries are placed at checkouts for impulse buys.

Background music covers up the hustle and bustle so that shopping seems relaxed. Promotional announcements are made.

1. A **consumer** is someone who buys **goods** (things) and uses **services** (such as a dentist).

2. **Needs** are essential (food). **Wants** are non-essential (takeaways).

3. **Factors that influence consumer decisions:** Resources (time and money), peer pressure, fashion trends, advertising, personal values, culture (Christmas trees) and merchandising (ways retailers encourage you to buy).

4. **Impulse buying** means buying without thinking it through. It often leads to **buyer's remorse** (regret).

5. **Factors to be considered when buying a product:** Money available, value (shop around), quality, suitability, durability (will a garment lose its shape after the first wash?), design and finish, safety, brand name, environmental impact, after-sales service, maintenance, size and comfort (shoes).

6. **Sources of consumer information:** Newspaper and magazine articles, advertisements, word of mouth, manufacturers' brochures, salespeople, internet, text alerts.

7. **Shopping trends:** Decrease in counter service, increase in self-service, increase in shopping centres, Sunday and later opening hours, better facilities for shoppers, increased internet shopping.

8. **Types of shops:** Multiple chain, voluntary chain, independent, specialist, department stores, other (internet, discount, mail order, markets, auctions).

9. **Grocery shopping guidelines:** Check what is in the house already. Plan meals for the week. Write an accurate list and stick to it. Don't shop too often. Bulk buy some items (toilet rolls). Check expiry dates. Don't shop when you are tired or hungry. Bring shopping bags.

10. **Barcodes:** A series of lines and spaces read by a scanner. They print an itemised receipt and allow easy stock control.

11. **Methods of payment:** Cash, cheque and card, debit card, credit card.

12. **Shopping terms:** Bulk buying, loss leader, own brands, unit pricing.

13. **How supermarkets encourage spending:** Heavy goods and trolleys are placed at the entrance. Fresh bread is placed near the entrance. Mirrors and lighting make fruit and vegetables look fresher. Luxury items are at eye level, essentials are lower down. Items that go together are placed together (toothpaste, toothbrushes and mouthwash). Special offers are displayed away from their normal place to give a 'bargain' impression. Essential items are at the far end of the shop. Items are placed at checkouts for impulse buys. Music makes the atmosphere more relaxed.

1. What is a consumer? Name four goods that you buy regularly. Name four services that you use/buy regularly. What is the difference between a need and a want in relation to being a consumer?

2. Describe six factors that can influence consumer decisions.

3. What is impulse buying? What is meant by buyer's remorse?

4. Outline six factors that should be considered when buying a product.

5. List six sources of consumer information.

6. Explain four shopping trends that have occurred in recent years.

7. List three advantages and disadvantages of (a) counter service and (b) self-service shopping.

8. Name four different types of shopping outlets and give an example of each.

9. Outline six shopping guidelines that should be followed.

10. What are barcodes? Give one advantage and one disadvantage of them.

11. What is an itemised receipt?

12. What are customer loyalty cards? What advantage do they have for the shop?

13. Explain six methods that supermarkets use to encourage you to buy more.

14. Describe four methods that can be used to pay for goods.

15. What do each of the following terms mean? (a) Loss leader (b) Bulk buying (c) Unit pricing (d) Own brand

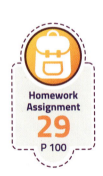

Homework Assignment
29
P 100

Teacher's CD Slide presentation • Student activity pack with revision crossword • Class test • Student learning contract

Key words

- Advertising techniques
- Classified advertisement
- Legal control of advertising
- Voluntary control of advertising
- Marketing
- Market research

Learning outcomes

After completing this chapter and the homework, assignments and activities that accompany it, you should:

- Be able to list where companies advertise, describe the characteristics of an effective advertisement and list the functions of advertising.
- Be able to describe the seven basic advertising techniques used by companies.
- Know what a classified advertisement is.
- Be able to describe the advantages and disadvantages of advertising and describe how advertisements are controlled (both by law and by the industry itself).
- Be able to define marketing and market research and understand their importance.

Advertising

Advertising is a feature of modern life. We are constantly exposed to it through:

- TV and radio
- Newspapers and magazines
- Cinema and DVDs
- The internet (emails and sponsored links on search engines)

- Billboards and bus shelters
- Buses and trains
- Sports grounds and sports sponsorship
- Direct mail and text messaging
- Social media sites such as Facebook
- Carrier bags, logos on clothing, etc.

An effective advertisement must:
- Catch your attention
- Make you want the product
- Persuade you to go out and buy the product

Functions of advertising

- To introduce a new product to the market
- To provide information on products, such as what they do
- To increase sales
- To make people familiar with a brand or logo

Advertising techniques

There are **seven** basic advertising techniques used by companies to encourage you to buy their products.

Advertising techniques	

1. **Humour** catches your attention.

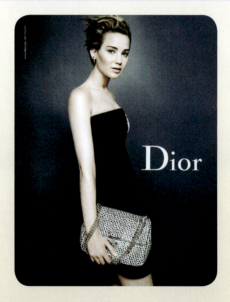

2. **Glamour and romance:** 'If you buy this product, you too can look like this/find romance.'

3. Traditional, wholesome images: 'This product is healthy.'

4. Happy family images: 'This product will make your family happy and healthy.' What do you think the image is advertising?

5. Famous personalities: Well-known people are used to promote products.

6. Slogans: 'I'm lovin' it.'

7. Statistics: 'Nine out of 10 cats prefer it.' The Advertising Standards Authority is clamping down on slogans like this, though, as they can be misleading. Colgate has been asked not to use their famous slogan 'eight out of every 10 dentists prefer it' because it is misleading – the reality is that eight out of every 10 dentists recommend Colgate, but not ahead of other brands.

Classified advertisements

Classifieds are ads placed in newspapers and magazines. They are used to sell goods such as cars and furniture, to let and sell property, etc.

PETS

ABANDONED ANIMALS need kind homes for Labrador (f) 1 yr. spayed; puppy, 12 weeks (m) house-trained, lovely nature; Border Collie (m) 2 yrs; kittens and young adult cats. Tel: 123-4567

LOVING HOMES wanted for Whippet (m) 4 yrs; black & white Cocker Spaniel (f) 6 yrs; Bloodhound (m) 5 yrs. All dogs very loving with excellent temperaments. Foster homes and fundraisers urgently needed. Tel: 345-6789

PET RESCUE urgently need kind homes for Dalmatian (m) 7 yrs, owner deceased; pair of gentle Collies (f) 2 yrs; German Shepherd (m) 3 yrs, house-trained; Sable Terrier (f) 1 yr, owner deceased; King Charles Spaniel (f) 10 months, very gentle; Long-haired Lurcher (like Wolfhound) (f) 2–3 yrs; black Setter type (f) 6 mths; tri-coloured Terrier (f) 2 yrs; affectionate and needy cats and kittens – all colours. Tel: 234-5678

Advantages and disadvantages of advertising

Advantages	Disadvantages
• Provides information • Creates jobs in advertising • Creates jobs in factories and shops because of increased sales • Keeps the cost of TV, newspapers and magazines down	• Heavily advertised goods are often expensive, such as Apple iPods • Encourages people to want only famous brand names • Encourages overspending • Sometimes stereotypical images are used, such as women being really concerned that their whites are white • Spoils the landscape (billboards) • Interrupts TV viewing

Advertising control

Because everyone in our society is exposed to advertising, it must be controlled. Advertising is controlled by the law and by the industry itself (voluntary control).

The law

- **The EU Misleading Advertising Regulations:** These can prevent the publication of misleading advertisements.
- **Consumer Information Act, 1978:** Advertisements must be truthful.
- **Employment Equality Act:** Protects against discrimination, such as 'single female required for busy restaurant'.

Voluntary control

Advertisers are encouraged by the Advertising Standards Authority to produce ads that are legal, decent, honest and truthful.

Marketing

Nowadays, marketing plays a big part in industry. Marketing is about finding out consumers' wants and needs and finding ways to satisfy them.

Market research means gathering information about consumers' likes, dislikes, wants and needs. Information is gathered by questionnaires, phone interviews and through the use of loyalty cards, etc.

Marketing is... finding out customers' wants and needs and satisfying them.

Case study

Through market research, Pepsi-Cola found that both males and females were concerned with the high levels of sugar in soft drinks. Males, however, were unwilling to be seen as 'wimps' by drinking diet drinks. Pepsi overcame this by creating a diet drink with a macho image: Pepsi Max.

1. **Advertisements:** Ads are a feature of modern life. To be effective, they must catch your attention, make you want the product and make you go out and buy it. Functions: To introduce new products, provide information, increase sales or familiarise people with a brand or logo.

2. **Advertising techniques:** Humour, glamour/romance, wholesome traditional images, happy family images, use of famous people, slogans, statistics.

3. **Advantages/disadvantages**
   - **Advantages:** Provides information, creates jobs, keeps cost of newspapers/magazines/TV/radio down.
   - **Disadvantages:** Encourages people to want only famous, heavily advertised brands, overspending, sometimes stereotypical images are used, spoils the landscape (billboards), interrupts TV and radio programmes.

4. **Advertising control:** By law: EU Misleading Advertisements Regulations, Consumer Information Act, 1978, Employment Equality Act. Advertising Standards Authority encourages voluntary control.

5. **Marketing:** Finding out consumers' wants and needs and finding ways to satisfy them. **Market research** is gathering information.

1. Name six different places where you find advertising. List the four functions of advertising.
2. Describe four advertising techniques. Name a product that uses each technique.
3. Where would you find a classified advertisement? Name four products or services commonly advertised in this way.
4. List four advantages of advertising.
5. List four disadvantages of advertising.
6. Define the term *marketing*.
7. What is market research?

Test Yourself
eTest.ie

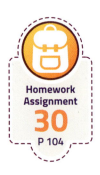

Homework
Assignment
30
P 104

CHAPTER 17

Consumer Protection and Making a Complaint

Teacher's CD

Slide presentation ▪ Student activity pack with revision crossword ▪ Class test ▪ Student learning contract

Key words

- ✔ Consumer rights
- ✔ Redress
- ✔ Monopoly
- ✔ Consumer responsibilities
- ✔ Ombudsman
- ✔ Legal contract
- ✔ Guarantee
- ✔ Competition and Consumer Protection Commission
- ✔ Consumers' Association
- ✔ Trade organisations
- ✔ Small claims court

Learning outcomes

After completing this chapter and the homework, assignments and activities that accompany it, you should:

- Understand the five basic consumer rights: choice, quality, information, redress and safety.
- Be able to explain the responsibilities you have as a consumer.
- Understand what a sales contract is and who it is between.
- Be able to describe the following consumer laws and understand the implications each has for you, the consumer: the Sale of Goods and Supply of Services Act, 1980 and the Consumer Information Act, 1978.
- Know how to effectively make a complaint in person and in writing.
- Be able to name and describe the function of both statutory and voluntary agencies that offer consumer information and advice.
- Know what the function of the small claims court is and how to make a small claim.

Consumer rights

As consumers, we have **five** basic rights. A right is something you are entitled to.

The right to choice
This means having a wide variety of goods and services to choose from. Having choice means that manufacturers must produce high-quality goods or they will not sell.

The right to information
This means that information written on goods or about services must be true. For example, if a chair is labelled 'genuine leather', it must be leather.

The right to redress
- Repair (item is fixed free of charge)
- Replacement (for example, a new pair of shoes)
- Refund (money back)

The right to quality
Goods must be able to do what they are meant to do and be of good quality. Manufacturers usually test goods for quality before they leave the factory. This is called **quality control**.

The right to safety
Goods and services must be safe for consumers to use. Electrical items, children's clothes and toys must follow strict safety rules. Dangerous goods, such as bleach, must carry warning symbols.

A **monopoly** is when only one company provides a good or service, such as Iarnród Éireann. What is the disadvantage of monopolies?

Consumer responsibilities

Your rights as a consumer are listed above. As a consumer, you also have responsibilities. You should:

- Be well informed about the products you are buying and your consumer rights.
- Examine products and services carefully before you buy.
- Read instructions and labels. Heed warnings.
- Use products only for the use intended. For example, if you use a Brillo pad to clean a non-stick frying pan, you would have no comeback.
- Shop around for value for money and avoid unnecessary waste.

Consumer law

Consumers are protected in three ways:

- The law
- Government organisations, such as the Ombudsman and the Competition and Consumer Protection Commission
- Voluntary organisations, such as the Consumers' Association of Ireland

Contract

When you buy something in a shop or pay for a service, a **legal contract** is formed between you (the buyer) and the seller, for example the shopkeeper or plumber. The contract **is not** between you and the manufacturer of the goods, for example Tommy Hilfiger.

The two most important consumer laws are:

- The Sale of Goods and Supply of Services Act, 1980
- The Consumer Information Act, 1978

The Sale of Goods and Supply of Services Act, 1980

Under this Act, goods must:

- **Be of merchantable quality:** This means they should be fit for sale and not faulty.
- **Be fit for their purpose:** For example, you should be able to walk in a pair of shoes without them falling apart.
- **Be as described:** For example, if a food product is labelled 'gluten-free', it should be so.
- **Correspond to (be the same as) samples:** For example, if you pick out a particular model of bathroom suite in a shop, the suite delivered to your house should be the same as the sample.

Under this Act, services, such as plumbing and hairdressing, must:

- Be carried out by someone with the necessary skills to do the job properly.
- Be carried out with care.
- Use good-quality materials. For example, a restaurant should use quality ingredients to make the food they serve.

If goods or services are faulty, you are entitled to compensation – that is, a repair, replacement or refund.

Services must be carried out with care and skill

This Act does not cover you if:

- The fault was pointed out to you before the sale, for example goods reduced in price and marked as **seconds** or **imperfect**.
- You misuse the goods.
- There is no fault and you simply change your mind (though some shops will exchange goods anyway).

Slightly imperfect wallpaper €5 per roll

The Consumer Information Act, 1978

This Act states that information or claims made about goods and services must be true. The Act covers information in advertisements, on packaging, on shop notices and given by shop salespeople. False claims about the prices of goods are also illegal under this Act (this includes present, previous and recommended retail prices).

Examples of claims made about goods and services

100% wool

Guaranteed Irish

1-hour repairs

Costa del Sol apartment to let, 3 mins from beach

Immaculate 3-year-old Toyota Avensis, only 23,000km

Breaches of the Consumer Information Act should be notified to the Competition and Consumer Protection Commission.

A guarantee

A guarantee is a promise made to you by the manufacturers of the goods you buy. The guarantee, which must be written, usually states that the goods, if faulty, will be replaced or repaired free of charge. There is usually a time limit on the guarantee, for example one year. Guarantees are in addition to, not instead of, your rights under consumer law.

No cash refunds.	Credit notes only.	No exchange on sale items.

No receipt, no refund!

Notices like these are illegal if they refer to the refund or exchange of **faulty goods**. Remember, if you simply change your mind about an item, the shop does not have to refund your money or exchange the item.

Making a complaint

From time to time, we all buy goods that turn out to be faulty. Knowing how to make a complaint effectively makes the experience better and less stressful for all involved.

When you first notice a fault:
- Stop using the goods.
- Find your receipt.
- Know your rights.
- Make your complaint to the shop where you bought the goods as soon as possible.

Remember: The shop where you bought the goods, and not the manufacturer, should deal with your complaint.

At the shop
- Ask for the customer services manager, or in a small shop, the manager.
- Calmly explain what is wrong.
- State exactly what you want done, such as a repair, refund or replacement.
- If you get no satisfaction, ask for the name of the managing director of the company, leave the shop and put the complaint in writing.

Remember! No claim if:

🛒 The fault was pointed out at the time of purchase.

🛒 You abused the goods.

🛒 You simply changed your mind and there is no actual fault.

Writing a letter of complaint

Write or type a neat letter to the managing director of the company.

Customer address

11 Highlands
Clones
Co. Monaghan

Company address

Mr James Callaghan
Callaghan Sports
Main Street
Clones
Co. Monaghan

23 September 2015

Dear Mr Callaghan,

Details of:
- Exactly what you bought
- Where you bought it
- State that you are enclosing a copy of the receipt

I wish to make a complaint about a pair of Nike Airforce 1 Low iD runners that I purchased in your shop on Main Street on 1 September last. Please find attached a copy of my receipt.

Clear details of the complaint

After wearing the runners on just three occasions, the sole began to separate from the upper and I was unable to wear them. As the runners were not badly treated, the fault is most certainly with them. I returned the runners to your Clones branch, but your shop assistant was unable to help me.

Details of action you would like taken

It is quite clear that there was a fault in the runners when I bought them. I would like a refund for the total amount of €135.

Yours sincerely,

Anna Tuite

Wait a couple of weeks for a reply. You could then follow up with a phone call. If you still get no satisfaction, you may wish to go to the small claims court or to one of the following organisations for further advice.

Agencies that provide consumer information and advice

Statutory (government-run) agencies

The Ombudsman

The Office of the Ombudsman deals with complaints against government-run organisations, such as the HSE or An Post. Complain to the organisation itself first – only complain to the Ombudsman as a last resort.

Office of the Ombudsman
Oifig an Ombudsman

Competition and Consumer Protection Commission

The Competition and Consumer Protection Commission (CCPC) was established by the government in October 2014 to replace the National Consumer Agency.

The CCPC:

- Enforces consumer laws
- Helps control the advertising industry
- Promotes consumer awareness
- Controls safety and labelling of food and textiles

consumerhelp.ie

Non-statutory (voluntary) agencies

Consumers' Association of Ireland

- Advises consumers
- Provides consumer information, such as teachers' packs and leaflets
- Has an information website
- Produces a monthly consumer magazine called *Consumer Choice* that gives unbiased information on goods and services currently on the market

Trade organisations

Some groups of businesspeople, such as auctioneers (MIAVI) and publicans (Vintners Association), come together to form a trade organisation. These organisations develop codes of good practice for their members and will deal with complaints.

RESTAURANTS ASSOCIATION
OF IRELAND

Small claims court

To make a complaint in the small claims court, you must fill in an application form from the small claims registrar in your local district court. The small claims court deals with claims up to the value of €2,000.

Rapid Revision

1. **Consumer rights:** Choice, quality, information, redress (repair, replacement or refund) and safety.
2. **Monopoly:** When only one company supplies a good or service.
3. **Consumer responsibilities:** Be well informed. Examine products before purchase. Follow instructions and warnings. Use goods only for the use intended. Shop around for value.
4. **Contract:** When you buy goods and services, you enter into a legally binding contract with the retailer, not the manufacturer.
5. **Sale of Goods and Supply of Services Act, 1980:** Goods must be of merchantable quality, fit for purpose, as described and correspond to samples. Services must be carried out with skill and care and use quality materials. The Act does not cover you if the fault was pointed out before sale, product misuse, no fault or you change your mind.
6. **Consumer Information Act, 1978:** Claims made about goods and services must be true.
7. **A guarantee:** A promise by the manufacturer to replace or repair goods if they become faulty within a certain timeframe. A guarantee is in addition to your rights under consumer law.
8. **Notices:** No cash refunds, credit notes only, no exchange on sale items, no receipt, no refund, illegal if they refer to faulty goods.
9. **Complaints about faulty goods:** First complain in person – come prepared, have your receipt, calmly explain what is wrong and state exactly what you want done (such as a refund). Put your complaint in writing if you get no satisfaction.
10. **Letter of complaint:** Address and date the letter. Explain what you bought and enclose a copy of the receipt. Give exact details of the complaint and state what action you would like taken.
11. **Consumer agencies**
    *   **Statutory:** The ombudsman (complaints about government-run agencies) and Competition and Consumer Protection Commission (enforces consumer laws, controls advertising, promotes consumer awareness, controls safety and labelling of goods).
    *   **Voluntary:** Consumers' Association of Ireland (gives advice and information), trade organisations develop codes of practice for their members.
12. **Small claims court:** Deals with claims under €2,000. You can get applications from the local district court.

1. Describe five basic consumer rights and four consumer responsibilities.

2. What is a monopoly? Give an example of one in Ireland.

3. Name the three ways consumers are protected.

4. In relation to buying goods and services, what is a contract? Who is the contract between?

5. Describe the Sale of Goods and Supply of Services Act, 1980.

6. What is a guarantee?

7. Describe the Consumer Information Act, 1978.

8. Who should be notified regarding breaches of the Consumer Information Act?

9. What should you do when you first notice a fault in something you have purchased?

10. When you are returning to the shop with faulty goods, what should you do?

11. Outline what should be included in a letter of complaint about faulty goods.

12. Name and describe the function of one statutory agency dealing with consumer issues.

13. Name and describe the function of one non-statutory agency dealing with consumer issues.

14. What is the procedure for going to the small claims court? Claims going to the court cannot exceed a certain amount – what is this amount?

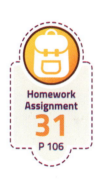

Homework Assignment
31
P 106

Teacher's CD

Slide presentation ▪ Student activity pack with revision crossword ▪ Class test ▪ Student learning contract

Key words

- ✓ Quality marks
- ✓ Quality control
- ✓ Product labelling
- ✓ Care labels
- ✓ Safety symbols
- ✓ Warning symbols

Learning outcomes

After completing this chapter and the homework, assignments and activities that accompany it, you should:

- Understand the term *quality control* and be able to identify a range of quality and standard marks.
- Be able to describe the characteristics of a good service.
- Know what information product labels should carry.
- Be able to identify a range of safety and warning symbols and understand what each means.
- Be able to describe the functions, types and disadvantages of packaging.

Quality of goods

The term **quality** describes the standard of goods and services. Before goods leave a factory, they are examined and tested to ensure that they reach a certain set standard. This is called **quality control**.

The quality and standard marks on the next page are awarded to goods and services that are of a good quality or standard. These marks will be on the goods themselves or on their box or label.

Quality and standard marks

This **Quality Mark** is awarded to Irish companies for quality goods and services. It can be withdrawn if standards drop.

The **Guaranteed Irish** symbol is awarded to high-quality goods made in Ireland.

The **Irish Standards Mark** can be found on any product that has been certified to an Irish standard.

The **European Standards Mark** is awarded by the EU to goods that have reached a high standard of safety. It is found on children's toys, clothes, buggies, electrical goods, etc.

The **BSI Kite Mark** is awarded by the British Standards Institution (BSI) to goods and services, such as crash helmets, garage servicing and repairs, to show they have been independently assessed and meet appropriate standards of safety and performance, etc.

Quality of services

A good-quality **service** will have:

- Friendly staff who know what they are doing
- Clean, well laid-out premises
- Wheelchair access
- Little queuing or waiting
- Clean toilet facilities

Product labelling

Product labels should give you the following information:

- Quality symbol
- Warnings about the dangers of misuse
- Name and address of the manufacturer
- Description of product, what it is made from, weight, colour, number of items, etc.
- Instructions for use, care and cleaning

Product safety

Product safety is concerned with two things:

☙ The safety of the user of the product

☙ That the product itself is not destroyed by being used, cared for or stored incorrectly

Product labels carry instructions as well as warning and safety symbols. These try to ensure the safe use of the product. The more common ones are shown here.

Instructions

Instructions tell you how to use the product safely. They may come as a separate booklet, which should be kept in a safe place.

Care labels

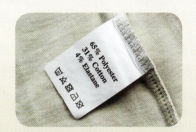

Care labels tell us how to wash, dry and iron a garment.

Food labels

Best before 30.01.16
Date stamping/expiry date

Safety symbols show that products have been tested for safety

Flame-resistant mark: Found on furniture, etc. Fabric carrying this symbol does not burn easily.

C € (European Standards mark)

European Standards mark: Products carrying this symbol, such as children's toys and nightwear, have passed strict safety tests.

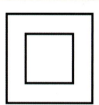

Doubly insulated mark: Found on small electrical appliances.

Warning symbols: Found on potentially dangerous products

Government warnings.

Harmful irritant: This product will damage the skin and eyes, for example bleach.

Highly flammable: Will burst into flames easily, for example aerosols.

Packaging

With the increase in self-service shopping (such as in supermarkets) and in the use of convenience foods, the amount of packaging has also increased.

Functions of packaging

- Advertises the product
- Makes it easier to store
- Protects the product (food) from contamination
- Preserves food, such as in cans
- Provides essential information, such as instructions for use
- Carries the barcode

Types of packaging

Plastic   Paper   Glass   Metal

Good packaging is:

- Environmentally friendly
- Strong
- Light
- Easily opened and resealed (if necessary)

Disadvantages of too much packaging

- Bad for the environment
- Uses up natural resources, such as trees
- Causes litter and pollution, for example plastics
- Is expensive
- Prevents us from seeing what we are getting for our money, for example ready meals

See also Chapter 30: Community Services and the Environment

Rapid Revision

1. **Quality:** Describes the standard of goods and services. **Quality control:** Goods are examined and tested to ensure they reach a set standard.
2. **Quality marks:** Quality Mark, Guaranteed Irish symbol, Irish Standards Mark, European Standards Mark, BSI Kite Mark.
3. **Quality service:** Friendly, skilled staff. Clean, wheelchair-accessible premises. Little queuing. Clean toilet facilities.
4. **Product labels:** Quality symbol, warnings, name and address of manufacturer, description of product and instructions for use.
5. **Product safety:** Concerned with the safety of the user and the care of the product. Products carry instructions, care labels, food must have labels, flame-resistant mark, European Standards Mark, doubly insulated mark, government warnings, harmful irritant mark, highly flammable mark.
6. **Packaging**
   - **Functions:** Advertisement, easy to store, protects product, preserves food, provides information, carries barcode.
   - **Types:** Plastic, paper, glass, metal.
   - **Disadvantages:** Bad for the environment, uses resources (trees), causes litter and pollution, expensive and stops us from seeing the product.

Revision Questions

1. What is meant by quality control? Draw each of the following symbols in your copy: (a) Quality Mark (b) Guaranteed Irish (c) European Standards Mark (d) BSI Kite Mark.
2. List five characteristics of a good service.
3. List five pieces of information found on product labels.
4. Product safety concerns itself with two things – what are they?
5. What are care labels?
6. Draw each of the following safety symbols in your copy: (a) flame-resistant mark (b) doubly insulated mark (c) European Standards Mark.
7. Draw each of the following warning symbols in your copy: (a) harmful irritant (b) highly flammable.
8. List four functions of packaging. Name four different types of packaging. Describe four characteristics of good packaging. List four disadvantages of over-packaging goods.

Test Yourself
eTest.ie

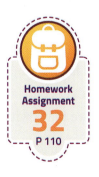

Homework Assignment
32
P 110

CHAPTER 19
Money Management

Teacher's CD

Slide presentation • Student activity pack with revision crossword • Class test • Student learning contract

Key words

- Money management
- Budget
- Resources
- Statutory deductions
- Voluntary deductions
- Income tax
- Pay Related Social Insurance
- Universal Social Charge
- Pension levy
- Tax credits
- Deposit account
- Current account
- Credit
- Home filing system

Learning outcomes

After completing this chapter and the homework, assignments and activities that accompany it, you should:

- Know the money management process and create a weekly budget for yourself.
- Understand the following income-related terms: gross income, income tax, tax credits, PRSI, Universal Social Charge, pension levy, superannuation, net income, voluntary deductions (private health insurance or private pension payments).
- Be able to list all the essential items of expenditure that are experienced by a household. Be able to describe the advantages of budgeting.
- Know the savings and credit options available to the consumer and the advantages and disadvantages of each.
- Be able to describe the advantages of a home filing system.

Money management is planning our spending wisely so that we have enough for our needs and avoid debt. A **budget** is the actual plan for spending and saving. A good budget balances income (the money we have) with expenditure (what we spend).

The money management process is continuous and involves five stages. Budgeting is part of this process.

The money management process

START

1. **Identify goal or aim:** To balance income and spending.

2. **Identify resources:** Money, energy, time.

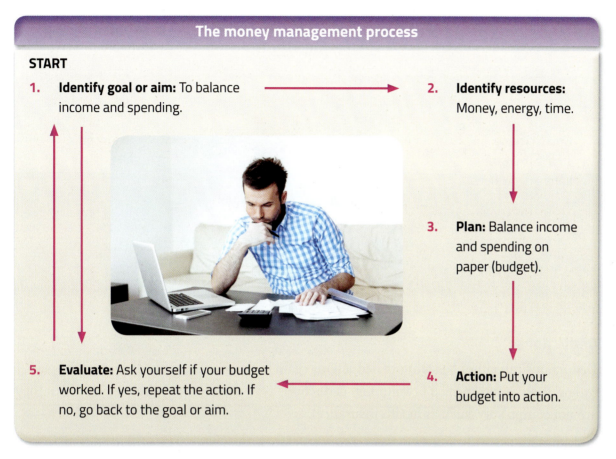

3. **Plan:** Balance income and spending on paper (budget).

5. **Evaluate:** Ask yourself if your budget worked. If yes, repeat the action. If no, go back to the goal or aim.

4. **Action:** Put your budget into action.

Teenage budget

1. Find out your exact income. Write it down.
2. List and price items you spend your money on. List savings too.
3. Try to balance both figures. **Overspending** happens if you borrow to buy things you cannot afford.

Teenage weekly budget: Balancing income with expenditure

Some costs, such as snacks, are weekly costs. For other costs, such as clothes, which you may not buy every week, an average weekly figure is worked out. For instance, if you spend €40 per month on clothes on average, your average weekly spending on clothes is €10.

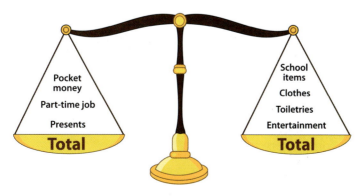

Household budget

The household budget must balance income with expenditure. Income may come from:

- Earnings from employment
- State benefits, such as one-parent family payment or jobseeker's allowance

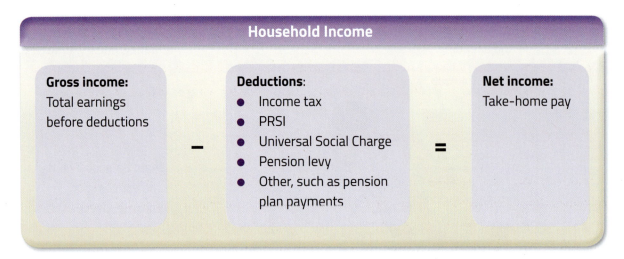

Deductions

Deductions can either be **statutory deductions** (paid to the government – they must be paid by law, such as income tax) or **voluntary deductions** (you decide to pay these yourself but they are not compulsory, such as health insurance).

Statutory deductions

Income tax

Income tax is money that is either:

- Deducted from your wages by your employer on your behalf and paid to the government (if you are a Pay As You Earn (PAYE) worker)
- Paid directly to the government by you (if you are self-employed)

Income tax pays for government-provided services such as hospitals, schools, roads, gardaí, etc.

Pay Related Social Insurance (PRSI)

A percentage of your gross income is taken in PRSI (most younger people are currently on the high rate of 4%). This money pays for benefits, including some dental treatments, contributory pensions and benefits paid when you are ill or out of work.

Other income deductions

In permanent government jobs (teachers, nurses, gardaí), payments towards your pension (superannuation) are compulsory.

Universal Social Charge

The USC is an additional charge or tax that came into effect in January 2011. For people under 65, this charge has to be paid if earnings exceed €10,036 per year. The percentage of income paid depends on gross earnings and increases as earnings rise. The USC does not apply to social welfare payments.

Pension levy

A pension levy, or tax, came into effect on 1 March 2009 for public sector workers (workers paid by the government). The amount you pay depends on your income and is taken as a percentage.

Tax credits

Under the tax credit system, every individual is given a number of tax credits every year. The number of tax credits you get depends on your personal circumstances.

Each week or month (or annually if you are self-employed), a person's **gross tax** is calculated. This gross tax is reduced by the **tax credit** due to the person for that week or month to get the net, or actual tax payable. Unused credits can be carried to the next week or month.

Gross tax **less** tax credits **equals** net tax (what you actually pay).

Voluntary deductions

Employees can also decide to have **voluntary deductions** taken from their pay. Examples include health insurance payments, savings and pension payments (unless you are a government worker, in which case pension payments are compulsory).

Household expenditure

As stated earlier, the household budget must balance income with household expenditure. The costs of basic needs such as food, clothing and shelter must be met first. Other necessities, such as transport, must then be met before luxury items are purchased.

- Clothes and shoes
- Crèche payments
- Educational expenses (books, uniforms)
- Food
- House insurance
- Household bills (electricity, gas)
- Housing (rent or mortgage)

Basic needs such as food must be bought first

- Luxuries (entertainment, holidays)
- Medical expenses (doctor, dentist, chemist)
- Medical insurance (Aviva, Quinn, VHI)
- Savings
- Transport (car, bus and train fares)

Advantages of budgeting

- There is more security and less financial worry.
- Overspending on impulse buys is less likely.
- Areas of overspending become obvious and can be cut down on.
- It sets a good example for children.
- Money can be set aside for major bills and seasonal spending, such as Christmas.

Saving and credit

When you decide to buy something that you do not have enough money for, two options are open to you:

- Save for the item
- Buy it on credit (borrowing)

Saving

Saving for an item and then paying for it in full, in cash, has advantages in that you earn interest rather than pay it, the item costs less in the end than if you borrowed for it and there is no risk of getting into debt. However, saving for an item means that you have to wait to get the item, something that we have become less willing to do.

Where can you save?

- Credit union
- Bank or building society
- Post office

Before deciding where to save, find out:

- Who offers the highest rates of interest?
- Do they offer student incentives such as no bank charges?
- How easy is it to lodge and withdraw money?

In banks and building societies, there are two basic types of account:

- Deposit account (savings)
- Current account

Money left in a deposit account will earn interest. A current account, on the other hand, is designed for everyday use. Money does not stay in it long and earns no interest. Bills can be paid by direct debit from a current account.

Opening a student deposit account

To open a student deposit (savings) account, you must:

- Fill out the bank or building society application form.

- Get a letter from your school saying you are a student there. The letter should also state your name, address and date of birth. Alternatively, you can produce official identification such as your passport.

Buying on credit

Credit buying means **buy now, pay later**. Credit encourages you to buy more than you can afford and has many disadvantages:

- Interest is charged and the item ends up costing much more.

- People run up debts.

On the other hand, if you use credit wisely it does have advantages in that you can use the item while paying for it and some very large items could not be bought without credit, such as houses and cars.

Where can you get credit?

- **Credit cards**.
- Bank/building society or credit union **loans**.
- **Bank overdraft:** The bank allows your account to go into the red, but charges interest on money owed.
- **Hire purchase:** Pay for goods in instalments. You don't own the item until it is paid for in full.
- **Catalogues** such as Family Album allow customers to pay for goods in instalments.

Some companies, such as car firms, offer interest-free loans to allow people to buy goods. These are an improvement in that you do not pay interest, but they encourage overspending and bills to mount up.

Home filing

A home filing system should contain all the family's important paperwork: bills, receipts, school reports, guarantees, bank statements, etc. Keeping a household filing system has many **advantages**:

- Bills are not mislaid and can therefore be paid on time.

- Time is not wasted searching for paperwork, since it is all in one place.

- Guarantees and receipts are at hand if you have a problem with goods purchased.

- Past and present bills can be compared.

- School progress can be monitored from year to year.

Home filing system

There are many simple yet effective home files on the market. Generally they cost from about €30 upwards.

Rapid Revision

1. **Money management:** Means planning spending to fulfil our needs and avoid debt. A **budget** is a plan for our money so that income balances with or is more than expenditure.

2. **Money management process:** Identify a goal or aim, identify resources, plan, put plan into action, evaluate and readjust plan if required.

3. **Gross income:** Wages before deductions. **Net income:** Wages after deductions.

4. **Statutory deductions:** Income tax, PRSI, Universal Social Charge, pension levy, pension payments (if you are a permanent government worker).

5. Depending on your personal circumstances (single, married), you are given a certain number of **tax credits** each week, month or year (self-employed). These tax credits come off your tax bill and your net tax amount is calculated (the tax you actually pay).

6. **Voluntary deductions:** Health insurance, saving and pension payments (non-government workers).

7. **Advantages of budgeting:** Less financial worry, less overspending, areas of overspending are highlighted, sets good example for children and money can be set aside for major bills and seasonal spending (for holidays).

8. **Saving:** Credit union, bank or building society, post office. Find out interest rates, if they offer incentives and how easy it is to lodge and withdraw money. Account types include deposit (savings) and current account.

9. **Buying on credit:** Encourages you to buy more, interest is charged and you can run up debts, but you can use the item while paying for it. Where: Credit cards, loans, overdrafts, hire purchase, pay in instalments (Family Album). Some car companies offer car loans with relatively low interest rates.

10. **Home filing:** Paperwork is not mislaid. Time is not wasted searching for paperwork. Guarantees and receipts are in one place. Past and present bills can be compared. School progress can be monitored year to year.

1. What is meant by the term *money management*? Describe the money management process (Higher Level only).
2. What is a budget? List four advantages of budgeting. Describe how you would plan a teenager's budget.
3. What is meant by gross and net income? Describe three statutory deductions that must be paid from income.
4. What are the advantages of saving for an item rather than getting it on credit? Name three places where you can save your money.
5. Name and describe four different sources of consumer credit.

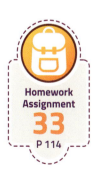

Homework
Assignment
33
P 114

Unit 3
Social and
Health Studies

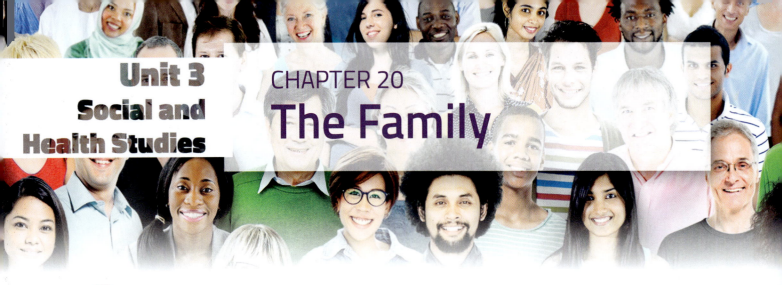

Teacher's CD

Slide presentation ▪ Student activity pack with revision crossword ▪ Class test ▪ Student learning contract

Key words

- Nuclear family
- Extended family
- Lone-parent family
- Blended family
- Cohabiting couple
- Same-sex couple
- Census
- Functional family
- Dysfunctional family
- Family roles
- Family responsibilities
- Boundary (rule)
- Role confusion
- Gender roles
- Stereotyping
- Gender stereotyping
- Gender role stereotyping
- Gender equality

Learning outcomes

After completing this chapter and the homework, assignments and activities that accompany it, you should:

- Be able to describe the four types of family common in Irish society today.
- Be able to describe the changes that have occurred in families in Ireland over the past three decades.
- Be able to discuss the functions of the family and understand the difference between a functional and dysfunctional family. Apply this understanding to a real case study.
- Understand the rights of children within the family unit.
- Understand the relationship between roles and responsibilities within the family unit and how conflict can occur when role confusion occurs. Apply this knowledge to your own life.
- Understand and be able to apply the concepts of gender roles, stereotyping, gender stereotyping, gender role stereotyping and gender equality to real life.

Types of family

- **Nuclear family:** Father, mother, child or children living in the same house.
- **Extended family:** Includes grandparents, uncles, aunts and cousins all living together or near each other.
- **Lone-parent family:** A family headed by a parent who may be unmarried, separated, divorced or widowed.
- **Blended family:** When parents and their children from previous relationships form a new family. Parents may also have children together.

Changes to the family

- **Increase in the number of people getting married:** A reversal of recent martial trends has seen a 9% increase in marriage rates between 2006 and 2011. Why do you think that at a time of economic recession, more people are choosing to get married?

- **Increase in the number of lone-parent families:** In the past in Ireland, the only type of one-parent family seen as acceptable was where a parent had died. Today, as a result of divorce, increased marital separation and a social acceptance of single unmarried parents, one in four families in Ireland is headed by one parent. Some 85% of lone parents are women, and statistically this group has the lowest disposable income.

- **Cohabiting couples:** For various reasons, many couples decide not to get married, but rather live together and rear their children. As of the 2011 census, 7.7% of all families with children in Ireland are headed by cohabiting couples. This figure has actually declined since the 2006 census – why do you think this is so?

- **Increase in the number of blended families:** Because of increased levels of divorce and separation, more children are growing up in blended families, whereby they live with their parent's new partner and their children. Ireland still has a fairly low divorce rate – 9.7% of marriages end in divorce. Many more divorced people (particularly men) are getting remarried. There was a 550% increase in remarriages between 1996 and 2011.

- **Increased number of same-sex couples:** There are an increasing number of families in Ireland headed by same-sex couples. The 2011 census recorded 4,042 such units.

- **Increased number of adult children living at home:** Due to financial pressures and other factors, Ireland has seen an increase in the number of adult children living at home with their parents. The figure now stands at 440,000.

- **Increased isolation:** Nowadays, many couples move away from their extended family to find work, etc. Childrearing can be more difficult, as there are no family members nearby to help out.

Functions of the family

A **functional** family will provide us with our physical, intellectual, language, emotional and social needs (PILES). A **dysfunctional** family will only provide some of them.

- **Physical needs:** Food, clothing, health, warmth, safety and shelter.
- **Intellectual needs:** Encouragement and support with schoolwork, a stimulating environment.
- **Language needs:** Conversation, reading stories to children.
- **Emotional needs:** Love, security, support.
- **Social needs:** Healthy, respectful relationships with adults and other children, guidance on what is right and wrong, boundaries, giving children a clear understanding of the **norms** of society (for example, it is the 'norm' in Irish society not to spit in public).

Rights of children

- Love and security
- Care
- Education
- Protection from neglect or abuse

Children can be neglected as a result of parents being too busy

Case study

Read the following case study on Jake Ryan. Which of his needs do you think are or are not being adequately met?

Jake Ryan is the nine-year-old son of Christine, who is a lone parent. Jake's father, Alan, left the family home when he was just over two years of age and Jake does not remember him living at his apartment. Alan lives with his new partner in the same general area, but has irregular contact with Jake, as he now has a second family and his new partner does not like him spending too much time with Jake and Christine. Christine is a heavy smoker and frequently drinks too much. She has a low-paid job in retail but hates it because she finds it so draining. All she feels able for in the evenings is lying on the couch and watching telly. Jake is currently in fourth class but is finding schoolwork difficult. He has literacy and numeracy difficulties, just like his mother did. He tends to bully other kids in his class who he sees as brighter than him. He is small for his age, but is excellent at sports – he recently was made captain of the under-10 soccer team.

Roles and responsibilities within the family

Every family member has rights, but each also has responsibilities. A **responsibility** is something that is expected of us. What responsibilities a family member has will depend on their role in the family. **Roles** include that of a child, adolescent, parent or grandparent.

Child	Adolescent	Adult
• To respect household boundaries (rules) • To show respect for all family members • To participate well in school • To help out in the home	• To respect household boundaries (rules) • To show respect for all family members • To help out in the running of the home • To behave in an acceptable way in society	• To provide for the family's needs • To set reasonable boundaries (rules) for members of the household • To show respect for all family members • To behave in an acceptable way in society, setting a good example

Conflict in the family

Relationships between family members will generally be good if each person fulfils the responsibilities connected to their role. There is often conflict between adolescent family members (teenagers) and their parents because of **role confusion**, with each side seeing the same situation differently. For example, a parent feels they have a responsibility to ensure that their teenage son or daughter is safe, so asks them to be home by 10pm. The teenage son or daughter feels they are old enough to make decisions for themselves about when they return home (see also 'Dealing with conflict' on page 257).

Gender roles

Gender means being either male or female. In the past, males and females had very different gender roles, meaning they were expected to behave very differently from each other. For example, many men were expected to go out to work and do very little housework or childrearing. Women were expected not to work outside the home and to do all the housework and childrearing.

Stereotyping

Stereotyping means having an oversimplified, fixed and often wrong idea about a group of people, such as 'all Americans are loud'.

Gender stereotyping means having a fixed and often wrong idea about men's and women's personalities and life expectations. Examples of gender stereotyping:

- **Personalities:** Women are emotional; men are not.
- **Life expectations:** Women want to find a husband and have children; men want a career.

Gender role stereotyping means having a fixed and often wrong idea about how men and women should behave in society, for example 'women should do the childrearing and housework and men should go out to work'. In Irish society today, more than 50% of women work outside the home, yet many are expected to carry on their traditional roles as well, resulting in many women feeling burned out.

Gender equality means treating men and women equally. Both can be who and what they want to be without being judged or discriminated against. Are men and women treated equally in Irish society?

'Supermum'

Rapid Revision

1. **Types of family:** Nuclear, extended, lone-parent, blended.
2. **Changes to the family:** Increase in numbers getting married, increase in lone-parent families, decrease but still large numbers of cohabiting couples, increase in blended families and individuals remarrying after divorce, increase in adult children living with parents, increased isolation.
3. **Functions of the family:** A **functional** family will provide for family members' physical, intellectual, language, emotional and social needs. A **dysfunctional** family will only provide for some of them.
4. **Children's rights:** Love and security, care, education and protection from neglect or abuse.
5. **Roles and responsibilities:** A **role** is the part you play in the family (child, parent). **Responsibilities** depend on the individual's role (children have a responsibility to respect the boundaries or rules of the family). **Role confusion** occurs when family members are unsure of or resist their roles and do not fulfil their responsibilities.
6. **Gender roles:** The expectations there are of males and females in society. **Gender stereotyping** is having a fixed and often incorrect idea about men and women's personalities and life expectations.
7. **Gender equality:** Treating men and women equally.

Revision Questions

1. Describe four different family structures.
2. Describe four changes to family life and structure that have occurred in Ireland over the last number of decades.
3. What is meant by a dysfunctional family?
4. List three types of needs provided for by the family. Give one example of each.
5. Name four children's rights within the family.
6. What is meant by a responsibility? List four responsibilities adolescents have within the family.
7. Define the term *gender stereotyping*. What is treating men and women equally called?

Test Yourself
eTest.ie

Homework
Assignment
34
P 120

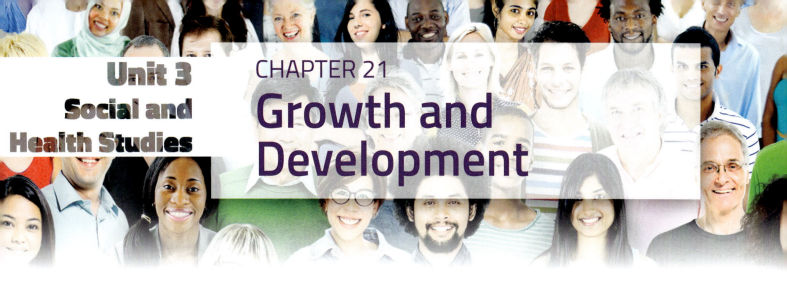

Teacher's CD

Slide presentation • Student activity pack with revision crossword • Class test • Student learning contract

Key words

- Heredity
- Environment
- Nature vs. nurture debate
- Physical development
- Intellectual development
- Language development
- Emotional development
- Social development
- Puberty
- Peer group
- Peer pressure
- Moral development
- Social norms

Learning outcomes

After completing this chapter and the homework, assignments and activities that accompany it, you should:

- Be able to discuss the issues involved in the nature vs. nurture debate.
- Be able to list and describe the five areas of development and be able to discuss how each area can be best promoted in children and adolescents.
- Be able to describe the physical signs of puberty in adolescents, both male and female.
- Be able to describe the three characteristics of adolescent thought and how these thought processes affect how some adolescents behave in society.
- Be able to describe how to deal with conflict effectively.

Growth and development

Our growth and development as human beings are influenced by two things:

Heredity: What has been passed on by our parents.

Environment: How we are brought up; our surroundings.

The extent to which these two factors influence development is often called the **nature vs. nurture debate**.

During our lives, we go through four stages of development:

- Childhood
- Adolescence
- Adulthood
- Old age

As human beings, there are also five different areas of development.

Type of development and what it means

Physical

- Growth of the body, such as getting taller
- Increased co-ordination and ability to do things, like ride a bike

Intellectual

- Development of memory, concentration, understanding, problem-solving skills, imagination and creativity

Language

- Development of speech, reading and writing skills

Emotional

- Learning to handle your emotions (anger, fear) in a positive way
- Development of self-esteem (how you feel about yourself)

Social

- Developing friendships and relationships with others
- Learning what behaviours are acceptable in society (social norms), for example using a tissue
- Knowing right from wrong (moral)

 Chapter 37: Childcare option

Development during adolescence

Adolescence (age 11–18), like early childhood, is a time of rapid development.

Physical development

- Co-ordination improves, such as the ability to dance or to play sports.

- The ability to complete skilled tasks increases.

- Physical and sexual development takes place during puberty, caused by sex hormones (see the illustrations below). Puberty is occurring earlier nowadays than it did in the past. This is because children are heavier than in the past and many have better nutrition.

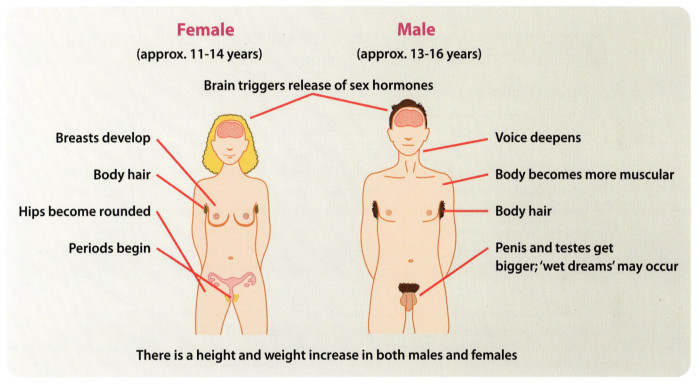

Female
(approx. 11-14 years)

Male
(approx. 13-16 years)

Brain triggers release of sex hormones

Breasts develop

Body hair

Hips become rounded

Periods begin

Voice deepens

Body becomes more muscular

Body hair

Penis and testes get bigger; 'wet dreams' may occur

There is a height and weight increase in both males and females

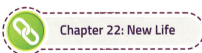
Chapter 22: New Life

Intellectual development

During adolescence, most young people become capable of more complex thought. Younger children tend to think more in the here and now – about what they can now see, hear, smell or touch. They do not think about the past and the future as much. Most adolescents, on the other hand, become able to plan, understand abstract concepts such as justice and democracy and think about or carry out more than one thing at a time.

A stimulating environment is important for intellectual development. Passive activities such as playing computer games or watching TV do not stimulate the mind as much as more intellectually active activities such as conversation, reading or playing board games.

The psychologist David Elkind believed that adolescents think differently to adults in three basic ways and that these differences influence adolescents' behaviour.

- **Imaginary audience:** The belief that others are watching you and are as concerned with your behaviour and appearance as you are yourself. This results in adolescents being influenced by fashion trends and being easily embarrassed by events.
- **Personal fable:** The belief that their experiences are unique, for example everyone else is allowed out except me.
- **Invincibility:** While adolescents are aware of the dangers of risky behaviours, there is a stronger sense at this time that 'it will not happen to me'. This results in, for example, adolescents driving or sitting in cars that are being driven too fast.

Case study

Margaret Hughes is 14 years old. She is in 2nd year in a large co-educational secondary school in a large town in County Louth. Margaret lives in a small rural area 12 miles away from her school on her father's farm. Her mother and father are old compared to her friends' parents, as her mother was 40 when she had her and her father was even older, at 45. Margaret (who hates her old-fashioned name) was dreading the parent–teacher meeting, as her mother is a bit overweight and wears sort of old-fashioned clothes. She knows that her mum and dad will ask her teachers loads of questions, which she is mortified about. Her parents waited for many years to have her and they both love her dearly. They tend to be a bit overprotective of her compared to her friends' parents and this really annoys her. She has not asked any of her friends out to stay in her house, as she lives on a farm and she knows her parents will become really involved, fussing over them having enough food and being comfortable.

Which aspects of Elkind's theory do you think are at play in this case study? How do you think Margaret will see things when she is 10 years older?

Language development

Language development means the development of a child's ability to speak, read and write. A 2009 report by the Programme for International Student Assessment showed that 17% of all Irish 15-year-olds and almost one in four teenage boys lack the literacy skills to function effectively in today's society. Ireland's international ranking in terms of literacy and numeracy has steadily declined over the past number of decades. Why is this so?

Children and teenagers need to develop their language skills by holding frequent conversations with their parents and peers and by reading and writing every day. Most Junior Certificate textbooks (including this one) require a reading age of approximately 14 years. Students reading below this level are at a severe disadvantage because most of the material presented to them in school requires this level of ability.

Emotional development

Emotional development means learning to deal with emotions in a positive way. It also means the development of a positive self-image and self-esteem. Life experiences and how important people such as our parents treat us are very important to positive emotional development. For example, a child or adolescent who is constantly criticised or put down by his or her parents may become very negative and have poor self-esteem. This often manifests itself in the child or teenager becoming very negative or critical of others, such as their classmates.

During adolescence:

- Sexual feelings develop.
- Adolescents are often very concerned about how others see them (see 'imaginary audience' on page 256). The advertising industry uses these insecurities to sell their goods.
- Conflict increases.

Conflict is a normal part of development for many adolescents. Conflict is usually about housework, money, appearance, substance use or abuse (such as drinking), schoolwork, curfew, boy/girlfriends and sexual behaviour. Adolescents usually want more independence than their parents will allow.

Dealing with conflict

If you are fighting with a parent or someone else:

- Do not get aggressive or blame them.
- Do not ignore the problem – it will not go away.
- Do listen and calmly discuss the issue and try to work out a solution.

Social development

Social development involves the following three skills:

1. Learning how to communicate and relate effectively with others
2. Learning the 'norms', or ways to behave in society
3. Developing a strong sense of right and wrong (moral development)

1. Developing social relationships

During adolescence, the peer group becomes very important. Your peer group is people your own age who share similar interests. Adolescents usually spend less and less time with their family and more time with their peer group. Peer pressure is when your peer group puts pressure on you to do something, for example to smoke. **Peer pressure** is not always bad. Can you think of an example of positive peer pressure in your life?

2. Understanding social norms

Our sense of right and wrong is often influenced by the norms of the society and home we live in. Norms are acceptable ways of behaving, such as putting rubbish in the bin, not damaging other people's property, etc. People's understanding of norms are developed in early childhood, which is why it is difficult to change attitudes later in life, such as towards littering.

3. Moral development

Moral development occurs in two stages. Some people never reach stage two.

Stage 1: Actions are driven by a desire for rewards or a fear of punishment – 'I won't steal from my mother's purse because if she notices, she'll kill me.' Some adults remain at this stage, such as career criminals.

Stage 2: Actions are led by your own sense of right and wrong – 'I won't steal from my mother's purse because she has worked hard for that money and stealing is wrong.'

Rapid Revision

1. **Nature vs. nurture debate:** The extent to which a person's genetic make-up (handed down from their parents) or their environment influences how they develop.
2. **Life stages:** Childhood, adolescence, adulthood, old age.
3. **Areas of development:** Physical, intellectual, language, emotional and social (PILES).
4. **Physical development during adolescence:** Males develop later than females, triggered by sex hormones in both. Females: Breasts develop, body hair, hips become rounded, periods, height and weight gain, 11–14 years. Males: Voice breaks, more muscle, body and facial hair (later), penis and testes enlarge, wet dreams, height and weight gain, 13–16 years.
5. **Intellectual development during adolescence:** Thoughts become less about the here and now. There is more thinking about the past and future. Capable of abstract thought. Stimulation is vital. Characteristics: Imaginary audience, personal fable, invincibility.
6. **Language development during adolescence:** Up to 25% of adolescents have literacy difficulties. Frequent conversation, reading and writing are vital.
7. **Emotional development during adolescence:** Sexual feelings develop. Some become self-conscious. Conflict increases. Dealing with conflict: No aggression or blame, do not ignore, discuss and resolve.
8. **Social development during adolescence:** Three areas: social relationships, understanding social norms, moral development. All are very much influenced by one's environment, parents and peers.

1. Human growth and development are said to be influenced by two factors. What are they?
2. What are the five areas of development and what does each one mean?
3. List five physical changes that occur in (a) females and (b) males during puberty.
4. Describe emotional development during adolescence.
5. Outline the dos and don'ts of dealing with conflict.
6. What is meant by the terms *peer group* and *peer pressure*?
7. What is a norm? Give an example.

Homework Assignment
35
P 123

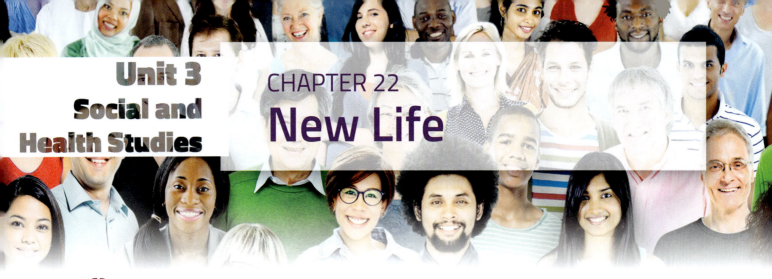

Teacher's CD

Slide presentation • Student activity pack with revision crossword • Class test • Student learning contract

Key words

- Menstrual cycle
- Menopause
- Ovum
- Ovulation
- Fertilisation
- Fallopian tubes
- Uterus
- Progesterone
- Oestrogen
- Testes
- Sperm
- Semen
- Ejaculation
- Testosterone
- Scrotum
- Embryo
- Foetus
- Placenta
- Umbilical cord
- Labour
- Episiotomy
- Afterbirth
- Caesarean section

Learning outcomes

After completing this chapter and the homework, assignments and activities that accompany it, you should:

- Be able to describe and understand the female menstrual cycle. Know how good hygiene can be maintained during menstruation.
- Be able to describe both the male and female reproductive systems, including identifying reproductive organs on a diagram.
- Understand how fertilisation or conception takes place.
- Be able to describe pregnancy, from fertilisation to birth.
- Understand the need for responsible sexual behaviour and the possible consequences of irresponsible behaviour.

The menstrual cycle (menstruation – periods)

Certain changes occur in a woman's body every month. These changes are referred to as the **menstrual cycle**. It begins at puberty and continues until **menopause** (which normally occurs between 45 and 55 years of age, when periods stop).

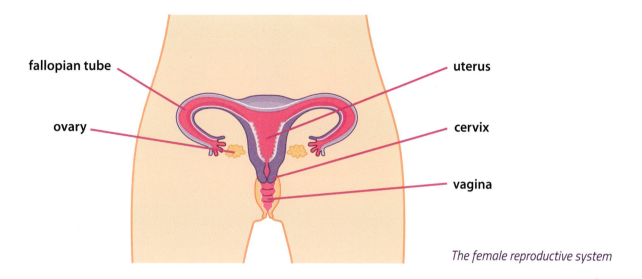

fallopian tube

ovary

uterus

cervix

vagina

The female reproductive system

During menstruation:

1. An egg, or ovum, is released from one of the female's ovaries. This is called **ovulation**.
2. The egg goes into the **fallopian tube** nearby and waits to be fertilised by a male sperm.
3. If the egg is not fertilised, it travels down into the womb and out of the body. The girl or woman then has her monthly period.
4. If the woman has sex, sperm comes up to the fallopian tube and may join with the egg. This is called **fertilisation** or **conception**.
5. The egg makes its way to the **uterus** (womb) and attaches itself to the womb wall. The woman is then pregnant.
6. The female hormones **progesterone** and **oestrogen** cause:
   - Ovulation
   - Changes during puberty (breasts develop, growth of pubic hair)
   - Changes during pregnancy

Hygiene during menstruation

- Change pads or tampons every 3–4 hours.
- Wash your pubic area well every day.
- Wash your hands before and after changing a pad or tampon.
- Wear tight-fitting underwear with pads to prevent leaking.
- Buy dark-coloured underwear to wear during periods.

The male reproductive system

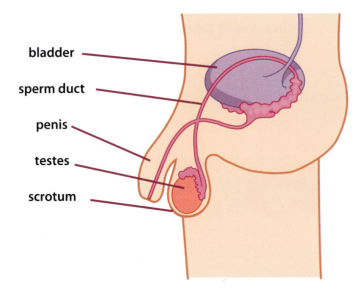

bladder

sperm duct

penis

testes

scrotum

The male reproductive system

1. From puberty onwards, the male **testes** produce **sperm**. The testes lie outside the body in a sac called the **scrotum**.

2. During sexual intercourse, the blood vessels of the penis fill with blood and it becomes stiff and erect. This allows the man to insert his penis into the woman's vagina. When the man reaches orgasm, sperm travel quickly through two sperm ducts and spurt out through the penis into the woman's body. While travelling to the penis, the sperm mix with fluids that nourish the sperm and allow them to swim. This mixture is called **semen**.

3. At the moment of **ejaculation**, many thousands of sperm are released near the woman's cervix. They begin swimming towards the fallopian tubes in an effort to fertilise an egg, which may or may not be there. In the end, only one sperm fertilises the egg.

4. The male hormone **testosterone** is made in the testes and causes:
   - Sperm production
   - Other changes during puberty (facial hair)

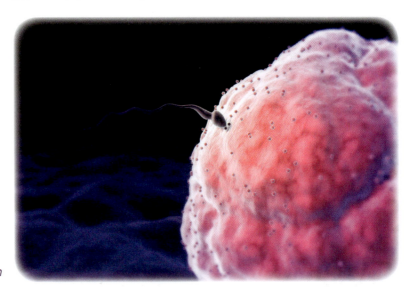

The moment of conception

Pregnancy

1. A few days after conception, the egg travels along the fallopian tube to the womb, where it attaches itself to the womb wall. It is now called an **embryo**. At eight weeks it is called a **foetus**.

2. Sometimes the egg does not remain implanted and an early miscarriage occurs.

3. The **placenta** forms where the embryo is attached. The **umbilical cord** then forms, joining the placenta to the baby. The umbilical cord is the baby's lifeline, supplying food and oxygen.

4. Unfortunately, harmful viruses, such as rubella and HIV, and harmful substances such as alcohol, nicotine and other drugs can also pass to the baby.

5. A baby's due date is calculated as 40 weeks from the first day of the woman's last period.

6. From about 32 weeks, the baby's head will face downwards. When the baby is about to be born, the waters usually break and contractions start. This is called **labour**. As labour progresses, contractions will become stronger and more frequent. Some women decide to have an epidural, which is an anaesthetic injected into the spine for pain relief.

7. Sometimes labour is **induced**. This involves giving the woman hormones to start labour.

8. During birth, the head is delivered first. (Babies coming feet first are described as being in the breech position. Because of the risk of suffocation, they are usually delivered by Caesarean section.)

9. Often a cut is made in the vagina to make the opening bigger and to stop tearing. This is called an **episiotomy**.

10. Once the head is out, the rest of the body and the **afterbirth** are delivered.

11. The World Health Organization (WHO) estimates that 10–15% of births worldwide will be by **Caesarean section**. Ireland has much higher rates than this – on average, 30% of babies are born this way, though it is as high as 40% at some hospitals. During a C-section, the woman's lower abdomen and uterus are cut open and the baby is removed. Common reasons for a C-section are a large baby, small pelvis, breech baby (feet first), twins (smaller twin coming first) or a very premature baby.

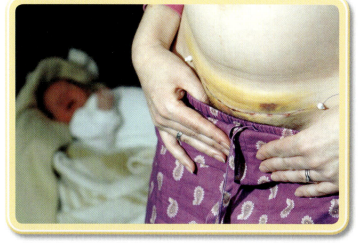

A Caesarean scar

Responsible sexual behaviour

The teenage birth rate has declined, from a high of 3,087 in 2001 to almost half that figure (1,639) in 2012. Studies show that many teenagers (especially teenage girls) have sex because of various pressures rather than because they really want to. Most people believe that sex is best kept for close, long-term relationships and that casual sex can be damaging for the individual, both physically and psychologically.

Casual sex can lead to:

- Unplanned pregnancy
- Feelings of being used
- Sexually transmitted infections (STIs), such as genital warts, chlamydia, herpes or AIDS
- While any woman can develop cervical cancer, there is an increased incidence of cervical cancer in women who were sexually active before the age of 18

Alcohol or other drugs are often involved when people make risky decisions about sexual activity.

Rapid Revision

1. **Menstrual cycle:** Changes that occur in a woman's body each month from puberty to menopause. An egg (ovum) is released and travels to the fallopian tube. If the ovum is fertilised it travels to the uterus (womb) and attaches itself to the womb wall. If the ovum is not fertilised, the woman has her period as normal. The cycle is controlled by female sex hormones (progesterone and oestrogen). Good hygiene is important.

2. **Male reproductive system:** From puberty, testes produces sperm. During sexual intercourse, the male penis becomes erect and sperm is released (ejaculation). Male sex hormone is testosterone.

3. **Pregnancy:** After conception, the egg travels to the uterus and attaches itself. The egg is now called an embryo; it is called a foetus from 8 weeks. Where the egg attaches forms the placenta and umbilical cord (nourishes the growing baby). The due date is 40 weeks from the first day of the last period. Labour begins as the uterus contracts. The woman may have an epidural (pain relief) and an episiotomy (incision to prevent vagina tearing). The baby will normally come head first. Some babies are born by Caesarean section.

4. **Responsible sexual behaviour:** Most people feel that sex is best kept for close, long-term relationships. Casual sex risks unplanned pregnancy, feelings of being used and sexually transmitted infections. Alcohol and other drugs are often involved when people take risks.

Revision Questions

1. What is menopause?
2. Describe what occurs in the female body during menstruation.
3. Draw and label a diagram of (a) the female and (b) the male reproductive system.
4. What are the functions of testosterone in males?
5. Give a step-by-step description of pregnancy from conception to birth.
6. What is the function of the placenta and umbilical cord?
7. What is a Caesarean section? Why would one be carried out?
8. Outline four risks associated with casual sex.

Test Yourself
eTest.ie

Homework
Assignment
36
P 126

CHAPTER 23
The Human Body

Slide presentation ▪ Student activity pack with revision crossword ▪ Class test ▪ Student learning contract

Key words

- Milk teeth
- Permanent teeth
- Crown
- Root
- Enamel
- Dentine
- Pulp cavity
- Cementum
- Plaque
- Gum disease
- Fluoride
- Dental products
- Epidermis
- Dermis
- Malpighian layer
- Nerves
- Sweat gland
- Oil gland
- Pore
- Fat layer
- Personal hygiene
- Antiperspirant
- Deodorant
- Acne
- Skin cancer
- Respiratory system
- Pharynx
- Larynx
- Epiglottis
- Trachea
- Bronchi
- Bronchioles
- Alveoli
- Exchange of gases
- Circulatory system
- Artery
- Vein
- Capillary
- Heart
- Septum
- Vena cava
- Pulmonary arteries
- Pulmonary veins
- Right and left atrium
- Right and left ventricles
- Aorta
- Pulse
- Blood
- Plasma
- Red blood cells
- White blood cells
- Platelets
- Coronary heart disease

Learning outcomes

After completing this chapter and the homework, assignments and activities that accompany it, you should:

- Know how many teeth a baby and an adult should have. Be able to name and describe the functions of the four types of adult teeth. Be able to label a diagram of the structure of the tooth. Know what causes tooth decay and gum disease and apply this knowledge while caring for your teeth and gums.
- Understand the structure and functions of the skin. Know how to maintain good personal hygiene and promote healthy skin.
- Understand the structure of the respiratory system and be able to describe the passage of air through it. Understand how gases are exchanged in the lungs and how this connects with the rest of the respiratory system and the circulatory system.
- Understand the structure of the circulatory system and be able to describe the passage of blood through it. Understand how the respiratory system links with it. Be able to describe arteries, veins and capillaries in terms of their structure and function. Know what blood is composed of and what its functions are in the body. Understand the concept of coronary heart disease and how it can best be prevented.

The human body

In this chapter, you will study:

- The teeth
- The skin and personal hygiene
- The respiratory system
- The circulatory system (Higher Level only)

The teeth

Healthy teeth are very important. They are attractive and allow you to speak properly and chew food.

A baby's 20 milk teeth generally appear by age two and a half and fall out from age seven. An adult, on the other hand, has 32 permanent teeth. The four wisdom teeth are the last to appear, in the mid to late teens.

Types of adult teeth

There are four different types of teeth, each with a different function.

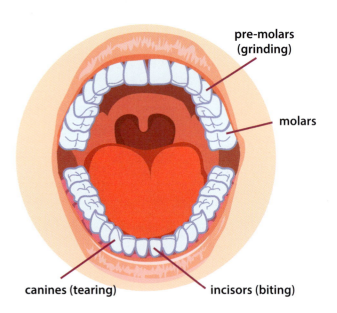

Structure of the tooth

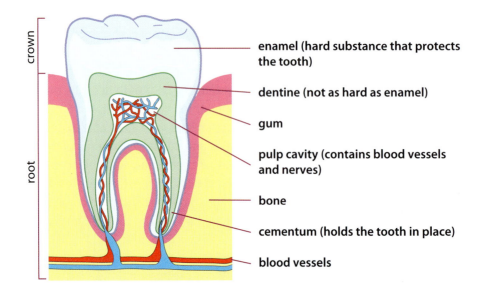

Tooth decay and gum disease

Unhealthy teeth are unattractive and can cause the person to become very self-conscious, have bad breath and suffer from gum and stomach infections.

Plaque

Plaque is the yellowish coating that forms on teeth between brushings. Plaque contains food and bacteria. If teeth are not brushed, the bacteria begin digesting the food and acid is produced. This acid burns into the tooth and causes it to decay or rot. A toothache is not felt until the acid has burned through to the pulp cavity. Why?

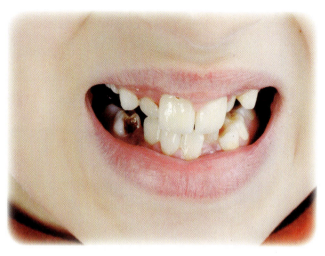

Tooth decay

Gum disease

Gum disease occurs when acid attacks the gums, leaving them infected, sore and swollen.

Fluoride

Fluoride is often added to water supplies and toothpaste. Fluoride strengthens teeth and helps prevent decay.

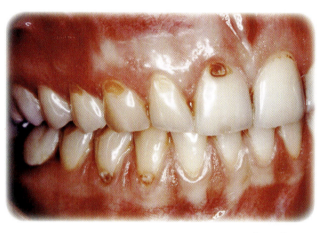

Brushing teeth

Teeth have four surfaces: outer, inner, chewing surface and between teeth. All four surfaces should be cleaned thoroughly by brushing and flossing.

Gum disease

Dental products

Use dental floss to clean between the teeth safely. Floss before brushing – never use metal objects to do this because it damages the enamel. Mouthwash helps kill the acid-producing bacteria in plaque. Use after brushing. The circular action of a good electric toothbrush does not damage gums.

Caring for teeth and gums

There are five basic rules for caring for the teeth and gums:

- Eat calcium-rich foods and raw fruit and vegetables.
- Avoid sugary food and drinks.
- Brush after meals with a soft toothbrush. Replace your brush regularly.

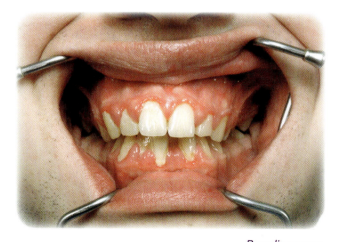

Receding gums

👥 Have a dental check-up every six months. Never use your teeth to open bottles, etc., as this damages the enamel.

👥 Do not brush teeth too aggressively, as this will cause your gums to recede or pull back from the teeth.

Teeth

1. Children have 20 milk teeth, adults have 32. Types of teeth are incisors, canines, pre-molars and molars. Crown of tooth above gum, root below. Parts of tooth are enamel, dentine, pulp cavity (containing nerves and blood vessels). The tooth is anchored in the jawbone with cementum.

2. Tooth decay and gum disease are caused by plaque. This yellow substance contains food and bacteria. Bacteria produce acid, which rots teeth and gums. Fluoride added to toothpaste and water helps strengthen teeth. Teeth should be brushed and flossed between meals. Eat calcium-rich foods and avoid sugary foods and drinks. Have regular dental check-ups and do not brush too aggressively (causes receding gums).

The teeth

1. Name the four different types of teeth an adult has and describe the function of each type.
2. What part of the tooth is (a) above the gum (b) below the gum?
3. Draw and label a diagram of the structure of the tooth.
4. List some problems caused by unhealthy teeth. What is gum disease and how is it caused?
5. What is plaque? How does it affect teeth?
6. What is fluoride? What is it for?
7. Name two dental products and explain what they do.
8. List five points that should be remembered when caring for teeth and gums.

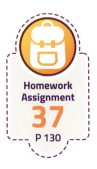

Homework
Assignment
37
P 130

The skin and personal hygiene

The skin is a very important organ in the body. It is an excretory organ, meaning that it gets rid of waste products from the body such as water and salts (sweat).

Structure of the skin

The skin has two layers:

- Epidermis (the surface you can see)
- Dermis (under the surface)

The epidermis is the outermost layer of the skin. As you can see in the illustration, the top layer of the epidermis consists of flat, dead cells. These cells are constantly brushed off and replaced from beneath. The Malpighian layer lies further into the epidermis. This layer contains a pigment (colour) called melanin. The more melanin you have, the darker your skin is. Melanin protects the skin from the sun.

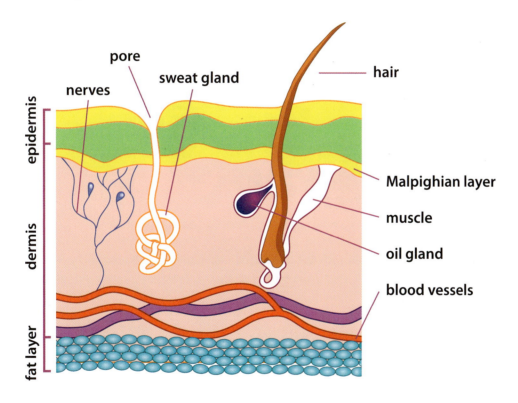

The dermis is under the epidermis and contains the following.

- **Blood vessels** carry blood to the skin.
- **Nerves** allow us to feel pain, cold, heat and touch.
- **Sweat glands** remove water and salts from the body.
- **Oil glands** keep skin soft.
- **Hair** helps keep the body warm.
- **Fat layer** helps keep the body warm.

Functions of the skin

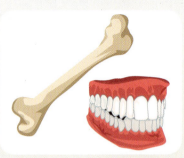

Vitamin D
Vitamin D is made by the skin from sunlight. It is needed for healthy bones and teeth.

Protection
The epidermis stops bacteria from getting into the body. It also prevents the loss of body fluids (burn victims are prone to infection and dehydration).

Temperature control
Blood vessels in the skin widen when we are hot. The skin turns red, thus giving off unwanted heat. Sweat glands produce sweat, which cools us down.

Organ of touch
Nerves in the skin allow us to feel pain, cold, heat, etc.

Insulation and energy store
The fat layer keeps us warm and acts as an energy store.

Personal hygiene

Even while at rest, our sweat glands are constantly producing sweat (about 1 litre per day). When this sweat dries, it mixes with oil from the oil glands and sits on the surface of the skin. If it is not washed off, bacteria begin to grow and body odour (smell) is the result. During the teenage years, sweat and oil glands become very active and teenagers are much more prone to body odour than children.

To avoid body odour:

- Shower every day and also after sports. Use soap or gel.
- Use deodorant or antiperspirant (an antiperspirant prevents sweating, whereas a deodorant just perfumes sweat).
- Girls should shave underarm hair, as hair traps sweat and can cause body odour.

- Change socks and underwear daily.
- Girls should be particularly careful during periods, as body odour can be a problem at this time.

Acne

Acne is a skin condition that usually starts during the teenage years. Because of hormonal changes, a teenager's skin produces extra oil, which can block pores and cause whiteheads, blackheads and spots. Acne normally appears on the T-zone (forehead, nose and chin) or on the shoulders or chest.

Acne cannot be prevented, but it may be helped by:

- Avoiding fatty foods, such as chocolate and crisps
- Not squeezing spots, as this spreads acne and can lead to scarring
- Drinking plenty of water
- Using medicated soap, such as Biactol

Many teenagers experience problems with acne

If acne is very bad, consult your doctor, as he or she may prescribe antibiotic creams and tablets.

How to promote healthy skin

- Have a good skincare routine – cleanse, tone and moisturise your face every day.
- Avoid wearing too much make-up and never sleep with it on.
- Wash the rest of your body daily and use a body moisturiser.
- Eat a healthy diet with plenty of fresh fruit and vegetables.
- Drink at least eight glasses of water per day.
- Take exercise daily and get enough sleep.
- Avoid smoking and alcohol.
- Wear sun cream on your face every day.

Skin cancer

Skin cancer is the most common cancer in Ireland. Due to our skin type, Ireland has one of the highest rates of skin cancer in Europe – it affects one in every eight men and one in every 10 women. Yet 90% of skin cancers can be avoided by:

- Avoiding too much sun – just because you are wearing sun factor does not mean you can stay out indefinitely in the sun, especially if abroad

👥 Wearing sun cream **every day** (factor 25, even in Ireland)

👥 Never using sun beds

👥 Covering your skin, particularly if you have moles or birthmarks

People with fair or freckled skin are more prone to skin cancer. They should avoid unprotected exposure to the sun.

Children's skin is easily damaged. They must wear a high-factor sun cream.

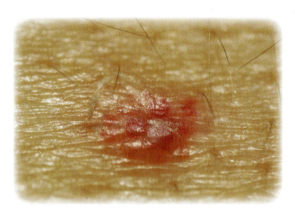
Skin cancer

Sunbathing = skin cancer and wrinkles

Caring for your hair, hands and feet		
Caring for your hair	**Caring for your hands**	**Caring for your feet**
• Wash your hair at least once a week.	• Wash your hands, especially after using the toilet.	• Wash daily and dry well between your toes.
• Use conditioner on the ends.	• Keep nails clean and filed.	• Wear good supportive footwear.
• Rinse well to prevent dandruff.	• Use hand cream.	• Cut nails straight across.
• Avoid too many hair treatments or blow-drying.	• Use rubber gloves when doing the washing up or other jobs, such as gardening.	• Change socks daily.
• Trim your hair every six weeks.		

Skin

1. **Structure:** Skin has two layers: the epidermis (surface) and dermis (beneath the surface). The Malpighian layer contains melanin, which colours the skin and protects it from the sun. The dermis contains blood vessels, nerves, sweat glands, oil glands, hair and a fat layer.

2. **Functions of the skin:** Makes vitamin D, protection, temperature control, organ of touch, insulation and energy store.

3. **Personal hygiene:** Bacteria grow on sweat and oil on the skin. If not washed off, this causes body odour. During adolescence, sweat and oil glands are very active. Shower daily, especially after exercise. Use antiperspirant. Girls should shave underarm hair. Change socks and underwear daily. Girls should be very conscious of hygiene during periods.

4. **Acne:** Hormonal changes can cause skin to become oily and develop whiteheads, blackheads and spots. Acne cannot be prevented, but it can be helped by avoiding fatty foods, by not squeezing spots and blackheads (which causes infection), drinking water and using a medicated soap. Sometimes antibiotic cream will be prescribed.

5. **Promoting healthy skin:** Follow a good skincare routine, avoid too much make-up or sleeping with it on, sleep, get plenty of exercise, drink lots of water, avoid smoking and alcohol, wear sun cream every day and cover moles in the sun.

6. **Skin cancer:** Irish people are very prone to skin cancer. To prevent it, avoid the sun, apply sun protection cream and never use sun beds.

7. **Care of hair, hands and feet:**
   - **Hair:** Wash at least once a week, use conditioner on the ends, rinse very well, avoid too many hair treatments and trim every six weeks.
   - **Hands:** Wash after using the toilet, keep nails clean and filed, use hand cream and wear rubber gloves.
   - **Feet:** Wash daily, dry between the toes, wear good footwear, cut nails straight across and change socks daily.

The skin

1. Name the three layers of the skin.
2. Draw and label a diagram of the skin.
3. Describe five functions of the skin.
4. What causes body odour? List five ways body odour can be avoided.
5. What causes acne? Suggest some ways acne can be helped.
6. List six ways of promoting healthy skin. Include information on how the risk of skin cancer can be minimised.
7. How should we care for our (a) hair (b) hands and (c) feet?

Homework
Assignment
38
P 133

Respiratory system

The respiratory system takes oxygen from the air when we breathe in and brings it to the cells of the body to make energy. This is called **oxidation**. Carbon dioxide is produced as waste and is removed by the respiratory system when we breathe out. The respiratory tract (below) is part of this system.

1. Air passes through the mouth and nose, where it is warmed. Some dust is filtered by the hairs in the nose.
2. Air then passes by the **pharynx** and **larynx** (voice box) and **epiglottis**. The epiglottis is a flap of skin that covers the windpipe when we swallow to stop food from going down the windpipe.

3. Air then passes into the **trachea**, or windpipe. The trachea divides into branches called **bronchi**. Each bronchus divides again and again to form tiny **bronchioles**.
4. At the end of each tiny bronchiole is an **air sac**, or **alveolus** (plural: **alveoli**). Oxygen and carbon dioxide are exchanged here.

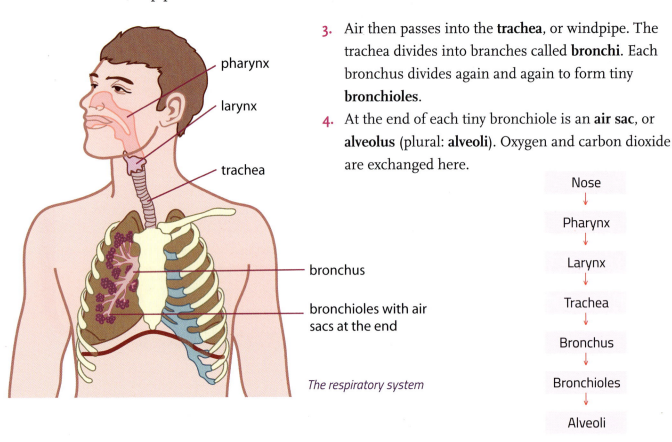

pharynx

larynx

trachea

bronchus

bronchioles with air sacs at the end

The respiratory system

Nose
↓
Pharynx
↓
Larynx
↓
Trachea
↓
Bronchus
↓
Bronchioles
↓
Alveoli

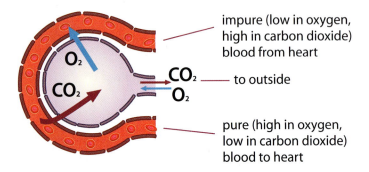

O_2

CO_2

impure (low in oxygen, high in carbon dioxide) blood from heart

CO_2 — to outside
O_2

pure (high in oxygen, low in carbon dioxide) blood to heart

Exchange of gases

The exchange of gases happens in the air sacs (alveoli) of the lungs. The air sacs are surrounded by capillaries. Carbon dioxide is removed from the blood in the capillaries and oxygen is added in its place. This oxygen-rich blood then returns to the heart and is pumped around the body.

Functions of the lungs

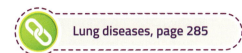 Take in oxygen

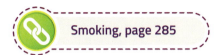 Remove carbon dioxide and water vapour

🔗 Lung diseases, page 285

🔗 Smoking, page 285

Respiratory system

1. **Function:** The respiratory system takes oxygen from the air we breathe and brings it to cells, where it is burned for energy. Carbon dioxide is a waste product of this process and is breathed out.

2. **Structure:** The respiratory system consists of the nose and mouth, pharynx, larynx (voice box), epiglottis, trachea, two bronchi, bronchioles and alveoli (in the lungs).

3. **Exchange of gases:** Occurs in the lungs. Alveoli are surrounded by tiny capillaries. Oxygen leaves the alveoli and enters the capillaries. Carbon dioxide leaves the capillaries and enters the alveoli to be breathed out.

4. **Functions of lungs:** To take in oxygen and remove carbon dioxide from the bloodstream.

The respiratory system (Higher Level only)

1. What is meant by oxidation? What is the main waste product produced by the respiratory system following oxidation?

2. Draw and label a diagram of the respiratory system and then describe the passage of air through it.

3. Where and how does the exchange of gases occur?

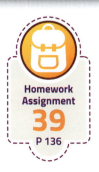

Homework
Assignment
39
P 136

H Circulatory system

The circulatory system consists of the heart, the blood vessels and the blood. The circulatory system's job is to carry blood full of oxygen and nutrients around the body and then to collect waste products, such as carbon dioxide.

The heart is a strong muscular organ that pumps blood either to the lungs (to get oxygen) or around the body. It lies between the lungs in the middle of the chest and is about the size of your fist. The heart has four chambers, with a wall called the septum dividing the left and right sides.

Blood flow through the heart

1. Impure blood (full of carbon dioxide) comes into the heart from the rest of the body through the vena cava into the right atrium. The right atrium contracts (squeezes in), pushing the blood through valves into the right ventricle.
2. The blood is then pushed out of the heart through a valve into the pulmonary artery and to the lungs.
3. In the lungs, carbon dioxide is exchanged for oxygen.
4. The blood then returns through the pulmonary veins to the left atrium.
5. The left atrium contracts, pushing blood through a valve into the left ventricle.
6. The left ventricle then contracts, pushing blood through a valve into the aorta.
7. The aorta brings the oxygen-rich blood around the body.
8. The body uses this oxygen and produces carbon dioxide. This carbon dioxide is brought back to the vena cava and the cycle begins again.

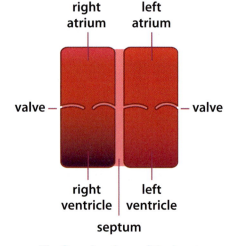

The four chambers of the heart

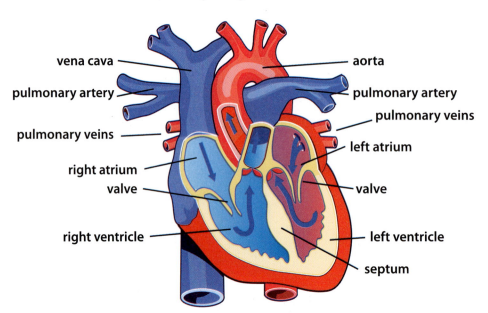

Pulse

The heartbeat is the sound of the valves in the heart opening and closing. Each time the heart beats, blood is forced into the arteries – this can be felt as a pulse. The average pulse is 72 beats per minute. It is usually taken by placing the first two fingertips on the wrist, as shown in the photograph, and counting.

Taking a pulse

Blood vessels

Blood vessels are tubes that carry blood around the body. There are three types:

- **Artery:** Arteries carry blood away from the heart under pressure. They have thick elastic walls.

- **Vein:** Veins carry blood to the heart. The blood is not under much pressure, so valves are needed to stop it from flowing backwards. They have thin walls.

- **Capillary:** Capillaries join arteries and veins. Their walls are only one cell thick. This allows oxygen and nutrients to pass through into the body's cells.

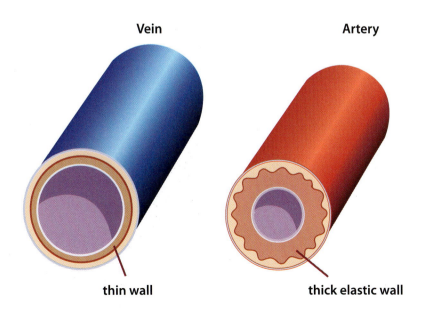

| **Vein** | **Artery** |
| thin wall | thick elastic wall |

The blood

An adult has approximately 5 litres of blood in their body.

Composition

- **Plasma:** A yellowish liquid in which the blood cells float.
- **Red blood cells:** These disc-shaped cells contain haemoglobin, which carries oxygen around the body. Iron is needed to make haemoglobin.
- **White blood cells:** These fight infection. They surround the germs causing the infection and destroy them. Pus is the result of white blood cells and germs fighting each other.
- **Platelets:** Small cells that clot blood when we get a cut to form a scab.

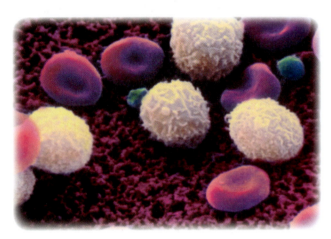

Red blood cells, white blood cells and platelets (the platelets appear green in this photo)

Functions of the blood

- Transports oxygen, carbon dioxide, nutrients, hormones, enzymes and waste around the body
- Fights infection (white blood cells)

Coronary heart disease (CHD)

Sometimes the arteries of the heart become blocked by cholesterol. If this happens, a heart attack occurs and the person's life is at risk. The risk of coronary heart disease is mostly hereditary. It can be reduced by decreasing the amount of animal fat in the diet.

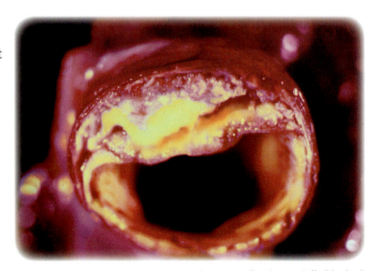

An artery that is partially blocked by cholesterol

Chapter 4, page 35 – dietary causes of CHD and strokes

Circulatory system

1. **Circulatory system:** Heart, blood vessels and blood. Function is to carry blood rich in oxygen and nutrients to the cells and to collect waste products for excretion.

2. **The heart:** Four chambers divided by septum, right atrium and ventricle, left atrium and ventricle.

3. **Blood flow through the heart:** Vena cava, right atrium, valves, right ventricle, pulmonary arteries, lungs, pulmonary veins, left atrium, valves, left ventricle, aorta, cells.

4. **Pulse:** Blood being forced into arteries from the heart is felt as a pulse. The average is 72 beats per minute.

5. **Blood vessels:** Arteries (bring blood from heart, thick elastic walls), veins (bring blood to heart, thin walls, valves to prevent backward blood flow), capillaries (very thin walls just one cell thick, join arteries and veins).

6. **Blood:** Plasma (straw coloured, blood cells float in it), red blood cells (disc shaped, carry oxygen), white blood cells (irregularly shaped, fight infection), platelets (small cells that help with clotting). Functions of blood are to transport oxygen, hormones, nutrients and enzymes around the body and to transport waste to organs of excretion (carbon dioxide to the lungs).

7. **Coronary heart disease (CHD):** When arteries become blocked with cholesterol. Risk is mostly hereditary, but you can reduce the risk with a low-cholesterol diet.

The circulatory system (Higher Level only)

1. What is the circulatory system composed of?
2. What is the main function of the circulatory system?
3. Draw and label a diagram of the heart and describe in words the passage of blood through the heart.
4. What is a pulse? Describe how it is taken.
5. Name and describe the three types of blood vessels in the body.
6. List and describe the function of the four constituents of blood.
7. What is coronary heart disease? How can the risk of CHD be reduced?

Test Yourself
eTest.ie

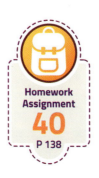

Homework Assignment

40

P 138

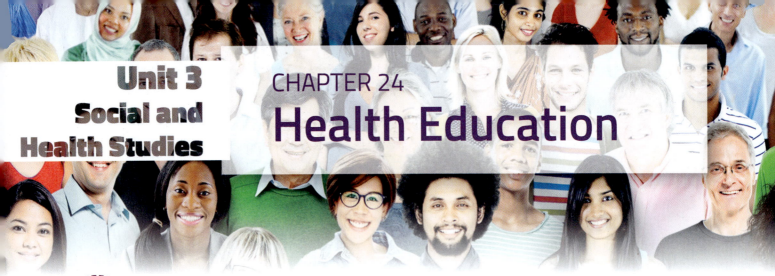

Unit 3
Social and Health Studies

CHAPTER 24
Health Education

Slide presentation ▪ Student activity pack with revision crossword ▪ Class test ▪ Student learning contract

Key words

- ✔ Balanced diet
- ✔ Leisure time
- ✔ Aerobic exercise
- ✔ Mental health
- ✔ Self-esteem
- ✔ Stress
- ✔ Health hazards
- ✔ Emphysema
- ✔ Passive smoking
- ✔ Problem drinker
- ✔ Social drinker
- ✔ Short-term effects
- ✔ Long-term effects
- ✔ Legal drugs
- ✔ Illegal drugs
- ✔ Restricted drugs
- ✔ Depressants
- ✔ Hallucinogens
- ✔ Sedatives
- ✔ Opiates
- ✔ Stimulants

Learning outcomes

After completing this chapter and the homework, assignments and activities that accompany it, you should:

- Be able to define good health and be able to describe the seven guidelines for good health.
- Be able to describe what we should reduce and increase in our diets for better health.
- Be able to describe the benefits of exercise.
- Understand why adequate sleep, rest and relaxation are important for good health and be able to describe how these can be promoted.
- Know what positive mental health is and how it can be promoted.
- Understand the concept of self-esteem and the factors that can cause a person to have low or high self-esteem.
- Know what stress is, what effects it can have on the body, both in the short and long term, and be able to describe some ways of coping with stress.
- Be able to describe the effects of smoking on the body. Understand the terms *emphysema* and *passive smoking*. Understand the effects that smoking can have on an unborn baby during pregnancy.
- Understand what safe limits are for alcohol. Be able to describe the short- and long-term effects of alcohol abuse on the mind, body, family and society. Know where people can get help.
- Be able to classify drugs in terms of their legal status and effects on the mind and body. Be able to discuss the effects of drug use on the individual, family and society.
- Understand the ways in which society tries to promote health and prevent the use of health hazards.

In this chapter you will study:

- Good health
- Health hazards

Health

The World Health Organization (WHO) describes health as **a complete state of physical, mental and social well-being, and not simply the absence of disease or infirmity**. With this definition in mind, we can list seven general guidelines to good health.

Good health guide

1. Eat a balanced diet.

2. Get enough rest and sleep.

3. Avoid cigarettes, drugs and alcohol.

4. Have good personal hygiene.

5. Take regular exercise.

6. Treat those around you with respect – you in turn will be treated with respect.

7. Think positively about yourself and your experiences (mental well-being).

Healthy diet

Try to follow a balanced diet. Remember the healthy eating guidelines:

- Eat less food that is high in fat, salt or sugar (crisps, cakes, highly processed foods).
- Increase fibre intake by eating more fruit, vegetables, brown bread, brown rice, etc.
- Drink plenty of water.

 Chapter 3: A Balanced Diet

Exercise

Exercise is vital to good health. Most children do not need to be told to take exercise – they just do it automatically. Unfortunately, during the late teens and early twenties, many people give up sport and regular exercise. This results in unfitness and weight gain. Habits formed during this time can stay for life.

Benefits of exercise

Reduces stress

Keeps weight off

Keeps heart and lungs healthy

Maintains good muscle tone and bone density

Relaxation and sleep

Getting enough sleep is vital to good health. For a good night's sleep, avoid having large meals, tea or coffee late in the evening. Stop doing homework or studying at least one hour before bedtime, as your body and mind need to be relaxed for you to sleep well.

Stress is the most common cause of sleeplessness. It is better to treat the stress itself rather than the sleeplessness alone (for example, with sleeping pills, which can be habit-forming).

Leisure time

Leisure time is time spent away from work, school or study. Some people waste their leisure time and then complain about being bored. They say things like, 'There is absolutely nothing to do in this area or town.' This is rarely true. Sometimes leisure facilities are there but people either do not know about them or are unwilling to use them.

Aerobic exercise, such as jogging, step aerobics or playing active sports, works the heart and lungs, making them stronger and healthier.

Mental health

In general, a mentally healthy person:

- Feels positive about themselves (positive self-image or high self-esteem)
- Feels positive about the people and world around them
- Is able to cope with life most of the time

Mental health guidelines

- Look after your physical health (good diet, exercise, relaxation and sleep).
- Do not smoke or use drugs. Keep alcohol within healthy limits.
- Think positively about yourself (see the self-esteem section below).
- Form a few close, trusting friendships. Do not neglect these friendships, for instance if you have a new boyfriend or girlfriend.
- Discuss problems and feelings with a trusted friend.
- Have a good routine in your life, including regular sleep and meals.
- Make good use of leisure time.
- Avoid too much stress.

Mental and physical health rely on each other – neglect one and the other suffers

Self-esteem

People who like themselves and have confidence in their abilities have **high self-esteem**. Those who do not think much of themselves or their abilities have **low self-esteem**.

Why do some people have low self-esteem?

During childhood, how others treat us plays an important part in the development of our self-esteem. Children who are neglected, abused, criticised or live with family problems such as alcohol abuse or poverty are more likely to have low self-esteem. In adulthood, how we treat ourselves has a lot to do with our self-esteem.

The issues below are sometimes linked with low self-esteem:

 Alcohol or drug abuse

 Being very critical of others

 Bullying (bullies usually have low self-esteem)

 Leaving school early

 Mental illness (depression)

 Overeating

 Possessiveness

 Smoking

 Staying in abusive relationships

 Teen pregnancy

Stress

Stress is a normal reaction to difficulties in our lives. Some stress is healthy or else we would become bored. Problems occur when we experience too much stress.

Common effects of stress on the body and mind	
Body	**Mind**
Short term:	• Anger
• Faster breathing	• Anxiety
• Increased heartbeat	• Being easily irritated
• Indigestion	• Feeling depressed
• Sweating	• Feeling unable to cope
• Forgetfulness	• Frustration
	• Low self-esteem
Long term:	• Tearfulness
• Backache	• Tension
• Frequent headaches	• Tiredness
• High blood pressure	
• Prone to infection	
• Skin problems, such as eczema	
• Stomach ulcers	

Coping with stress

There are two basic ways of coping with stress:

 Get rid of the cause of the stress, for example by reducing your workload.

 Do something to relieve the symptoms. Eat well. Take physical exercise. Take time to relax. Get enough sleep. Talk over your problems with someone you trust.

Health hazards

Every year in Ireland, thousands of people die prematurely because they expose themselves to health hazards such as smoking, excessive alcohol or illegal drugs use.

Smoking

Effects of smoking

- Nicotine (the drug in cigarettes) is highly addictive
- Strokes (blood clots in the brain)
- Discoloured teeth and hair, bad breath
- Skin becomes wrinkled and aged
- Heart disease
- Tar in tobacco causes lung cancer, frequent bronchitis (lung infections) and emphysema (see below)

Emphysema

Emphysema is a serious, incurable lung disease. Ninety per cent of people with the disease are smokers. Someone with emphysema has a lot of trouble breathing or doing anything that needs energy, such as climbing stairs.

Smoking causes premature ageing of the skin

Passive smoking

Passive smoking means inhaling other people's smoke. Frequent passive smokers run the same health risks as smokers.

Smoking during pregnancy

- If you smoke, your baby smokes too.
- There is an increased risk of the baby miscarrying or being stillborn.
- Babies of smokers are smaller and more likely to be premature. While even very premature babies often live nowadays, they can be left with permanent problems, such as cerebral palsy, blindness, deafness and lung problems.
- Smoking near a baby either before or after it is born increases the risk of cot death.
- The children of smokers are more likely to smoke themselves.

Babies of smokers are much more likely to be born premature

It is widely believed that giving up smoking is as difficult as giving up heroin. So why do so many young people start each year? Curiosity? Image? Peer pressure? What do you think?

Alcohol

When taken in moderation, alcohol can be a positive social substance. Historically, however, the Irish have had a very unusual relationship with alcohol. We have tended to either not drink at all or else drink to excess. In fact, it is estimated that one in 10 Irish adults are problem drinkers (previously called alcoholics).

A person is considered to be a problem drinker when alcohol is causing a problem in their home, at school, in their social life or at work, such as missing a day of work because of a hangover.

Moderate social drinking

Safe alcohol limits spread over the week

- Fully grown men: 21 units per week
- Fully grown women: 14 units per week
- One unit = half a pint of beer or lager, a glass of wine or a small measure of spirits
- Drinking more than five units at one time is considered binge drinking by the World Health Organization.

Short-term effects of alcohol abuse

Effects of alcohol abuse on the mind and body

Short term:

- Face turns red
- Loss of inhibitions, such as having unprotected sex
- Mood alters: drinker may become aggressive, sad, etc.
- Vomiting
- Lack of co-ordination, such as staggering
- Poor driving skills – a 17-year-old male driver is 40 times more likely to have an accident after one and a half to two units of alcohol

Long term:

- Addiction
- Brain damage
- Mental illness (depression)
- Heart disease
- Liver disease (cirrhosis)
- Cancer of the mouth or stomach
- Foetal alcohol syndrome (birth defects caused by drinking during pregnancy)

Effects of alcohol abuse on the family

- General unhappiness and uncertainty in the family: 'Will he/she be drunk tonight?'
- Separation and divorce
- Violence in the home
- Financial problems

Effects of alcohol abuse on society

- **Road accidents:** One in three road deaths is related to alcohol.
- **Crime:** Links between crime and alcohol abuse are well documented. For example, 76% of all rape defendants had been drinking at the time of the alleged crime, alcohol has been identified in 97% of all public order offences and almost 50% of all homicides were committed while the perpetrator was under the influence of alcohol.
- **Cost:** Cost of treating people for alcohol-related health problems.
- **Absenteeism:** People not turning up for work because of alcohol abuse.

This is the author of 'A Child Called It'. He lived his life with parents addicted to alcohol.

Help for those affected by alcohol abuse

- Alcoholics Anonymous (help for the problem drinker themselves):
  (01) 842 0700; www.alcoholicsanonymous.ie
- Al-Anon (help for families and friends of problem drinkers):
  (01) 873 2699; www.al-anon-ireland.org
- Al Ateen (help for the teenage children of problem drinkers):
  (01) 873 2699; www.al-anon-ireland.org

Note: These are all central numbers and websites. They will direct you to local services.

Drugs

Classification

Drugs can be classified in two ways: according to their effect on the body (see the table below) or their legal status.

Legal status

Drugs can be legal (caffeine, nicotine, alcohol), illegal (cannabis, cocaine) or restricted (such as Valium, which is only available through a prescription).

Type	Examples	Effects
Depressants	Alcohol	• Slows down the nervous system, making the person relaxed but uncoordinated
Hallucinogens	LSD, magic mushrooms, ecstasy, cannabis, solvents	• Causes changes in mood and thought patterns • May hear and see things in a different way to reality
Sedatives	Sleeping tablets, cannabis, tranquillisers (e.g. Valium)	• Relief of tension/anxiety • Causes sleep, physical and psychological dependence
Opiates	Heroin, methadone, morphine	• Feelings of euphoria (intense pleasure) but highly addictive
Stimulants	Caffeine, nicotine, ecstasy, cocaine	• Increases heart rate and breathing • Prevents sleep • Feelings of intense well-being and energy (ecstasy and cocaine)

Effects of drug abuse on the individual and their families

- Health problems, such as HIV from sharing dirty needles, weight loss or cancer if the drug is smoked.
- Physical, psychological and social addiction makes it difficult for the addict to cope with life without the drug.
- Loss of self-respect – an addict will do anything to get the drug.
- Loss of ambition – for example, regular cannabis use can have a huge effect on a young person's desire to do well at school, in sport, etc.
- Mental illness, such as depression or paranoia.
- Families and children of addicts may suffer poverty, worry, neglect and abuse.

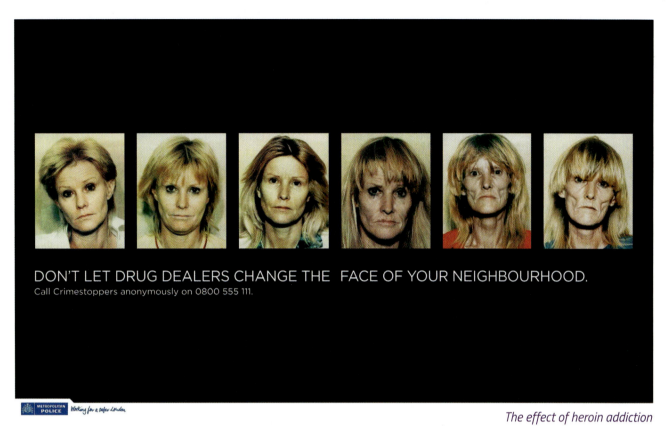

DON'T LET DRUG DEALERS CHANGE THE FACE OF YOUR NEIGHBOURHOOD.
Call Crimestoppers anonymously on 0800 555 111.

METROPOLITAN POLICE   Working for a safer London

The effect of heroin addiction

Effects of drug abuse on society

- Crime – many addicts steal to support their habits
- Cost to the taxpayer
- Addicts strain an already stretched healthcare system
- Welfare payments for addicts unfit to work

Health promotion

Most countries ban or limit the use of substances that are hazardous to health. There are laws banning drink driving and some drugs. Health promotion tactics include health warnings on cigarettes and drug education in schools.

For further information on any health issue, www.healthpromotion.ie is a useful site and will direct you to other relevant sites, such as www.drugs.ie.

1. **Good health guide:** Balanced diet, adequate sleep and rest, avoid health hazards, good personal hygiene, take exercise, treat yourself and others with respect and think positively.

2. **Stress:** Too much stress causes physical and mental problems.
    *   **Physical:** High blood pressure, headaches, more prone to infection, skin problems, ulcers.
    *   **Mental:** Anger, anxiety, feeling unable to cope, tiredness.
    *   **Coping with stress:** Eliminate the cause. If that is not possible, then deal with the symptoms, eat well, exercise, rest and talk to someone.

3. **Smoking:** Nicotine is a highly addictive drug. Smoking causes discolouration of hair, skin and teeth, bad breath, skin ageing, lung cancer and emphysema, heart disease and strokes. Smoking during pregnancy increases the risk of miscarriage, stillbirth, prematurity and cot death. The children of smokers are more likely to smoke themselves.

4. **Alcohol:** One in 10 Irish adults is a problem drinker. Safe limits are 21 units a week for men, 14 for women.
    *   **Short-term effects:** Loss of inhibitions, mood altered, vomiting, loss of co-ordination.
    *   **Long-term effects:** Addiction, brain damage, mental illness, heart and liver disease, cancer of mouth and stomach, foetal alcohol syndrome. Alcohol abuse also has a negative effect on family life and society in general.

5. **Drugs**
    *   **Classification** by legal status (legal, illegal and restricted) and by the effect on the mind and body: depressants (alcohol), hallucinogens (ecstasy), sedatives (Valium), opiates (heroin), stimulants (cocaine).
    *   **Effects of drug use:** Health problems (cancer if the drug is smoked), loss of self-respect, loss of ambition, increased risk of mental illness, family of abuser suffers, increased crime, cost to taxpayer, healthcare and social welfare payments.

6. **Health promotion:** Laws ban or restrict certain substances. Government warnings and campaigns try to change behaviours.

Revision Questions

1. How does the World Health Organization define health?
2. List seven guidelines for good health.
3. List three basic healthy eating guidelines.
4. List four benefits of exercise. What is aerobic exercise? What is its main benefit?
5. What can you do/not do before bedtime to help ensure you get a good night's sleep?
6. Give eight guidelines for positive mental health.
7. What is self-esteem? Why might some children have low-self esteem?
8. List five issues linked with low self-esteem in adolescents and young adults.
9. List four long-term effects of stress. Suggest three ways of coping with stress.
10. Describe five effects of smoking on the body.
11. What is passive smoking? What are its effects?
12. What are the effects on an unborn baby of smoking during pregnancy?
13. What are considered to be safe weekly alcohol limits for fully grown men and women?
14. When would someone be considered a problem drinker?
15. What effects can alcohol abuse have on (a) the individual (b) the family (c) society?
16. Where can problem drinkers and their families get help?
17. How can drugs be classified? Give one example of each class.
18. What effects can drug abuse have on (a) the individual (b) the family (c) society?

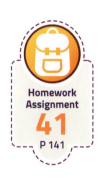

Homework
Assignment
41
P 141

Unit 4
Resource Management and Home Studies

A good management system

A good management system allows you to achieve what you set out to achieve. It involves five steps.

1. **Goals:** Decide what it is you want to achieve, for example to provide healthy family meals for the week.
2. **Resources:** Think about everything you need to carry out the tasks involved (time, food, equipment, etc.).
3. **Plan:** For example, make out menus for the week, make a shopping list, etc.
4. **Action:** Carry out the action: make a shopping list, buy the food and cook the food.
5. **Evaluate:** How well did you achieve your goals? If they were not achieved, why not? What could you do better next time?

Weekly cleaning roster/work routine

1. List all the jobs that need to be done and divide them up according to how often they have to be done: daily (dishes, make the beds), weekly (vacuum the stairs, change the bed linen) or occasionally (wash windows).
2. Divide the jobs according to how much free time the person has and how old they are. For example, a young child cannot be expected to cook dinner.
3. Make sure two or three weekly jobs are done every day and that one occasional job is done every week.
4. Try out the roster and change it if necessary.

Case study

Alan and Deirdre Burke both work full time and have two teenage sons: Cian, aged 16, and Daniel, aged 14. While both children are very academic and work hard at school, they need help with home management, as the house is never really clean and is always a mess, with books, shoes and clothes lying everywhere. Both parents have well-paid but pressurised jobs and find that they are often too tired in the evenings or at weekends to do much housework. The two boys do virtually no housework – they hardly even bring their clothes down for the wash, which often results in their rooms being an absolute mess. The bed linen is changed infrequently and the bathrooms are cleaned irregularly. In terms of cooking, the family eats out at least twice a week and uses a lot of convenience foods. The house is nice and in a very expensive area, but the garden is really overgrown and the house looks a bit shabby, as the windows are rarely cleaned and there are weeds growing up through the cobble lock in the driveway. Deirdre gets a burst of energy every now and then and buys lots of potted plants for outside, which all inevitably die from lack of watering.

How would you help this family manage their home more efficiently?

Unit 4
Resource Management and Home Studies

A good management system

A good management system allows you to achieve what you set out to achieve. It involves five steps.

1. **Goals:** Decide what it is you want to achieve, for example to provide healthy family meals for the week.
2. **Resources:** Think about everything you need to carry out the tasks involved (time, food, equipment, etc.).
3. **Plan:** For example, make out menus for the week, make a shopping list, etc.
4. **Action:** Carry out the action: make a shopping list, buy the food and cook the food.
5. **Evaluate:** How well did you achieve your goals? If they were not achieved, why not? What could you do better next time?

Weekly cleaning roster/work routine

1. List all the jobs that need to be done and divide them up according to how often they have to be done: daily (dishes, make the beds), weekly (vacuum the stairs, change the bed linen) or occasionally (wash windows).
2. Divide the jobs according to how much free time the person has and how old they are. For example, a young child cannot be expected to cook dinner.
3. Make sure two or three weekly jobs are done every day and that one occasional job is done every week.
4. Try out the roster and change it if necessary.

Case study

Alan and Deirdre Burke both work full time and have two teenage sons: Cian, aged 16, and Daniel, aged 14. While both children are very academic and work hard at school, they need help with home management, as the house is never really clean and is always a mess, with books, shoes and clothes lying everywhere. Both parents have well-paid but pressurised jobs and find that they are often too tired in the evenings or at weekends to do much housework. The two boys do virtually no housework – they hardly even bring their clothes down for the wash, which often results in their rooms being an absolute mess. The bed linen is changed infrequently and the bathrooms are cleaned irregularly. In terms of cooking, the family eats out at least twice a week and uses a lot of convenience foods. The house is nice and in a very expensive area, but the garden is really overgrown and the house looks a bit shabby, as the windows are rarely cleaned and there are weeds growing up through the cobble lock in the driveway. Deirdre gets a burst of energy every now and then and buys lots of potted plants for outside, which all inevitably die from lack of watering.

How would you help this family manage their home more efficiently?

Unit 4
Resource Management and Home Studies

CHAPTER 25

Home Management

Teacher's CD

Slide presentation ▪ Student activity pack with revision crossword ▪ Class test ▪ Student learning contract

Key words

- ✓ Home management
- ✓ Resources
- ✓ Goals
- ✓ Evaluation
- ✓ Cleaning roster
- ✓ Work routine

Learning outcomes

After completing this chapter and the homework, assignments and activities that accompany it, you should:

- Know the principle tasks that are involved in running a home and understand the reasons why good home management is important.
- Be able to list the four resources required for efficient home management.
- Understand the five stages involved in a good home management system and be able to apply this to real-life situations.
- Be able to compile a weekly cleaning roster/ work routine for a household.

The tasks involved in running the home include:

🏠 Budgeting

🏠 Child care

🏠 Cleaning and maintenance

🏠 Cooking

🏠 Gardening

🏠 Laundry

🏠 Shopping

Some of these tasks need to be done daily, others weekly or less often. In order to make sure they get done, planning is needed.

Home management is the efficient running of the home. When a home is run efficiently, money is not wasted, the home is kept clean and tidy, laundry is done and the family tends to eat more healthily. Because of today's busy lifestyles, efficient home management is even more important. **All family members should be involved in the running of the home.** Good home management means using **resources** wisely to achieve **goals.**

Well, someone's got to do it, dear.

Resources

Resources are what we use to carry out the tasks listed above. There are four basic resources.

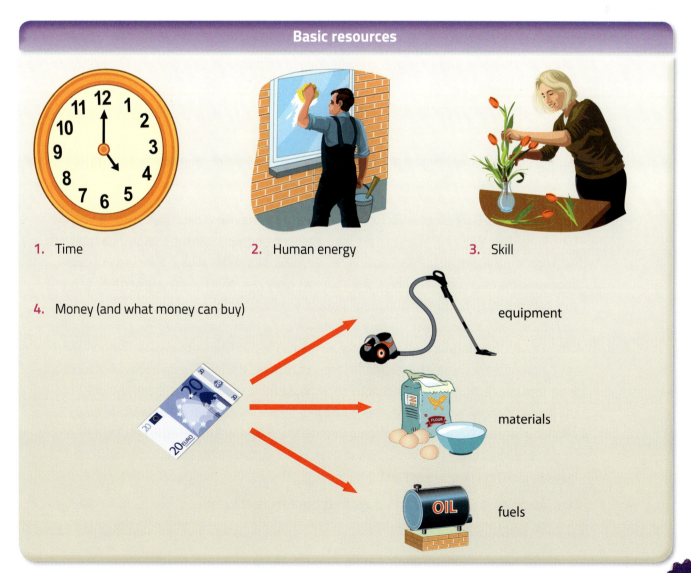

Basic resources

1. Time
2. Human energy
3. Skill
4. Money (and what money can buy)

equipment

materials

fuels

A good management system

A good management system allows you to achieve what you set out to achieve. It involves five steps.

1. **Goals:** Decide what it is you want to achieve, for example to provide healthy family meals for the week.
2. **Resources:** Think about everything you need to carry out the tasks involved (time, food, equipment, etc.).
3. **Plan:** For example, make out menus for the week, make a shopping list, etc.
4. **Action:** Carry out the action: make a shopping list, buy the food and cook the food.
5. **Evaluate:** How well did you achieve your goals? If they were not achieved, why not? What could you do better next time?

Weekly cleaning roster/work routine

1. List all the jobs that need to be done and divide them up according to how often they have to be done: daily (dishes, make the beds), weekly (vacuum the stairs, change the bed linen) or occasionally (wash windows).
2. Divide the jobs according to how much free time the person has and how old they are. For example, a young child cannot be expected to cook dinner.
3. Make sure two or three weekly jobs are done every day and that one occasional job is done every week.
4. Try out the roster and change it if necessary.

Case study

Alan and Deirdre Burke both work full time and have two teenage sons: Cian, aged 16, and Daniel, aged 14. While both children are very academic and work hard at school, they need help with home management, as the house is never really clean and is always a mess, with books, shoes and clothes lying everywhere. Both parents have well-paid but pressurised jobs and find that they are often too tired in the evenings or at weekends to do much housework. The two boys do virtually no housework – they hardly even bring their clothes down for the wash, which often results in their rooms being an absolute mess. The bed linen is changed infrequently and the bathrooms are cleaned irregularly. In terms of cooking, the family eats out at least twice a week and uses a lot of convenience foods. The house is nice and in a very expensive area, but the garden is really overgrown and the house looks a bit shabby, as the windows are rarely cleaned and there are weeds growing up through the cobble lock in the driveway. Deirdre gets a burst of energy every now and then and buys lots of potted plants for outside, which all inevitably die from lack of watering.

How would you help this family manage their home more efficiently?

1. **Running a home:** Tasks involved are budgeting, childcare, cleaning and maintenance, cooking, gardening, laundry and shopping.

2. **Home management:** Efficient running of the home is essential for happiness and well-being. All family members should be involved.

3. **Resources:** Time, energy, skill, money and what it can buy.

4. **Management system:** Set goals, think about the resources required, make plans, carry out the actions and evaluate.

5. **Cleaning rosters/routines:** List all the jobs that have to be done. Decide which ones are daily, weekly and occasional jobs. Divide the jobs out. Make sure weekly and occasional jobs are factored in.

1. List six tasks involved in running a home.
2. What is good home management? What are its main advantages?
3. List four resources needed for good home management.
4. Describe the five steps of a good home management system.
5. How would you plan a weekly cleaning roster for a family?

Test Yourself
eTest.ie

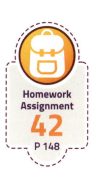

Homework Assignment

42

P 148

CHAPTER 26

Home Design and Room Planning

Teacher's CD

Slide presentation • Student activity pack with revision crossword • Class test • Student learning contract

Key words

- ✓ Types of accommodation
- ✓ Physical needs
- ✓ Emotional needs
- ✓ Social needs
- ✓ Function
- ✓ Form
- ✓ Primary colours
- ✓ Secondary colours
- ✓ Tertiary colours
- ✓ Warm colours
- ✓ Cool colours
- ✓ Pastels
- ✓ Neutral colours
- ✓ Shade
- ✓ Tint
- ✓ Pattern
- ✓ Texture
- ✓ Proportion
- ✓ Emphasis
- ✓ Balance
- ✓ Rhythm
- ✓ Ergonomics
- ✓ Work triangle
- ✓ Soft furnishings

Learning outcomes

After completing this chapter and the homework, assignments and activities that accompany it, you should:

- Be able to list and describe the main types of accommodation available in Ireland.
- Be able to explain how a home provides for our physical, emotional and social needs.
- Be able to explain the factors that influence our choice of housing.
- Understand the principles of design and be able to apply them to interior design.
- Be able to describe the factors that must be considered when planning a room.
- Understand the principle of ergonomics and the kitchen work triangle.
- Know the different types of floor coverings, wall finishes, soft furnishings and lighting choices available for interior decoration.

Shelter is a basic human need. Even though house prices in Ireland are still relatively high, over 75% of families in Ireland are homeowners. This is a much higher figure than many of our European neighbours – for example, in Germany the figure is 46%.

Types of accommodation

🏠 **Houses:** Bungalow, two to three storeys, detached, semi-detached, terraced.

🏠 **Apartments:** Purpose-built or a large house divided into flats or bedsits (one room).

🏠 **Institutions:** Convents, hostels (such as Homeless Aid), boarding schools, nursing homes.

🏠 **Sheltered housing:** A number of small housing units built together, for example for elderly or disabled people. There is a warden and sometimes a doctor or nurse on call.

🏠 **Caravan or mobile home:** Used by the Irish Travelling community. Young people sometimes live in mobile homes on site while their house is being built to save spending money on rent.

Ireland has the lowest number of people living in apartment accommodation, at just 4% – the EU average is 42%

Making a house a home

A house simply provides shelter; a home also contains people and their unique possessions. It provides for other needs as well.

🏠 **Physical needs:** Shelter, warmth and protection.

🏠 **Emotional needs:** Safety, security, love, privacy (curtains are one of the first things people buy for a new home).

🏠 **Social needs:** It is at home that we learn our basic social skills, such as table manners, as children. People feel comfortable and can be themselves at home.

Choosing a home

Choice of housing is usually influenced by:

🏠 **Cost:** Is it within my price range?

🏠 **Location:** Is it close to work, family, etc.?

🏠 **Size:** Is it big enough for my needs, such as a growing family?

🏠 **Style of house:** Do I like the overall style of the house, how it is laid out, etc.?

Design

Good design is when something is safe, functional, attractive to look at and hard-wearing.

Features of design include:

- 🏠 Function
- 🏠 Form (shape and line)
- 🏠 Colour
- 🏠 Pattern
- 🏠 Texture

Function

Products that are well designed do what they are meant to do or serve their function. For example, a vegetable peeler must be able to peel vegetables and a lunchbox must stay closed in a schoolbag.

What shapes do you see in this modern kitchen?

Form (shape and line)

Shape

Most objects in the home, rooms and even houses themselves use four basic shapes: square, rectangle, triangle and circle.

Line

Lines in rooms, houses, furniture, clothing or objects can be vertical, horizontal or curved. Each creates a different effect.

Vertical lines cause the eye to look up and down. They make things look taller and narrower. For example, if you wanted to make the ceiling in a room look higher, you could use vertically striped wallpaper.

Horizontal lines make things look shorter and wider. For example, if you wanted to make the ceiling in a room look lower in order to make the room look cosier, you could use horizontal striped wallpaper.

Curved lines appear soft and feminine.

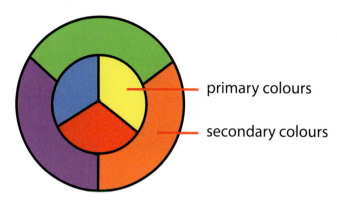

primary colours

secondary colours

The colour wheel

Colour

Colour is an important element of design, especially interior design. Paint a room white and you will create a feeling of light and space. Paint that same room plum and it will feel smaller and cosier.

The colour wheel

- 🏠 **Primary colours:** Blue, yellow, red.
- 🏠 **Secondary colours:** Two primary colours mixed together – green, orange, purple.
- 🏠 **Tertiary colours:** One primary colour and one secondary colour mixed together. For example, blue + green = turquoise.

Describing colours

Colours can be described as being warm, cool, neutral or pastel. Each of these can be used to create a different effect in the home.

Warm colours: Vibrant, warm colours such as reds, oranges, pinks and purples are very rich. When used alone they make a room look much smaller than it is. They are best used in small amounts with neutrals or pastels. For example, paint three walls with neutrals or pastels and paint one wall a warm, rich colour.

Warm colours

Cool colours

Pastels

Neutral colours

Cool colours like blue and green create an atmosphere that is cool and restful. Cool colours are best used in warm, sunny rooms.

Pastels like light blue, green, pink and yellow are also restful. Pastels are ideal for bedrooms.

Neutral colours: Black, white, cream and beige are often called neutral colours. Interest can be added to neutral colours by adding splashes of strong colour.

✳ A shade: Black is added to a colour to darken it.
✳ A tint: White is added to a colour to lighten it.

Pattern

Pattern can add interest to a room. Too much pattern makes a room look crowded and untidy. It is possible, however, to have several different patterns in a room if you keep the colours the same.

Good use of pattern

Texture

Texture describes how an object feels: rough, smooth, warm or cool.

🏠 **Smooth texture**, such as the texture of tiles and painted surfaces, gives a cool, clean, hygienic feel.

🏠 **Rough texture**, such as the texture of carpets and curtains, absorbs sound and gives a warm, cosy feel.

Smooth textures are clean and hygienic

Rough textures add warmth and interest

Elements of design

There are four important elements in design. These apply well to interior design.

🏠 **Proportion:** This relates to the size of objects. Pieces of furniture in a room should be *in proportion* to each other and to the room. For example, a large antique table would be *out of proportion* in a small apartment.

🏠 **Emphasis:** When the eye is drawn towards something in the room. This is called the *focal point*, such as a fireplace.

🏠 **Balance:** When there is an equal spread of colour, pattern and texture in a room.

🏠 **Rhythm:** This is where a colour, shape or pattern links or ties a room together.

Rhythm: blue stripes are being used to tie this this room together – curtains, cushions and candles.

Room planning

When planning or redecorating any room, consider each of the following.

🏠 **Likes and dislikes** of the person planning or living with the room.

🏠 **Money available** for decoration.

🏠 **Function:** Which room are you planning? If it is a sitting room, it needs to be comfortable and relaxing. A kitchen, on the other hand, needs to be hygienic and easy to work in.

🏠 **Existing fixtures and fittings:** Doors, windows, fireplaces and radiators cannot easily be moved and need to be considered in a plan.

🏠 **Heating and lighting:** This must be decided upon early, as rewiring, etc. may need to be done.

🏠 **Storage:** A room with little storage will be difficult to keep tidy. Plan plenty of storage space.

🏠 **Traffic flow:** Furniture should be placed so that people can walk around the room without bumping into it. Do not put too much furniture into a room.

🏠 **Colour:** The colour you choose for a room will often depend on its aspect, that is, whether it is north or south facing. North-facing rooms tend to get less sun, so warm colours are often used. South-facing rooms get lots of sun, so cool colours can be used.

🏠 **Pattern and texture:** The use of pattern and texture can add interest to a room.

Floor plan

When planning a room, it is a good idea to make a floor plan. The room outline should be drawn **to scale** on graph paper. Fixtures such as doors and windows are then drawn in. Furniture can be drawn to scale, cut out and then moved around on the floor plan until the best arrangement is achieved.

A floor plan

Kitchen design

A kitchen must:

- 🏠 Be hygienic and easy to keep clean
- 🏠 Be efficient – there should not be too much walking between the fridge, sink and cooker
- 🏠 Have enough storage space
- 🏠 Be bright and well ventilated
- 🏠 Be safe to work in

Ergonomics

Ergonomics is the study of how efficiently people work. Design has a lot to do with ergonomics. In a badly designed workplace, frequently used pieces of equipment will not be conveniently located.

The work triangle

The fridge, sink and cooker are the three pieces of equipment used most in the kitchen. It makes sense to put them near each other in an invisible triangle. There should be work surfaces in between.

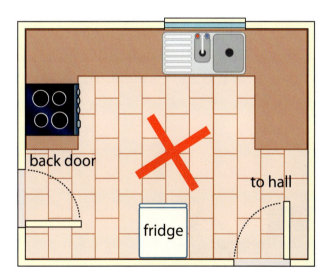

Too much walking between the fridge, sink and cooker

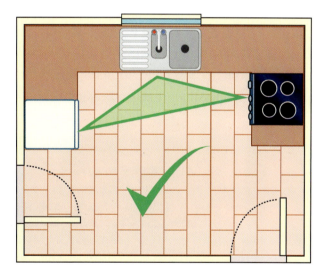

A well-designed kitchen – note the work triangle

Flooring

There is a wide variety of types of flooring on the market. The type you choose will depend on the type of room it is being used for, personal taste and money available. Common floor coverings include carpets, wooden floors and laminates, tiles and vinyl.

Walls

Walls may be painted, papered or tiled. What wall covering is chosen will usually depend on the type of room being decorated, the condition of the walls, personal taste, fashion trends and cost. Because so much of a room is taken up with wall space, care should be taken when choosing colours for walls. Avoid using paper or paint that is too overpowering. Sometimes a rich paper or paint can be used on one **feature wall**.

A room can have a feature wall, perhaps papered or in stone

Soft furnishings

Soft furnishings can be used in every room in the house. They include curtains, blinds, cushions, rugs, duvet covers, pillows and throws, lampshades, soft covers on chairs, tablecloths and table runners. Soft furnishings create interest in a room and also make the room appear warmer and cosier.

A bed dressed with soft furnishings

Lighting

Good lighting is needed to prevent eyestrain and accidents in the home. Lighting is also a great interior design tool and can add a special atmosphere to a room. Most rooms have a large central light. This light can be supported by other, smaller ones, such as table lamps, standard lamps, wall lights, spotlights, etc. (see the photograph).

Spotlight

central light

table lamp

Rapid Revision

1. **Types of accommodation:** Houses (bungalow, two or three stories, detached, semi-detached, terraced), apartments, institutions, sheltered housing, caravans and mobile homes.
2. A **home** provides for its inhabitants' physical, emotional and social needs.
3. **Choosing a home:** Cost, location, size and style of house.
4. **Features of design:** Function, form (shape, and line), colour, pattern and texture. Proportion, emphasis, balance and rhythm (Higher Level only).
5. **Planning a room:** Considerations are likes and dislikes, money available, function of room, existing features and fittings, heating and lighting (consider these early), storage, traffic flow, colour, pattern and texture.
6. **Floor plan:** It is a good idea to make a floor plan out to scale on graph paper. Draw and cut out furniture to scale so that it can be moved around on the plan.
7. **Kitchen design:** Must be hygienic and easy to clean and it must be efficient (not too much walking between appliances). There should be enough storage space. It should be bright, well ventilated and safe.
8. **Ergonomics** (Higher Level only)**:** The study of how effectively people work. An ergonomic, well-designed kitchen will require little unnecessary walking between appliances.
9. **Work triangle:** An invisible triangle formed between the fridge, cooker and sink.
10. **Flooring:** Choice will depend on location, function, likes and dislikes and the style of the room.

11. **Walls:** May be painted, papered or tiled. Choice will depend on the function of the room, the condition of the walls and personal likes and dislikes.

12. **Soft furnishings:** Curtains, blinds, cushions, rugs, bed linen, lampshades, tablecloths and runners. Soft furnishings add interest and texture.

13. **Lighting:** Good lighting is essential and adds interest and atmosphere. Types include central light, spotlights, table and floor lamps and picture lights.

Revision Questions

1. List five different types of accommodation.
2. List the needs that are provided by a home.
3. What four factors normally influence one's choice of home?
4. What are the principle features or characteristics of a well-designed object?
5. Describe the following five features of design: (a) function (b) form (c) colour (d) pattern (e) texture.
6. What effect does lots of texture create in a room?
7. What is meant by the following terms? (a) Emphasis (b) Balance (c) Proportion (d) Rhythm
8. List six considerations when planning a room.
9. What is a floor plan? Why is it a good idea to have one?
10. List five features of a well-designed kitchen.
11. What is meant by the term *ergonomics*? What is the work triangle?
12. What factors may influence someone's choice of floor covering for a room? List three different types of floor covering and one room in the house where it is commonly found.
13. What factors may influence someone's choice of wall covering for a room?
14. What are soft furnishings? What are their functions?
15. What are the functions of good lighting in the home? Name three types of lighting that can be used in interior design.

Test Yourself eTest.ie

Homework Assignment
43
P 149

CHAPTER 27
Services to the Home

Teacher's CD

Slide presentation • Student activity pack with revision crossword • Class test • Student learning contract

Key words

- Fuse box
- Electricity meter
- Night Saver electricity
- Electrical circuit
- Circuit breaker
- Live wire
- Neutral wire
- Earth wire
- Doubly insulated
- Wind turbine
- Solar panels
- Natural gas
- Bottled gas
- Gas safety
- Water treatment
- Mains water pipe
- Service water pipe
- Tungsten filament bulb

Learning outcomes

After completing this chapter and the homework, assignments and activities that accompany it, you should:

- Understand how electricity is supplied to the home and what safety measures exist. Be able to wire an electrical plug correctly and understand the principles of electrical safety in the home. Understand how wind and solar energy can be used in the home.
- Understand the different types of gas that can be used in the home and for what purposes. Understand the principles of gas safety and know what to do if there is a suspected gas leak.
- Understand how domestic water is treated for human consumption. Understand how it can be heated in the home. Be able to unblock a sink and know how to deal with a burst pipe.
- Know the different types of lighting and light bulbs available today.

- ✔ Halogen bulb
- ✔ Fluorescent tube
- ✔ Compact fluorescent lamp (CFL)
- ✔ Light-emitting diode (LED)
- ✔ Conduction
- ✔ Convection
- ✔ Radiation
- ✔ Thermostat
- ✔ Insulation
- ✔ Building energy rating (BER)
- ✔ Ventilation
- ✔ Condensation
- ✔ Conservation

- ● Understand the three methods of heat transfer and apply this knowledge to methods of home heating. Know the different types of fuel available to heat homes and be able to list the advantages and disadvantages of each. Understand how room thermostats and central heating timers work. Understand the principle behind insulation and be able to discuss how the attic, walls, floors, windows and doors can be treated to provide insulation and eliminate draughts.
- ● Understand how buildings are rated in terms of their energy efficiency.
- ● Understand what each of these terms means and how they relate to each other. Know the different ways a home can be well ventilated and how condensation and its associated problems can be avoided.
- ● Be able to describe the ways in which energy can be conserved in the home.

Electricity

Electricity is a form of energy produced and/or supplied in Ireland by the Electricity Supply Board (ESB), Airtricity and Bord Gáis. Electricity is produced by the movement of either wind or water or by burning fuels such as gas, turf, oil or coal.

When the electricity leaves the power station, it travels in huge **service cables** to a **main fuse** on the outside of our homes. Electricity enters the house through the **fuse box** and then goes to all the light fittings and sockets in the house.

The amount of electricity used is recorded by an **electricity meter**. Sometimes there are two meters: one for cheaper **Night Saver** electricity (night-time) and one for the daytime. Households are sent a bill every two months.

An electricity meter

Modern fuse boxes do not contain actual fuses. Instead, they contain switches called **circuit breakers**. These switches click off if there is a fault. They are easily switched on again when the fault is corrected.

A modern fuse box

Electrical circuit

Electricity always travels in a circuit, or circle. A fuse or circuit breaker is a deliberate weak link in this circuit. If anything goes wrong, the fuse will blow or the switch will flick off on the **circuit breaker** and the circuit will break. This stops the electricity flowing. Circuit breakers can be found in the main fuse box of the house and in fuses in electric plugs.

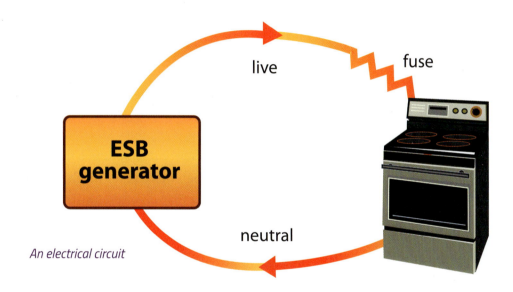

An electrical circuit

All electrical appliances must have at least two wires:

🏠 Live (brown)
🏠 Neutral (blue)

The **live wire** brings electricity to the appliances in our homes. The **neutral wire** returns to the ESB/Airtricity/Bord Gáis generator. A third wire, called the **earth wire** (yellow and green), is for safety. If something goes wrong, electricity will flow to the ground through this earth wire and not through the person using the appliance. Appliances with no earth wire should be doubly insulated and carry this symbol.

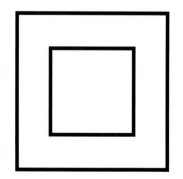

The doubly insulated symbol

How to wire a plug

🏠 Open the plug top.

🏠 Clamp the wire into the plug top.

🏠 Trim three small wires to size.

🏠 Screw each wire into the correct place.

🏠 Replace the fuse and the top of the plug.

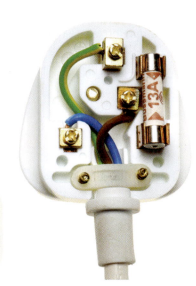

Brown = live
Blue = neutral
Green and yellow = earth

A domestic wind turbine

Domestic wind turbines

With rising fuel costs, an increasing number of households are producing their own electricity. One way of doing this is by having a domestic wind turbine like the one pictured. Turbines supply the household with electricity and excess energy produced can be sold to the national grid. At times when there is no wind, electricity can be bought from the ESB, Bord Gáis or Airtricity in the normal way. Some systems have huge batteries that allow for energy to be stored for times when there is no wind. Turbines are expensive to buy but they pay for themselves within a few years.

Domestic solar panels

Solar panels are usually mounted on the roof of the house. Each panel contains photovoltaic cells, also known as **solar cells**. When sunlight falls on the cells, they convert the sun's energy into direct current (DC) power. Panels are connected via a cable to an **inverter**, which converts the DC power into AC power, which is the type of electricity used in the home. Solar panels typically last for 25 years.

Domestic solar panels

Electrical safety

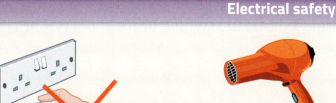

Never touch anything electrical with wet hands.

Never bring portable electrical appliances (except a razor) into the bathroom.

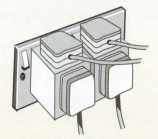

Don't overload sockets.

The bathroom light switch must be outside the door on a pull cord.

Replace damaged flexes – do not try to repair them.

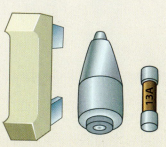

Use the correct size of fuse.

Gas

There are two types of gas available in Ireland.

🏠 **Natural gas:** Natural gas is piped ashore in gas pipelines from under the seabed. These large gas pipelines branch off and a smaller line enters the house through a meter control valve. This records how much gas is used. It is also where the gas can be turned off if necessary.

🏠 **Bottled gas:** Available in tanks or cylinders.

Uses

Gas can be used for a whole host of appliances in the home. It can be used to fuel a central heating system, individual gas fires or heaters, for cooking (cookers and barbecues), outdoor heating and gas-powered tumble dryers.

A natural gas fire is clean and attractive, but not very warm

Gas safety

🏠 Gas can be dangerous. Appliances should be fitted only by a qualified person and serviced regularly.

🏠 Gas needs proper ventilation. Gas used in a badly ventilated room can, and does, kill. Never block wall vents.

If you smell gas, act quickly

Do open doors and windows.

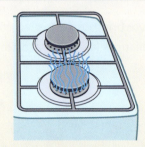

Do check if the flame has gone out on an appliance and the gas has been left on.

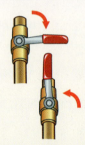

If not, turn the gas off at the meter valve.

Do call the gas company from a neighbour's house or from your mobile phone once you are out of the house.

Don't smoke or light matches. Never use a lighted flame to look for gas leaks – it is explosive.

Don't use anything electrical – even a light switch or mobile phone – inside, as they can give off a tiny spark and cause the gas to ignite.

Water

Water is the most basic service to our homes. Fresh water is supplied to our homes by the corporation (urban), county council (rural) or by private water schemes (rural). Water is collected in a lake or a man-made reservoir. From there it goes to a treatment plant to be cleaned.

Note: Individual households not on any of these schemes will have to dig their own well when building their house.

Water treatment

🏠 It is filtered to remove impurities.

🏠 Chlorine is added to kill bacteria.

🏠 Fluoride is added for strong bones and teeth.

Clean water travels in a **mains pipe** to the houses of the area. Water enters each individual house through a **service pipe**. There is a valve on this pipe that can turn the water off. Fresh water goes directly to the kitchen sink and also fills the tank in the attic. Water from this tank supplies the toilet, cold taps in the bathroom and the cylinder in the hot press.

Water can be heated in the house in a number of ways:

🏠 Immersion heater in the tank in the hot press

🏠 Instantaneous water heaters, such as electric showers

🏠 Back boiler behind an open fire or stove

🏠 Central heating system that also heats the water

🏠 Solar panels

The kitchen sink

The kitchen sink is usually placed under a window. There are several reasons for this:

🏠 Light

🏠 Ventilation

🏠 Easily plumbed

🏠 It is nice to look out the window while working

Kitchen sinks are usually made from stainless steel (Belfast sinks are ceramic) because it is hygienic, durable and does not stain. All sinks have an S-bend or U-bend. The S- or U-bend stops germs and smells from coming back up the plughole. Sinks can become blocked by substances, especially grease.

A ceramic double Belfast sink

How to unblock a sink

1. Cover the overflow with a cloth. Place a plunger over the plughole and plunge up and down. If this does not work, try step 2.
2. Put washing soda in the plughole and rinse down with boiling water. Plunge again. If this does not work, try step 3.
3. Place a basin under the U-bend, unscrew it and remove whatever is blocking the sink with a piece of wire clothes hanger. Flush out and replace the U-bend.

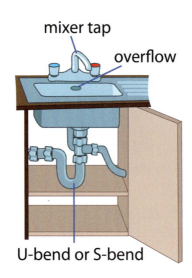

mixer tap

overflow

U-bend or S-bend

Burst pipes

Pipes may freeze in cold weather. Water expands when frozen and in this way cracks the pipes. It is not until the pipes thaw again and flooding occurs that we notice a problem.

What to do:

🏠 Turn off the water at the mains.

🏠 Turn off the heating.

🏠 Run cold taps to clear the pipes.

🏠 Call a plumber.

Lighting

Types of lighting

1. The sun is a type of lighting.
2. Under an EU directive, manufacturing of the ordinary (tungsten filament) light bulbs has been banned since September 2013, making way for the new, more energy-efficient types.
3. Halogen bulbs are a variation on the tungsten filament bulb in that they have a tungsten filament but are also filled with halogen gas, which makes them more efficient. Halogen bulbs give off a good light, but they are expensive and heat up, so care must be taken with regard to where they are placed.

South-facing rooms tend to get most sunlight

Tungsten filament bulb

A bathroom with halogen spotlights

Fluorescent bulbs give off a cold, clinical light, so they are not used very much in the home

CFL bulb

LED bulb

4. Fluorescent tubes are glass tubes that are 0.5–2.5m long. They last for approximately 3,000 hours but give off a cold, clinical light.

5. Compact fluorescent lamps (CFLs) are expensive to buy but last approximately 8,000 hours. They are cheap to run (they use 80% less electricity than tungsten) but give a cold, clinical light.

6. Light-emitting diodes (LEDs) are bulbs without a filament. They are very economical and long lasting and they do not heat up like halogen bulbs. However, they are not very bright.

Heating and insulation

Methods of heat transfer

Heat can be transferred from a heat source such as a fire to a person in three ways: conduction, convection or radiation.

- **Conduction:** Heat travels along something solid and the entire object becomes hot. A storage heater heats by conduction. Heat travels through bricks in the heater, the bricks become hot and begin giving off heat (by convection).

- **Convection:** Air or water is heated, rises and is replaced by cool air or water and the cycle continues. A fan heater heats by convection. It takes cold air in at the bottom, the element inside warms the air and gives off hot air at the top.
- **Radiation:** Heat rays heat the object or person they shine on. A bar fire heats by radiation. It heats whatever it shines on, not the air in between.
- **Combination:** Complex systems, such as oil or gas-fired central heating, use all methods of heat transfer: conduction, convection and radiation.

A storage heater

A fan heater

A bar heater

Ways a home can be heated

- **Central heating:** A boiler or stove (fuelled by gas, oil, wood, wood pellets, etc.) is connected by metal pipes to radiators in each room or to a network of rods under the floor (under-floor heating). Water heated by the boiler or stove runs to the radiators or the under-floor pipes, heating each room as it goes. The main advantage of central heating is that it keeps the whole house at a comfortably warm temperature. It is also cheaper than heating each room with individual heaters.

- **Individual heaters:** Storage heaters use off-peak electricity and can be left on. Others are used for shorter periods of time, such as gas 'supersers', open fires and stand-alone stoves. Individual heaters are expensive if they are used as the only source of heat in a house, but they can be useful as an extra source of heat on particularly cold nights or as a feature or focal point, such as an open fire.

A wood-burning stove

Fuels

There is a wide variety of fuels available to households. Each type has advantages and disadvantages.

Fuel	Advantages	Disadvantages
Oil	• Convenient and easily available • Gives off a strong heat	• Cost varies, depending on world oil prices • It's a fossil fuel, which is not good for the environment • Storage tank is unsightly and oil can be stolen from it
Gas	• Clean and efficient • Can be used for both heating and cooking • Natural gas is available on the mains, so it won't run out • Sourced in Ireland	• Natural gas is not available in all parts of the country • Gas cylinders are awkward and can run out • Dangerous if leaks occur or if used in unventilated rooms
Coal and slack	• Widely available • Gives off a strong heat • Little waste, can be bought in quantities required	• Dirty to use and store • It's a fossil fuel, which is not good for the environment • It's a hassle to clean out the fire after use • Can't be lit on its own
Wood	• Cheap and freely available • Environmentally friendly if wood is sourced from renewable forests • Visually attractive	• Burns quickly and doesn't give off as much heat as other fuels • Bulky, difficult to store • Environmental impact if wood is not sourced from renewable forests
Wood pellets	• Cheaper than oil or gas • Gives off a strong heat • Environmentally friendly if wood waste or wood from a renewable source is used	• Not widely available • If bought in bulk, storage can be a problem
Briquettes and turf	• Cheap and widely available • Sourced in Ireland	• Burn quickly and don't give off as much heat as other fuels

Wood pellets

Thermostats and timers

Thermostats and timers control when your heating system is switched on and off.

Thermostats can be set for a certain temperature, such as 21°C in a living room. Once that temperature is reached, the thermostat switches the heating system off.

Thermostats can be on:

🏠 The central heating boiler itself

🏠 Each radiator

🏠 The wall in each room (these can be dial or digital)

Digital room thermostat

Radiator thermostat

Timers can be set to switch the heating on or off at various times during the day or night. For example, the heating can be set to come on two hours before you return home in the evening.

Insulation

Insulation means trapping heat in the house. A house with poor insulation loses up to 75% of its heat and will be cold, draughty and expensive to run. Windows, roofs, walls, floors and doors should all be insulated with materials that are bad conductors of heat. Bad conductors do not let heat pass through them easily. Examples of bad conductors are air, fabric, fibreglass and polystyrene.

Digital central heating timer

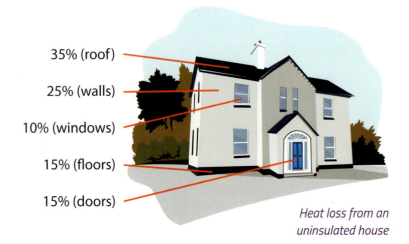

35% (roof)

25% (walls)

10% (windows)

15% (floors)

15% (doors)

Heat loss from an uninsulated house

Attic

Fibreglass, wool, condensed foam or foam pellets are laid on the floor of the attic to prevent heat loss through the roof.

Walls

Modern houses have cavity walls. This means that there are two rows of blocks or bricks (or one row and a timber frame) with a gap between them. Trapped air, along with other insulation materials, stops heat from escaping from the house through the walls.

Floors

Carpet and carpet underlay are both bad conductors/good insulators.

An insulated attic

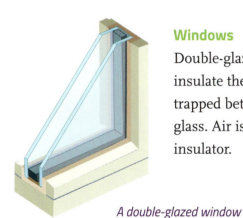

Windows

Double-glazed windows help insulate the house because air is trapped between the panes of glass. Air is a bad conductor/good insulator.

A double-glazed window

Cavity wall insulation

Draughts

Heavy curtains or draught excluders can prevent heat loss through windows, doors and letterboxes.

A letterbox draught excluder

A door draught excluder

 You could make a draught excluder for your own home for one of your textile projects – see page 408

Building energy rating (BER)

A building energy rating (BER) is similar to the energy label on your fridge, with a scale of A to G. A-rated homes are the most energy efficient, while G is the least efficient. Since 1 January 2009, a BER certificate is compulsory for all homes being sold or rented. So if you want to sell or rent a house, you need to have your house assessed by a registered BER assessor in order to get your certificate. The assessor will also advise you on how you can improve the energy rating of your home.

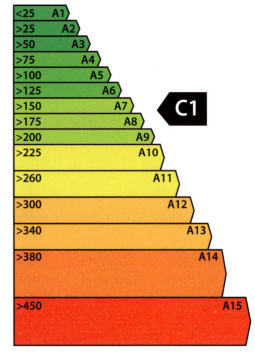

<25	A1
>25	A2
>50	A3
>75	A4
>100	A5
>125	A6
>150	A7
>175	A8
>200	A9
>225	A10
>260	A11
>300	A12
>340	A13
>380	A14
>450	A15

C1

BER certificate

Ventilation and condensation

Ventilation

A good ventilation system replaces stale air with fresh air without causing a draught.

Ventilation is needed to:

- 🏠 Provide fresh air (rich in oxygen)
- 🏠 Remove stale air (high in carbon dioxide)
- 🏠 Control humidity (the amount of moisture in the air)
- 🏠 Prevent condensation
- 🏠 Prevent the room from getting too warm and stuffy

Methods of ventilation include doors, windows, fireplace, wall vents, extractor fans (kitchen and bathrooms) and cooker hoods.

Condensation

Condensation occurs when warm, humid air (full of water vapour) comes in contact with a cold surface, such as a window. If a room frequently has a lot of condensation, then dampness can result. This will cause wallpaper and paints to mould, metals to rust and wood to rot. It will also cause the room to smell musty and unpleasant.

Condensation can be controlled by good ventilation, good insulation and a good heating system.

Mould caused by condensation

Conserving resources in the home

- Choose appliances with a good energy efficiency rating (A or B).
- Fit the hot water cylinder with a lagging jacket (new cylinders come ready insulated).
- Have showers instead of baths – they use less water.
- Fit thermostats and timers and only heat rooms if they are being used.
- Use CFL bulbs and switch off lights when not in use.
- Don't leave TVs, computers, DVD players and computer games on standby, as they use electricity in this mode – switch them off.
- Wait until there is a full load before using the dishwasher or washing machine.
- If possible, dry clothes outside.
- Only boil the amount of water you need in the kettle.
- Insulate the home well and exclude draughts.
- Consider alternative energies, such as wind and solar energies.

1. **Electricity:** Travels from power station in large service cables to the meter and main fuse box outside each home. Enters the house through the main fuse box and from there to the light fittings and sockets. Night Saver electricity is cheaper. The fuse box contains a deliberate weak link in the circuit so that if anything goes wrong, the electrical current will be broken.

2. **Wiring:** All electrical appliances have a live (brown) and a neutral (blue) wire. Some also have an earth wire (green and yellow). The live wire brings electricity to the appliance, the neutral wire goes back to the generator and the earth wire brings power to the ground if there is a fault. Appliances without an earth wire must be doubly insulated.

3. **Alternative energies:** Wind and solar power can be converted into electricity.

4. **Electrical safety:** Never touch anything electrical with wet hands. Never bring portable electrical appliances into the bathroom. Don't overload or repair sockets, plugs or flexes. The bathroom light switch should be outside the door or on a pull cord. Use the correct fuse size.

5. **Gas:** Two types: natural, piped gas and bottled gas. Can be used for heating, cooking or drying clothes.
   - **Gas safety:** Appliances should be installed by a qualified gas fitter. Proper ventilation is vital.
   - **Suspected gas leak:** Open doors and windows. Check if the flame on the cooker has gone out. Turn gas off at the mains. Call the gas company. Do not smoke, turn on light switches or use a mobile phone.

6. **Water:** Travels from reservoir to water treatment plant, where it is filtered and chlorine and fluoride are added. Clean water travels through the mains pipe to an area and through service pipes to individual homes. Water can be turned on or off at the valve. Fresh water goes to the kitchen sink and attic tank. Water is heated in an immersion heater in the hot press, instantaneous heaters (electric showers), back boilers, central heating, solar panels.

7. **Kitchen sink:** Put under a window for light, ventilation, easily plumbed and nice to look out. Usually stainless steel or ceramic. U- or S-bend stops smells coming back up the sink.
   - **To unblock a sink:** Cover the overflow and plunge over the plughole. If that doesn't work, rinse with boiling water and washing soda, then unscrew the S- or U-bend and unblock – put a bucket under the bend!

8. **Burst pipes:** Water expands when frozen, so it causes pipes to burst. Turn off at mains, run cold water, turn off the heating and call a plumber.

9. **Types of lighting:** Sunlight, tungsten filament (illegal to manufacture now), halogen, fluorescent tubes, CFLs and LEDs.

10. **Heat and insulation:** Methods of heat transfer: conduction (storage heaters), convection (fan heater), radiation (bar heater), central heating (all three). Homes can be centrally heated (from central boiler) or each room can be heated individually (more costly, but can provide a focal point, such as an open fire).

11. **Fuels:** All fuels have advantages and disadvantages.
    - **Oil:** Convenient and produces a lot of heat, but is costly, is a fossil fuel and requires a large storage area.
    - **Gas:** Clean and efficient, natural gas won't run out and it is Irish, but not available everywhere, gas cylinders are awkward and it can be dangerous.
    - **Coal and slack:** Widely available and produces a lot of heat, but dirty, is a fossil fuel and cleaning is required.
    - **Wood:** Cheap, widely available, can be environmentally friendly and is visually attractive, but burns quickly, is bulky to store and may not be environmentally friendly.
    - **Wood pellets:** Cheap, give off strong heat and are environmentally friendly, but not widely available and they are bulky.
    - **Briquettes and turf:** Cheap, Irish and light easily, but burn quickly and do not give much heat.

12. **Thermostats and timers**
    - **Thermostats:** Switch off once the desired temperature has been reached. Placed on boiler, rooms or individual radiators.
    - **Timers:** Can be set to come on and off as the family desires.

13. **Insulation:** Up to 75% of heat can be lost from an uninsulated home. Insulation means trapping heat in the house. The roof, windows, walls, floors and doors should all be insulated. Good insulators are bad conductors (air, fabric, fibreglass and polystyrene).

14. **BER rating:** Since 2009, all homes being sold or rented must have a building energy rating (BER). This rating decides how energy efficient a home is. A certificate is issued.

15. **Ventilation and condensation**
    - **Ventilation:** Good ventilation replaces stale air with fresh air without a draught. Methods include doors, windows, fireplaces, wall vents, extractor fans and cooker hoods.
    - **Condensation:** When warm, humid air contacts cold surfaces, it causes dampness, mould and rust.

16. **Conservation:** Choose appliances with a good rating. Use lagging jackets, thermostats and timers and CFL bulbs. Switch off appliances at night, especially lights. Run full loads of laundry. Boil only the amount of water required in the kettle. Insulate your home. Consider alternative energies (wind and solar).

Revision Questions

1. How is electricity produced in Ireland? How/where is domestic electricity usage recorded?
2. What is a circuit breaker? What is its function? How does a fuse work?
3. What are each of the following wires in a domestic plug called and what is their function: (a) blue (b) brown (c) green/yellow?
4. Draw the doubly insulated symbol. What does this symbol mean? Where would it be found?
5. Describe six points regarding electrical safety.
6. Name the two types of gas used by households in Ireland. What should you do/not do if you smell gas at home?
7. Why is (a) chlorine and (b) fluoride added to domestic water supplies?
8. Describe five ways water can be heated in the home.
9. Why is the kitchen sink normally placed under a window? What is the purpose of a U- or S-bend on a sink?
10. Describe how you would unblock a sink.
11. Why do water pipes sometimes burst in winter? What should you do if you have a burst pipe?
12. Name and describe the three different methods of heat transfer. Name one form of heating that uses each method.
13. List the advantages and disadvantages of the following types of fuel: (a) oil (b) gas (c) coal and slack (d) wood (e) wood pellets (f) turf (g) briquettes.
14. What is a heating thermostat? What is it used for in the home?
15. What is insulation? What type of materials are good insulators? How can attics, walls, floors and windows be insulated?
16. Suggest one way draughts may be excluded from both doors and windows.
17. What is a building energy rating certificate? Why do homeowners need to have one for their home?
18. What is good ventilation? Why is good ventilation necessary in the home?
19. What is condensation? Why is it unwanted in the home?
20. How can condensation be controlled in the home?
21. Suggest six different ways resources can be conserved in the home.

Test Yourself
eTest.ie

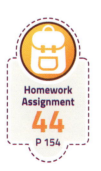

Homework
Assignment
44
P 154

CHAPTER 28
Technology in the Home

Teacher's CD

Slide presentation • Student activity pack with revision crossword • Class test • Student learning contract

Key words

- Motor
- Heating element
- Energy efficiency label
- Guarantee
- After-sales service
- Watts
- Standing time
- Turntable
- Split level cooker
- Solid fuel cooker
- Fan oven
- Ceramic hob
- Dual ring
- Induction hob
- Dual grill
- Self-cleaning oven
- Autotimer
- Timer
- Thermostat
- Automatic defrost
- WEEE directive
- White goods disposal charge

Learning outcomes

After completing this chapter and the homework, assignments and activities that accompany it, you should:

- Appreciate how technological advances have made running a home much less time-consuming than in the past.
- Know that there are three basic types of appliance: motor only, heating element only and motor and heating element combined.
- Know what should be considered when buying electrical appliances. Be able to give an example of each.
- Understand how a microwave cooker works, the advantages and disadvantages of microwave cooking, what it can be used for in cookery and how to use it safely. Know what factors should be considered when buying a microwave. Be able to clean a microwave correctly.
- Know the different types of cooker available and be able to list the modern features available. Know what factors should be considered when buying and positioning a cooker in the kitchen. Be able to clean a cooker and hob correctly.
- Know the different types of fridges and freezers available and be able to list the modern features. Know the rules for using a refrigerator. Be able to defrost and clean a freezer and refrigerator correctly.
- Understand the reasons for the WEEE directive and what it means for the consumer.

Advances in technology have made running the home very different than it was even 30 or 40 years ago.

- 🏠 Washing and caring for clothes have been made much easier by automatic washing machines, tumble dryers and electric steam irons.

- 🏠 Dishwashers and vacuum cleaners (including central vacuum systems) allow us to wash dishes and clean carpets and floors more efficiently.

- 🏠 Food preparation and storage are aided by equipment such as freezers, refrigerators, microwaves, food processors, modern cookers, etc.

- 🏠 The internet can be used for shopping, gathering information, booking holidays, banking online, sending email, etc.

Motor only

Modern household appliances

There are three basic types of household appliance:

- 🏠 Appliances with a motor (noisy), such as a vacuum cleaner, electric knife or food processor.

- 🏠 Appliances with a heating element, such as a toaster, heater, kettle or cooker.

- 🏠 Appliances with both a motor and an element (may not be a heating element), such as a washing machine, dishwasher, fridge and freezer.

Heating element only

Buying electrical appliances

- 🏠 **Cost:** Compare different models and the same models in different shops.

- 🏠 **Safety:** Buy from a reliable shop. Check for safety labels (see below).

- 🏠 **Energy efficiency label:** The appliance should ideally have an A or B rating.

- 🏠 **Size:** Will the appliance fit in the space you have for it?

- 🏠 **Special features:** Do not spend money on appliances with lots of special features if you will never use them.

- 🏠 **Demonstration:** If necessary, ask to have a demonstration on how to use the appliance.

- 🏠 **Check the guarantee:** It should be for at least one year.

- 🏠 **After-sales service:** Ask about this.

Heating element and motor

Irish Standards mark

European Standards mark

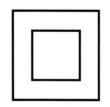

Doubly insulated mark

Energy efficiency label

The microwave

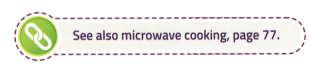
See also microwave cooking, page 77.

The microwave oven produces energy waves called microwaves. These waves hit food and cause the molecules in it to vibrate. This produces heat, which cooks the food. Some microwave ovens are more powerful than others. They range from 600 watts to 1,200 watts (1,200 watts is the most powerful). Cooking time decreases as wattage increases. Food continues to cook for a few minutes after it has been removed from the microwave, so it should not be eaten for a few minutes. This is called **standing time**.

Advantages of microwave ovens

- Microwaves cook food very quickly, which suits today's busy lifestyle.
- It is a healthy cooking method – no extra fat is added and the fast cooking means there is little loss of nutrients.
- It thaws food quickly, which suits today's busy lifestyle.
- It can reheat food quickly and thoroughly.
- It is a small, convenient appliance that uses little fuel.

Disadvantages of microwave ovens

- It does not brown food (unless a browning dish is used).
- It is not suitable for all foods, such as large joints of meat.
- It does not make meat tender.
- Foods that have an uneven thickness are not suitable, as the thin parts overcook while the thicker parts remain undercooked.
- Foods with large amounts of sugar and fat tend to burn.
- Special microwave recipes are needed, as many conventional recipes will not work in the microwave.

An integrated microwave oven

Uses of microwave ovens

🏠 Cooks, thaws and reheats most foods (except if browning is needed)

🏠 Melts jam, chocolate, jelly, etc. quickly, but be careful not to overheat

🏠 Ripens avocados, bananas or tomatoes (on low heat; pierce the skin first)

Safe use of the microwave

🏠 Do not put anything metallic into the microwave. Use glass, china or heat-resistant plastic instead.

🏠 Prick anything with a skin, such as tomatoes, potatoes or sausages, before cooking to prevent bursting.

🏠 Cover foods with a plate so that they do not spatter the oven.

🏠 Be careful to mix foods thoroughly before eating – food may be cool on the outside and red hot in the middle.

🏠 Leave to stand for a few minutes before eating, as food continues to cook during this time.

🏠 Wipe up spills immediately, as they will be more difficult to remove later.

🏠 Do not switch on the microwave when it is empty, as this can cause damage.

Buying a microwave

Read the general guidelines on page 327 for buying electrical appliances.

Consider these special features that may be available in a microwave:

🏠 Does the oven have a turntable? (This helps ensure even cooking.)

🏠 What is its wattage? (The higher the wattage, the more powerful the oven.)

🏠 Many modern microwave ovens have lots of special features, such as temperature probes, automatic programming facilities and a browning element. Do not spend money on a complicated microwave however if you are unlikely to use its features.

Cleaning a microwave

🏠 Prevent food spills and spatters in the first place by using a big enough container and by covering food loosely while it cooks.

🏠 Wipe up spills as soon as they occur, as they will be removed much more easily.

🏠 Remove the turntable and wash it in warm soapy water.

🏠 Wash the inside of the microwave with warm soapy water and a cloth. Harsh abrasives or scrubs will scratch the metal interior and should not be used.

🏠 Polish the exterior of the oven with a soft cloth and glass cleaner, such as Windolene.

The cooker

Types of cooker

- 🏠 Gas cooker

- 🏠 Electric cooker with gas hob

- 🏠 Split level – the hob can be built into the worktop and the oven at waist level; one can be gas and the other electric

- 🏠 Solid fuel cookers (Aga) often heat water and radiators as well as cook, but they are very expensive to buy

An Aga solid fuel cooker

Modern features

- 🏠 **Fan ovens:** A fan oven blows hot air around the oven, which cooks food more quickly (set the cooking temperature 10°C lower than what the recipe calls for).

- 🏠 **Top oven:** The grill can also be used as a small oven.

- 🏠 **Ceramic hob:** Easy-to-clean, heat-resistant glass surface.

- 🏠 **Dual rings:** Can be set so that only the middle part of the ring heats, such as for small saucepans (see the illustration).

- 🏠 **Induction hob:** Electric hob, heats and cools instantly. Need to use cast iron or specific stainless steel saucepans (see the photo).

Dual ring

A modern induction hob

- 🏠 **Dual grill:** Full grill or one side only heats up for small amounts of food.

- 🏠 **Self-cleaning ovens:** Door locks; oven reaches very high temperatures; food burns off; ash can then be swept out.

- 🏠 **Autotimers:** Three clocks, may be digital (see below).

  - 🏠 Set clock 1 for the time you want the oven to come on at, such as 3pm.

  - 🏠 Set clock 2 for the time you want the oven to switch off at.

  - 🏠 Set clock 3 at the present time, such as 7:30am.

Clock 1	Clock 2	Clock 3

Autotimer

🏠 **Timers** are less complex. You set the timer for a certain amount of time, such as one hour. The oven switches on there and then (it cannot be set for later in the day, like autotimers). It switches off when the time is up.

Buying a cooker

🏠 See the general guidelines for buying electrical appliances on page 327.

🏠 Should you buy a gas or electric cooker? If your house does not have natural gas, you may want to choose an electric one, as bottled gas can be inconvenient. Gas cookers, on the other hand, heat up quickly and are easily controlled.

🏠 Do not pay for a cooker with extra features if you are unlikely to use them.

Caring for and cleaning cookers

🏠 Wipe up spills straightaway. (Why?)

🏠 Wash the grill pan after each use. (Why?)

🏠 Never drag saucepans over a ceramic hob – they will scratch it. Use a special ceramic hob cleaner.

When cleaning a cooker:

🏠 Protect your hands, clothes and surroundings.

🏠 Remove all removable parts. Wash and dry them in warm soapy water.

🏠 Use a special oven cleaner to dissolve burnt-on food in the oven itself.

🏠 Wash out, rinse and dry the oven.

🏠 Wash, dry and polish the exterior of the cooker and replace all removable parts.

Positioning a cooker

🏠 The cooker needs to be positioned within the work triangle (see page 305).

🏠 Position close to electrical or gas connections.

🏠 Position away from refrigerators or freezers.

🏠 Position gas cookers away from draughts to avoid the risk of fire.

The refrigerator

Fridge with icebox

Fridge-freezer

Integrated fridge-freezer

Features of a modern refrigerator

- Thermostatically controlled
- Door of fridge can be made to match kitchen units (see photo of the integrated fridge above)
- Cold drinks dispenser and ice maker
- Moulded door storage and moveable plastic-coated shelves
- Automatic defrost – the fridge or fridge-freezer switches itself off every now and then so that ice does not build up and the icebox or freezer is kept defrosted
- Salad drawers

Choosing a refrigerator

See the general guidelines for buying electrical appliances on page 327.

Rules for using a refrigerator

- Do not position the fridge near the cooker or a radiator, as its motor will have to work harder to keep the fridge cool.
- Never put hot food in the fridge.
- Cover food before putting it in the fridge. This stops it from drying out and absorbing strong smells such as onions.

- Do not over-pack the fridge and make sure to clean the fridge out regularly, throwing out anything that is out of date.
- Put meat (especially raw meat) on a plate so it does not drip onto other food. Store it in the coldest part of the fridge, near the icebox.
- Close the door immediately after use.
- Defrost the freezer compartment regularly.
- If a fridge is not in use (for instance, if you are going on holiday), clean it thoroughly and leave the door open.

Care and cleaning

Defrosting the icebox

1. Choose a time when the icebox or freezer is fairly empty.
2. Some models have an automatic defrost (see page 332). If not:
   - Remove all food and wrap it in a good insulator, such as newspaper.
   - Allow ice to melt into the drip tray, then empty the drip tray.
   - When all the ice is gone, wash out with warm water and bread soda, then dry the icebox or freezer.
   - Plug the refrigerator back in and return the food items.
   - Never use a knife to remove ice.

Cleaning the refrigerator

1. Choose a time when the fridge is fairly empty.
2. Remove all food and wrap it in a good insulator, such as newspaper.
3. Remove all moveable shelves and parts.
4. Clean the fridge with a solution of 2 tablespoons of bread soda mixed with 1 litre of water.
5. Rinse with plain warm water. Dry. Replace the shelves and food.
6. Wash the outside with warm water and washing-up liquid. Dry well.

Disposing of electrical appliances

Under European law (EU Directive on Waste Electrical and Electronic Equipment 2005, better known as the WEEE directive), electrical appliances can no longer be disposed of in landfill sites by owners themselves. For environmental reasons, appliances must be brought to special collection points (most large electrical outlets have a collection point), where they will be collected and recycled in an environmentally friendly way.

In order to cover the cost of this, customers must now pay a white goods disposal charge when purchasing a new appliance. The charge depends on the size and type of appliance. For example, a large American-style fridge has a disposal charge of €30, whereas a smaller under-the-counter fridge has a charge of €10. Other large appliances, such as cookers and washing machines, are €5 (2014 figures).

1. **Advances in technology:** Technology makes the task of running the home much easier, with automatic washing machines, tumble dryers, steam irons, dishwashers, vacuum cleaners, freezers, refrigerators, microwaves, food processors, modern cookers and internet shopping.

2. **Types of appliance:** With a motor (vacuum cleaner), with a heating element (toaster) and both (washing machine).

3. **Buying electrical appliances:** Consider cost, safety, energy efficiency label, size, special features, demonstration, guarantee and after-sales service.

4. **Microwave:** Microwaves cause molecules in food to vibrate and this cooks food. Wattage ranges from 600 to 1,200 watts. Food continues to cook after it is removed from the microwave (standing time).

   - **Advantages:** Cooks, thaws and reheats food quickly. Healthy method of cooking. Small, convenient appliance.
   - **Disadvantages:** Does not brown food, not suitable for large joints, does not tenderise meat and not suitable if food has uneven thickness. Foods with a lot of sugar or fat burn easily. Many conventional recipes are unsuitable.
   - **Safety:** Don't use metallic cookware. Prick food with a skin. Cover food so it doesn't spatter. Mix foods thoroughly before eating. Leave to stand. Wipe up spills immediately. Do not switch on when empty.
   - **Buying:** Don't pay for extra features if you won't use them.
   - **Cleaning:** Prevent spills by covering food while cooking. Wipe up spills immediately. Use hot soapy water, not abrasives. Polish the outside with a soft cloth and glass cleaner.

5. **Cooker:**
   - **Types:** Gas, electric, combination, split level, solid fuel.
   - **Features:** Fan oven, top oven, ceramic hob, dual rings and grill, induction hob, self-cleaning ovens, autotimers and timers.
   - **Buying:** Consider general guidelines. Consider the type: gas or electrical (do you have a natural gas supply?). Do not pay for features you won't use.
   - **Care and cleaning:** Wipe up spills immediately. Wash the grill pan after use. Never drag saucepans across a ceramic hob. Protect your hands, clothing and surroundings. Remove all removable parts and wash in hot, soapy water. Dry thoroughly. Use oven cleaner. Wash, rinse and dry the oven interior and polish the exterior.
   - **Positioning:** Within work triangle. Close to connections and away from fridge, freezer, curtains and draughts.

6. **Refrigerator:**
   - **Types:** Fridge with icebox, fridge-freezer, integrated.
   - **Features:** Thermostatically controlled, integrated, cold drinks dispenser and icemaker, moulded door storage, automatic defrost, salad drawers.
   - **Buying:** Consider general guidelines. Ensure it is the correct size to meet the family's needs.
   - **Rules for using:** Do not position near a heat source. Never put hot food in a fridge. Cover food. Do not over-pack. Clean regularly. Put high-protein foods (meat) on a plate in the coldest place (top). Keep the door closed. Defrost the freezer regularly. If not in use, unplug, clean and leave the door open.

- **Defrosting:** Choose a time when it is almost empty. Wrap food in newspaper, turn off and allow ice to melt. Wash out with warm water and bread soda. Plug back in and return food. Never use a knife to remove ice. Clean the fridge with bread soda and water.

7. **Disposing of electrical appliances:** Waste Electrical and Electronic Equipment Directive (WEEE, 2005). Individuals cannot dispose of white goods in landfill. You must pay tax when buying goods, which covers the cost of disposal when the appliance becomes obsolete. Cost ranges from €5 to €30.

Revision Questions

1. Describe four technological advances that have impacted on the running of the home today.
2. What are the three types or categories of household appliance? Give one example of each.
3. List six guidelines for buying household appliances.
4. How does a microwave cook food? List four advantages and four disadvantages of microwave cooking.
5. Describe three uses of the microwave oven in cookery.
6. List six points for using a microwave safely.
7. Describe four guidelines that should be followed when buying a microwave oven.
8. Name four different types of cooker on the market today. Describe six features of modern cookers.
9. Outline four points for caring for and cleaning a cooker.
10. Outline four points that should be considered when deciding where to position a cooker.
11. Name three different types of refrigerator. List four features of a modern refrigerator?
12. Describe how an icebox should be defrosted. Give six guidelines for cleaning a refrigerator.
13. What does the EU Directive on Waste Electrical and Electronic Equipment 2005 mean for consumers?

Test Yourself
eTest.ie

Homework Assignment
45
P 159

CHAPTER 29
Home Hygiene, Safety and First Aid

Teacher's CD

Slide presentation ▪ Student activity pack with revision crossword ▪ Class test ▪ Student learning contract

Key words

- Home hygiene
- Cleaning agents
- Detergents
- Abrasives
- Multi-purpose cleaners
- Window cleaners
- Polish
- Metal polishes
- Bleach
- Disinfectants
- Alternative cleaning agents
- Fire drill
- Fire extinguisher
- Fire blanket
- Smoke detector
- First aid
- First aid kit
- Resuscitation
- Burn
- Scald
- Shock

Learning outcomes

After completing this chapter and the homework, assignments and activities that accompany it, you should:

- Understand why home hygiene is important and know how to keep your home hygienic.
- Be able to list and give examples of the following range of cleaning agents and understand what each is used for: water, detergents, abrasives, multi-purpose cleaners, window cleaners, polish, metal polishes, bleaches, disinfectants and alternative products such as vinegar, bread soda, lemon juice and cola.
- Know what the most common causes of accidents in the home are. Be able to describe how the following types of accidents can best be avoided: electrical, fire, falls, choking and suffocation, scalds, poisoning and drowning.
- Be able to describe the three main aims of first aid. Know how to react in case of a serious accident, including how to resuscitate a patient.
- Know what items should be included in a basic first aid kit. Know what basic first aid treatments should be administered for the following: burns and scalds, bleeding, choking, shock and poisoning.

Home hygiene

A good standard of hygiene in the home is essential for good health. Bacteria thrive in damp, dirty conditions and cause food poisoning and disease.

General guidelines for good hygiene in the home

- Ensure there is good ventilation – bacteria love stuffy, damp conditions.
- Keep the house warm and dry.
- Open curtains and windows daily – sunlight and fresh air help to destroy bacteria.
- Kitchens and bathrooms should have smooth, easy-to-clean surfaces such as tiles.
- Empty kitchen bins daily and the large dustbin weekly. Wash and disinfect them regularly.
- Keep toilets and sinks spotless – disinfect once a week.
- Carpets and floors should be vacuumed or washed at least once a week (more often if necessary).
- Bed sheets and pillowcases should be washed at as high a temperature as the fabric will allow and changed weekly.

Hygiene in the kitchen and bathroom are most important

Cleaning agents

Nowadays there is a huge number of different cleaning agents on the market. Many are poisonous, so:

- Store only in their original containers – dangerous products will often have a childproof container.
- Keep out of the reach of children (do not store under the sink).
- Store in a dry place.
- Follow directions carefully.
- Wear gloves and protective clothing while using.
- Rinse away all traces of the cleaning agent after use.

Cleaning agent	Examples	Use
Water	—	Warm (washing), cold (soaking)
Detergents	Washing powder, soap, washing-up liquid, dishwasher powder	Washing clothes and dishes
Abrasives	Cream cleaners (such as Cif), Brillo pads	Stubborn stains on scratch-resistant surfaces, such as ceramic bathroom sinks and metal saucepans (not non-stick)
Multipurpose cleaners	Cillit Bang, Flash liquid	Used on most work surfaces and floors
Window cleaners	Windolene	Cleans windows without streaking
Polish	Pledge, Mr Sheen (sprays), solid wax	Polishing furniture
Metal polishes	Brasso, Silvo, silver cloths	Polishing metal (brass and silver)
Bleaches	Parazone, Domestos	Kill germs, remove stains
Disinfectants	Dettol, Savlon	Kill germs
Alternative products	White vinegar	Removes limescale from around taps, cleans windows
	Bread soda (with water)	Cleaning fridges and toilets
	Lemon juice	Removes blood and grass stains, also bleaches whites
	Cola and denture tablets	Both (separately) remove stains from toilets (leave overnight)

Do not use bleaches and toilet cleaners, such as Harpic, together, as a poisonous gas is given off when they are mixed.

Accidents in the home

Causes

- 🏠 Carelessness or curiosity (children especially)
- 🏠 Badly designed homes, such as hidden steps or poor lighting
- 🏠 Faulty equipment
- 🏠 Incorrect storage of dangerous substances

Accident prevention

Electricity

🏠 Electricity and water do not mix – never touch anything electrical with wet hands.

🏠 Wire electrical appliances correctly with the correct size of fuse.

🏠 Check for safety symbols on appliances.

🏠 Never take anything electrical, such as a heater or hairdryer, into the bathroom.

🏠 Never overload sockets or repair flexes with tape.

🏠 Fit childproof covers on electric sockets.

A childproof electrical cover

Fire

🏠 Never leave matches or cigarette lighters where children can get them.

🏠 Fit a full fireguard.

🏠 Do not hang a mirror over the fireplace. (Why?)

🏠 Use an electric deep-fat fryer, not a chip pan.

🏠 Stub cigarettes out completely and never smoke in bed.

🏠 Check that nightwear is fire resistant (especially children's).

🏠 Unplug electrical appliances before going to bed.

🏠 Close doors at night – this stops a fire from spreading.

> Have an exit plan and make sure everyone knows the best way to get out of the house if there is a fire.

Fire safety equipment

A smoke alarm – check the battery on the same day every week

A fire extinguisher – aim it at the base of the fire

A fire blanket – keep in the kitchen and throw over a small fire to smother it

Fire drill

Few people realise how quickly a house fire spreads until they witness one. Fire drills are vital so that all occupants know what to do in the event of a fire.

Small fire

🏠 Use a fire extinguisher or a fire blanket to put out the fire.

🏠 Never put water on burning oil or an electrical appliance.

🏠 If a chip pan catches on fire, do not bring it outside – the oxygen will feed the fire. Try to put the lid on to smother the flames.

🏠 Call the fire brigade if necessary.

Large fire

🏠 Get out, following your exit plan. Crawl along the floor, as there is more oxygen low down.

🏠 Call the fire brigade.

🏠 Do not re-enter the house.

Falls

🏠 Have a light switch at the top and the bottom of stairs.

🏠 Make sure the carpet is not loose.

🏠 Never leave objects, such as toys, on the stairs.

🏠 Use a stair gate at the top and bottom if there are young children in the house.

🏠 Avoid frayed carpets and over-polished floors.

🏠 Have grips on the sides of baths and showers. The bottom of the shower or bath should have a non-slip surface (especially for elderly people).

🏠 Be careful on newly washed floors and wipe up spills immediately.

Children

Accidents are the biggest cause of injury and death of children in this country. Each year, approximately one in five children has an accident at home that is serious enough to need treatment by a doctor or in hospital.

All children have accidents, no matter how safe the home or how careful the parents. Nevertheless, parents can reduce the risk of accidents by taking the following precautions:

🏠 **Never** leave a young child unsupervised in the house.

🏠 **Only** buy equipment and toys with safety symbols attached.

Type of accident	How to prevent it
Choking and suffocation 	• Keep plastic bags and small, hard objects out of reach of children. • Never leave a baby or a young child alone while feeding. • Be careful with curtain cords, etc.
Scalds 	• Have a short safety flex on kettles. • Do not use tablecloths. (Why?) • Keep hot drinks away from the edges of tables. • Never drink tea or coffee with a child in your lap. • Turn saucepan handles inwards on the hob. • Put cold water into the bath first.
Falls 	• Fit window locks. • Fit stair gates. • Do not allow children onto balconies alone. • Strap babies into buggies and highchairs.
Poisoning 	• Keep medicines locked away. • Medicines should be stored in childproof containers. • Lock other dangerous substances away, such as alcohol, bleach, weed killer and rat poison.
Burns 	• Fit a fire guard. • Never leave matches, lighters or petrol within reach of children. • Be careful when using an iron – do not allow the flex to dangle. • Make sure nightwear is flame-resistant.
Drowning 	• Never leave a child alone in the bath or anywhere there is water.

First aid

Aims of first aid

🏠 To preserve life, such as giving mouth-to-mouth resuscitation (see below)

🏠 To prevent the condition getting worse, for example to stop the bleeding (see page 344)

🏠 To promote recovery, such as putting the patient in the recovery position (see page 344)

A serious accident

1. Do not move the patient unless it is absolutely necessary.
2. Check for breathing.
3. If the patient is not breathing, start mouth-to-mouth resuscitation and chest compressions.
4. Do not give the patient anything to eat or drink (they may need to fast for an anaesthetic later).
5. Ring 999 and give clear directions to the accident scene.

The ABCs of resuscitation

A is for AIRWAY	B is for BREATHING	C is for CIRCULATION
		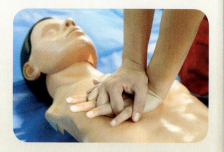
Tilt the casualty's head back and lift the chin. This will open the airway.	If the casualty is not breathing, breathe for them. Cover their mouth with yours and blow air into their lungs.	Apply chest compressions to support circulation. Two breaths – 30 compressions, two breaths – 30 compressions, and so on.

Why not do a basic first aid course?

Contact the Irish Red Cross Society, 16 Merrion Square, Dublin 2.
Telephone: (01) 676 5135; www.redcross.ie; email: redcross@iol.ie. They will put you in touch with your local branch.

First aid kit

Every home should have a well-stocked first aid kit. It should contain the following items.

antiseptic lotion

assorted adhesive plasters

cotton wool

crepe bandages

a card of needles

safety pins

tweezers

calamine lotion

sterile eye pads

cotton buds

scissors

examination gloves pairs

pocket face mask

individually wrapped disinfectant wipes

individually wrapped triangular bandages

individually wrapped sterile *unmedicated wound dressing* (medium, large and extra large)

paramedic shears

thermometer

Basic first aid treatments

Burns and scalds

Minor (not serious)

1. Stop the burning – pour cold water on the burn for 10 minutes.
2. Gently remove rings, watches, belts, etc. before the area swells.
3. Reduce the risk of infection – cover with a clean, non-fluffy dressing.
4. **Do not** put any creams on the burn.

Major (serious)

1. Put out the fire by wrapping the victim in a blanket or coat or by rolling them on the ground.
2. Call an ambulance.
3. Pour cold water on the burn.
4. Resuscitate if necessary.
5. **Do not** remove any clothing stuck to the burn.
6. Gently remove rings, watches, etc. before the area begins to swell.

Bleeding

1. Try to stop the bleeding by applying pressure to the wound with your fingers for 10 minutes.
2. If there is glass or something else in the wound, press on either side of it.
3. If it is a limb, raise it up to help stop the bleeding.
4. Wrap in a bandage.
5. Call an ambulance if bleeding is severe.

The Heimlich manoeuvre

Choking

🏠 **A child:** Place face down on your lap with the head lower than the body. Slap sharply between the shoulder blades.

🏠 **An adult:** Slap sharply between the shoulder blades. If this does not work, try the Heimlich manoeuvre (see the photo).

Shock

Shock in this sense does not mean emotional shock. Physical shock usually occurs when there has been a heart attack, a severe loss of blood or a loss of body fluids through severe diarrhoea or vomiting.

Symptoms

Pale, clammy skin; rapid, shallow breathing; sweating but cold; nausea; thirst; weak pulse; dizziness and fainting.

Treatment

1. Treat the cause of shock, such as bleeding.
2. Lay the patient down with their legs raised.
3. Loosen clothing. Cover with a coat or blanket.
4. Do not give the person anything to eat or drink.

Poisoning

Approximately 170 people die each year in Ireland from poisoning.

1. Call an ambulance or take the patient immediately to casualty.
2. Find out what the patient has taken and bring the container to the hospital.
3. **Do not** try to make the patient vomit.
4. Resuscitate if necessary – put in the recovery position.

The recovery position is the safest position for the casualty

1. **Home hygiene:** Required for good health. Guidelines: Good ventilation, house warm and dry, open curtains and windows daily, kitchen and bathrooms should have hygienic surfaces, empty bins, disinfect toilets and sinks weekly, vacuum carpets and floors at least weekly, change bed linen weekly.

2. **Cleaning agents:** Store in original containers, lock away, keep dry, follow directions, wear gloves, rinse off. Detergents (washing powder, liquid, dishwasher powder) clean dishes and clothes. Abrasives (Cif and Brillo) clean scratch-resistant surfaces. Multipurpose (Cillit Bang) work on most work surfaces and floors. Window cleaners (Windolene) clean glass. Polish (Pledge) cleans furniture. Metal polishes (Brasso or Silvo) clean brass and silver. Bleach (Parazone) kills germs and removes stains from sinks and toilets. Disinfectants (Dettol) kill germs. Alternatives (white vinegar, bread soda, lemon juice, cola) remove limescale, clean fridges, remove blood and grass stains and remove stains from toilets. Do not use different products together.

3. **Causes of accidents:** Carelessness, curiosity (children), poor home design, faulty equipment, incorrect storage.

4. **Accident prevention**
   - **Electricity:** No wet hands, correct fuse, safety symbols, no electrical equipment in bathroom, never overload or repair, use childproof covers.
   - **Fire:** No lighters or matches left around, full fireguard, no mirror over fireplace, deep-fat fryer (not chip pan), extinguish cigarettes, no smoking in bed, fire-resistant nightwear, unplug appliances at night, close doors at night.
   - **Fire safety:** Have a smoke alarm, extinguisher and fire blanket. Agree on a fire drill. Never put water on oil or an electrical fire. Do not bring fire outside into air. Call the fire brigade if necessary. If there is a large fire, get out and stay out.
   - **Falls:** Prevention is vital. Have good lighting on stairs, no objects on stairs, use stair gates, avoid frayed carpets or overly polished floors, fit grab rails on baths, showers and toilets, and wipe up spills immediately.

5. **Child safety:** Supervise closely and buy only safe toys.
   - **Choking and suffocation:** Keep plastic bags, small objects and curtain cords out of reach. Never leave children unsupervised.
   - **Scalds:** Use short flexes. Do not use tablecloths. Keep hot drinks away from table edges. Never have a hot drink with a child on your lap. Turn saucepan handles inwards. Put cold water in the bath first.
   - **Falls:** Use window locks and stair gates. Don't allow children onto balconies alone. Strap children into buggies and highchairs.
   - **Poisoning:** Lock away poisonous materials. Store in a childproof place. Use the original containers.
   - **Burns:** Use a full fire guard. Never leave matches etc. around. Make sure there are no dangling flexes. Only buy flame-resistant nightwear.
   - **Drowning:** Never leave a child alone anywhere near water.

6. **Aims of first aid:** To preserve life, to prevent the condition getting worse and to promote recovery.
   - **Serious accident:** Don't move the patient. Check their pulse. Resuscitate if necessary. Don't give the patient food or water. Call 999.
   - **Resuscitation:** Open the airway, breathe for the patient and compress to get heart going again.

7. **First aid treatments**
- **Burns and scalds: Minor:** Pour cold water on the burn. Remove restricting items before swelling occurs. Reduce the risk of infection by applying a loose, non–fluffy dressing. Do not use creams. **Major:** Put out the fire (roll on the ground or in a blanket). Call an ambulance. Pour cold water on the burn. Resuscitate if necessary. Do not remove clothing. Remove restricting items before swelling occurs.
- **Bleeding:** Try to stop the bleeding by applying pressure on or around the wound. Raise the limb if injured. Wrap in a bandage. Call an ambulance if needed.
- **Choking: Child:** Place the child face down on your lap and slap between their shoulder blades. **Adults:** Heimlich manoeuvre.
- **Shock: Causes:** Heart attack, severe loss of blood or other bodily fluids. **Symptoms:** Pale, clammy skin, shallow breathing, sweating, cold, nausea, thirst, weak pulse, dizziness and fainting. **Treatment:** Lay with legs raised, loosen clothing, cover, no food or drink.
- **Poisoning:** Call an ambulance or take the patient to casualty. Bring the container. Do not try to make the patient vomit. Resuscitate if required and put into the recovery position.

Revision Questions

1. Why is good home hygiene important? Outline six general guidelines for good hygiene in the home.
2. What six points should be remembered while using and storing cleaning agents safely?
3. What cleaning agents would you use for the following?
   (a) Cleaning the bath
   (b) Cleaning a tiled kitchen floor
   (c) Removing limescale from around taps
   (d) Cleaning the fridge
   (e) Cleaning a stained toilet
4. What are the four main causes of accidents in the home?
5. Outline five general guidelines for preventing electrical accidents in the home.
6. Outline six ways fire can be prevented in the home.
7. Name three pieces of fire safety equipment that should be found in the home.
8. What is a household fire drill? Why is it necessary in the home?
9. How would you deal with (a) a small fire and (b) a large house fire?
10. How can individuals help prevent the following household accidents?
    (a) Choking and suffocation
    (b) Scalds
    (c) Poisoning
    (d) Burns
    (e) Drowning

11. What are the three aims of first aid?

12. Describe what is involved in the ABCs of resuscitation.

13. Name six items that should be found in a first aid box.

14. What should you administer for first aid for the following?

    (a) A minor burn/scald

    (b) A major burn/scald

    (c) Bleeding

    (d) Choking (child and adult)

15. What are the symptoms of shock? How should shock be treated?

16. What should you do if you suspect someone has been poisoned?

Homework
Assignment
46
P 164

CHAPTER 30
Community Services and the Environment

Teacher's CD

Slide presentation ▪ Student activity pack with revision crossword ▪ Class test ▪ Student learning contract

Key words

- Environmental pollution
- Air pollution
- Smog
- Acid rain
- Climate change
- Global warming
- Greenhouse gases
- Deforestation
- Fossil fuels
- Incineration
- Intensive livestock rearing
- Ozone layer
- Water pollution
- Biodegradable waste
- Inorganic waste
- Recycling
- Sustainable energy
- Carbon emissions
- Community services
- Community amenities
- Statutory services
- Voluntary services

Learning outcomes

After completing this chapter and the homework, assignments and activities that accompany it, you should:

- Be able to define the term *environmental pollution* and know what human activities cause it.
- Know what the main causes of air pollution are and what effects it has on our world. Understand what smog, acid rain, global warming and the ozone layer are and what effects they have on our environment.
- Understand the main causes of water pollution and the effects it has on humans and wildlife.
- Be able to differentiate between organic and inorganic waste. Understand and apply the three Rs of waste management: reduce, reuse and recycle.
- Understand and put into action the ways that you can become a more environmentally friendly person.
- Know the ways in which our government is trying to promote environmental friendliness. Be able to list the organisations associated with environmental protection.
- Be able to differentiate between statutory and non-statutory services and give examples of each.
- Know what the concept of amenities means. Be able to give examples of natural and man-made amenities in your area.

'We don't have to stop using the earth's resources, but we do have to stop wasting them.' (ENFO)

Environmental pollution

Environmental pollution is the term used to describe the ways in which the waste products of human activity harm the natural environment. Environmental pollution is one of the most serious problems facing mankind and all other animals and plants on earth today.

When asked, most people say they would like to see pollution reduced. Unfortunately, most of the pollution that threatens our health and the health of the planet comes from products people want and are unwilling to do without, such as unnecessarily large cars and houses, foreign travel, etc.

Air pollution

According to the World Health Organization, about one-fifth of the world's people are exposed to dangerous levels of air pollution. Air pollution occurs when factories and vehicles, etc. release large amounts of gas, smoke and dirt into the air. Burning rubbish in incineration plants can release smoke and heavy metals such as mercury into the atmosphere.

Effects of air pollution

Air pollution causes:

- Lung problems such as asthma, bronchitis and cancer
- Smog
- Acid rain
- Climate change
- Decrease in the ozone layer

Smog

Smog is one of the most common types of air pollution. Smog is a brown, hazy mixture of gases and smoke. Smog forms when these gases react with sunlight. This reaction then creates hundreds of harmful chemicals, which make up smog.

Smog is still a problem in many cities today. It causes many health problems, such as increased lung infections, asthma and irritation of the linings of the eyes, nose and throat. It also decreases the body's ability to fight infection and disease.

Dublin had a smog problem in the 1980s, which prompted the government to allow only smokeless fuels to be burned in Irish cities and large towns. This action led to a 70% reduction in smog levels in Ireland.

Acid rain

Acid rain is rain or snow that is unusually acidic. It has harmful effects on plants, aquatic animals, buildings and human health (cancer). Acid rain is mostly caused by human emissions of sulphur and nitrogen (as a result of burning fossil fuels), which react in the atmosphere to produce acids.

Climate change

Climate change is any long-term significant change in expected average weather patterns. The main reason for climate change is global warming. Global warming occurs because we are producing increasing amounts of greenhouse gases such as carbon dioxide. These gases trap heat on the earth's surface, which raises the temperature (global warming).

Effects of acid rain on forestry

Causes of increased greenhouse gas production

🏠 **Increased CO_2 emissions:** There are more cars and trucks on the roads. Households and industry burn fossil fuels, such as oil.

🏠 **Deforestation:** Because plants use CO_2 and give off oxygen, cutting down large areas of forest increases the amount of CO_2 in the atmosphere.

🏠 **Burning waste:** Large incineration plants.

🏠 **Large power plants** burning fossil fuels to produce electricity, such as the ESB.

🏠 **Intensive livestock rearing** produces methane, a greenhouse gas.

Effects of climate change

🏠 Flooding (because the icecaps in Antarctica are melting)

🏠 More stormy, wet weather

🏠 The appearance of insects such as mosquitoes in countries like Ireland, which increases the risk of disease in these countries

🏠 Previously fertile land becoming dry and barren, resulting in extreme poverty and starvation

Flooding and drought are both effects of climate change

Ozone layer

The ozone layer is a layer of gas (O_3) found nine to 18 miles above the earth's surface. Ozone is important because it shields us from the sun's harmful (cancer-causing) UV rays.

During the 1970s, scientists discovered that holes were forming in the ozone layer, mainly as a result of two groups of substances: CFCs and halons. CFCs were found in aerosol sprays, fridges and freezers, fast food cartons and air conditioning systems. Halons were in some types of fire extinguishers.

Nowadays, as a result of the Montreal Protocol (an international agreement) that came into force in 1989, there is a ban on CFCs and halons in most countries in the world, and the ozone layer is now repairing itself. Experts believe that it will recover fully by 2050.

Water pollution

Water pollution is the contamination of water by substances such as human sewage, agricultural run-off and chemical waste from industrial plants.

According to the World Heath Organization, approximately 5 million people die every year from drinking polluted water – that is more than the population of Ireland. The main effects of water pollution on humans are diseases such as cholera, dysentery and *E. coli* poisoning (see page 54). Water pollution also causes the death of fish and damages birds, plants and other wildlife.

Waste disposal

One of the biggest problems facing society is waste disposal. Waste products can be:

- 🏠 **Organic or biodegradable:** This means that it can be easily broken down by nature, such as paper and vegetable peels.
- 🏠 **Inorganic:** This means that the waste cannot be easily broken down and is harmful to the environment, such as plastic, glass and metal. However, while some inorganic waste does not break down easily, it can be **recycled.**

If waste is not recycled, then it must be disposed of in one of two ways: dumped and buried in landfill sites or burned in incinerators. Both of these methods can be damaging to us and the environment. We therefore need to remember the three Rs of waste management:

🏠 **Reduce** the amount of waste produced.

🏠 **Reuse** goods where possible, such as shopping bags, or reuse old clothes as polishing cloths.

🏠 **Recycle** both organic waste (compost bin) and inorganic waste (bottle bank).

Protecting the environment

What can you do to help protect the environment?

1. Be an eco-friendly shopper.

   🏠 Avoid over-packaged goods. For example, buy fruit, vegetables and meat loose rather than pre-packaged.

   🏠 If goods are packaged, make sure the packaging is recycled or recyclable.

   🏠 Look for the EU Ecolabel. This shows that the product is environmentally friendly and does not harm the environment.

   🏠 Bring a shopping bag.

2. Recycle.

   🏠 Recycle bottles, cans, paper, plastic, batteries and mobile phones. There is probably a recycling centre near you, it just takes a little effort.

   🏠 Recycle clothes by donating them to charity shops.

   🏠 Recycle organic waste, such as vegetable peels, by having a compost bin or compost heap (some local authorities sell compost bins at a reduced price).

A home compost bin

The recycling symbol

3. Don't litter and don't tolerate those who do.

4. Use less water.

   🏠 Showers use less than half the water baths do.

   🏠 Fix dripping taps.

🏠 Do not turn on the dishwasher or washing machine for small amounts. Use the half-load setting or economy wash if you must wash less than a full load or if the load is not very dirty.

5. Walk or cycle to school or work if possible.

6. Use less energy.

   🏠 Do not over-heat your home.

   🏠 Turn off lights when not in use.

   🏠 Use energy-saving bulbs (CFLs).

7. When choosing electrical appliances, choose energy-efficient models (A or B labels – see page 327).

Government action

🏠 **The plastic bag levy.**

🏠 **Car tax based on carbon emissions:** All new cars registered since July 2008 are now taxed based on their rates of carbon emissions rather than engine size. Cars are graded A to G (A is best, with the lowest carbon emissions). Grade A cars are taxed at €120 per year, whereas owners of grade G cars must pay €2,330 in car tax annually (figures as of 2014). Most cars fall somewhere in between these two figures.

🏠 **Sustainable Energy Ireland:** This is a government organisation set up in 2002 to promote and help develop sustainable energy in Ireland. For example, they give grants to people who want to improve the energy efficiency of their home, such as by installing better insulation.

🏠 **Recycling centres:** Over the past number of years, the government has improved recycling facilities throughout the country. In general, people do not have to travel far to a centre.

🏠 **Government-sponsored websites:** These provide useful information on the environment and what you can do to help. Sites include www.change.ie, www.enfo.ie and www.sei.ie.

What other measures do you think the government could introduce to help us help the environment?

Organisations involved with environmental protection

🏠 Environment Protection Agency

🏠 Friends of the Earth

🏠 Green Party

🏠 Greenpeace

Community services

When people live together in urban (city or town) or rural (country) areas, they form a **community**. Most communities have a number of **services** and **amenities**.

Services

Statutory (government-run)

🏠 Education (schools, some pre-schools)

🏠 Gardaí

🏠 Health (hospitals, health centres)

🏠 Libraries

🏠 Local authority housing (council or corporation)

🏠 Postal services

🏠 Public transport

🏠 Social welfare

Voluntary services

🏠 GAA, soccer and rugby clubs

🏠 Homeless Aid

🏠 ISPCC

🏠 Meals on Wheels

🏠 Neighbourhood Watch

🏠 REHAB Foundation

🏠 Samaritans

🏠 Society of St Vincent de Paul

🏠 Youth clubs

The GAA is a voluntary service

Amenities

An amenity is another word for a leisure facility. Amenities can be natural (rivers, lakes, beaches) or man-made (parks, playgrounds, sports pitches, cinemas, museums, fitness centres, swimming pools).

1. **Environmental pollution:** When the waste products of human activity harm the environment.
2. **Air pollution:** Occurs when factories, incineration plants, homes and vehicles release gas, smoke and dirt into the air.

- **Effects:** Lung problems, smog, depleted ozone layer, acid rain and climate change.
- **Smog:** When gases and smoke in the air react with sunlight, creating dangerous chemicals. Ireland had a smog problem in the 1980s, but using smokeless fuel reduced this problem by 70%.
- **Acid rain:** Caused when emissions from burning fossil fuels react with the atmosphere, producing acid rain. Acid rain destroys forestry and buildings.
- **Climate change:** Long-term change in average weather patterns and global warming. Main cause: gases (CO_2) trap the earth's heat, raising temperatures. **Causes of climate change:** Increased CO_2 emissions, deforestation, incineration, power plants burning fossil fuels, intensive livestock rearing. **Effects:** Flooding, stormy, wet weather, appearance of unusual insects, fertile land becoming too dry or too wet.
- **Ozone layer:** The layer of gas (O_3) 18 miles above the earth's surface that protects us from the sun's harmful rays. CFCs and halogen gases were destroying the ozone layer. The Montreal Protocol (1989) banned CFCs and halogens. The ozone layer is repairing itself (experts believe by 2050).

3. **Water pollution:** Occurs when human sewage, agricultural run-off and chemical waste enter the waterways. Approximately 5 million people die every year from polluted water. Effects: Cholera, dysentery and *E. coli* poisoning.
4. **Waste disposal:** Types of waste are organic and inorganic. Inorganic waste must be reduced, reused or recycled.
5. **Protecting the environment:** Avoid overpackaged goods. Make sure packaging is recyclable. Look for the EU Ecolabel. Bring shopping bags. Recycle. Don't litter. Conserve water. Walk or cycle rather than drive. Conserve energy – don't overheat the home, use CFL bulbs and turn off lights when not in use and choose energy-efficient appliances.
6. **Government action:** Plastic bag levy, car tax based on carbon emissions, establishment of Sustainable Energy Ireland, establishment of nationwide recycling centres, government-sponsored websites, support of environmental protection agencies (Environment Protection Agency).
7. **Community services:** Statutory agencies (run by the government), such as schools and hospitals, and non-statutory agencies (not run by the government), such as the GAA.
8. **Amenities:** Leisure facilities can be natural (rivers) or man-made (playgrounds).

1. What is environmental pollution?
2. List two causes of air pollution. What are the five main effects of air pollution?
3. What is acid rain? What causes it?
4. Define climate change. What is the main reason for climate change? Describe the five main effects of climate change.
5. Name a greenhouse gas. Describe five causes of increased greenhouse gas production in modern society.
6. What is the ozone layer? What caused a hole to develop in the ozone layer during the 1970s?
7. List three causes of water pollution. List two effects of water pollution.
8. What are the two types of waste? Describe the three Rs of waste management.
9. Outline six ways you can help protect the environment.
10. List three ways the government has tried to reduce environmental pollution.
11. Name four organisations involved in environmental protection.
12. What are (a) statutory and (b) voluntary services? Give four examples of each.
13. Give two examples of natural and two examples of man-made amenities.

Test Yourself
eTest.ie

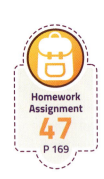

Homework Assignment
47
P 169

Unit 5
Textile Studies

Unit 5 Textile Studies

CHAPTER 31
Textiles in the Home

Teacher's CD

Slide presentation • Student activity pack with revision crossword • Class test • Student learning contract

Key words

- ✓ Textiles
- ✓ Soft furnishings
- ✓ Upholstery
- ✓ Carpets
- ✓ Bed linen
- ✓ Table linen
- ✓ Desirable properties
- ✓ Pile
- ✓ Light domestic use
- ✓ General domestic use
- ✓ Heavy domestic use
- ✓ Tog rating

Learning outcomes

After completing this chapter and the homework, assignments and activities that accompany it, you should:

- Know the different types of textiles used in the home.
- Understand that textiles can have different characteristics or properties that make them suitable or unsuitable for different purposes in the home. Be able to give examples of properties.
- Know what factors should be considered when choosing textiles for the home.
- Be able to give examples of soft furnishings and describe the functions of each example given. Know how to measure curtains and be able to list the properties that curtain fabric should have.
- Understand the two basic construction types and the factors that influence the price of carpets. Understand how carpets are graded and be able to list the desirable properties of carpets.
- Be able to list the different types of bed linen available, the fabrics suitable for each and the desirable properties of each.
- Understand what is meant by upholstery, what the desirable properties of upholstery are and name suitable fabrics.

What are textiles?

A textile is a fabric or cloth. The clothes we wear and many of the items in our homes are made from textiles.

Using textiles in the home

- **Soft furnishings:** These are items other than furniture that are used to decorate a room and make it more comfortable. Examples include curtains and blinds, cushions, rugs, wall hangings and lampshades.

- **Upholstery:** This is the name given to the fillings and covering fabrics that are used in furniture such as sofas, armchairs, mattresses and chair seats.

- **Carpets:** Many different types of carpets are available. Some are very hard-wearing, while others are cheaper and less so.

Textiles can be used to make a room warm and cosy. They also absorb sound.

- **Bed linen:** This includes sheets and pillowcases, duvets and duvet covers, blankets, bedspreads and throws.

- **Table linen and towels:** This includes tablecloths, napkins, table runners, placemats, dishcloths, tea towels, hand towels and bath towels.

Properties of textiles

A property is a characteristic or quality of a textile. When choosing a textile for a particular purpose, for example towels, the properties of the textile you choose are important. Imagine buying towels made from a non-absorbent, rough textile that you had to dry clean. Desirable properties are those that are most important. For example, desirable properties for a face towel would be that it is absorbent, soft and washable.

Examples of properties

Cool, soft, warm, absorbent, waterproof, washable, colour fast (won't run), soft, shiny, rough, smooth, delicate, light, heavy, hard-wearing, breathable, non-absorbent, crease-resistant, flame-resistant, resilient (bounces back into shape), stretchy, insulating, stain-resistant, transparent (lets light through).

Choosing fabrics for household items

Points to consider:

- Cost: Some fabrics, such as silk, are very expensive.
- Desirable properties, such as durable and stain resistant.
- Colour, pattern and style should fit in with the existing décor.

Soft furnishings

Soft furnishings include curtains and blinds, cushions, rugs, wall hangings and lampshades.

Curtains give privacy, insulate and decorate

Functions of soft furnishings:

- Curtains and blinds give us privacy.
- Curtains insulate the room and help to keep draughts out.
- Soft furnishings such as rugs and cushions make the room more comfortable.
- All soft furnishings absorb sound and so reduce noise in the room.
- They finish off a room, making it more attractive.
- They allow us to express our personal taste.

Curtains

Measuring curtains

- **Length:** From rail to 5cm below the windowsill for short curtains; from rail to 2cm off the floor for long curtains.
- **Width:** 2.5 times the width of the window or rail.
- **Suitable fabrics:** Cotton, linen, velvet, dralon (best lined).

Properties

Curtains should:

- Hang well
- Be fade resistant
- Be washable or dry cleanable
- Be fire resistant
- Be pre-shrunk
- Have a close weave

Carpets

Carpets can be one of the most expensive purchases for the home, so they should be chosen wisely. Carpets can be:

 Woven (expensive)

 Non-woven (less expensive)

With woven carpets, tufts of carpet fibres are woven into a heavy cloth backing. Non-woven carpet tufts, on the other hand, are glued into or onto a rubber or cloth backing.

The **pile** of a carpet describes the tufts on the surface of the carpet. The pile can be long or short, twisted or straight, dense (tightly packed) or loose. The density of the pile is very important. If the pile is dense (a lot of tufts per square centimetre), then the carpet will be soft and luxurious. However, it will also be expensive.

A cheap, non-woven carpet with low pile density

Classification or grading of carpets

Carpets are graded according to how hard-wearing (durable) they are.

 Light domestic: Suitable for bedrooms.

 General domestic: Suitable for living rooms.

 Heavy domestic: Suitable for halls, stairs and living rooms.

An expensive woven carpet with high pile density

What type of carpet you buy will depend on which room it is for and how much money you have to spend. Ideally a room with a lot of traffic, such as a living room, hallway or stairs, should have a good-quality carpet. A less expensive carpet, on the other hand, would be fine for a bedroom.

Properties

A good carpet will be:

 Resilient (bounce back after being walked on)

 Warm

 Hard-wearing

 Stain-resistant

Carpets are generally made from:

- ✂ **Wool** because it is warm and resilient.
- ✂ **Nylon and acrylic** because they are hard-wearing and cheap.
- ✂ The best carpets (although they are the most expensive) are made from a mix of wool (80%) and nylon (20%).

Bed linen

Household item	Made from	Points to remember
Sheets, pillowcases, duvet covers	Cotton, polycotton, polyester	Need to be washable, easily dried and absorbent.
Bedspreads and duvets (a bedspread is like a duvet except it is not covered with a separate cover – it is made from decorative fabric)	Covering: Cotton, polyester or polycotton. Filling: Polyester or duck down	The warmth of a duvet or bedspread is measured by a tog rating – 4.5 to 15 tog (warmest). Duvets and bedspreads need to be warm, light and washable.
Blankets	Wool, wool and nylon or acrylic mixed	Wool blankets are warm but expensive; wool mixed with acrylic or nylon is hard-wearing as well; acrylic on its own is cheaper but not as warm.
Throws, cushions	Cotton, wool, satin, acrylic, silk	These usually complement the rest of the bed linen.

An attractively dressed bed

Upholstery

Upholstery is the covering and filling on sofas, armchairs, mattresses and chair seats.

 Desirable properties: Durable, stain-resistant, closely woven, easy to clean, fire-resistant.

 Suitable fabrics: Heavy cotton, linen, wool, leather, velvet and dralon (like velvet).

Upholstered furniture

1. A **textile** is a fabric or a cloth. Textiles are used a lot in the home for soft furnishings, upholstery, carpets, bed linen, table linen and towels.

2. **Properties of textiles:** When choosing a textile for a particular purpose, you must consider its properties. For example, it is important that the textile chosen for a bath towel would be absorbent, soft and washable.

3. **Choosing fabrics for household items:** Consider cost, desirable properties, colour, pattern and style.

4. **Soft furnishings:** Curtains, blinds, cushions, rugs, wall hangings and lampshades. Curtains give privacy, absorb sound, decorate and insulate. Rugs and cushions absorb sound, decorate and make the room more attractive. All soft furnishing decorate and allow us to express our personal taste.

5. **Measuring curtains:** Length from rail to 5cm below windowsill for short curtains or 2cm off the floor for long curtains. Width should be 2.5 times the width of the rail. Suitable fabrics are cotton, linen, velvet and dralon. Properties: Hang well, fade-resistant, washable or dry cleanable, fire-resistant, pre-shrunk and close weave.

6. **Carpets:** Can be woven (expensive) or non-woven (less expensive). The pile describes the tufts on the surface of the carpet (dense or loose). The denser the pile, the better the carpet, but it will be more expensive.
   - **Grading:** Light domestic, general domestic, heavy domestic.
   - **Properties:** Resilient, warm, hard-wearing and stain-resistant. Best carpets are 80% wool (warm and resilient) and 20% nylon (hard-wearing).
7. **Bed linen:** Sheets, pillowcases, duvet covers (cotton, polycotton; must be washable and absorbent), bedspreads and duvets (filling is polyester or duck down; warmth is measured by tog rating 4.5–15), blankets (wool, wool nylon or acrylic mixed; must be warm), throws and cushions (usually complement the décor).
8. **Upholstery:** Coverings and fillings on sofas, armchairs, mattresses and chair seats.
   - **Desirable properties:** Durable, stain-resistant, closely woven, easy to clean, fire-resistant. Heavy cotton, linen, wool, leather, velvet and dralon are suitable.

Revision Questions

1. Describe five uses of textiles in the home.
2. What is meant by the properties of a textile?
3. Name three points that should be considered when choosing fabrics for household items.
4. List four functions of soft furnishings in the home.
5. List four properties that would be desirable in curtain fabric.
6. How do woven and non-woven carpets differ in terms of their construction?
7. What is a carpet pile? How are carpets graded? What factors should you consider when buying a carpet? List four properties of a good carpet.
8. Why is a carpet made from wool (80%) and nylon (20%) an ideal mix?
9. Suggest two suitable fabrics for sheets, pillowcases and duvet covers. Name three fabric properties that would be important.
10. What is a tog rating?
11. What is upholstery? List four desirable properties of upholstery fabric. List three fabrics suitable for upholstery.

Test Yourself
eTest.ie

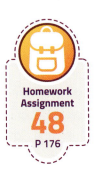
Homework Assignment
48
P 176

CHAPTER 32

Clothing, Fashion and Design

Slide presentation • Student activity pack with revision crossword • Class test • Student learning contract

Key words

- ✓ Fashion trends
- ✓ Fashion fads
- ✓ Haute couture
- ✓ Prêt-à-porter
- ✓ Off-the-peg
- ✓ Accessories

Learning outcomes

After completing this chapter and the homework, assignments and activities that accompany it, you should:

- Know what the six functions of clothing are.
- Know what fashion trends are and understand how the fashion industry, famous personalities, historical events, economy and technology influence them.
- Be able to discuss the factors that influence your choice of clothes and the factors you should consider when buying clothing.
- Know what accessories are and be able to give examples.
- Understand the principles involved in clothing design.

Clothing

One of the most important uses of textiles is clothing. Natural fabrics such as cotton, wool and linen are used together with man-made fabrics such as nylon, polyester and acrylic.

Functions of clothing

There are six basic functions of clothing.

Functions of clothing

1. Protection from the weather

2. Safety

3. Modesty (levels of modesty vary between cultures and situations)

4. Self-expression

5. Identification – uniforms

6. Creating an image or impression

Jumpsuits were popular in the 1980s and seem to be making a comeback!

Fashion and design

Fashion is a word used to describe clothes or other items that are trendy or popular at any given time. Fashion changes constantly. **Fashion trends** are changes in fashion. Most people also see that fashion trends form cycles of fashion. For example, 1980s drainpipe jeans and batwing tops have returned in an almost identical form almost 30 years later as skinny jeans and batwing. **Fashion fads** are short-term fashion trends, such as wearing leg warmers.

Fashion trends are influenced by:

- The fashion industry
- Famous people and the media
- Historical events and the economy
- Technology

The fashion industry

It is in the interest of the fashion industry that fashion is always changing. Otherwise, how would the industry continue to make money? Twice a year, fashion shows are held in Paris, London, New York and Milan, where the world's top fashion designers show off their new designs. These **haute couture** clothes are hand made, one of a kind and very expensive. For example, you could pay more than €25,000 for a suit.

Top designers such as Prada, Versace and Christian Dior also produce less expensive machine-made clothes. These ranges, called **prêt-à-porter** (ready-to-wear) clothes, are still expensive and are only available in designer boutiques.

Chain stores such as A-Wear, Next, Cocoon and Dunnes Stores then buy or recreate these looks and sell them cheaply as **off-the-peg clothes**.

Famous people

Pop stars, sports stars, models, actors and actresses all influence current fashion trends through the media.

Historical events and the economy

- During World War II fabric was scarce, so skirts became straight and shorter.
- During times of economic recession, aggressive, anti-establishment fashions become more popular, such as punk and Goth.

Technology

As new fabrics are developed, they influence fashion.

Haute couture – high fashion

Famous people influence fashion trends

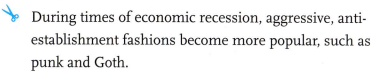

Despite the economic recession, young people do not tend to dress in anti-establishment clothing

Buying clothes

What influences your choice?

- **Age:** As you get older, your idea of what is nice changes.
- **Cost:** How much money you have influences where you shop and what type of clothes you buy.
- **Fashion:** Fashion trends often influence our likes and dislikes. For example, skinny jeans are in fashion for teenage girls today, so most teenagers like skinny jeans and don't like bootcut jeans.
- **What suits you:** Sometimes people follow fashion trends even when they do not suit them. For example, low-rise or skinny jeans do not suit someone who is overweight, yet many will still wear them because they are in fashion.
- **Peer pressure:** You may be influenced by what your peers are wearing.
- **Lifestyle and occupation:** A student would be likely to dress differently to a bank manager, for example.
- **Culture:** Some cultures have a dress code, such as Muslims.

Factors to consider when buying clothing

- Can I afford it? Is it good value for money?
- Do I need it?
- Does it suit my figure, hair colour, skin colour?
- Does it fit me well? Is it comfortable?
- Is it good quality?
- Is it washable or will it have to be dry cleaned (expensive)?
- Does it suit the occasion, for example a job interview?

Accessories are worn with an outfit to complete it. Examples include jewellery, belts, hats, shoes, bags, etc. Some accessories also have a function – for example, a bag is used to carry things.

Designing clothes

When designing clothes, there are two basic aims. The item must:

 Function as it should

 Look good

As with interior design (see page 300–303), certain design guidelines or factors, when followed, can achieve these aims.

Design guidelines or factors

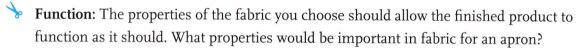

Function: The properties of the fabric you choose should allow the finished product to function as it should. What properties would be important in fabric for an apron?

Colour: Choose colours that suit your hair, skin and eye colour. For example, bright red may not suit a person with red hair. Some colours never go out of fashion, such as black, white, navy and denim.

Pattern: Avoid too much, especially large patterns.

Texture: Texture is the feel of a fabric. Can you name a clothing fabric with a smooth or a rough texture?

Line: Horizontal lines (stripes) make a person look wider. Vertical lines make a person look taller and slimmer. Curved lines, such as those in a flowing dress, are feminine.

Shape: The shape or outline of a garment. A well-cut garment can flatter any figure.

The same principles of proportion, emphasis, balance and rhythm also apply to clothing and textile design (see interior design, page 303).

Pictured opposite is an example of a school uniform. What do you think of it? Consider the principles of design above.

1. **Functions of clothing:** Protection, safety, modesty, self-expression, identification and creating an image or impression.

2. **Fashion** describes clothes or other items that are popular or trendy at a given time. **Fashion trends** are changes in fashion. **Fashion fads** are short-term fashion trends. Trends are influenced by the fashion industry, famous people and the media, historical events and the economy, and advances in technology that make new fabrics available.

3. **Fashion industry:** Always changing. Top designers produce hand-made, one-of-a-kind haute couture clothes for fashion shows twice a year. Top designers then make machine versions of some of these clothes (prêt-à-porter). Chain stores then recreate these looks and sell them off the peg.

4. **Buying clothes (influences):** Your age, cost, fashion, what suits you, peer pressure, lifestyle and occupation, culture.

5. **Factors to consider:** Can I afford it? Do I need it? Does it suit my figure? Does it fit comfortably? Is it good quality? Is it washable? Does it suit the occasion?

6. **Accessories:** Worn to complement an outfit (belts, jewellery, ties, hats, shoes, bags, etc.).

7. **Clothing design:** Items must function well and look good. Design factors are function, colour, pattern, texture, line, shape, proportion, emphasis, balance and rhythm.

1. List the six functions of clothing.
2. What are (a) fashion trends and (b) fashion fads? Give an example of each.
3. What do the following fashion terms mean: (a) haute couture (b) prêt-à-porter and (c) off-the-peg clothes?
4. Describe four factors that influence fashion trends.
5. What six factors may influence people when buying clothes?
6. What are accessories? Give two examples.
7. Describe the six basic design principles.
8. What is meant by each of the following in relation to clothing design: (a) proportion (b) emphasis (c) balance (d) rhythm?

Test Yourself
eTest.ie

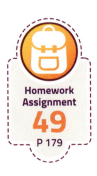

Homework Assignment
49
P 179

Unit 5 Textile Studies

CHAPTER 33
Fibres and Fabrics

Teacher's CD

Slide presentation ▪ Student activity pack with revision crossword ▪ Class test ▪ Student learning contract

Key words

- ✓ Fibres
- ✓ Yarn
- ✓ Fabric
- ✓ Natural fibres
- ✓ Man-made fibres
- ✓ Synthetic
- ✓ Regenerated
- ✓ Properties of fibres and fabrics
- ✓ Wool
- ✓ Silk
- ✓ Cotton
- ✓ Linen
- ✓ Viscose
- ✓ Rayon
- ✓ Acetate
- ✓ Nylon
- ✓ Polyester
- ✓ Acrylic
- ✓ Elastane (Lycra)
- ✓ Denier
- ✓ Bonded fabrics
- ✓ Ply
- ✓ Weaving
- ✓ Knitting
- ✓ Fabric finishes
- ✓ Dyeing
- ✓ Colourfast
- ✓ Burning tests

Learning outcomes

After completing this chapter and the homework, assignments and activities that accompany it, you should:

- Be able to classify fibres into natural and man-made and give examples of each.
- Be able to describe the source, production, properties and uses of wool, silk, cotton, linen, regenerated fibres (viscose, rayon and acetate) and synthetic fibres (nylon, polyester, acrylic and elastane (Lycra)).
- Understand how fibres are made into fabrics by weaving, knitting and bonding.
- Be able to name a range of fabric finishes, state what the function of each finish is and where they are used.
- Be able to describe the different ways colour and pattern are added to fabrics.
- Be able to describe the burning test for wool, silk, cotton, linen, viscose and nylon.

Fibres are tiny hair-like threads. They are twisted together into yarn and the yarn is then made into fabric.

fibres → yarn → fabric

Classification of fibres

Fibres can be divided or classified into two groups: natural fibres and man-made fibres. Each group can be divided again.

Natural fibres	Man-made fibres
• **Animal:** Wool, silk • **Plant:** Cotton, linen	• **Synthetic:** Polyester, nylon, acrylic • **Regenerated:** Viscose, acetate

Natural fibres (animal)

Wool

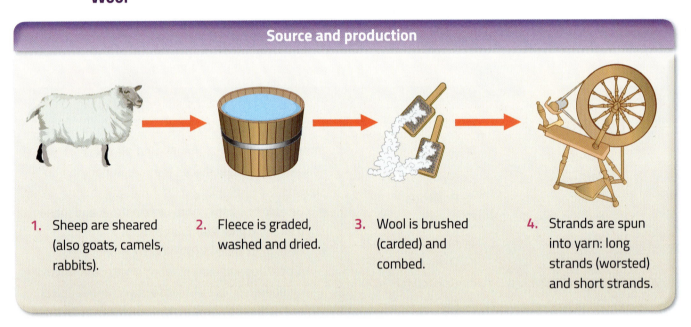

Source and production

1. Sheep are sheared (also goats, camels, rabbits).

2. Fleece is graded, washed and dried.

3. Wool is brushed (carded) and combed.

4. Strands are spun into yarn: long strands (worsted) and short strands.

Long strands (worsted) are used to make wool fabric

Short strands are used for knitting wool

WOOLMARK ®
100% wool

WOOLMARK BLEND ®
Wool blend (wool + another fibre)

Properties

✂ **Good:** Wool is a warm, absorbent fabric that does not burn easily. Wool carpets are hard-wearing and resilient (do not stay flattened when walked on).

✂ **Bad:** Untreated wool shrinks if washed at too high a temperature or if tumble dried. Coarse qualities can irritate the skin.

Uses of wool

✂ **Short fibres:** Jumpers, blankets, carpets.

✂ **Long fibres:** Long worsted fibres are used to make different types of wool fabric, such as gabardine, tweed and crepe.

A suit made from wool

Silk

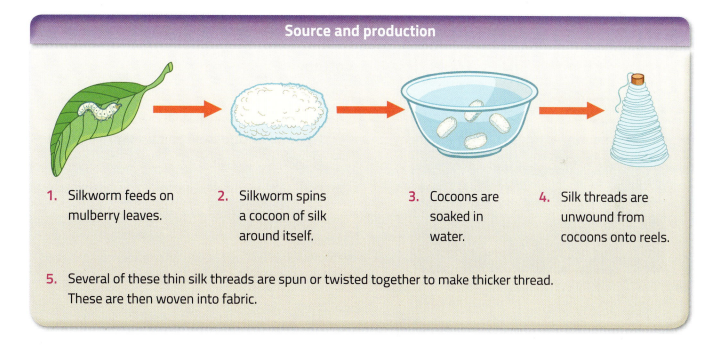

Source and production

1. Silkworm feeds on mulberry leaves.

2. Silkworm spins a cocoon of silk around itself.

3. Cocoons are soaked in water.

4. Silk threads are unwound from cocoons onto reels.

5. Several of these thin silk threads are spun or twisted together to make thicker thread. These are then woven into fabric.

Properties

✂ **Good:** Silk is absorbent, crease-resistant, strong, smooth, light and drapes (falls) well.

✂ **Bad:** Silk is expensive. It is also easily damaged by careless washing, moths, sunshine and chemicals and it is flammable (burns easily).

Uses of silk

Silk is a luxury fabric and is used for shirts, evening dresses, etc. In the home, silk can be used for paintings, cushion covers and curtains (line them – why?).

Pure silk symbol

Types of silk

Chiffon (very light), taffeta, wild silk, satin.

A silk dress

Source and production

Cotton bolls

↓

picked
cleaned
graded
combed
spun

↓

Yarn

Natural fibres (plant)
Cotton
Properties

- **Good:** Cotton is absorbent, cool, strong, washes and dries well and is easy to dye and bleach.

- **Bad:** Cotton creases, shrinks and burns easily. It can be damaged by mildew (mould).

Uses of cotton

Clothes, towels, sheets and curtains.

100% cotton symbol

Types of cotton

- Flannelette (fluffy sheets)
- Denim
- Towelling (towels)
- Muslin (a light, see-through fabric)

Linen

Muslin curtains

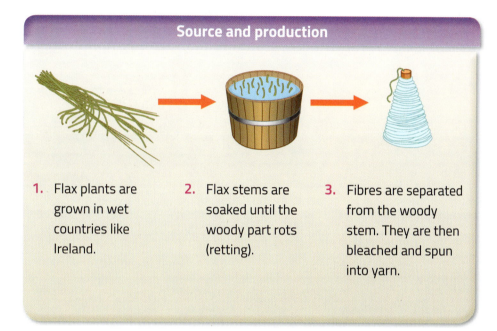

Source and production

1. Flax plants are grown in wet countries like Ireland.
2. Flax stems are soaked until the woody part rots (retting).
3. Fibres are separated from the woody stem. They are then bleached and spun into yarn.

Symbol for linen

Properties

- **Good:** Linen is absorbent, cool, strong and washes well.
- **Bad:** Linen is expensive, creases and shrinks easily. It is difficult to dye and is damaged by mildew.

Flax plants

Uses and types of linen

Irish linen is famous the world over. Linen products range from heavy damask tablecloths and sheets to finer lawn and cambric clothing.

Man-made fibres

Man-made fibres can be either **regenerated** or **synthetic**.

Regenerated

Viscose, rayon, acetate.

A linen outfit

Source and production – regenerated

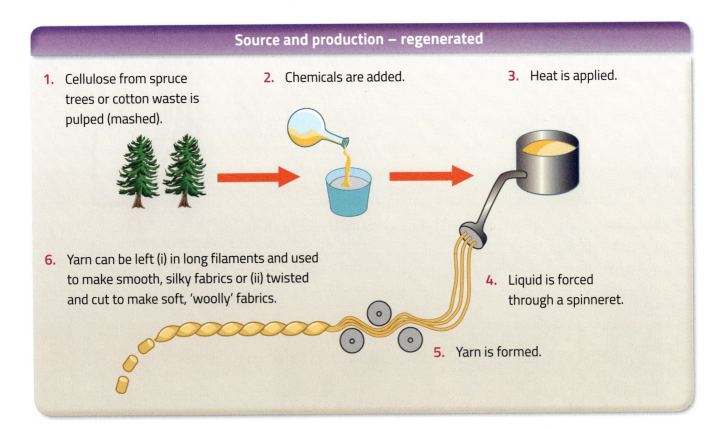

1. Cellulose from spruce trees or cotton waste is pulped (mashed).

2. Chemicals are added.

3. Heat is applied.

6. Yarn can be left (i) in long filaments and used to make smooth, silky fabrics or (ii) twisted and cut to make soft, 'woolly' fabrics.

4. Liquid is forced through a spinneret.

5. Yarn is formed.

Properties

- **Good:** Regenerated fabrics are absorbent and cool to wear.
- **Bad:** They are not hard-wearing and they tear easily after a lot of washing.

Uses of regenerated fibres

Fabrics made from regenerated fibres, such as rayon and viscose, are used to make silky blouses, dresses, etc. (see the photograph).

Synthetic

Nylon, polyester, acrylic, elastane (Lycra).

An acrylic jumper

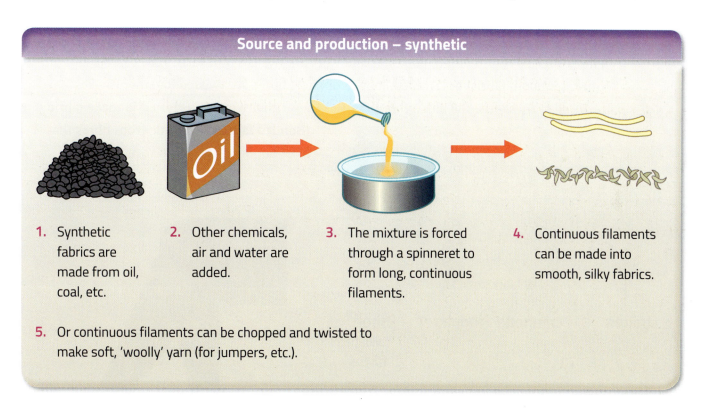

Source and production – synthetic

1. Synthetic fabrics are made from oil, coal, etc.

2. Other chemicals, air and water are added.

3. The mixture is forced through a spinneret to form long, continuous filaments.

4. Continuous filaments can be made into smooth, silky fabrics.

5. Or continuous filaments can be chopped and twisted to make soft, 'woolly' yarn (for jumpers, etc.).

Properties

- **Good:** Synthetic fabrics are all strong and hard-wearing. Acrylic and polyester are warm (acrylic jumpers, polyester filling in duvets and coats). Nylon repels water, so it is good for tents, rain gear, etc.

- **Bad:** All synthetics are flammable. Some, such as nylon, cling and are clammy in summer, as they don't absorb moisture. Damaged by careless washing.

Uses of synthetic fibres

- **Acrylic:** Jumpers, fake fur, dresses, carpets.
- **Nylon:** Umbrellas, swimsuits, tents, raincoats, tights, blended with wool for carpets.
- **Polyester:** Usually blended with cotton in trousers, blouses and shirts. Used to make the filling in duvets and coats.
- **PVC:** Fake leather goods.
- **Elastane (Lycra):** Added to other fabrics to make a garment stretchy, such as swimwear.

Elastane (Lycra)

Making fibres into fabrics
Yarn

Fibres such as cotton, linen, polyester and wool are twisted into yarn. **Yarn** can be straight (makes smooth fabric) or crimped, looped or short fibres are twisted together (makes textured fabrics – see the illustration). Yarn is then either woven or knitted to make fabric.

(**Bonded fabrics** are made from fibres that have not been spun into yarn.)

straight   crimped   looped   short
                                        twisted
                                        fibres

Denier refers to the thickness of man-made fibres. The lower the denier, the finer or thinner the yarn. Denier ranges from 1 to 70+ (very thick).

Ply refers to the number of yarns twisted together. It usually applies to knitting wool. Wool can be anything from single ply to 20 ply, which is very chunky.

40 denier tights

Yarn to fabric

Weaving

Most weaving is done on a loom. Warp threads (vertical) are put onto the loom first and weft threads are then woven through them. The selvedge is the edge that the weft threads make; it doesn't fray.

A loom. Weft threads run across.

Knitting

Knitting can be done by hand or by machine. Most people, when they think of knitting, think only of jumpers, hats and scarves. Many fabrics are also knitted, as you can see if you look closely at them. All knitted fabrics are stretchy. Tracksuits, T-shirts, jumpers and tights are all made from knitted fabrics.

Knitted fabric

Bonded fabrics

Bonded fabrics are made from fibres that have not been spun into yarn. They are made by sticking fibres together by applying moisture, pressure and heat.

    Examples: Felt (snooker tables, hats), wadding (filling inside duvets, coats, carpet underlay) and disposable fabrics (J-cloths, hospital gowns).

The covering on a snooker table is made from bonded fabric

1. Hair-like fibres are twisted into **yarn** and then made into **fabric**.
2. **Classification**
   - **Natural:** Animal (wool, silk) and plant (cotton, linen).
   - **Man-made:** Regenerated (viscose, acetate) and synthetic (nylon, polyester, acrylic).
3. **Wool**
   - **Production:** Animals are sheared. The fleece is graded, washed and dried, brushed (carded) and combed, then spun into yarn. Long fibres are made into wool fabric (worsted) and short fibres are used for knitting wool.
   - **Properties:** Warm, absorbent, does not burn, hard-wearing and resilient, but shrinks and can be coarse on skin.
   - **Uses:** Short fibres for knits, long fibres for wool fabrics.
4. **Silk**
   - **Production:** The silkworm spins a cocoon. The cocoons are soaked. The threads are unwound and several silk threads are spun together to make silk thread, which is then woven into fabric.
   - **Properties:** Absorbent, crease-resistant, strong, smooth, light and drapes well, but it is expensive, easily damaged by careless washing, moths and sunshine, and burns easily.
   - **Uses:** Luxury fabric evening dresses, cushions and wall hangings.
   - **Types:** Chiffon, taffeta, wild silk and satin.
5. **Cotton**
   - **Production:** Cotton bolls are picked, cleaned, graded, combed and spun into yarn, then woven into fabric.
   - **Properties:** Absorbent, cool, strong and washes, dries and bleaches well, but creases, shrinks and burns easily and is affected by mildew.
   - **Uses:** Clothing, towels, sheets and curtains.
   - **Types:** Flannelette, denim, towelling, muslin.
6. **Linen**
   - **Production:** Flax plant is soaked and the woody part rots. The interior of the plant is bleached and spun into yarn, then woven into fabric.
   - **Properties:** Cool, absorbent, strong and washes well, but it is expensive, creases and shrinks, is difficult to dye and is damaged by mildew.
   - **Uses:** Tablecloths, napkins and clothing.
   - **Types:** Damask (thick) and lawn (finer).
7. **Regenerated fabrics:** Examples are viscose, rayon and acetate.
   - **Production:** Made from wood pulp or cotton waste. Chemicals are added and heat is applied. The liquid is forced through a spinneret. Yarn is formed and can be woven into fabric or made into knitting yarn.
   - **Properties:** Absorbent and cool but not hard-wearing.
8. **Synthetic:** Examples are nylon, polyester, acrylic and elastane (Lycra).
   - **Production:** Made from oil and coal. Other chemicals and water are added. The liquid is forced through a spinneret. Long filaments are made into fabric, short filaments into soft, 'woolly' yarn.
   - **Uses:** Acrylic: Jumpers, fake fur, dresses, carpet. Nylon: Umbrellas, swimsuits, tents, raincoats, tights, blended with wool for carpets. Polyester: Blended with cotton for clothing, filling in duvets, etc. PVC: Fake leather goods. Elastane is added to other fabrics for elasticity.
   - **Properties:** Strong, hard-wearing, acrylic and polyester are warm and nylon is water-resistant, but they are flammable and not absorbent.

Yarn to fabric

Weaving

Most weaving is done on a loom. Warp threads (vertical) are put onto the loom first and weft threads are then woven through them. The selvedge is the edge that the weft threads make; it doesn't fray.

A loom. Weft threads run across.

Knitted fabric

Knitting

Knitting can be done by hand or by machine. Most people, when they think of knitting, think only of jumpers, hats and scarves. Many fabrics are also knitted, as you can see if you look closely at them. All knitted fabrics are stretchy. Tracksuits, T-shirts, jumpers and tights are all made from knitted fabrics.

Bonded fabrics

Bonded fabrics are made from fibres that have not been spun into yarn. They are made by sticking fibres together by applying moisture, pressure and heat.

Examples: Felt (snooker tables, hats), wadding (filling inside duvets, coats, carpet underlay) and disposable fabrics (J-cloths, hospital gowns).

The covering on a snooker table is made from bonded fabric

1. Hair-like fibres are twisted into **yarn** and then made into **fabric**.
2. **Classification**
   - **Natural:** Animal (wool, silk) and plant (cotton, linen).
   - **Man-made:** Regenerated (viscose, acetate) and synthetic (nylon, polyester, acrylic).
3. **Wool**
   - **Production:** Animals are sheared. The fleece is graded, washed and dried, brushed (carded) and combed, then spun into yarn. Long fibres are made into wool fabric (worsted) and short fibres are used for knitting wool.
   - **Properties:** Warm, absorbent, does not burn, hard-wearing and resilient, but shrinks and can be coarse on skin.
   - **Uses:** Short fibres for knits, long fibres for wool fabrics.
4. **Silk**
   - **Production:** The silkworm spins a cocoon. The cocoons are soaked. The threads are unwound and several silk threads are spun together to make silk thread, which is then woven into fabric.
   - **Properties:** Absorbent, crease-resistant, strong, smooth, light and drapes well, but it is expensive, easily damaged by careless washing, moths and sunshine, and burns easily.
   - **Uses:** Luxury fabric evening dresses, cushions and wall hangings.
   - **Types:** Chiffon, taffeta, wild silk and satin.
5. **Cotton**
   - **Production:** Cotton bolls are picked, cleaned, graded, combed and spun into yarn, then woven into fabric.
   - **Properties:** Absorbent, cool, strong and washes, dries and bleaches well, but creases, shrinks and burns easily and is affected by mildew.
   - **Uses:** Clothing, towels, sheets and curtains.
   - **Types:** Flannelette, denim, towelling, muslin.
6. **Linen**
   - **Production:** Flax plant is soaked and the woody part rots. The interior of the plant is bleached and spun into yarn, then woven into fabric.
   - **Properties:** Cool, absorbent, strong and washes well, but it is expensive, creases and shrinks, is difficult to dye and is damaged by mildew.
   - **Uses:** Tablecloths, napkins and clothing.
   - **Types:** Damask (thick) and lawn (finer).
7. **Regenerated fabrics:** Examples are viscose, rayon and acetate.
   - **Production:** Made from wood pulp or cotton waste. Chemicals are added and heat is applied. The liquid is forced through a spinneret. Yarn is formed and can be woven into fabric or made into knitting yarn.
   - **Properties:** Absorbent and cool but not hard-wearing.
8. **Synthetic:** Examples are nylon, polyester, acrylic and elastane (Lycra).
   - **Production:** Made from oil and coal. Other chemicals and water are added. The liquid is forced through a spinneret. Long filaments are made into fabric, short filaments into soft, 'woolly' yarn.
   - **Uses:** Acrylic: Jumpers, fake fur, dresses, carpet. Nylon: Umbrellas, swimsuits, tents, raincoats, tights, blended with wool for carpets. Polyester: Blended with cotton for clothing, filling in duvets, etc. PVC: Fake leather goods. Elastane is added to other fabrics for elasticity.
   - **Properties:** Strong, hard-wearing, acrylic and polyester are warm and nylon is water-resistant, but they are flammable and not absorbent.

Yarn to fabric

Weaving

Most weaving is done on a loom. Warp threads (vertical) are put onto the loom first and weft threads are then woven through them. The selvedge is the edge that the weft threads make; it doesn't fray.

A loom. Weft threads run across.

Knitting

Knitting can be done by hand or by machine. Most people, when they think of knitting, think only of jumpers, hats and scarves. Many fabrics are also knitted, as you can see if you look closely at them. All knitted fabrics are stretchy. Tracksuits, T-shirts, jumpers and tights are all made from knitted fabrics.

Knitted fabric

Bonded fabrics

Bonded fabrics are made from fibres that have not been spun into yarn. They are made by sticking fibres together by applying moisture, pressure and heat.

Examples: Felt (snooker tables, hats), wadding (filling inside duvets, coats, carpet underlay) and disposable fabrics (J-cloths, hospital gowns).

The covering on a snooker table is made from bonded fabric

Fabric finishes

Finish (trade name)	Function	Use
Waterproofing (Scotch Guard)	Stops water from soaking through	Anoraks, waterproof sportswear (golf jackets, tents)
Water-repellent (Scotch Guard)	Makes fabric shower-proof	Shower-proof coats, jackets
Stain-repellent (Scotch Guard)	Stops stains from soaking into fabric	Clothes, carpets and upholstery
Flame-resistant	Fabric won't catch on fire easily	Children's nightwear, upholstery fabrics, for example on sofas
Brushing	Makes fabric feel warmer and softer	Flannelette sheets
Crease-resistant	Reduces creasing, no need to iron	Shirts, trousers, sheets, curtains
Permanent pleating	Pleats won't fall out	Skirts and trousers
Stretch (Lycra)	Woven into fabric to give stretch	Swimwear, trousers, cycle shorts, underwear
Non-shrink	Stops shrinking	Clothing, furnishing fabrics
Moth proofing	Stops moths attacking fabrics and making holes in them	Wool and silk
Anti-static	Stops clothes from clinging	Synthetic underwear, clothing and carpets
Polishing	Makes fabric smooth and strong (mercerising)	Cotton thread and fabric
Stiffening	Gives a sharp, crisp finish	Cuffs and collars

Adding colour and pattern to fabric

✂ **Weaving:** Different coloured yarns are woven together on the loom to create different effects, such as checks and tartans.

An example of pattern woven into a fabric

- **Dyeing:** In the past, natural products such as berries and leaves were used to dye fabric. Today, chemical dyes are used. Chemical dyes, unlike natural dyes, are colourfast, meaning they do not run. Dye can be used to create pattern in batik and tie dye.

- **Printing:** Printing applies colour to one side of the fabric using a block, screen or roller.

Tie dyeing

Printed fabrics

Fibre and fabric identification – burning tests

Burning tests are used to identify fibres and fabrics. Observe the following:

 How the test fibres or fabrics burn

 The odour given off

 The residue (what is left after burning)

Fibre	Odour	How it burns	Residue
Wool or silk	Burning hair	Slowly	Dark ash
Cotton, linen, viscose	Burning paper	Quickly	Paper-like ash
Nylon	Celery	Melts	Hard bead

1. Hair-like fibres are twisted into **yarn** and then made into **fabric**.
2. **Classification**
   - **Natural:** Animal (wool, silk) and plant (cotton, linen).
   - **Man-made:** Regenerated (viscose, acetate) and synthetic (nylon, polyester, acrylic).
3. **Wool**
   - **Production:** Animals are sheared. The fleece is graded, washed and dried, brushed (carded) and combed, then spun into yarn. Long fibres are made into wool fabric (worsted) and short fibres are used for knitting wool.
   - **Properties:** Warm, absorbent, does not burn, hard-wearing and resilient, but shrinks and can be coarse on skin.
   - **Uses:** Short fibres for knits, long fibres for wool fabrics.
4. **Silk**
   - **Production:** The silkworm spins a cocoon. The cocoons are soaked. The threads are unwound and several silk threads are spun together to make silk thread, which is then woven into fabric.
   - **Properties:** Absorbent, crease-resistant, strong, smooth, light and drapes well, but it is expensive, easily damaged by careless washing, moths and sunshine, and burns easily.
   - **Uses:** Luxury fabric evening dresses, cushions and wall hangings.
   - **Types:** Chiffon, taffeta, wild silk and satin.
5. **Cotton**
   - **Production:** Cotton bolls are picked, cleaned, graded, combed and spun into yarn, then woven into fabric.
   - **Properties:** Absorbent, cool, strong and washes, dries and bleaches well, but creases, shrinks and burns easily and is affected by mildew.
   - **Uses:** Clothing, towels, sheets and curtains.
   - **Types:** Flannelette, denim, towelling, muslin.
6. **Linen**
   - **Production:** Flax plant is soaked and the woody part rots. The interior of the plant is bleached and spun into yarn, then woven into fabric.
   - **Properties:** Cool, absorbent, strong and washes well, but it is expensive, creases and shrinks, is difficult to dye and is damaged by mildew.
   - **Uses:** Tablecloths, napkins and clothing.
   - **Types:** Damask (thick) and lawn (finer).
7. **Regenerated fabrics:** Examples are viscose, rayon and acetate.
   - **Production:** Made from wood pulp or cotton waste. Chemicals are added and heat is applied. The liquid is forced through a spinneret. Yarn is formed and can be woven into fabric or made into knitting yarn.
   - **Properties:** Absorbent and cool but not hard-wearing.
8. **Synthetic:** Examples are nylon, polyester, acrylic and elastane (Lycra).
   - **Production:** Made from oil and coal. Other chemicals and water are added. The liquid is forced through a spinneret. Long filaments are made into fabric, short filaments into soft, 'woolly' yarn.
   - **Uses:** Acrylic: Jumpers, fake fur, dresses, carpet. Nylon: Umbrellas, swimsuits, tents, raincoats, tights, blended with wool for carpets. Polyester: Blended with cotton for clothing, filling in duvets, etc. PVC: Fake leather goods. Elastane is added to other fabrics for elasticity.
   - **Properties:** Strong, hard-wearing, acrylic and polyester are warm and nylon is water-resistant, but they are flammable and not absorbent.

9. **Fibres** can be straight, crimped, looped or short and twisted. This will affect the type of product produced. **Denier** refers to the thickness of man-made yarn and ranges from 1 to 70+ (very thick). **Ply** refers to the number of yarns twisted together and ranges from 1 to 20.

10. **Yarn to fabric:** Warp threads (vertical) are put on the weaving loom first, then weft threads are woven through (horizontal). Knitting is done by hand or machine. Knitted fabrics are stretchy (tracksuit fabric). Bonded fabrics are made from fibres, not spun into yarn. They use heat to 'stick' fibres together (felt).

11. **Fabric finishes:** Waterproofing, water-repellent, stain-repellent, flame-resistant, brushing, crease-resistant, permanent pleating, stretch, non-shrink, moth proofing, anti-static, polishing and stiffening.

12. **Applying colour and pattern:** Weaving, dyeing, printing.

13. **Fabric identification:** Burning tests for wool or silk (burning hair, slowly, dark ash), cotton, linen or viscose (burning paper, quickly, paper-like ash), nylon (celery, melts, hard bead).

1. Fibres can be either natural or man-made. Describe how each is further classified, giving one example of each.

2. Describe how wool is produced. Describe two positive and two negative properties of wool. List three uses of wool.

3. Describe how silk is produced. Describe three positive and three negative properties of silk. List three uses of silk. Name three different types of silk fabric.

4. Describe how cotton is produced. Describe three positive and three negative properties of cotton. List three uses of cotton. Describe three types of cotton fabric.

5. Describe how linen is produced. Describe three positive and negative properties of linen. Name two uses of linen.

6. Describe how regenerated fibres are produced. Describe two positive and one negative property of regenerated fabrics. Name three regenerated fabrics.

7. Describe how synthetic fibres are produced. Describe two positive and two negative properties of synthetic fabrics. Name and describe a possible use of four synthetic fabrics.

8. What is the difference between woven and bonded fabrics?

9. What does the term *denier* describe?

10. What is meant by ply in relation to fibres and fabrics?

11. Describe the three ways fibres can be made into fabrics.

12. Describe the function and uses of each of the following fabric finishes: (a) stain-repellent (b) flame-resistant (c) brushing (d) anti-static (e) mercerising.

13. Describe three ways colour can be added to fabric.

14. Describe how the following fibres can be identified using a burning test: (a) wool (b) linen (c) nylon.

Homework Assignment
50
P 181

Unit 5 Textile Studies

CHAPTER 34
Fabric Care

Teacher's CD

Slide presentation ▪ Student activity pack with revision crossword ▪ Class test ▪ Student learning contract

Key words

✓ Care labelling
✓ Washing instructions
✓ Drying instructions
✓ Ironing instructions
✓ Bleaching instructions
✓ Dry cleaning instructions
✓ Bar symbols
✓ Delicate fabrics
✓ Stain removal
✓ Colour catcher and colour run products
✓ Detergents
✓ Fabric conditioners

Learning outcomes

After completing this chapter and the homework, assignments and activities that accompany it, you should:

● Be able to understand the care labels on clothing and apply this information to real life.
● Know what method of stain removal to apply to different types of stain.
● Understand the function of each ingredient in detergents and be able to name the different types of detergent.
● Understand the function of fabric softeners.
● Understand and be able to apply the guidelines for washing, drying and ironing clothes.

Caring for clothes

Before storing:

 Mend.

 Remove stains, wash or dry clean.

 Fold knitwear and store flat in a drawer.

 Close zips and button.

 Hang on shaped or padded hangers.

Care labelling

Care labels that are sewn into clothing and household textiles carry five basic symbols.

Care labels				
Washing instructions	Drying instructions	Ironing instructions	Bleaching instructions	Dry cleaning instructions

Washing instructions

There are three basic factors to consider when machine washing:

- **Water temperature.**
- **Wash action:** How fast the machine moves the clothes around during the cycle.
- **Spin length:** Spin (full) or short spin.

Water temperature is written inside the washtub symbol.

The bar symbol under the washtub tells you the correct wash action and spin length for the item you are washing.

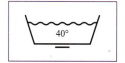

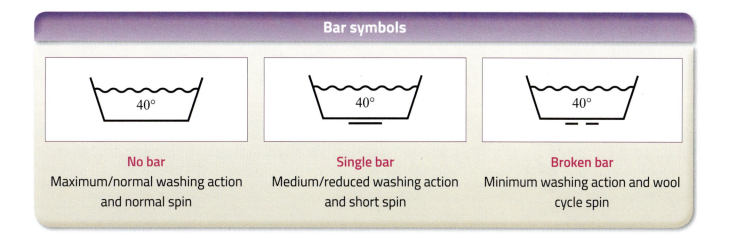

Bar symbols		
No bar	**Single bar**	**Broken bar**
Maximum/normal washing action and normal spin	Medium/reduced washing action and short spin	Minimum washing action and wool cycle spin

Tables like this one are found on washing detergent packets. They explain how fabrics can be washed and spun.

Textile/machine code	Machine wash	Hand wash	Fabric
95°	Maximum wash in cotton cycle	Hand-hot or boil, spin or wring	White cotton, linen; no special finishes
60°	Maximum wash in cotton cycle	Hand-hot or boil, spin or wring	Cotton, linen, viscose; no special finishes; colours fast at 60°C
50°	Medium wash in synthetic cycle	Hand-hot, cold rinse, short spin	Polyester-cotton mixes, nylon, polyester, cotton, viscose articles with special finishes, cotton-acrylic mixes
40°	Maximum wash in cotton cycle	Warm, spin or wring	Cotton, linen, viscose where colours are not fast at 60°C
40°	Medium wash in synthetic cycle	Warm, do not rub; spin, do not wring	Acrylics, acetate and triacetate, including mixes with wool; polyester-wool blends
40°	Minimum wash in wool cycle	Warm, do not rub; spin, do not wring	Wool, wool mixes, silk
	Hand wash only	See individual care label	Some pleated fabrics
	Do not wash	Do not wash	See individual care label

Drying instructions

| Dry flat (wool) | Line dry | Drip dry | Tumble dry | Do not tumble dry |

Ironing instructions

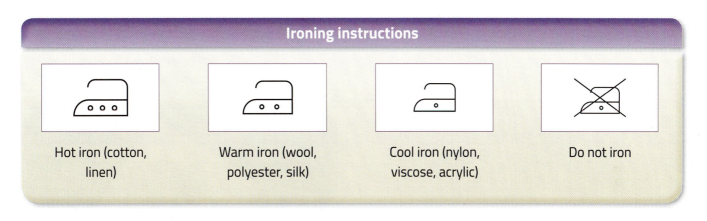

| Hot iron (cotton, linen) | Warm iron (wool, polyester, silk) | Cool iron (nylon, viscose, acrylic) | Do not iron |

Dry cleaning instructions

The letters tell the dry cleaner which chemicals to use

Do not dry clean

Bleaching

Bleach can be used

Do not bleach

Preparing a wash

- Empty pockets.
- Repair any clothes that need mending.
- Remove stubborn stains before washing.
- Close zips and buttons.
- Sort clothes according to their colour and their care labels. The colour in some clothes is colourfast, meaning it will not run. Other clothing has colours that are not colourfast. These clothes need to be washed separately, as their colour will run into other clothing in the wash.

Washing should be sorted into whites, colours and dark clothing

A care label. What sort of garment do you think this was attached to?

Delicate fabrics – wool and silk

- Wash by hand.
- Use a mild detergent.
- Rinse twice.
- Squeeze to remove excess water.
- Roll in a towel to remove water.
- Drip or dry flat.

Stain removal

- Act quickly or the stain will set.
- Do not rub the stain into the fabric – blot or scrape off as much as you can.
- Use the mildest treatment first, such as soaking in cold water.
- If you have to use a chemical stain remover, first test it somewhere on the garment that will not be seen.
- Remove stains before washing.

Commercial stain removers

There is a wide variety of stain removers on the market today. For example, some Stain Devils are specific to a certain type of stain, such as grass, while others are more general, such as Vanish products.

Colour catcher and colour run remover products

Colour catchers try to prevent strong colours from running into lighter colours in the wash by trapping the excess colour on a fabric sheet. Colour run removers try to remove unwanted colour from light-coloured clothing.

Stain	How to remove it
Protein stains (blood, egg, gravy)	If the stain is fresh, soak it in cold water, then wash. If the stain is older, soak it in warm water with an enzyme (biological) detergent, then wash.
Chewing gum	Freeze, then pick off. You may have to use a grease solvent, such as Benzene, or a Stain Devil.
Ink, grass	Dab with methylated spirits and wash.
Chocolate	Dab with glycerine and wash in hot water.
Tea, coffee, perspiration (sweat)	Soak in warm water with an enzyme (biological) detergent, then wash.
Grease and oil	Wash in hot water and dab with a grease solvent, such as Benzene, if necessary.
Mildew (grey spots on cotton and linen)	Whites: Soak in a mild bleach solution. Colours: Treat with hydrogen peroxide.

Detergents

Detergents such as Persil and Ariel help remove dirt and stains from clothes. Detergents contain a range of ingredients, each with its own job to do.

- **Emulsifiers:** Attach themselves to the dirt at one end and to the water at the other. This takes dirt off clothes and into the washing water.
- **Bleach:** Helps to remove stains and keep whites whiter.
- **Enzymes:** Remove protein-based stains, such as blood.
- **Water softener:** Softens hard water, allowing the detergent to work more effectively.
- **Perfume:** Gives clothes a nice scent.

Types of detergent

- Powder, tablet or liquid detergents
- Hand washing (for delicates, such as Woolite)
- Low-foaming (automatic powders for modern washing machines)
- Biological (contain enzymes that break protein stains down under 40°C; powder also washes at other temperatures)
- Eco-friendly detergents

Detergents

Fabric conditioners

Fabric conditioners

These are added during the final rinse. They soften clothes, reduce static cling and reduce wrinkling. Some liquid detergents also contain conditioner.

The washing machine
Guidelines for use

- If you can, wait until you have a full load before using the machine.
- Use a low-foaming (automatic) detergent.
- Use the economy button if clothes are not very dirty.
- Know which programmes are suited to which fabrics.

Drying

Clothes can be line dried, dried in outdoor all-weather lines (see the photo), dried indoors on a clotheshorse or tumble dried.

Be careful when tumble drying, as some clothes will shrink (wool) or discolour (synthetic underwear) if tumble dried. Tumble drying, while quick and great for removing creases, is expensive.

This all-weather line has been invented and produced in Ireland by www.lennonlines.ie.

Ironing

Most modern irons are steam irons. They contain a heating element, water tank and thermostat that controls how hot the iron gets.

Guidelines for use

- Store the iron sitting upright.
- Unplug to fill the water tank and empty after use.
- Use pre-boiled water in hard water areas to prevent limescale build-up.
- Set the iron to the correct temperature (look at the care label).
- Iron on the wrong side unless you want a shine, such as linen tablecloths.

Non-iron fabrics

Cotton fabric treated with a chemical resin stops non-iron shirts and blouses from wrinkling. All you need to do is hang them up after washing.

Rapid Revision

1. **Caring for clothes:** Mend, remove stains, wash or dry clean, fold knits, close zips and hang on padded hangers.
2. **Care labels:** These include washing, drying, ironing, bleaching and dry cleaning instructions.
   - **Washing instructions:** Three factors: wash temperature, wash action and spin length. The bar symbol is for the spin length: no bar, single or broken.
   - **Drying:** Dry flat, line dry, drip dry, tumble dry, do not tumble dry.
   - **Ironing:** Hot iron (three dots) for cotton and linen, warm iron (two dots) for wool, polyester and silk, cool iron (one dot) for nylon, viscose and acrylic. Sometimes fabrics are non-iron.
   - **Dry cleaning:** The symbol inside the circle tells the cleaner which chemicals to use.
   - **Bleaching:** Triangle: bleach or not.
3. **Preparing a wash:** Empty pockets, repair, remove stains, close zips and buttons, sort clothes (whites, colours and darks). Determine if clothes are colourfast or non-colourfast.
4. **Stain removal:** Act quickly – don't let the stain set. Soak in water and apply the appropriate stain remover. Commercial stain removers are available (Stain Devils, Vanish).
5. **Detergents:** Contain emulsifiers, bleach, enzymes, water softeners and perfume. Types: Powder, tablet or liquid detergents, delicates (Woolite), low-foaming (automatic), biological (work at under 40°C), eco-friendly.
6. **Fabric conditioners:** Soften clothes and reduce static cling and wrinkling.

7. **Washing clothes:** Wait until you have a full load. Use automatic detergent. Use the economy setting where possible and know which programmes are suitable.

8. **Drying:** Clothes can be line dried, dried on an all-weather line, dried indoors or tumble dried. Not all clothes can be tumbled dried – wools shrink and some synthetics discolour.

9. **Ironing:** Modern steam irons have the water reservoir separate from the actual iron. They produce much more steam and give rapid results. Some fabrics are non-iron and just need to be hung up after washing.

Revision Questions

1. Draw the following care label: hand wash only, do not bleach, do not tumble dry, warm iron, may be dry cleaned.
2. What five points should you consider while preparing a basket of clothing for washing?
3. How should you wash delicate fabrics such as wool and silk?
4. What guidelines should you follow for effective stain removal?
5. How would you try to remove the following stains: (a) blood (b) chewing gum (c) grass (d) chocolate (e) coffee (f) mildew?
6. Name five ingredients found in clothing detergents and state the function of each ingredient.
7. What are the three main functions of fabric conditioners?
8. Describe four guidelines for using a washing machine.
9. List two disadvantages of using a tumble dryer.
10. Describe five guidelines for using an iron.
11. How have non-iron fabrics been treated to reduce wrinkling?

Test Yourself
eTest.ie

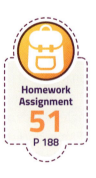
Homework
Assignment
51
P 188

Teacher's CD Slide presentation • Student activity pack with revision crossword • Class test • Student learning contract

Key words

- Tacking
- Temporary stitch
- Running
- Backstitch
- Hemming
- Slip hemming
- Tailor tacking
- Crewel needles
- Skein of embroidery thread
- Stem stitch
- Satin stitch
- Long and short stitch
- Chain stitch
- Thread guides
- Tension wheel
- Bobbin and case
- Spool pin
- Stitch selector
- Stitch width selector
- Buttonhole knob
- Stitch length regulator
- Foot pedal
- Straight stitch
- Zigzag stitch
- Buttonhole stitch
- Machine embroidery
- Flat seam
- Seam finishes
- Nap fabrics
- One-way design
- Selvedge
- Bias
- Straight of grain
- Notches

Learning outcomes

After completing this chapter and the homework, assignments and activities that accompany it, you should:

- Understand the guidelines for hand sewing and be able to work the following hand stitches: tacking, running, backstitching, hemming, slip hemming and tailor tacking. Know what each of these stitches is used for.
- Be able to work the following embroidery stitches and know what each one is used for: stem stitch, satin stitch, long and short stitch and chain stitch.
- Be able to thread and use a sewing machine correctly and use it for your practical needlework tasks (see Chapter 36). Understand the factors you should consider when choosing and caring for a sewing machine. Know the causes of various machine faults.
- Be able to work a flat seam and know how to finish it appropriately so that it is neat and does not fray.
- Understand the factors you should consider when choosing fabric for home sewing.
- Understand what selvedge threads are and that pattern pieces should be cut out so that selvedge threads run down the length of the garment. Be able to follow the guidelines for cutting fabric out while making your practical needlework tasks.
- Understand what bias binding is and what it can be used for.

393

Hand sewing guidelines

- Use a single thread that is not too long.
- Pin and tack if necessary.
- Start and finish with a secure stitch, such as a backstitch.
- Small, even stitches are strongest.
- A thimble can be used for tough fabrics such as denim.

Essential sewing equipment: scissors, measuring tape, thread, pins, needle, stitch ripper, thimble, pinking shears (not essential)

Common stitches

The best way to learn how to hand sew is to:

- Ask for a demonstration.
- Study some samples of the stitches you want to learn.
- Practise.

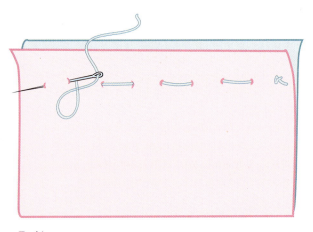

Tacking

Tacking

Tacking is a temporary stitch. It is used to:

- Hold pieces of fabric together for permanent stitching
- Help keep machine stitching straight
- Hold a garment together for fitting

Finish tacking with a backstitch – two or three stitches on top of each other.

Running

Running is like small tacking. Begin with a backstitch.

Two rows of running stitch are used to gather fabric if you do not have a sewing machine. **Gathering** is used when you want to join a wide piece of fabric to a narrower one, such as gathering fabric into the waistband of a skirt.

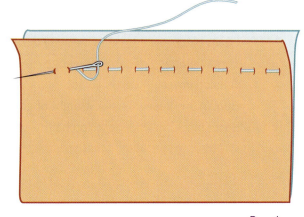

Running

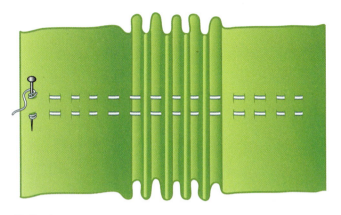

Gathering

A gathered waistband

Gathering (machine or running)

1. Loosen the machine tension.
2. Machine or run two rows 1cm from the top of the fabric to be gathered. Leave threads.
3. Gently pull the gathering threads until you get the correct size. Secure with a pin (see the illustration).

Backstitching

Backstitching is a strong stitch used for seams instead of machining. Start with a backstitch. Put the needle in at the end of the last stitch and out 2mm in front. Repeat. There is little or no gap between stitches.

Hemming

Hemming is a strong slanted stitch used for stitching down collars and waistbands.

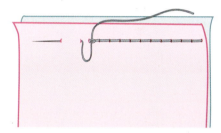

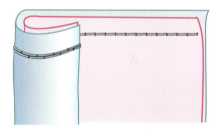

Backstitching

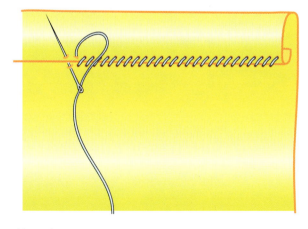

Hemming

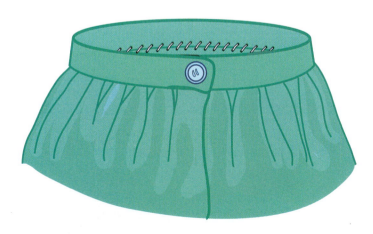

Hemming is used to stitch down collars and waistbands

Slip hemming

Slip hemming is used to sew up hems on skirts, trousers and dresses. If done well, it is almost invisible on the right side.

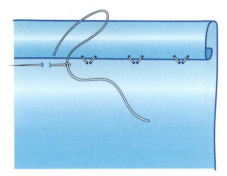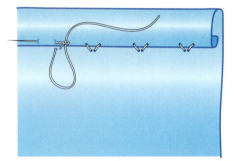

Two stages of slip hemming

Tailor tacking

Tailor tacking is used to transfer markings from paper patterns to fabric.

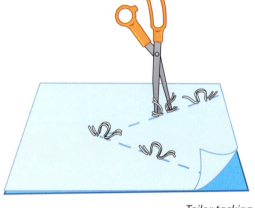

Tailor tacking

Embroidery

- Embroidery is used to decorate fabrics.
- Embroidery thread is made up of six strands. Use two or three strands at a time.
- Use crewel needles (they have a large eye).
- Start with a few running stitches along the line to be embroidered. These secure the stitching and are covered as you work embroidery stitches over them.
- Finish by weaving thread through stitches at the back.

Common embroidery stitches

- Ask for a demonstration.
- Examine samples.
- Practise.

Hand embroidery

Skeins of embroidery thread

Stem stitch

Use stem stitch to outline stems, etc.

Satin stitch

Use satin stitch to fill in small areas, such as petals and leaves.

Long and short stitch

Use long and short stitch to fill in larger areas.

Chain stitch

Chain stitch is usually used to outline.

Stem stitch

Satin stitch

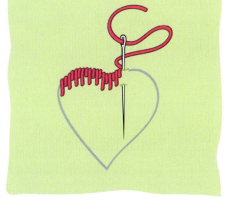

Long and short stitch

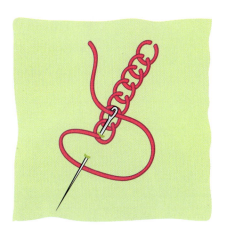

Chain stitch

The sewing machine

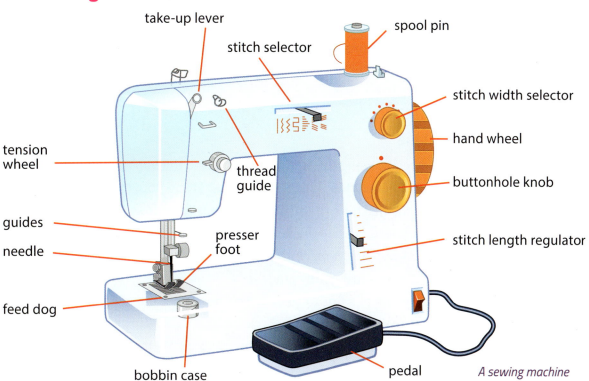

take-up lever

stitch selector

spool pin

stitch width selector

hand wheel

buttonhole knob

tension wheel

thread guide

stitch length regulator

guides

needle

presser foot

feed dog

bobbin case

pedal

A sewing machine

Threading

This varies from machine to machine (read the user instructions), but generally:

- Have thread coming from the back of the spool to the thread guide (1).
- Around tension wheel (2) to take-up lever (3).
- Through thread guides (4) and through needle (5), usually from the front to back, although it can be from left to right depending on the machine.
- Thread the bobbin and insert. Bobbin thread will be brought up by turning the hand wheel.

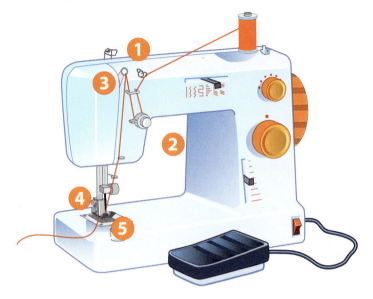

A bobbin and a bobbin case

Stitch tension

Two threads form a machine stitch: one from the top spool and the other from the bobbin. Tension (the tightness of the thread) must be equal between both threads. If the tension is too tight, it causes the fabric to pucker. If it is too loose, it will cause the thread to loop. The tension can be adjusted by twisting the tension wheel or regulator on the machine (top thread), or the small tension screw on the bobbin case (bottom thread).

Using the sewing machine

1. Thread the machine correctly, using the same thread in both the bobbin and the top spool. Make sure the thread is not too thick for the fabric. Bring both threads away from you, towards the back of the machine (if the needle threads from front to back).

2. Raise the presser foot and needle. Slide the fabric into position and then lower the presser foot and needle into the fabric. Begin machining.

3. Do not push or pull the fabric – just gently guide it.

4. If you must stop in the middle of a line or to turn a corner, lower the needle into the fabric (you can then start again exactly where you left off).

5. When you finish, you can secure the stitching by reversing back a few stitches or by hand sewing a few backstitches.

Common machine stitches

- **Straight stitch:** Used for seams and hems.
- **Zigzag:** Mainly used for seam finishing. A slight zigzag can be used for seams and hems on stretchy fabric.
- **Buttonhole stitch:** Machine buttonholes.
- **Machine embroidery:** To decorate.

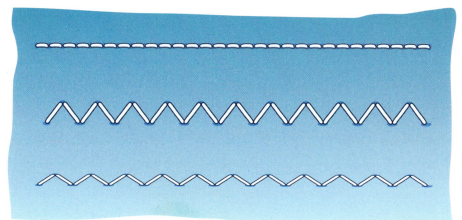

Straight stitch

Zigzag stitch

Slight zigzag stitch

Choosing a sewing machine	Caring for a sewing machine
• Cost: Compare models and compare the same models in different shops. • Buy a reliable brand from a reliable shop. • Buy an elaborate machine only if you intend to use its special features. • Check the guarantee and after-sales service. • Ask for a demonstration.	• Carefully read the care instructions that come with the machine. • Cover the machine when it's not in use. • Clean dust from moving parts with the small brush provided with the machine. • Oil the machine occasionally (see the care instructions for where to oil it). • Occasionally have the machine serviced and repaired by a sewing machine mechanic.

Machine faults: Possible causes

Fault	Possible causes
Needle breaks	• Needle has been put in back to front • Needle is blunt and cannot get through the fabric properly • Fabric is too thick • Sewing over zips or pins • Presser foot is loose and the needle is hitting it
Thread breaks	• Machine is not threaded properly • Thread is too fine or of poor quality • Faulty needle or needle is in back to front

Fault	Possible causes
Looped stitches (underneath)	• Top tension is too loose • Top and bobbin threads are not the same • Presser foot is not down • Machine is not threaded correctly
Slipped stitches	• Blunt needle • Needle is in back to front • Needle is the wrong size for the fabric
Puckered seam	• Tension (top or bobbin) is too tight • Blunt needle • Top and bottom threads are different • Stitch is too long (fine fabrics, such as satin, need a shorter stitch)

Seams

Seams are used to join pieces of fabric together to make clothing and other textile items. The flat seam pictured here is the most common type.

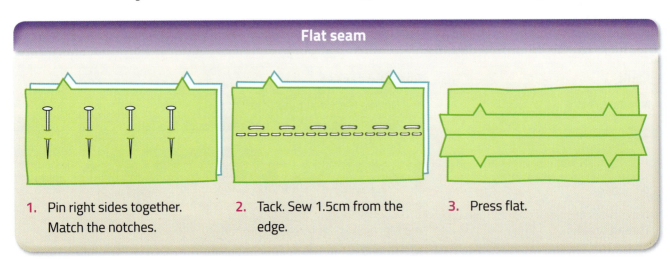

Flat seam

1. Pin right sides together. Match the notches.

2. Tack. Sew 1.5cm from the edge.

3. Press flat.

Seam finishes

Raw edges may be finished in one of four ways: zigzag stitch, edge machining, pinking shears or with an overlocking machine. Seam finishes prevent fraying.

A special overlocking machine can be used to finish raw edges

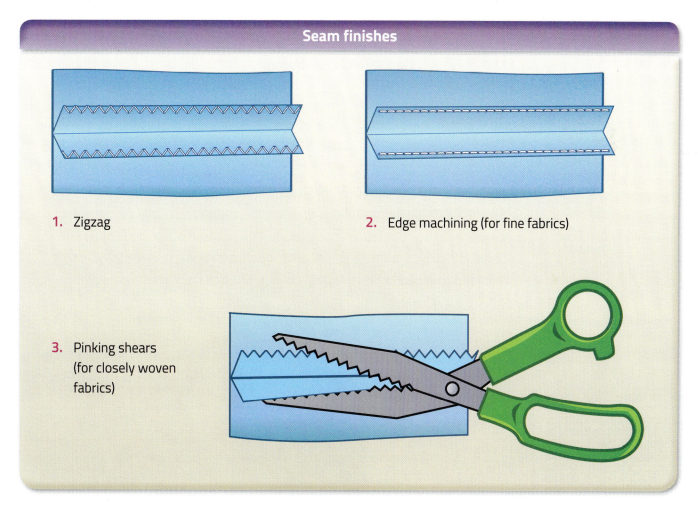

Seam finishes

1. Zigzag

2. Edge machining (for fine fabrics)

3. Pinking shears (for closely woven fabrics)

Choosing a fabric for home sewing

✄ Choose a fabric that is easy to work with. Avoid slippery or stretchy fabrics, as these are difficult to sew. Medium-weight cotton is good for beginners.

✄ Fabrics that have a nap, such as velvet, or a one-way design are more difficult to cut out properly and need more fabric.

- Fabrics are sold in different widths. The wider the fabric you buy, the less you will need.

- Calculate the amount of fabric you will need using the grid on the back of your pattern envelope.

- Check the wash and care instructions on the fabric roll.

- Buy anything else you need. A list of requirements or notions (matching thread, zip, buttons, etc.) will be on your pattern envelope.

Beginners should avoid fabrics with a nap or a one-way design

Note: Nap fabrics are smooth when brushed one way and rough when brushed the other way, such as velvet.

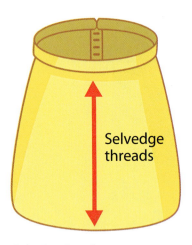

Selvedge threads

Selvedge

Selvedge threads, also called warp threads, are strong threads that run up and down the length of the fabric. When cutting out pattern pieces, it is important that the selvedge runs down the length of the piece. This allows the finished garment to hang well.

Bias: If fabric is cut on the bias (see the illustration), it is stretchy. Strips of bias binding can be used to neaten armholes or necklines or for piping.

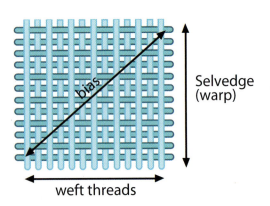

Piping is a common use for bias binding

Cutting out

1. Arrange the pattern pieces on the fabric. Straight-of-grain arrows should run parallel with selvedge edges. Place fold arrows on the fold. (Pattern instructions will suggest a layout.)

2. Pin the pattern pieces in position.

3. Using a sharp scissors, cut around each pattern piece. Leave a 1.5cm seam allowance if not already allowed. (Most patterns include this allowance, in which case cut fabric to the exact size of the pattern pieces.)

4. Keep fabric flat on the table with one hand. Do not lift up the fabric to cut it. Cut notches outwards.

5. Transfer important pattern markings such as buttonhole location using notches, tailor tacks or tailor's chalk and a tracing wheel and carbon, as pictured here.

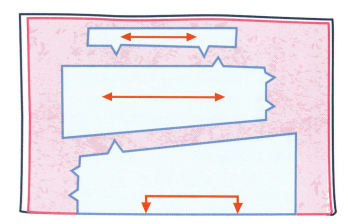

Tailor tacking　　　　　　　*Tailor's chalk*

A tracing wheel and carbon

Tailor tacking is always used. Tailor's chalk and a tracing wheel may also be used.

1. **Hand sewing guidelines:** Use a short single thread. Pin and tack if necessary. Start and finish with a secure stitch (backstitch). Use small, even stitches. Use a thimble for tough fabrics. Essential equipment: Scissors, measuring tape, thread, pins, needles, stitch ripper, thimble, pinking shears.

2. **Hand stitching**
   - **Tacking:** A temporary stitch that holds the garment together for fitting and permanent stitching. Keeps machining straight. Begin with a backstitch.
   - **Running:** Like small tacking. Usually two rows of running stitch are used for gathering.
   - **Backstitching:** A strong stitch used instead of machining.
   - **Hemming:** A strong slanted stitch used for stitching down collars and waistbands.
   - **Slip hemming:** Used to sew up hems. If done correctly, it is almost invisible on the right side.
   - **Tailor tacking:** Used to transfer markings from pattern pieces to fabric.

3. **Embroidery:** Used to decorate fabrics. Use embroidery thread and crewel needles. Start with a few secure stitches.
   - **Stem stitch:** Used to outline stems, etc.
   - **Satin stitch:** Used to fill small areas (petals).
   - **Long and short stitch:** Used to fill larger areas.
   - **Chain stitch:** Used to outline.

4. **Sewing machine parts:** Spool pin, take-up lever, thread guides, tension wheel, needle, feed dog, stitch width and length selectors, pedal, buttonhole knob, hand wheel, bobbin and case.

5. **Stitch tension:** Machine stitching has a top and bottom thread tension (tightness), which must be equal between both threads. Tension can be adjusted using the tension wheel or the tension screw on the bobbin case.

6. **Using the sewing machine:** Thread the machine correctly. Use the same thread in both the top and the bottom. Raise the presser foot and insert the fabric. Gently guide the fabric – do not push or pull. If you need to stop or turn a corner, insert the needle into the fabric. Reverse a few stitches at the end to secure. Common machine stitches are straight, zigzag, buttonhole, embroidery.

7. **Buying and caring for a sewing machine**
   - **Buying a machine:** Compare prices, buy a reliable brand, do not pay for an elaborate machine if you will not use the functions, check the guarantee and after-sales service and ask for a demonstration.
   - **Caring for a machine:** Read the instructions, cover when not in use, clean dust off moving parts, oil and have the machine serviced occasionally.

8. **Machine faults:** Needle breaking, thread breaking, looped stitches (back), slipped stitches, puckered seam. Know the possible causes of each.

9. **Seams:** A flat seam is the most common. Seam finishes neaten and prevent fraying: zigzag, edge machining, pinking (for closely woven fabrics) and overlocking.

10. **How to choose fabric:** Avoid slippery, stretchy fabrics or those with a nap or one-way design. Consider the fabric width when calculating the amount needed. Notions (buttons and zips) will also be listed on the back of the pattern.

11. **Selvedge (warp) threads** run down the length of the fabric. **Weft threads** run horizontally. **Bias** is cut diagonally across the fabric to make it stretchy and is used for piping.

12. **Cutting out:** Arrange the pattern pieces according to the pattern layout instructions. Pin in position. Keep fabric flat and cut out with sharp scissors. Transfer pattern markings using tailor tacks, notches, tailor's chalk or a tracing wheel and carbon.

1. Suggest five guidelines for home sewing.
2. Name eight items of sewing equipment commonly used in hand sewing.
3. What is (a) a temporary and (b) a permanent stitch? Give an example of each.
4. Draw a diagram of each of the following types of stitch and suggest one use for each:
   (a) tacking (b) running (c) backstitching (d) hemming (e) slip hemming.
5. Name and describe a use for four different types of embroidery stitch.
6. With machine stitching, why does thread tension need to be equal on the top and bottom?
7. List five guidelines for using a sewing machine.
8. Name three common machine stitches and suggest one use for each.
9. Suggest four guidelines that should be followed when buying a sewing machine.
10. Suggest the possible causes of each of the following machine faults: (a) needle breaking (b) thread breaking (c) looped stitches underneath (d) a puckered seam.
11. Name one type of seam. Suggest three ways seams may be finished.
12. List five guidelines for choosing fabrics for home sewing.
13. What is bias binding and what can it be used for?
14. Describe in detail how fabric should be cut out.
15. Suggest three ways pattern markings can be transferred to fabric pieces.
    Your finished pieces will not be examined directly, but you may be asked questions about one or other of them in section B, question 6 of your examination paper (especially at Ordinary Level).

Test Yourself
eTest.ie

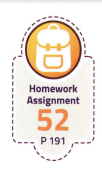

Homework Assignment
52
P 191

Unit 5 Textile Studies

CHAPTER 36
Practical Needlework Tasks

Teacher's CD

Slide presentation ▪ Student activity pack

Key words

✓ Design brief
✓ Analysis of brief

Learning outcomes

After completing this chapter and the homework, assignments and activities that accompany it, you should:

- Be able to read and analyse two briefs: one about making a household item and the other about an item of clothing.
- Develop the sewing skills required to create the two items to a high standard.
- Be able to describe in detail what you have done.

As part of the Junior Certificate Textile Studies section, you must make two simple textile items:

- A household item
- An item of clothing

Household item
Sample brief

Design and make a household item. The item must be made from textiles and cost no more than €15 to make. You must be able to complete the item in approximately four weeks.

Analysis

What are the points that you must consider?

- A textile must be used.
- The item must be for the home.
- It must cost no more than €20.
- It must not be too difficult for you to make. Consider your sewing skills and the short time given to make the item.

Research

Look through books and magazines for ideas and costs of fabrics.

List possible solutions

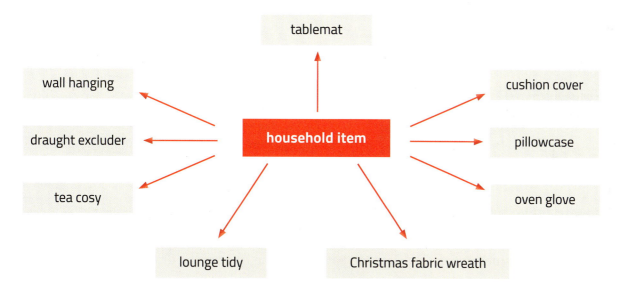

Decide on a solution

Give a reason.

Action

Make the item.

Evaluate

Did you do everything you were asked to do in the brief?

Making a household item – draught excluder

You will need:

- One long piece of fabric (94cm × 26cm) for the back of the excluder. It should match the fabrics chosen for the front of the excluder.

- Seven patches of fabric that are 16cm × 26cm. The fabric patches chosen should match each other and the long piece of fabric chosen for the back. (Craft shops sell what are called 'fat quarter bundles' of matching fabric. Depending on the number of fabric pieces in the bundle, fabrics can be shared among students, thus reducing the cost.)

A fat quarter bundle of fabric

- Pieces of complementary coloured felt fabric (for appliqué) that match or complement the fabric patches chosen for the front of the excluder. Cut these pieces into heart shapes or whatever patterns you like.

- Contrasting embroidery thread for appliqué.

- Buttons or other sew-on items to decorate the front of the excluder.

- Matching thread, needles, pins, etc.

- 7kg long-grain rice to fill the excluder (buy own brand rice to save money – approximately €1 per kg) or wadding (this is lighter and cheaper but probably not as effective as rice for draught exclusion).

How to make a draught excluder

1. Cut out all the fabric for the excluder. Iron it flat.
2. Appliqué any decorative shapes to the patches for the front of the draught excluder together with any decorative buttons, etc.
3. Pin, tack and machine sew the patches of fabric for the draught excluder together (allow a 1.5cm seam allowance), right sides together along their long side (26cm). Altogether, they should be 91cm long. Press the seams flat with an iron.
4. Pin, tack and machine sew the front of the excluder to the back (right sides together, allowing a 1.5cm allowance). Leave one end unstitched (in order to fill it).
5. Turn the excluder right side out. Fill with the rice or stuff with the wadding.
6. Machine or top sew the open end closed.

Finished draught excluder

Item of clothing

The second textile item that you must make as part of the basic Junior Certificate Home Economics course is an item of clothing. The usual difficulty with this part of the course is finding ideas for an item of clothing that you will actually wear and use.

One idea is to make a festive apron (the example shown is for Christmas). This item makes a lovely gift for someone who likes to cook.

Festive apron

You will need:

 Pattern pieces (see next page)

 1 metre of festive fabric

 Matching thread

How to make the festive apron

Preparation

1. For the main body of the apron, cut out a piece of fabric 65cm × 60cm. For the patch pocket, cut out a piece that is 12cm × 15cm.
2. Make the pattern pieces for the main body of the apron and patch pocket (see the diagrams below).
3. Cut out the fabric. Be as economical as you can, as you will need the remaining fabric for frills and for tying the apron round your waist and neck.
4. Cut out long strips to measure 3.5m × 6cm (for frills) in total. Strips will have to be joined.
5. Cut out two strips that are 70cm × 10cm (for waist ties).
6. Cut one strip that is 24cm × 8cm (for the neck strap).

Construction

1. Overlock or use a machine zigzag stitch to sew around the main part of the apron.
2. Edge machine around one side of the frill fabric. Join the frill where necessary so that a piece measuring 3.5m × 6cm is formed.
3. Using a seam iron, press 2cm pleats into the fabric. This should reduce the frill to 2m × 6cm, which is the circumference of the apron. Pin and tack the pleats in place.
4. With the right sides together, pin, tack and sew the frill to the circumference of the apron. Use a straight machine stitch. Iron the pleats down.
5. Make the strips for the waist ties and the neck strap by folding and ironing the pieces in half along their length (right sides together) and sewing 1.5cm all round. Do not sew the top edge, as it needs to be open to turn the strips right side out. Turn right side out, turn in and sew the top edge. Iron flat and attach to the apron.

6. Pin and tack in the edges of the patch pocket. Apply to the apron using a straight machine stitch.

7. Iron your apron and wrap it up for a wonderful Christmas present.

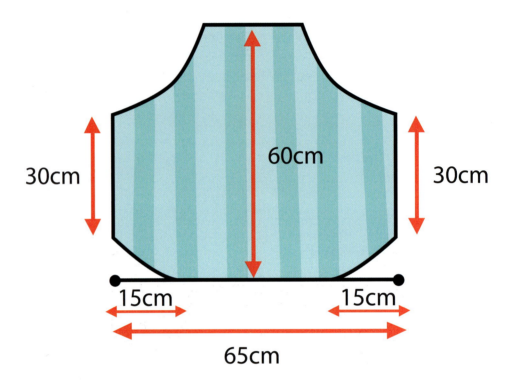

30cm

60cm

30cm

15cm

15cm

65cm

Homework Assignment

53

P 198

Unit 6
Options

CHAPTER 37
Childcare Option

Slide presentation

Learning outcomes

By the end of this section of the course you will have selected a topic of your choice related to childcare and development and prepared a written report on it. You may also have chosen to make an item promoting a childd's development and prepared a written report.

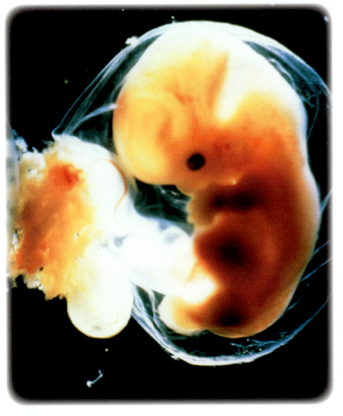

Six weeks

Development of the foetus in the uterus (womb)

Revise pregnancy and birth (page 263) and nutrition during pregnancy (pages 29–30).

While pregnancy generally lasts 40 weeks, many babies are born prematurely (less than 40 weeks) or are overdue (more than 40 weeks). Rapid development takes place in the uterus during pregnancy.

Week 6

The embryo is now approximately 2.5cm long. The heart is beating and arms and legs are beginning to form. It is important that the mother does not allow harmful substances such as alcohol to pass to the baby at this stage, as all the organs are forming.

Week 12

The embryo is now called a foetus and is approximately 8.5cm long. All the organs, both external (outside) and internal (inside), are formed. They must now mature.

Week 28

The foetus is now about 35cm long and weighs approximately 1.1kg (2.4lb). A baby born at this stage has a 75% chance of survival in an intensive care baby unit.

Weeks 38 to 40

The baby is now at full term. He or she is covered in a waxy substance called vernix, which stops the baby's skin from drying out. Full-term babies are on average 50cm long and weigh approximately 3.4kg (7.5lb).

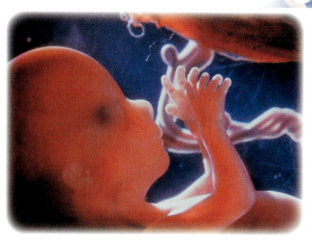

Twelve weeks

Twenty-eight weeks

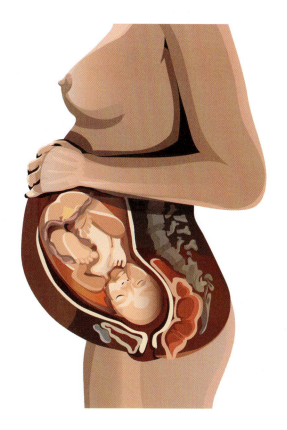

Child development

Child development means the development of every aspect of the child:

- 🐻 Physical development
- 🐻 Intellectual and language development
- 🐻 Social and emotional development

Physical development

- Height and weight increase.
- Gross motor skills develop. This means co-ordinating large body movements, such as crawling, walking, running and jumping.
- Fine motor skills develop. This means co-ordinating small body movements, especially with the hands, such as feeding with a spoon, picking up small objects or holding a pen or pencil.
- Fresh air and exercise are vital to healthy physical development.
- Children should be given opportunities to learn and develop to their full potential.

Development of gross motor skills

Intellectual and language development

Intellectual and language development are closely linked.

Intellectual development

- Reasoning: If I eat my dinner, I will be allowed out to play.
- Problem solving: If I make the base of this block tower wider, it won't keep falling over.
- Concept formation: A pig is a pink animal with a curly tail.
- Concentration and memory.

Development of fine motor skills

Language development

- Listening and understanding
- Talking, reading and writing

Children learn a lot through imitation

Social and emotional development

Social development

Social development involves three things:

- Learning the norms (acceptable ways of behaving) in their particular society, such as eating with a knife and fork

- How to relate well to others, such as sharing and taking turns

- Developing a sense of right and wrong, for example it is wrong to throw litter on the ground

Emotional development

Emotional development means learning to cope with feelings and development of self-esteem and self-image (how you see yourself).

Promoting healthy development

While hereditary factors (traits the child inherits from his or her parents) do influence a child's developmental progress, the child's environment (how the child is brought up) is equally (if not more) important.

Healthy physical development

Parents should:

- Provide a well-balanced diet that contains plenty of freshly prepared food.

- Avoid too much exposure to convenience and fast foods.

- Make sure the child gets plenty of fresh air and sleep.

- Make sure the child gets plenty of opportunity for physical activity and play. For example, the parent could involve the child in sports from an early age.

- Give the child plenty of opportunities to practise their fine motor skills, such as feeding themselves. Later on, give them opportunities to write, draw, make and do activities, etc.

Healthy intellectual and language development

Parents should:

- Listen and talk to their child.

- Encourage their child's efforts.

- Read stories to their child and provide plenty of reading material for them, such as by visiting the local library every week. Children should be exposed to books from an early age.

- Expose their child to a variety of interesting activities, such as cooking, gardening, nature walks, etc.

- A child who is exposed to these things has a much better chance of reaching their full potential than a child who experiences few of these things.

Note: The National Strategy on Literacy and Numeracy (2011–2020) reported that approximately one in 10 Irish children has literacy difficulties. This figures rises to one in three in areas described as socially and economically disadvantaged. An earlier OECD study found a strong correlation between literacy levels and the number of books in a child's home.

Healthy social and emotional development

Parents should:

🐻 Make sure that their child has a stable, secure family life with predicable routines.

🐻 Give their child plenty of physical contact and affection.

🐻 Give plenty of encouragement and praise.

🐻 Set clear boundaries for their child, with fair and consistent discipline.

🐻 Set a good example – much of a child's social behaviour is learned through imitation. For example, if a child hears bad language, they will use bad language.

🐻 Parents should not overprotect their child. If a child is overprotected, this can cause the child to believe that his or her parents do not think they are capable, which can in turn affect their self-image and self-esteem.

🐻 Give their child independence and an appropriate amount of responsibility, for example in dressing, feeding, tidying away toys and making their own decisions.

Stages of child development from birth to three years

The table below outlines the norms of development from birth to three years. Norms mean the average age at which children do certain things. There will be variation between children. Often a child may be more advanced in one area than another. For example, they may be fast to walk, but slower to speak.

Stage	Physical development	Intellectual and language development	Social and emotional development	Suitable toys and activities for age group
Birth	• Reflexes are present at birth, such as the stepping reflex (see the photo) • No head control • Can see 25cm from nose	• Startled by loud noises	• Cries to make needs known	• Plenty of physical contact • Breastfeeding helps mother and baby to bond • Constantly talk to the baby in a soothing voice • Play music to the baby

Stage	Physical development	Intellectual and language development	Social and emotional development	Suitable toys and activities for age group
6 weeks	• When lying on front, can lift head up for a few seconds	• Recognises familiar voices • Gurgles and coos	• Smiles at about 6 weeks • Looks at parent's face intently when feeding • Cries to make needs known	• Give the baby things to look at, such as mobiles • Plenty of close physical contact • Talk to and interact with the baby constantly • Music
3 months	• Body is now uncurled – legs and arms are outstretched • Kicks vigorously • Head is steady • Plays with own hands	• Chuckles • Turns head towards sounds	• Gets excited at voices and sounds, such as bathwater running, or the sight of a bottle	• Things to kick, such as baby gyms (homemade are just as good) • Music
6 months	• Sits with support • Turns head from side to side to look around • Holds hands up to be lifted • When standing, can take weight on legs and enjoys bouncing up and down • Puts everything into mouth (see the photo)	• Squeals aloud in play • Babbles tunefully, for example *a dah aroo goo ga* • Out of sight is out of mind – no sense of object permanence, so they will not look for a fallen or hidden object	• Still friendly towards strangers (fear of strangers develops around 7 months)	• Picture books • Bath toys • Toys to bang, such as a drum with wooden spoons • Activity centre

Stage	Physical development	Intellectual and language development	Social and emotional development	Suitable toys and activities for age group
9 months	• Can sit alone • Rolls along on the floor • Tries to crawl and sometimes succeeds • Can stand holding on (see the photo) • Passes toys from hand to hand • Uses finger to point	• Shouts to attract attention • Understands simple words, such as *bye-bye* or *no* • Babbles *da da*, *ma ma* • Playful vocal sounds – for example, if you say 'Jack has a bad cough', the baby will pretend to cough	• Can hold and bite a biscuit • Clings to known adult, afraid of strangers • Plays peek-a-boo • Claps hands	• Songs and action rhymes • Encourage crawling • Toys that roll • Give finger foods
12 months	• Some babies 'bear walk' before walking • May walk alone • Can crawl up stairs (care is needed, as they can't come down safely) • Can pick up small objects, such as crumbs • Points to what he or she wants	• Knows own name • Understands simple instructions, such as 'Give the ball to Daddy' • Understands how to use everyday objects, such as a hairbrush • Waves bye-bye	• Helps with dressing, for example holds foot out for shoe to be put on • Likes to be constantly in sight of a familiar adult • Can bring spoon to mouth, may tip it upside down and spill food	• Picture books • Push-along toys • Fetching games, such as get teddy • Songs and rhymes

Stage	Physical development	Intellectual and language development	Social and emotional development	Suitable toys and activities for age group
18 months	• Walks well carrying a toy • Runs carefully with eyes fixed on the ground, will therefore bump into things • Climbs onto adult chair and then turns around • Makes scribbles and dots on paper • Turns several pages of a book at once • Starts to show left- or right-handedness	• Recognises familiar faces • Uses 20+ recognisable words • Imitates everyday activities, like feeding a doll or sweeping the floor	• Can feed him or herself • Can take off shoes, socks and hat • Will play alone but still likes an adult to be nearby • Tells adult when nappy is soiled and wants it removed	• Dancing to music • Pull/push-along toys (see photo) • Crayons and paper • Bricks • Shape sorters • Encourage child to 'help' with household chores
2 years	• Can run and avoid obstacles • Walks up stairs and (often) down, holding rail or wall, two feet to a step • Throws a ball without falling over • Sits on a tricycle but can't use the pedals • Can remove paper wrapping from a sweet • Holds a pencil and scribbles • Turns pages singly	• 50+ recognisable words • Two- or three-word sentences – girls often talk earlier than boys • Refers to self by name • Constantly asks the names of objects and people • Can join in nursery rhymes and songs • Enjoys pretend play (see photo)	• Spoon-feeds without spilling • No comprehension of danger, e.g. will run onto road • Has temper tantrums (usually one or two per day) • Will not share willingly yet • Plays near other children, but not with them • Jealous of other siblings getting attention from important adults	• Jigsaws • Simple story books • Play dough • Painting • Threading toys • Musical instruments • Tricycle • Props for pretend play, such as a cash register for a shop

Stage	Physical development	Intellectual and language development	Social and emotional development	Suitable toys and activities for age group
3 years	• Rides a tricycle using the pedals • Kicks ball forcibly • Can avoid obstacles when running • Can cut out with safety scissors	• Can write X, V, H and T • Draws a person with a head and one or two other parts or features • May know the names of colours • Covers entire page with paint, often using only one colour • Asks a lot of questions: what, where, who?	• Eats with a fork and spoon • Can pull pants up and down • Toilet trained (step stool and training seat can help with independence – see the photo) • Plays with other children • Understands sharing • Shows affection for siblings	• Story books • Educational computer games • Crayons, paint and paper • Construction toys, such as Lego • Sand and water play • Cooking activities • Encourage child to 'help' with household chores • Large outdoor equipment, such as a slide • Make-believe toys

Feeding

Babies feed on milk alone for the first four months of life. Babies may be bottle or breastfed.

Breastfeeding

Advantages:

🐻 Nutrients are in the correct proportions for the baby's needs.

🐻 Antibodies are passed from the mother to the baby, so breastfed babies are better able to fight infection.

🐻 Breast milk is totally sterile, so there is no risk of food poisoning.

🐻 Breastfeeding encourages bonding.

🐻 Breast milk is free and always available.

🐻 Breastfeeding helps the mother to regain her figure after pregnancy.

🐻 Breastfed babies are less likely to be overweight, suffer from allergies or have colic or constipation.

Disadvantages:

- 🐻 Breastfeeding is a strain on the mother, who must do all the feeds. Breast milk can be expressed and used to bottle feed, but mixed feeding like this is often not recommended because a different suck is required for breast and bottle feeding.

- 🐻 Other members of the family, such as the father, may feel left out.

- 🐻 Breastfeeding can be sore to begin with.

- 🐻 There is sometimes a lack of breastfeeding facilities or bad attitudes of others to breastfeeding in public.

- 🐻 Because breast milk is more digestible, it does not stay in the stomach as long, so breastfed babies may feed more often and sleep less.

Bottle feeding

Advantages:

- 🐻 Formula milks are now available that copy breast milk exactly.

- 🐻 Bottle feeding gives the mother more freedom – night feeds can be shared between parents.

Disadvantages:

- 🐻 Badly made-up feeds can be dangerous. Never put extra scoops of formula into the bottle, as it can cause the baby to dehydrate or become very constipated.

- 🐻 Bottles that have not been sterilised properly can give the baby food poisoning and make him or her very ill.

- 🐻 Formula milks are expensive and making up feeds is time consuming.

- 🐻 Formula milk does not protect against infection and disease like breast milk does.

Formula milk

Infant formula milk is made from cow or soya milk. It is manufactured to resemble breast milk. Soya milk formula is given to vegan babies or babies with a cow's milk allergy.

Ready-made formula feeds are available for travel, but they are too expensive to use all the time

Making up a formula feed

1. Wash your hands carefully.
2. Scrub all baby-feeding equipment thoroughly with a bottle brush, washing-up liquid and hot water. Rinse.
3. Sterilise using one of the following four methods:

   🐻 Boil everything in a saucepan with the lid on for 3 minutes.

   🐻 Use a cold water sterilising tank. Sterilising fluid or tablets are added to cold water. Bottles, etc. must be completely covered with fluid for 30 minutes.

   🐻 Use a steam sterilising unit that clicks off automatically when the bottles are sterilised. Follow the manufacturer's instructions exactly.

   🐻 Sterilisers for use in the microwave are also available. Follow the instructions exactly.

4. First, pour the exact amount of cool boiled water into the sterilised bottles.
5. Second, add the correct number of level scoops of dried formula milk (the pack will tell you how many scoops to add).
6. Replace the teat and lid and shake well.
7. If you make up more than one feed, store the others in the fridge. Reheat carefully in a jug of boiling water (microwave reheating can be dangerous, as the outside of the bottle may be cool and the inside hot – shake well).
8. Hold the baby close when feeding. A baby should never be left alone to feed with a propped-up bottle.
9. Empty any leftover feed out. Rinse and wash the bottle, ready for sterilising.

A microwave steam steriliser

An automatic steam steriliser

Winding

All babies, but particularly bottle-fed babies, swallow some air while feeding. Winding helps bring up trapped wind and makes the baby more comfortable. To wind a baby, hold him or her up against your shoulder or hold under their chin on your knee and gently rub or pat the baby's back until the wind is released. Cover your shoulder with a tea towel, as some feed may also come back up.

Winding a baby

Colic

Colic is an attack of crying and what appears to be abdominal pain in early infancy (babies). Colic is a common condition and is estimated to affect at least 20% of babies during their first few months. Colic usually disappears within three or four months.

Simethicone drops, such as Infacol, are a supplement that can be added to a baby's bottle or breast milk before a feed. The drops are designed to help release bubbles of trapped air in the baby's digestive system, so they may be of some use if indigestion is contributing to their colic.

Weaning

Babies are usually ready for weaning at around 16 weeks. While babies may accept food earlier than that, babies should not be weaned too early, as their digestive systems are not developed enough to cope with solids. Breast- or bottle-fed babies have an instinct to feed, but eating solid food takes practice and babies may appear to be spitting out food even when they are not.

Baby food can be made in bulk and frozen in ice cube trays. That way, it can be used as needed.

Baby rice and puréed fruits and vegetables are suitable first foods. Never add salt or sugar to feeds and avoid foods containing gluten (wheat), as it can be difficult to digest.

Remember, eating habits that last a lifetime are created in childhood. Avoid giving children sugary or high-fat foods.

Commercial baby foods have improved greatly in recent times and now there is a huge variety on the market. Such foods are useful in emergencies but are expensive if used all the time.

Caring for the teeth

A baby's teeth start to appear at around six to seven months. Even though baby teeth (also called milk teeth) only last until around age seven, it is important that they are well cared for.

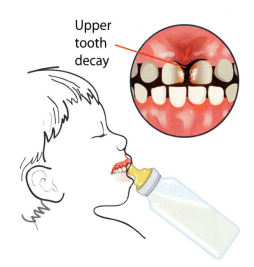

Upper tooth decay

Bottle rot

🧸 Never give babies juice to drink from a bottle, as this leads to bottle rot.

🧸 Even young babies can drink small amounts at a time from a cup or spoon.

🧸 Do not allow babies and toddlers to fall asleep with bottles of milk in their mouth, as this leads to bottle rot.

🧸 Once baby teeth appear, clean them using a cotton bud or later, a soft toothbrush. Teach toddlers to brush their own teeth as soon as they are able to.

🐻 Do not bribe children with sweets or dip soothers in sugar: you are encouraging a sweet tooth and may cause tooth decay.

🐻 Provide children with plenty of calcium-rich foods such as cheese, yoghurt and milk.

Bathing

Small babies need to be washed every day. Baby baths are available that allow even a very small baby to be supported and the freedom to kick their legs freely (see the photo). If the baby cannot be given a bath, then they should be 'topped and tailed'. This means that the baby's face and hands are washed first and the nappy area is washed last in order to avoid spreading infection.

Toilet training

While there is no set age at which toilet training should begin, children often show signs of being ready at around three years old. Girls often toilet train earlier than boys, perhaps because they generally have better verbal skills at this age and are able to say that they have to go. The main thing about toilet training is that the child should be allowed to progress at their own pace in a relaxed atmosphere. A low potty is often used initially, and then, when the child progresses to the toilet, a training seat and step may be used (see page 420).

Nowadays there seems to be a baby gadget for everything. Parents should be wary of spending money on unnecessary gadgets that are expensive and clutter up the house.

Clothing

A **layette** is the set of clothes needed for a newborn baby. It may include the following:

🐻 2 sleep suits (see the photo on page 425)

🐻 2 baby blankets

🐻 7 vests

🐻 7 babygros

🐻 3 cardigans

🐻 1 or 2 all-in snow suits

🐻 2 pairs of scratch mittens

🐻 7 bibs

A layette

Buying baby clothing

- 🐻 Clothing should be bought big enough to last two to three months.

- 🐻 Buy soft, flexible, washable fabrics with no hard seams or rough stitching.

- 🐻 Clothing should be flame-resistant.

- 🐻 Clothing should be easy to put on and take off.

- 🐻 Avoid buttons on inner garments, as they may press into the baby and be uncomfortable. Buttons on cardigans, etc. should be very well sewn on. Snap fasteners are safe and convenient.

A sleep suit

Nappies

Most babies wear disposable nappies, but for both economic and environmental reasons there has been a renewed interest in using cloth nappies. Brands such as Bum Genius and FuzziBunz have become popular. Where disposable nappies are used, there are ecologically friendly brands available that do not contain plastic. Nappies should be disposed of carefully.

Eco-friendly nappies are available to buy online and in some supermarkets

Healthcare

All babies in Ireland are entitled to free healthcare provided by the Health Service Executive (HSE).

Baby clinics run by the HSE provide health and developmental check-ups, such as sight, hearing and physical development. If they suspect the baby has a health or developmental difficulty, they will refer the baby to a more specialised service.

A **public health nurse** visits every mother and baby within a few days of them being discharged from hospital. Public health nurses give help and guidance on issues such as feeding, immunisations, etc.

Modern cloth nappies are becoming more popular

Immunisation works by stimulating the immune system to produce antibodies to fight particular diseases. Because either an altered version of the virus or bacteria (measles, mumps, rubella) or only a component of the virus or bacteria (tetanus, diphtheria, whooping cough) is injected into the baby, immunisation shots cannot cause the disease itself. Immunisations are available free of charge from a GP. GPs keep records of what injections a baby has had, but parents should keep an accurate record too.

Immunisation schedule (for babies born in September 2011 and after)

Age	Where	Vaccine
Birth	Hospital or clinic	BCG
2 months	GP	6 in 1 + PCV
4 months	GP	6 in 1 + Men C
6 months	GP	6 in 1 + Men C + PCV
12 months	GP	MMR + PCV
13 months	GP	Men C + Hib
4–5 years	GP or school	4 in 1 + MMR
1st year of secondary school	School	HPV (girls only)
6th year of secondary school	School	HPV (girls only)
1st year of secondary school	School	Tdap
Senior infants to 1st year of secondary school	School	MMR

BCG = Bacille Calmette-Guérin (tuberculosis vaccine)
6 in 1 = Diphtheria, haemophilus influenzae B (Hib), hepatitis B, pertussis (whooping cough), polio and
    tetanus
PCV = Pneumococcal vaccine
Men C = Meningococcal C
MMR = Measles, mumps, rubella
Hib = Haemophilus influenzae B
4 in 1 = Diphtheria, tetanus, polio, pertussis (whooping cough)
HPV = Human papillomavirus
Tdap = Tetanus, low-dose diphtheria, accelular pertussis

Childcare facilities

Since both parents work in many families, good childcare facilities have become very
important in Ireland. There are several childcare options available to working parents:

- Childminder (may be a relative)
- Live-in babysitter or au pair
- Crèche
- Pre-school or Montessori

Choosing childcare facilities

🐻 Choose childcare facilities that have an open door policy (parents can walk in at any time).

🐻 When visiting potential childcare facilities, parents should bring their child with them and observe how staff interact with him or her. Parents should observe if there are any children who are upset or not receiving attention.

🐻 Look for a variety of equipment, toys and educational material, such as jigsaws, play dough, books, etc. Children should have access to a safe outside area.

🐻 Children should not spend too much time watching TV or DVDs. Once a week is plenty.

🐻 Rooms should be spacious and clean, with plenty of natural light.

🐻 Children should have a separate sleep/nap area – cots should not be used as play pens. Children should not be sleeping in recliners and pushchairs.

🐻 Staff should be well trained and experienced. Parents should ask how long staff have been working there – a high staff turnover could indicate problems.

🐻 There should be good routines for eating, playing and sleeping.

🐻 Proper child to childcare worker ratios should be in place – 3:1 for babies under one year old, 6:1 for children between one and three years and 8:1 for children between three and six years.

🐻 There should be clean nappy-changing facilities.

🐻 Children should not have access to food preparation areas and meals prepared should be nutritionally balanced.

🐻 Exits should be easily accessed in case of an emergency, fire drills should be posted and practised and fire blankets, extinguishers and smoke alarms should be present.

🐻 Safety devices, such as socket covers, should be in place.

🐻 There should be emergency procedures in place if a child becomes ill and a policy preventing children from attending while ill.

🐻 Feedback should be given to parents daily on their child, such as what they have eaten, whether they have had wet and/or dirty nappies, etc. This is important if a child becomes ill after they leave for the day – doctors may need this information.

Babysitting guidelines

The Irish Red Cross produces an excellent handbook called 'A Handbook for Babysitters and Parents'. It can be downloaded from the Irish Red Cross website (www.redcross.ie). Babysitting could be an interesting topic for a Junior Certificate childcare project.

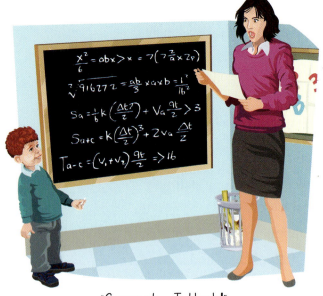

"Correct - I think!"

Children with extraordinary abilities also have frequently unmet special needs

Children with special needs

All children have needs: the need for food, shelter, clothing, love, security and understanding. Children with disabilities or extraordinary abilities have these same needs together with some additional ones.

A **disability** is something that can restrict the individual or make some things more difficult to do.

Classification of special needs

Special needs can be classified in a number of ways.

1. **Incidence (how often the special need occurs)**
    *   **High-incidence special needs:** These are special needs that occur relatively frequently in the general population, but symptoms are not very severe, for example borderline general learning difficulty, dyslexia, eczema, high-achieving children.
    *   **Low-incidence special needs:** These are special needs that do not occur frequently in the general population, but symptoms can be severe, for example cerebral palsy, autism, Down's syndrome.
2. **Cause and/or area of development affected by the special need**
    *   **Physical conditions:** Epilepsy, asthma, eczema, diabetes, HIV and AIDS, coeliac, dyspraxia.
    *   **Inherited conditions:** Sickle cell anaemia, cystic fibrosis, haemophilia, Duchenne muscular dystrophy.
    *   **Conditions affecting communication and control:** Dyslexia, dyscalculia, dyspraxia, autistic spectrum disorders, speech, language and communication impairment, emotional and behavioural difficulties, ADHD (attention deficit hyperactivity disorder).
    *   **Conditions affecting cognitive development:** General learning disability (borderline, mild, moderate, severe), dyscalculia (math)
    *   **Complex conditions:** Down's syndrome, fragile X syndrome, hearing impairment, visual impairment, spina bifida, hydrocephalus, cerebral palsy.

Always treat a child with special needs as the individual they are. Make sure that the child is considered first and the special need second. Refer to a child with Down's syndrome as 'a child with Down's syndrome' rather than a 'Down's syndrome child'.

Some common conditions and disabilities explained

It must be pointed out that only a very basic explanation is offered here for these complex disabilities.

Asthma

- **Cause:** The airways of the lungs become narrowed. Allergies, infection, exercise, the weather or emotional upset may bring on an attack.

- **Effects:** Breathing becomes difficult. If an attack is severe, the child may become anxious and afraid and require medical attention.

- **Special needs:** The child must avoid things or situations that they know bring on attacks, such as playing football on a cold, foggy morning. A reliever inhaler is used to widen the airways again and bring breathing back to normal. A preventer inhaler is used to help prevent attacks from occurring in the first place.

Autism

- **Cause:** Unknown, but genetic links strong.

- **Effects:** Autism is a complex, lifelong condition that affects the child's ability to socialise and communicate effectively. Some children with autism also have obsessive or ritualistic behaviour. Almost all will have an excessive need for sameness and routine in their lives. Most children with autism will never live independently, but can live independent lives with correct supports.

- **Special needs:** Safety is a big concern. The child often has no sense of danger. Routine and special education, such as applied behavioural analysis (ABA), are important.

Cerebral palsy

- **Cause:** The part of the brain that controls movement and posture is damaged or fails to develop. This may be caused by complications during pregnancy or accident/injury during or after birth.

- **Effects:** Movement of limbs is impaired or balance may be affected. Cerebral palsy ranges from mild to very severe (the child may be unable to move or speak).

- **Special needs:** Physiotherapy, speech therapy, occupational therapy (helping the person to develop new life skills).

Coeliac disease

See page 40.

Cystic fibrosis

- **Cause:** Hereditary disease (passed on in the genes).
- **Effects:** Body mucus is very thick, causing breathing problems, severe chest infections and digestive problems.
- **Special needs:** Antibiotic therapy for lung infections, physiotherapy, digestive enzymes taken at every meal, lung transplant.

Diabetes

See pages 41–42.

Down's syndrome

- **Cause:** Usually an abnormality on the twenty-first chromosome, although two other rarer forms exist. Associated with maternal age – at age 25–29 the incidence is one in 1,100, but by age 40 the incidence is one in 100.
- **Effects:** Learning difficulties, characteristic physical appearance, frequent illness, prone to chest infections and heart conditions.
- **Special needs:** A stimulating environment and a positive attitude will help the child to reach his or her full potential.

Dyslexia

- **Cause:** Dyslexia is inherited. It may be inherited from a parent, an uncle, aunt or grandparent.
- **Effects:** Dyslexia is a language-based learning disability in which a person has trouble reading and writing. It is estimated that while approximately 20% of children have reading and writing difficulties, only about 3% have dyslexia. Environmental factors such as a lack of books and reading at home are thought to be the main causes of reading difficulty, whereas children with dyslexia have difficulty reading despite adequate tuition.
- **Special needs:** Specific language learning techniques are used to overcome the problem. Using technology, such as Dragon NaturallySpeaking (a computer program that converts the student's speech into text), helps the child with schoolwork.

Hearing impairment

- **Cause:** Can be hereditary or caused by infections such as rubella during pregnancy or meningitis in the child after birth.
- **Effects:** Degree of hearing loss can range from slight hearing loss to profound deafness.
- **Special needs:** Cochlear ear implants are becoming more common. Hearing aids, speech therapy, sign language.

Spina bifida

🐻 **Cause:** The true cause is not known, but both genetic and environmental factors are thought to be involved (taking regular folic acid before and during pregnancy reduces the risk of spina bifida by 70%).

🐻 **Effects:** Gap in the bones of the spine, exposing the spinal cord. Several different types of spina bifida; ranges from little or no disability to paralysis.

🐻 **Special needs:** Children should be helped to partake in all the activities usual for their age group.

Visual impairment

🐻 **Cause:** Hereditary or caused by infections during pregnancy or birth, such as rubella.

🐻 **Effects:** Individual may be blind or partially sighted.

🐻 **Special needs:** If given good resources and support, many visually impaired children do very well in mainstream schools.

Irish family law

The structure of the Irish family has changed dramatically over the past few decades. As a result of all this change, Irish family law has needed to change and be updated. Some of the most common laws are listed and briefly explained below.

🐻 **Family Law (Maintenance of Spouses and Children) Act 1976:** In the event of separation or divorce, the earning partner must provide reasonable maintenance in order to support children. Failure to do so may result in deductions at source.

🐻 **Family Home Protection Act 1976:** Prevents the family home being sold without the consent of both partners.

🐻 **Family Law (Protection of Spouses and Children) Act 1981:** Gave the circuit and district courts power to grant barring and protection orders (added to by the Domestic Violence Act 1996).

🐻 **Status of Children Act 1987:** Abolished the status of illegitimacy and amended the law on maintenance and succession rights for non-marital children. Allowed unmarried fathers to apply for guardianship of their children. Provided for blood tests to establish paternity.

🐻 **Children Act 1989 and 2001:** Gave the HSE powers to care for children at risk.

🐻 **Child Care Act 1991:** Gave powers to the HSE to care for children who were ill treated, neglected or sexually abused. (Children First – published initially in 1999 and updated in 2011 provides national guidance for the protection and welfare of children at risk.)

🐻 **Maintenance Act 1994:** Simplified procedures for recovering maintenance debts from other countries.

- **Family Law Act 1995:** Raised the minimum age for marriage to 18 and requires three months' written notice to the local registrar.
- **Domestic Violence Act 1996:** Extended safety, barring and protection orders to non-spouses, gave the health boards powers to apply for orders and allowed arrest without warrant for breach.
- **Family Law (Divorce) Act 1996:** Allowed divorce and remarriage.
- **Children Act 1997:** Recognised natural fathers as guardians, allowed children's views to be considered in guardianship, access and custody matters, and allowed parents to have joint custody.
- **Education Act 1998:** Outlines the role of the Department of Education and Skills in providing education for all children under 18 years.
- **Education of Persons with Special Needs Act 2004:** Outlines the government's obligation to provide education to children with special needs.

In addition to the law, there are a number of organisations available to families experiencing difficulties.

- **Family Mediation Service:** This is a state-run service that helps couples who have decided to separate to sort out difficult issues such as custody of children, maintenance, etc.
- **Irish Catholic Marriage Advisory Council (CMAC):** Provides a counselling service to couples whose marriages are in difficulty.
- **Women's Aid:** Provides temporary accommodation and counselling for women victims of domestic violence and their children.
- **Gingerbread:** A support group for lone parents.
- **Alcoholics Anonymous, Narcotics Anonymous, Al-Anon and Alateen:** Provide support for families and individuals affected by drug and alcohol abuse.

Childcare project

You will not be asked questions on the Home Economics written paper about the childcare option. Instead, the childcare option, like each of the other two options, is assessed through project work. Your project is worth 15% of your final Junior Certificate mark at both Ordinary and Higher Levels.

For this project, you must select a topic and then research and prepare a written report on it. The written report should not be more than 1,500 words (approximately five full typed pages or nine written pages). You will not get good marks for large amounts of writing copied closely from books or leaflets. Read the section below for ideas on how to research and present a good project.

Deciding on a topic

Some possible topics include:

- Feeding babies and young children
- A child developmental study (where you choose a child and follow his or her development over a period of time)
- Experiences of being a teenage mother or lone parent
- A babysitter's handbook
- A guide for new parents
- Make a child's toy as part of an overall study on child development
- A study of childhood illness and immunisations
- An investigation into childcare facilities in your area
- An investigation into a particular special need
- Safety and accident prevention in the home, first aid for babies

Research methods

A good project will have two kinds of research:

- **Primary research:** You gather information yourself. You can do this by using questionnaires, interviewing people, observing children at play and recording what you see, visiting a play school and recording what you see, etc.
- **Secondary research:** You read and use other people's primary research. Secondary research is taken from books, the internet, magazines, information leaflets, etc. It is important that you do not copy straight from these sources into your project, as you will lose marks.

Presentation of project

Each of the following should be included.

1. **Contents page**.
2. **Acknowledgements:** Thank anybody who helped you with your project, such as the people who gave you information.
3. **Aims:** List what exactly it is you want to investigate and find out. You should try to have approximately four or five good, strong aims.

> Example: If you chose to do your project on Down's syndrome, an example of an aim would be: 'I would like to find out what causes Down's syndrome.'

4. **Research:** Give details of all the different research you undertook as part of the project. Remember, you must use both primary and secondary research.

> Example: If you chose to investigate the topic of breastfeeding for your project, you could say the following as part of your research section:
> **Primary research:** *I interviewed a mother who had breastfed both her children, asking her about her experience (please see Appendix 1 for interview questions asked).*
> **Secondary research:** *I looked up breastfeeding on the internet and also got a number of interesting leaflets from the health promotion corner in my local hospital.*

5. **Main content of project:** Give details about what you found out about your topic. It should be presented in an organised way and follow the aims of your project closely.

> Example: If you chose to do a project on children with type 1 diabetes, you would write here about (1) causes, symptoms and diagnosis (2) living with diabetes (results of an interview with a parent of a child with diabetes) (3) statistics – results of internet investigation into how common it is in children (4) sample menus for a child with diabetes, etc.

6. **Conclusions:** Present the most important findings of your project.

> Example: Having investigated the topic of breastfeeding on the internet, by interviewing a mother and by reading leaflets on the subject, I found that the main advantages of breastfeeding are that it passes immunity from infection on from mother to baby, etc.

7. **Evaluation:** Review your aims and decide how well you achieved them. Explain why you feel you achieved or did not achieve them. If you were to do this project again, list the changes you would make.

> Example: One of the main aims of this project was to investigate the childcare options available for parents in this town. I certainly did this by carrying out thorough research and compiling a list of all childcare services available, etc.

8. **Bibliography/sources of information:** List where you got your information. Include books, magazines, leaflets, internet sites, etc.

9. **Appendix:** Include copies of interviews, questionnaires, letters you received, leaflets, etc.

Marking scheme

Below is a copy of the marking scheme used by examiners of your project. You should use it to make sure you have covered all areas.

Area	Marking criteria	Marks
Aim of project	Clear statement of aims Relevance to child development	10
Research methodology or problem solving	Information-gathering techniques used and/or investigation of task	20
Content	Relevance to aim, depth of treatment, testing information, practical work (such as models), accurate information, organisation of materials	40
Conclusion	Conclusions drawn from results of investigation, to include a critical evaluation of any product produced against stated aims	10
Originality	Indication of original input by way of analysis, interpretation and/or development of topic by the candidate	10
Layout	Layout, spelling/writing skills, quality of graphics, etc., finish of product	10

Teacher's CD

Slide presentation

Learning outcomes

By the end of this section of the course you will have researched a range of needlework-based crafts. You will have selected one craft and produced an item using this craft. You will also have put together a design and craftwork folder supporting your craft piece.

Craft has a long, rich history in Ireland. In the past, craft items such as knitted jumpers, baskets, woven fabrics, lace and embroidery would have been made in every household. Many such crafts were made firstly as functional items and only secondly as items of beauty.

The major sectors within the Irish craft industry today are pottery, glass, jewellery, textiles (particularly knitwear) and furniture. While Irish craft businesses are usually small in scale and spread all over the country, the industry does employ a significant number of people, particularly in isolated rural communities unsuited to large-scale manufacturing.

Hand-woven willow baskets

Eugene and Anke McKernan scarves

Contemporary Aran knits

The Irish Craft Council

The Irish Craft Council, which was formed in 1971, is the national agency for the development of the craft industry in Ireland. The main aims of the council are to:

- Research and market Irish crafts at home and abroad.
- Encourage excellence in the Irish crafts industry.
- Provide training courses in various Irish crafts.
- Provide information to those interested in the craft industry.
- Run exhibitions to promote Irish crafts, such as in the RDS.
- Provide a directory of Irish crafts where Craft Council members have their own webpage.

For an overview of the craft industry in Ireland today, visit the Craft Council's website at www.ccoi.ie or write to them at Crafts Council of Ireland, Castle Yard, Kilkenny; telephone (056) 776 1804.

Design and craftwork project

You will not be asked questions on the Home Economics written paper about the design and craftwork option. Instead, the design and craftwork option, like each of the other two options, is assessed through project work. Your project is worth 15% of your final Junior Certificate mark at both Ordinary and Higher Levels.

> **Brief**
> For this project, you must design and make a simple, cost-effective craftwork item from a textile.

The design and craftwork folder

Together with the craft item, you must present a written folder, which must contain the following.

1. A table of contents:
   - Analysis of brief (points 2, 3 and 4 below)
   - Solution (points 5, 6, 7 and 8 below)
   - Evaluation (points 9 and 10 below)
2. A statement of what you have been asked to do
3. A list of the most important things you have to consider
4. Evidence that you investigated a number of different crafts before deciding on one
5. Background information on the craft you have chosen. You could look on the internet for this, or in books and magazines from your Home Economics room or local library.

6. A plan of work similar to this sample plan:
   - Week 1: Make a list of all the materials and equipment I need and go buy them.
   - Week 2: Practise my craft on scraps of fabric.
   - Week 3: Complete sample drawings and designs; choose one, etc.
7. A list of all materials and equipment you used for making the craft item, with costings
8. A description with diagrams, sample designs, patterns, etc. of exactly how you made your craft item
9. An evaluation of the craft item: does it meet the brief? Why?
10. Proposed modifications: what would you change if you were to do it again and why?

The craft item itself

Stage 1: Research and choose a craft. You will have to consult with your teacher and carry out research in books, magazines, craft shops, etc. **You cannot use craft kits.** Some possibilities are:

- Appliqué
- Crochet
- Cross-stitch
- Embroidery
- Knitting

- Lace making
- Patchwork
- Quilting
- Rug making
- Weaving

> **Note:** Tie-dying, batik, stencilling or painting fabric can be used, but only in addition to a stitch-based craft, which must make up the main part of your work. For example, if you decide to create an underwater sea scene, you could paint parts of the background in undersea colours before using textured embroidery and beading to create the scene.

Stage 2: Decide what to make that would best suit your craft. Some possibilities are:

- Cushion covers (suits most of the crafts above)
- Lampshade (weaving, pleating, appliqué, embroidery)
- Peg bag (appliqué, embroidery, cross-stitch)
- Picture (appliqué, embroidery, cross-stitch, lace making)
- Rug (rug making)
- Table wear – placemats, napkins, tablecloths, tray cloths and table runners (most crafts above)
- Wall hanging (patchwork, appliqué, embroidery)

Stage 3: Practise your craft. You should practise on old scraps of material: keep these and present them in your design folder.

Stage 4: Finalise your design on paper.

Stage 5: Make your craftwork item.

Sample craft items

Knitted cushions are now very fashionable. You could add unusual buttons, a little beading or embroidery to make yours unique.

A peg bag – decorated with appliqué

Teacher's CD

Slide presentation

Learning outcomes

By the end of this section you will have had the opportunity to make an item of clothing and to learn about career opportunities in the textile industry.

Taking body measurements

Before you buy a pattern or fabric, you will need to know your correct body measurements, or the body measurements for the person you are making the item for.

General guidelines

👕 Use a tape measure that has not been stretched and do not pull it too tight, as it will not give the correct reading.

👕 Remove outer garments, such as jumpers, so that you are not measuring over too much bulk.

👕 If measuring yourself ask a friend to help, as it is very difficult to take your own measurements correctly.

👕 Check all measurements twice, as it is easy to make mistakes.

For most garments, you need to measure your:

👕 Chest (male) or bust (female)

👕 Waist

👕 Hips

For all of these, measure around the fullest (widest) part. To find your natural waistline, tie a piece of string around your waist – where it rests comfortably is your natural waistline.

You may need additional measurements for some garments:

- **Back length:** From the bone at the bottom of your neck to your natural waistline.

- **Sleeve length:** From your shoulder to your wrist, keeping your elbow bent.

- **Outside leg:** From your waist down to where the bottom of the hem will be.

- **Inside leg:** From your crotch to where the bottom of the hem will be.

- **Neck width:** Measure around the neck and add 1.2cm to the result (so that collars will not be too tight).

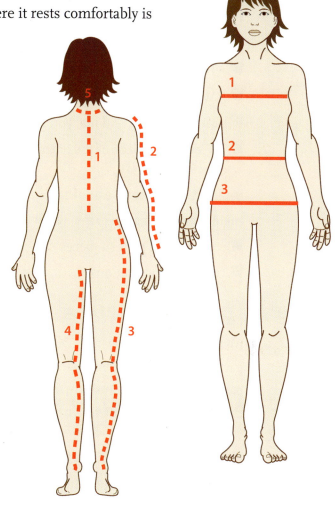

Making clothes
Choosing a pattern

Several different companies, such as Simplicity and Burda, make commercial patterns. These companies display their patterns in pattern catalogues, which are available for you to look at in textile shops or you can view and buy from their range online. Most of these companies make patterns that are suitable for beginners. These are often found in a special section of their catalogues or websites (www.simplicity.com or www.burdafashion.com).

Most patterns include more than one style (view) and a range of sizes

The pattern envelope

The pattern envelope (front and back) gives you information on:

- What the garment(s) should look like when it is finished
- How much fabric you need for each view and size of garment
- Which fabrics are suitable for the garment(s)
- Any extras, or notions, you need to make the garment(s)
- View of the back of the garment(s)

Inside the pattern envelope

Inside the pattern envelope, you will find two things:

- The actual pattern pieces
- A set of instructions

Pattern pieces

Inside the pattern envelope, you will find the pattern pieces for all the views pictured on the pattern envelope. Pattern pieces will be printed out on a number of very large pieces of tissue paper. You will have to study the pattern instructions to find out which pieces are needed for the particular garment you are making.

Pattern pieces will have the following information printed on them:

- The number of the pattern piece
- The name of the pattern piece, such as skirt back
- The following important markings

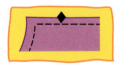

Notches
These show where the garment pieces should be joined. Cut notches outwards.

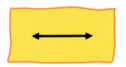

Straight grain
This arrow should be running along the selvedge (warp) of the fabric.

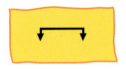

Fold line
This line should be placed along the fold of the fabric.

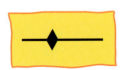

Cutting line
Most patterns have a cutting line that is 1.5cm outside the stitching line. This is where you cut out the fabric. **Note:** Some patterns do not have a cutting line, so you must allow the 1.5cm seam allowance yourself.

Balance marks

These show important points on the garment, such as the centre of the garment and the armhole.

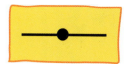

Construction marks

These show the position of darts, pockets, pleats, etc.

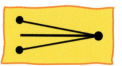

Stitching line

Machine stitch along this line.

Alteration lines

Pattern pieces can be made longer or shorter at these lines (see page 444).

Button positioning marks

These should be marked with a tailor tack to show where buttons are to be placed.

Buttonhole positioning marks

These show where buttonholes should be sewn. Notches, balance marks, button and buttonhole positioning marks should all be transferred from the tissue pattern to your fabric using tailor tacks (see page 403).

Stitching lines and construction marks may be transferred to fabric using a tracing wheel and paper.

Instruction sheets

These usually contain the following information:

- A sketch of the back of the garment(s)
- A labelled sketch of all the pattern pieces included
- A list of the pieces needed for each view
- Instructions for altering the pattern, for instance making it longer
- A sketch showing how pattern pieces can best be laid out on fabrics of different widths
- Cutting instructions
- Step-by-step instructions of how to make the garment

Altering patterns

While small adjustments can be made on the garment itself, for example letting out a seam slightly, larger adjustments must be made on the pattern pieces before placing them on the fabric.

To lengthen pattern pieces

Example: You want to add 3cm to the length of a pair of trousers.

1. Cut the pattern piece between the alteration lines.
2. On another piece of paper, draw two parallel lines 3cm apart.
3. Lay one pattern piece on each of the parallel lines. Stick in place using masking tape.
4. Redraw the cutting line. Trim excess paper.

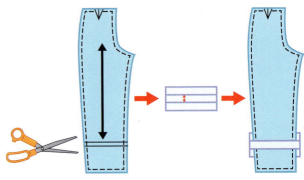

Lengthening pattern pieces

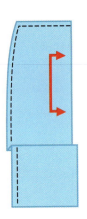
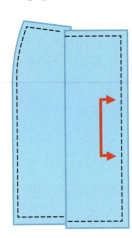

To decrease the length or width of a pattern

Fold the pattern piece on the alteration lines. The fold should measure half the width that you need to reduce. Tape into place and redraw the cutting line.

Decreasing the length or width

To increase the width

1. Draw two parallel lines on a piece of paper the correct distance apart. For example, if you want to increase the width by 3cm, the lines should be 3cm apart.
2. Tape the cut pattern piece along the two parallel lines. Redraw the fitting lines, etc.

Remember: If you increase the width of one part of the garment, the pieces it is attached to must also be increased to allow the pieces to join together.

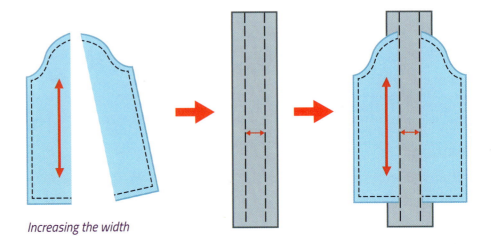

Increasing the width

Laying out pattern pieces

Your pattern instructions will include diagrams showing how your pattern pieces should best be laid out. Layouts will be different for different fabric widths.

In general:

👕 Press fabric on the wrong side before beginning pattern layout.

👕 Fold the fabric right sides and selvedge edges together.

👕 Pattern pieces are generally placed on the fold or laid on the fabric using the straight-of-grain lines (see page 403).

See also Chapter 35.

> **Using straight-of-grain lines**
> ● Lay the pattern pieces on the fabric so that the straight-of-grain arrow looks parallel with the selvedge edge. Pin one end of the arrow to the fabric.
> ● Measure from each end of the straight-of-grain arrow to the selvedge edge. When both ends are exactly the same distance from the selvedge, pin the other arrowhead in place. Then pin the rest of the pattern piece down.

Cutting out

See Chapter 35, page 403.

Transfer of pattern markings

It is vital to transfer important pattern markings from the tissue pattern pieces to the fabric. There are three main ways of doing this.

👕 **Tailor tacks** should always be used to show the location of important points on the pattern, such as end-of-bust darts or the position of buttons and buttonholes.

👕 **Waxed paper and a tracing wheel** are generally used to mark the sewing line. Two sheets of waxed paper are used, one against each piece of fabric on the wrong side. The wheel is rolled along the sewing line and the line comes out on the fabric. The line can be used as a guide to keep tacking and sewing straight.

👕 **Tailor's chalk** is sometimes used for marking the sewing line when pattern pieces have no seam allowance included.

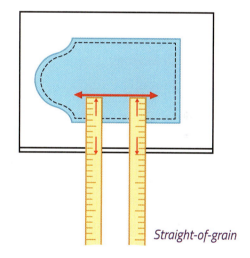

Straight-of-grain

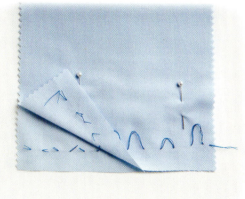

Tailor tacks

Fitting

It is important that the garment you are making fits well before you sew it up. A garment that fits well will:

- Be neither too loose nor too tight
- Hang well
- Be comfortable and look well

Guidelines

- Tack the large pieces (the front and back pieces) of the garment together.
- Tack any darts in place.
- Try the garment on. Sit, bend and raise your arms to make sure the garment is not too tight. You will be able to loosen or tighten the garment by letting out or taking in some of your seam allowances.
- Check that shoulder seams lie on the shoulder and that the armhole is not too tight or too loose.
- Check that the waist of the garment is on your natural waistline.
- Mark alterations with chalk or pins. Remove the garment and tack alterations. Try the garment on again before sewing.

Pressing

Pressing is important to give your garment a finished, crisp look. Pressing is different from ironing – with pressing, you lift the iron and press down on the fabric, lift and press, etc.

Guidelines

- Press after each stage of construction, for example after sewing the side seams. Do not wait until the end to press everything, as you will not get as good a result.
- Usually press on the wrong side of the fabric. If you must press on the right side, use a pressing cloth to protect the fabric.
- Use a steam iron set at the correct temperature for the fabric.
- Give the garment a final overall press when it is fully complete.

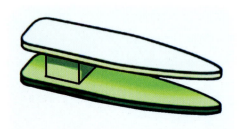

A sleeve board

Textile skills project

While there will be questions on Textile Studies (Unit 5) on the final examination paper, the textiles skills option, like the other two options, is assessed through project work alone and is worth 15% of your overall final mark for Home Economics. For this option, you must complete an item of clothing (worth 80 marks) and present a written support folder (worth 20 marks), the details of which are outlined below.

> **Brief**
>
> Make an item of clothing that includes a minimum of two processes, such as application of a collar, sleeves, zip, buttonholes, etc.

Support folder

You should include the following information in your support folder.

- Give details of what factors influenced you when choosing what garment to make, such as your sewing skills, availability of fabric, your body shape, fashion, your budget or if there was something you needed or a special occasion coming up, such as you made a child's dress because your aunt had a new baby girl.

- Give the details of the pattern you used and any changes you made to it.

- Give the details of the fabric you used (cost, amount you needed, type of fabric). Draw a wash care label for your garment.

- You could complete a fabric burning test to identify your fabric and present your results.

- Give details of the notions you had to buy to complete the garment (buttons, zip, etc.) and list and price them.

- What sewing equipment did you use? You could draw diagrams of some of the more unusual equipment, such as a sleeve board.

- Evaluate your item of clothing under the following headings:
  1. How well is it finished? Evaluate every part of the garment: seams, seam finishes, collar, zip, buttons, buttonholes, hems, pockets, etc.
  2. How well does it fit? Are there any puckers? Is the garment too tight or loose?
  3. What would you change the next time?

The textiles industry

The main textile industries in Ireland are:

- 👕 Fibre production and research
- 👕 Yarn production (making knitting wool)
- 👕 Fabric production, tweed, linen production
- 👕 Textile product production (Aran sweaters, wool and tweed suits, linen table wear, carpets)
- 👕 Fashion design – successful Irish designers include Paul Costello, Louise Kennedy, Quinn & Donnelly, John Rocha, Philip Treacy and Lulu Guinness
- 👕 Retail (shop assistants)

If you are interested in fashion design or in the textile industry generally (weaving, printing, etc.), a number of colleges around the country offer courses ranging from certificate to degree level. Ask your career guidance teacher for details.

Would you consider a career in fashion design?

FOOD TABLES

Tr = traces of the nutrient present

N = significant quantities of the nutrient present; values not known

Composition of foods (per kg)

	kcal	Protein (g)	Saturated fat (g)	Unsaturated fat (g)	Cholesterol (mg)	Carbohydrate (g)	Fibre (g)	Salt (mg)	Calcium (mg)	Iron (mg)	Carotene (µg)	Vitamin A (µg)	Vitamin D (µg)	Vitamin C (mg)	Water (g)
Cereal and cereal products															
Bran (wheat)	206	14.1	0.9	0.6	0	26.8	39.6	28	110	12.9	0	0	0	0	8.3
Cornflour	354	0.6	0.1	0.4	0	92.0	N	52	15	1.4	0	0	0	0	12.5
Croissant	360	8.3	6.5	13	75	38.3	2.5	390	80	20	0	21	0.2	0	31.1
Brown flour (wheat)	323	12.1	0.2	1.0	0	68.5	6.4	4	130	3.2	0	0	0	0	14.0
White flour (wheat)	341	9.4	0.2	0.7	0	77.7	3.6	0.3	140	2.0	0	0	0	0	14.0
Wheat germ	357	26.7	1.3	5.3	0	44.7	N	0.5	55	8.5	0	0	0	0	11.7
Brown rice (boiled)	141	2.6	0.3	0.7	0	32.1	1.1	1	4	0.5	0	0	0	0	66.0
White rice (boiled)	138	2.6	0.3	0.8	0	30.9	1.0	1	18	12	0	0	0	0	68.0
Noodles	62	2.2	0.1	0.3	6	22.2	1.0	15	5	0.3	0	2	Tr	0	84.3
Spaghetti	104	3.6	0.1	0.4	0	22.2	1.8	Tr	7	0.5	0	0	0	0	73.8
White sliced bread	217	7.6	0.3	0.6	0	46.8	3.7	530	100	1.4	0	0	0	0	40.4
Brown bread	215	9.2	0.5	1.2	0	1.6	41.6	550	54	2.7	0	0	0	0	38.3
All-Bran	261	14.0	0.6	1.9	0	46.6	30.0	900	69	12.0	0	0	1.6	0	3.0
Bran flakes	318	10.2	0.4	1.2	0	69.3	17.3	1000	50	20.0	0	0	2.1	25	3.0
Coco Pops	384	5.3	0.4	0.5	0	94.3	1.1	800	20	6.7	0	0	2.1	0	3.0
Common Sense	357	11.0	0.7	2.9	0	74.0	N	900	50	6.7	0	0	2.1	0	3.0
Cornflakes	360	7.9	0.1	0.4	0	85.9	3.4	1110	15	6.7	0	0	2.1	0	3.0
Frosties	377	5.9	0.1	0.3	0	93.7	1.2	800	11	6.7	0	0	2.1	0	3.0
Muesli	363	9.8	0.8	4.4	Tr	72.2	8.1	380	110	5.8	Tr	Tr	0	Tr	7.2
Porridge (made with milk)	116	4.8	2.7	2.0	14	13.7	0.8	620	120	0.6	21	53	0	1	74.8
Rice Krispies	369	6.1	0.3	0.5	0	89.7	1.1	1260	10	6.7	0	0	2.1	0	3.0
Shredded Wheat	325	10.6	0.4	1.8	0	68.3	10.1	8	38	4.2	0	0	0	0	7.6
Shreddies	331	10	0.2	0.9	0	74.1	10.9	550	40	2.8	0	0	0	0	4.0
Smacks	386	8.0	0.4	1.1	0	89.6	N	20	20	6.7	0	0	2.1	0	3.0
Special K	377	15.3	0.3	0.6	0	81.7	2.7	1000	70	13.3	0	0	2.8	0	3.0
Start	355	7.9	0.3	1.1	0	81.7	9.3	500	40	15.0	0	0	3.1	37	3.0
Weetabix	359	11.0	0.4	1.6	0	75.7	11.6	270	35	7.4	0	0	0	0	5.6
Biscuits															
Chocolate digestives	524	5.7	16.7	9.1	22	67.4	2.9	160	110	1.7	Tr	Tr	Tr	0	2.2
Cream crackers	440	9.5	N	N	N	68.3	6.1	610	110	1.7	0	0	0	0	4.3
Ginger nuts	456	5.6	7.2	7.2	N	79.1	1.8	330	130	4.0	N	0	0	0	3.4
Jaffa Cakes	363	3.5	N	N	21	67.8	N	130	55	1.5	0	14	0.1	2	18.0

Composition of foods (per kg)

	kcal	Protein (g)	Saturated fat (g)	Unsaturated fat (g)	Cholesterol (mg)	Carbohydrate (g)	Fibre (g)	Salt (mg)	Calcium (mg)	Iron (mg)	Carotene (µg)	Vitamin A (µg)	Vitamin D (µg)	Vitamin C (mg)	Water (g)
Cakes, buns and scones															
Rice Krispie buns	464	5.6	10.7	6.8	5	73.1	0.8	450	28	4.0	25	Tr	0.8	0	1.6
Madeira cake (queen cakes)	393	5.4	8.8	7.2	N	58.4	1.3	380	42	1.1	N	N	N	0	20.2
Sponge cake (jam filled)	302	4.2	1.6	2.4	N	64.2	1.1	420	44	1.6	N	N	N	0	24.5
Chocolate Swiss roll	337	4.3	11.3		8.6	58.1	2.4	350	77	1.1	N	N	N	0	17.5
Plain scones	362	7.2	4.9	9.1	29	53.8	2.2	770	180	1.3	125	140	1.2	Tr	22.9
Fruit scones	316	7.3	3.3	8.1	27	52.9	3.6	710	150	1.5	N	N	N	Tr	25.3
Wholemeal scones	326	8.7	4.8	9.0	27	43.1	5.0	730	110	2.3	115	130	1.2	0	26.9
Pastry															
Wholemeal pastry (cooked)	499	8.9	11.8	19.6	43	44.6	6.0	360	24	2.4	130	135	1.4	0	7.4
Mince pies	423	4.3	7.4	12.1	25	59.0	2.8	310	75	1.5	82	77	0.8	0	12.0
Pizza (basic)	235	9.0	5.5	5.7	16	24.8	1.8	570	210	1.0	250	65	0.1	3	51.7
Desserts															
Bread and butter pudding	297	5.9	5.9	3.1	53	49.7	3.0	310	120	1.6	45	100	0.2	Tr	29.3
Christmas pudding	291	4.6	4.5	4.7	45	49.5	2.7	200	79	1.5	9	23	0.2	0	30.4
Fruit crumble	198	2.0	2.1	4.4	12	34.0	2.2	68	49	0.6	145	64	0.7	3	54.8
Apple tart	260	3.0	4.8	7.9	18	34.0	2.2	200	59	0.8	115	55	0.6	3	47.9
Pancakes	301	5.9	7.1	8.3	68	35.0	0.9	53	110	0.8	14	60	0.2	1	43.4
Milk and milk products															
Whole milk	66	3.2	2.4	1.2	14	4.8	0	55	115	0.05	21	52	0.03	1	87.8
Skimmed milk	33	3.3	0.1	Tr	2	5.0	0	55	120	0.05	Tr	1	Tr	1	91.1
Semi-skimmed milk (low-fat)	46	3.3	1.0	0.5	7	5.0	0	55	120	0.05	9	21	0.01	1	89.8
Condensed milk	333	8.5	6.3	3.2	36	55.5	0	140	290	0.23	70	110	5.40	4	25.9
Evaporated milk	151	8.4	5.9	3.0	34	8.5	0	180	290	0.26	100	105	3.95	1	69.1
Human milk (colostrum)	56	2.0	1.1	1.4	31	6.6	0	47	28	0.07	135	155	1.03	7	88.2
Human milk (mature)	69	1.3	1.8	2.1	16	7.2	0	15	34	0.07	24	58	0.04	4	87.1
Baby milk formula	67	1.6	1.6	2.0	N	7.0	0	0.022	56	0.8	Tr	75	1.1		87.0
Soya milk	32	2.9	0.3	1.5	0	0.8	Tr	32	13	0.40	Tr	0	0	0	89.7
Cream (single)	198	2.6	11.9	6	55	4.1	0	49	91	0.1	125	315	0.14	1	73.7
Cream (double)	449	1.7	30	153	130	2.7	0	37	50	0.2	325	600	0.27	1	47.5
Cream (low-fat)	148	3.0	8.3	4.3	40	4.3	0	49	99	0.1	54	190	0.10	1	78.9
Cheese (Brie)	319	19.3	16.8	8.6	100	Tr	0	700	540	0.8	210	285	0.20	Tr	48.6
Cheese (Cheddar)	412	25.5	21.7	10.8	100	0.1	0	670	720	0.3	225	325	0.26	Tr	36.0
Cheese (low-fat Cheddar)	261	31.5	9.4	4.8	43	Tr	0	670	840	0.2	100	165	0.11	Tr	47.1
Cottage cheese	98	13.8	2.4	1.2	13	2.1	0	380	73	0.1	10	44	0.03	Tr	79.1
Edam	333	26	15.9	8.1	80	Tr	0	1020	770	0.2	150	175	0.19	Tr	43.8
Fromage frais (fruit)	131	6.8	13.7	4.7	70	13.8	Tr	35	86	0.1	N	82	0.04	Tr	71.9
Parmesan	452	39.4	20.5	10.4	100	Tr	0	1090	1200	1.1	210	345	0.25	Tr	18.4
Yoghurt (fruit)	105	5.1	1.5	1.0	10	15.7	N	82	160	Tr	16	39	0.04	1	73.1
Yoghurt (low-fat fruit)	90	4.1	0.4	0.2	4	17.9	N	64	150	0.1	4	10	0.01	1	77
Choc ice	277	3.5	10.8	5.9	30	28.1	Tr	91	130	0.1	5	1	Tr	N	N

Composition of foods (per kg)

	kcal	Protein (g)	Saturated fat (g)	Unsaturated fat (g)	Cholesterol (mg)	Carbohydrate (g)	Fibre (g)	Salt (mg)	Calcium (mg)	Iron (mg)	Carotene (µg)	Vitamin A (µg)	Vitamin D (µg)	Vitamin C (mg)	Water (g)
Milk and milk products (continued)															
Cornetto	260	3.7	6.7	5.5	2	34.5	N	91	120	N	N	N	Tr	N	N
Ice cream (vanilla)	194	3.6	6.4	2.7	31	24.4	Tr	69	130	0.1	195	115	0.12	1	61.91
Cheesecake	242	5.7	5.6	4.4	60	33.0	0.9	160	68	0.5	N	N	N	0	44.0
Jelly	61	1.2	0	0	0	15.1	0	5	7	0.4	0	0	0	0	84
Milk pudding	129	3.9	2.7	1.4	15	20.1	0.2	59	130	0.1	22	56	0.03	1	72.4
Trifle	166	2.4	5.2	3.5	33	19.5	0.5	63	68	0.3	33	70	0.17	4	68.1
Eggs and egg dishes															
Eggs (chicken)	147	12.5	3.1	5.9	385	Tr	0	140	57	1.9	Tr	190	1.75	0	75.1
Egg white	36	9.0	Tr	Tr	0	Tr	0	190	5	0.1	0	0	0	0	88.3
Egg yolk	339	16.1	8.7	16.6	1120	Tr	0	50	130	6.1	Tr	535	4.94	0	51.0
Scrambled eggs	247	10.7	11.6	8.6	350	0.6	0	1030	63	1.6	72	295	1.55	Tr	62.4
Omelette (cheese)	266	15.9	12.2	8.4	265	Tr	0	900	280	1.2	100	265	1.13	Tr	57.1
Quiche (plain)	314	12.5	10.3	10.2	140	17.3	0.7	340	260	1.0	100	185	0.93	Tr	46.7
Fats and oils															
Margarine (soft)	739	0.2	26.9	51	225	1.0	0	800	4	0.3	750	860	7.94	0	16.0
Olive oil	899	Tr	14.0	80.9	0	0	0	Tr	Tr	0.4	N	0	0	0	Tr
Sunflower oil	899	Tr	11.9	83.2	0	0	0	Tr	Tr	Tr	Tr	0	0	0	Tr
Meat and meat products															
Bacon – boiled (lean)	167	29.4	3.6	5.2	36	0	0	1350	15	1.9	Tr	Tr	Tr	0	62.7
Bacon – gammon steak	172	31.4	1.9	2.7	19	0	0	2210	10	1.5	Tr	Tr	Tr	0	57.0
Bacon – rasher (back), fried	465	24.9	15.9	22.6	143	0	0	1910	13	1.3	Tr	Tr	Tr	0	29.7
Ham	120	18.4	1.9	2.7	68	0	0	1250	9	1.2	Tr	Tr	Tr	0	72.5
Minced beef (average)	229	23.1	6.5	8	83	0	0	320	18	3.1	Tr	Tr	Tr	0	59.1
Beef – stewing steak	223	30.9	4.7	5.8	82	0	0	360	15	3.0	Tr	Tr	Tr	0	68.4
Lamb (loin chop, grilled)	355	23.5	14.4	12.6	107	0	0	72	9	1.9	Tr	Tr	Tr	0	46.6
Lamb (cutlet, grilled)	370	23.0	15.3	13.4	107	0	0	71	9	1.9	Tr	Tr	Tr	0	45.1
Pork (loin chops)	332	28.5	9.0	13.4	108	0	0	84	11	1.2	Tr	Tr	Tr	0	46.3
Chicken – roast	148	24.8	1.6	3.5	96	0	0	81	9	0.8	Tr	Tr	Tr	0	68.4
Chicken liver (fried)	194	26.9	2.1	2.4	610	0	0	240	15	9.1	0	12230	N	13	64.2
Duck – roast	189	25.3	2.7	6.5	160	0	0	96	13	2.7	N	N	N	0	64.2
Lamb's liver (fried)	232	22.9	4.0	5.7	330	3.9	0.1	190	12	10.0	60	22680	0.5	12	58.4
Lamb's kidney (fried)	155	24.6	2.1	2.4	610	0	0	270	13	12.0	0	110	N	9	66.5
Beef burgers	264	20.4	8.0	8.5	81	7.0	1.3	880	33	3.1	Tr	Tr	Tr	0	53.0
Black pudding	305	12.9	8.5	11.7	68	15.0	0.5	1210	35	20.0	Tr	41	Tr	0	44.0
Corned beef	217	26.9	6.3	5.1	93	0	0	950	14	2.9	Tr	Tr	Tr	0	58.5
Liver pâté	316	13.1	8.4	12.8	169	1.0	Tr	790	15	7.1	130	7330	N	N	50.6
Sausage rolls	459	8.0	11.8	18.2	43	37.5	1.8	530	76	1.3	80	85	0.9	0	22.3
Pork sausages (fried)	317	13.8	9.4	13.7	53	11.0	0.7	1050	55	1.5	Tr	Tr	Tr	N	44.9
Pork sausages (grilled)	318	13.3	9.5	13.7	53	11.5	0.7	1000	53	1.5	Tr	Tr	Tr	N	45.1

Composition of foods (per kg)

	kcal	Protein (g)	Saturated fat (g)	Unsaturated fat (g)	Cholesterol (mg)	Carbohydrate (g)	Fibre (g)	Salt (mg)	Calcium (mg)	Iron (mg)	Carotene (µg)	Vitamin A (µg)	Vitamin D (µg)	Vitamin C (mg)	Water (g)
Meat and meat products (continued)															
Steak and kidney pie	176	14.8	7.0	10.3	141	15.2	0.7	660	35	2.8	50	80	0.5	1	49.0
White pudding	450	7.0	31.8		22	36.3	3.1	370	38	2.1	Tr	Tr	Tr	0	22.8
Beef curry with rice	137	8.8	1.9	2.2	21	16.9	N	260	N	N	N	Tr	Tr	Tr	68.9
Beef stew	120	9.7	3.3	3.5	30	4.6	0.7	330	15	1.1	1100	1	Tr	1	77.3
Chicken curry with rice	144	7.8	2.3	2.8	28	16.9	N	230	250	N	N	N	N	1	68.4
Bolognese sauce	145	8.0	3.1	7.1	25	3.7	1.1	430	23	1.4	1275	Tr	Tr	4	74.7
Chilli con carne	151	11.0	3.0	4.9	27	8.3	3.2	250	29	2.2	145	Tr	Tr	9	67.6
Irish stew	123	5.3	3.5	3.1	20	9.1	1.0	360	10	0.6	2	Tr	Tr	3	76.2
Lasagne	102	5.0	1.9	1.6	11	12.8	0.5	430	71	0.7	N	N	N	Tr	75.2
Shepherd's pie	118	8.0	2.4	3.2	28	8.2	0.7	450	16	1.2	15	15	0.1	3	75.6
Fish and fish products															
Cod (baked, butter added)	96	21.4	0.5	0.4	48	0	0	340	22	0.4	Tr	2	Tr	Tr	76.6
Cod (fried in batter, oil)	199	19.6	0.9	8.8	N	7.5	0.3	100	80	0.5	Tr	N	Tr	Tr	60.9
Haddock (steamed)	98	22.8	0.2	0.4	48	0	0	120	55	0.7	Tr	Tr	Tr	Tr	75.1
Haddock (fried in crumbs)	174	21.4	0.7	7.1	N	3.6	0.2	180	110	1.2	Tr	Tr	Tr	Tr	65.1
Plaice (steamed)	93	18.9	0.3	1	50	0	0	120	38	0.6	Tr	Tr	Tr	Tr	78.0
Plaice (fried in batter)	279	15.8	1.5	15.5	N	14.4	0.5	220	93	1.0	Tr	Tr	Tr	Tr	52.4
Herring (grilled)	199	20.4	3.7	9.6	50	0	0	170	33	1.0	Tr	34	25.0	Tr	65.5
Mackerel (fried)	188	21.5	2.3	7.9	62	0	0	150	28	1.2	Tr	43	21.1	Tr	65.6
Salmon (canned)	155	20.3	1.5	5.9	34	0	0	570	93	1.4	Tr	35	12.5	Tr	70.4
Salmon (smoked)	177	17.8	0.8	3.2	50	0	0	1880	19	0.6	Tr	13	Tr	Tr	65.0
Tuna (canned in oil)	189	27.1	1.4	6.7	50	0	0	290	12	1.6	Tr	N	5.8	Tr	63.3
Tuna (canned in brine)	99	23.5	0.2	0.3	51	0	0	320	8	1.0	Tr	N	4.0	Tr	74.6
Prawns (boiled)	107	22.6	0.4	0.9	81	0	0	1590	150	1.1	Tr	Tr	Tr	Tr	70.0
Fish cakes (fried)	188	9.1	1.0	8.3	17	15.1	0.6	500	70	1.0	Tr	Tr	Tr	Tr	63.3
Fish fingers (grilled)	56.2	15.1	2.8	5.7	35	19.3	0.7	380	52	0.8	Tr	Tr	Tr	Tr	56.2
Fish pie	105	8.0	1.2	1.5	19	12.3	0.9	250	37	0.4	15	28	0.2	2	75.7
Vegetables															
New potatoes (boiled)	75	1.5	0.1	0.1	0	17.8	1.2	9	5	0.3	Tr	0	0	9	80.5
Old potatoes (boiled)	72	1.8	Tr	0.1	0	17.0	1.4	7	5	0.4	Tr	0	0	6	80.3
Chips (homemade, fried in vegetable oil)	189	3.9	0.6	5.7	0	30.1	3.0	12	11	0.8	Tr	0	0	9	56.5
Chips (frozen, fried in vegetable oil)	273	4.1	2.5	10.4	0	36.0	3.5	29	15	0.9	Tr	0	0	16	40.3
Oven chips (baked)	162	3.2	1.8	2.2	0	29.8	2.8	53	12	0.8	Tr	0	0	12	58.5
Chips fried in animal fat	273	4.1	7.5	5.3	12	36.0	3.5	30	15	0.9	N	N	Tr	16	40.3
Potato waffles (baked)	200	3.2	1.0	6.7	0	30.3	N	430	32	0.5	Tr	0	0	36	52.7
Baked beans	84	5.2	0.1	0.1	0.3	15.3	6.9	530	53	1.4	74	0	0	Tr	71.5
Green/French beans	25	1.7	Tr	Tr	0	4.7	N	Tr	36	1.2	180	0	0	7	90.0
Lentils	105	8.8	0.1	0.4	0	16.9	3.3	3	22	3.5	N	0	0	Tr	66.7

Composition of foods (per kg)

	kcal	Protein (g)	Saturated fat (g)	Unsaturated fat (g)	Cholesterol (mg)	Carbohydrate (g)	Fibre (g)	Salt (mg)	Calcium (mg)	Iron (mg)	Carotene (µg)	Vitamin A (µg)	Vitamin D (µg)	Vitamin C (mg)	Water (g)
Vegetables (continued)															
Soya beans	141	14.0	0.9	4.9	0	5.1	8	1	83	3.0	6	0	0	Tr	64.3
Tofu	73	8.1	0.5	1.0	0	0.7	0.3	4	510	1.2	2	0	0	0	85.0
Peas (frozen)	79	6.7	0.3	1.0	0	9.7	7.3	94	35	1.6	405	0	0	12	75.6
Processed peas	99	6.9	0.1	0.4	0	17.5	7.1	380	33	1.8	60	0	0	Tr	69.6
Broccoli	24	3.1	0.2	0.5	0	1.1	N	13	40	1.0	475	0	0	44	91.1
Brussels sprouts	35	2.9	0.3	0.8	0	3.5	2.6	2	20	0.5	320	0	0	60	86.9
Cabbage	16	1.0	0.1	0.3	0	2.3	2.3	8	33	0.3	210	0	0	20	93.1
Carrots	24	0.6	0.1	0.2	0	4.9	2.8	50	24	0.4	7560	0	0	2	90.5
Cauliflower	28	2.9	0.2	0.6	0	2.1	1.6	4	17	0.4	60	0	0	27	90.6
Celery	7	0.5	Tr	0.1	0	2.5	1.6	60	41	0.4	50	0	0	8	95.1
Courgette (cooked)	63	2.6	0.6	4.0	0	2.6	N	1	38	1.4	500	0	0	15	86.8
Cucumber	10	0.7	Tr	Tr	0	1.5	0.7	3	18	0.3	60	0	0	2	96.4
Curly kale	24	2.4	0.2	1.0	0	1.0	2.6	100	150	2.0	3375	0	0	71	90.9
Garlic	98	7.9	0.1	0.3	0	16.3	N	4	19	1.9	Tr	0	0	17	64.3
Leeks	21	1.2	0.1	0.4	0	2.6	2.4	2	24	1.1	735	0	0	17	92.2
Lettuce	14	0.8	0.1	0.3	0	1.7	1.3	3	28	0.7	355	0	0	5	95.1
Mixed vegetables (frozen)	42	3.3	Tr	Tr	0	6.6	N	96	35	0.8	2520	0	0	13	85.8
Mushrooms	13	1.8	0.1	0.3	0	0.4	2.3	5	6	0.6	0	0	0	1	92.6
Onions	36	1.2	Tr	0.1	0	7.9	1.5	3	25	0.3	10	0	0	5	89.0
Parsnips	66	1.6	0.2	0.7	0	12.9	4.3	10	41	0.6	30	0	0	17	78.7
Peppers	20	2.9	N	N	0	0.7	N	7	30	1.2	175	0	0	120	85.7
Spinach	19	2.2	0.1	0.6	0	0.8	3.1	120	160	1.6	3840	0	0	8	91.8
Sweetcorn (canned)	23	2.9	N	N	0	2.0	2.0	1140	8	1.2	140	0	0	14	92.5
Tomatoes	17	0.7	0.1	0.2	0	3.1	1.3	9	7	0.5	640	0	0	17	93.1
Turnip	12	0.6	Tr	0.1	0	2.0	2.0	15	48	0.2	20	0	0	10	93.1
Fruit															
Apples (eating)	47	0.4	Tr	0.1	0	11.8	2.0	3	4	0.1	18	0	0	6	84.5
Apricots	31	0.9	Tr	Tr	0	7.2	1.9	2	15	0.5	405	0	0	6	87.2
Avocado	190	1.9	4.1	14.3	0	1.9	N	6	11	0.4	16	0	0	6	72.5
Bananas	95	1.2	0.1	0.1	0	23.2	3.1	1	6	0.3	21	0	0	11	75.1
Blackberries	25	0.9	Tr	0.1	0	5.1	6.6	2	41	0.7	80	0	0	15	85.0
Blackcurrants	28	0.9	Tr	Tr	0	6.6	7.8	3	60	1.3	100	0	0	200	77.4
Cranberries	46	.6	tr	tr	0	9	4.6	2	8	.8	36	60	0	13.3	
Fruit cocktail (canned)	29	0.4	Tr	Tr	0	7.2	1.0	3	9	0.4	54	0	0	14	86.9
Fruit salad (homemade)	55	0.7	Tr	Tr	0	13.8	1.5	2	16	0.2	20	0	0	16	82.3
Gooseberries	19	1.1	N	N	0	3.0	2.9	2	28	0.3	110	0	0	14	90.1
Grapefruit	30	0.8	Tr	Tr	0	6.8	1.6	3	23	0.1	17	0	0	36	89.0
Grapes	60	0.4	Tr	Tr	0	15.4	0.8	3	23	0.1	17	0	0	3	81.8
Kiwis	49	1.1	N	N	0	10.6	2.3	4	25	0.4	37	0	0	59	84.0
Lemons	19	1.0	0.1	Tr	0	3.2	4.7	5	85	0.5	18	0	0	58	86.3
Mandarin oranges	32	0.7	Tr	Tr	0	7.7	0.3	6	17	0.5	95	0	0	20	89.6
Melon	19	0.6	Tr	Tr	0	4.2	0.9	8	20	0.3	1000	0	0	26	92.1

Composition of foods (per kg)

	kcal	Protein (g)	Saturated fat (g)	Unsaturated fat (g)	Cholesterol (mg)	Carbohydrate (g)	Fibre (g)	Salt (mg)	Calcium (mg)	Iron (mg)	Carotene (µg)	Vitamin A (µg)	Vitamin D (µg)	Vitamin C (mg)	Water (g)
Fruit (continued)															
Oranges	37	1.1	Tr	Tr	0	8.5	1.8	5	47	0.1	20	0	0	38	86.1
Passion fruit	36	2.6	0.1	0.2	0	5.8	N	19	11	1.3	750	0	0	23	74.9
Peaches (raw)	33	1.0	Tr	Tr	0	7.6	2.3	1	7	0.4	58	0	0	31	88.9
Peaches (canned in syrup)	55	0.5	Tr	Tr	0	14.0	0.9	4	3	0.2	75	0	0	5	81.1
Pears	40	0.3	Tr	Tr	0	10.0	2.8	3	11	0.2	18	0	0	6	83.8
Pineapple	41	0.4	Tr	0.2	0	10.1	1.3	2	18	0.2	18	0	0	12	86.5
Plums	36	0.6	Tr	Tr	0	8.8	2.3	2	13	0.4	295	0	0	4	83.9
Prunes (semi-dried)	141	2.5	N	N	0	34.0	12.8	11	34	2.6	140	0	0	Tr	31.1
Raisins	272	2.1	N	N	0	69.3	6.1	60	46	3.6	12	0	0	1	13.2
Raspberries	25	1.4	0.1	0.2	0	4.6	6.7	3	25	0.7	6	0	0	32	87.0
Rhubarb (stewed with sugar)	48	0.9	Tr	Tr	0	11.5	2.0	1	33	0.1	60	0	0	6	84.6
Strawberries	27	0.8	Tr	Tr	0	6.0	2.0	6	16	0.4	8	0	0	77	89.5
Nuts															
Almonds	612	21.1	4.7	48.6	0	6.9	12.9	14	240	3.0	0	0	0	0	4.2
Peanuts (roasted and salted)	602	24.5	9.5	40.7	0	7.1	6.9	400	37	1.3	0	0	0	0	1.9
Peanut butter	623	22.6	11.7	39.7	0	13.1	6.8	350	37	2.1	0	0	0	0	1.1
Walnuts	688	14.7	5.6	59.9	0	3.3	5.9	7	94	2.9	0	0	0	0	2.8
Sugars/snacks															
Honey	288	0.4	0	0	0	76.4	0	11	5	0.4	0	0	0	0	23.0
Jam (fruit)	261	0.6	0	0	0	69.0	1.0	16	24	1.5	Tr	0	0	10	29.8
Mincemeat	274	0.6	2.4	1.7	4	62.1	3.0	140	30	1.5	9	0	0	Tr	27.5
White sugar	394	Tr	0	0	0	99.9	0	Tr	2	0	0	0	0	0	Tr
Golden syrup	298	0.3	0	0	0	79.0	0	270	26	1.5	0	0	0	0	20.0
Treacle	257	1.2	0	0	0	67.2	0	96	500	9.2	0	0	0	0	28.5
Bounty bar	473	4.8	21.2	3.6	10	58.3	N	180	110	1.3	40	Tr	Tr	0	7.6
Milk chocolate	529	8.4	17.8	11.0	30	59.4	Tr	120	220	1.6	40	Tr	Tr	0	2.2
Crème eggs	385	4.1	16.8		N	58.0	Tr	55	120	0.8	55	47	0.6	0	5.3
Kit Kat	499	8.2	13.8	11.3	N	60.5	N	110	200	1.5	47	Tr	Tr	0	1.3
Mars bar	441	5.3	10.0	8.0	25	66.5	Tr	150	160	1.1	40	Tr	Tr	0	6.9
Twix	480	5.6	12.0	11.1	N	63.2	N	190	110	1.1	7	Tr	Tr	0	3.5
Popcorn	592	6.2	4.3	34.2	0	48.6	N	4	10	1.1	230	0	0	0	0.9
Crisps	546	5.6	9.2	21.9	0	49.3	10.7	1070	37	1.8	2	0	0	27	1.9
Crisps (low-fat)	456	6.6	6.2	14.6	0	63.0	13.7	1070	36	1.8	2	0	0	14	1.1
Corn snacks (e.g. Monster Munch)	519	7.0	11.8	18.7	0	54.3	N	1130	68	0.8	460	0	0	Tr	3.3
Drinks															
Cocoa (with whole milk)	76	3.4	2.6	1.3	13	6.8	0.2	70	110	0.2	20	50	0.03	Tr	84.6
Milkshake	90	2.9	2.0	1.0	10	13.2	Tr	55	100	1.0	51	21	0.05	1	80.0
Coca-Cola	39	Tr	0	0	0	10.5	0	8	4	Tr	0	0	0	0	89.8
Lucozade	67	Tr	0	0	0	18.0	0	28	4	Tr	0	0	0	3	81.7
Ribena (undiluted)	228	0.1	0	0	0	60.8	0	26	5	0.4	N	0	0	78	40.3

Composition of foods (per kg)

	kcal	Protein (g)	Saturated fat (g)	Unsaturated fat (g)	Cholesterol (mg)	Carbohydrate (g)	Fibre (g)	Salt (mg)	Calcium (mg)	Iron (mg)	Carotene (µg)	Vitamin A (µg)	Vitamin D (µg)	Vitamin C (mg)	Water (g)
Drinks (continued)															
Orange juice	36	0.5	0	0	0	8.8	0.1	10	10	0.2	17	0	0	39	89.2
			Alcohol content (g)												
Beer	32		3.1			2.3	0	9	8	0.01	0	0	0	0	96.7
Cider	36		3.8			2.6	0	7	4	Tr	0	0	0	0	96.3
Lager	29		3.2			1.5	0	4	4	Tr	0	0	0	0	96.2
Red wine	68		9.5			0.3	0	10	7	0.9	0	0	0	0	97.7
White wine	66		9.1			0.6	0	4	9	0.50	0	0	0	0	98.2
Spirits (e.g. vodka)	222		31.7			Tr	0	Tr	Tr	Tr	0	0	0	0	99.9
Soups and sauces															
Cream of chicken (tin)	58	1.7	3.8	N	4.5	N	460	27	0.4	0	0	0	0	0	87.9
Cream of mushroom (tin)	53	1.1	3.8	N	3.9	N	470	30	0.3	0	0	0	0	0	89.2
Cream of vegetable (tin)	37	1.5	0.7	N	6.7	N	500	17	0.6	18	0	0	0	0	86.4
Oxtail soup (packet)	27	1.4	0.5	N	3.9	0.3	400	11	0.3	0	0	0	0	0	92.5
Cheese sauce (whole milk)	197	8.0	7.5	6.4	39	9.0	0.2	450	240	0.2	105	150	0.55	1	66.9
White sauce (whole milk)	150	4.1	4.4	5.3	26	10.9	0.3	400	140	0.2	77	115	0.62	Tr	73.7
Mayonnaise (shop bought)	691	1.1	11.1	61.2	75	1.7	0	450	8	0.3	100	86	0.33	N	18.8
Tomato ketchup	98	2.1	0	0	0	24.0	N	1120	25	1.2	240	0	0	2	64.8

Index